MEANINGFUL INTEGRATION *Across* CURRICULUM

a collaborative approach

ANDREA P. BEAM

Kendall Hunt

publishing company

Cover image © Shutterstock.com

Kendall Hunt
publishing company

www.kendallhunt.com
Send all inquiries to:
4050 Westmark Drive
Dubuque, IA 52004-1840

CONTENTS

PREFACE

Writing daily lesson plans can be quite consuming for a new teacher, but developing curriculum can be even more cumbersome. It is the hope that this book will enlighten all pre-service teachers and seasoned teachers, alike, to not only prepare for their specific content, but create lessons that integrate other content areas as well. By developing curriculum for an entire school year, teachers will be able to emphasize the various contents, technology, and diversity that is necessary in our 21st-century learners.

The following text will enable all practitioners to develop integrated curriculum and write across curriculum, considering specific endorsement areas, best practices, and effective teaching strategies in reaching all levels of learners. While other curriculum textbooks currently on the market are theoretical in nature with very little discussion on practice, this book will approach curriculum from a "real world" perspective, allowing even first-year teachers to feel comfortable walking into a classroom and beginning their lessons from an integrated approach. After perusing an unlimited number of textbooks currently on the market, it was evident that most texts might only focus on one specific content area with no integration across other required areas. This text will not only provide an overview of what is curriculum, but it will be written for the audience of practitioners—those who will be working or are working in the field. It will also discuss all of the content areas, including math, science, social studies, English, physical education, music, theatre, and so forth, and share strategies in integrating other content areas within one specific topic of study. Not only will content integration be discussed, but other pertinent areas of curriculum will also be clarified, including how to work with students with exceptionalities, how to incorporate character education, assessment, collaboration, and technology. Special emphasis will be placed on the newly enacted edTPA initiative that many states have recently adopted.

This book should be used for pre-service teachers—those seeking initial licensure, but could be used for practicing educators who want to learn more about enhancing their craft with various integration required in K–12 public and private schools. The pre-service teachers will learn how to write a full year's worth of curriculum for a specific content area. Within their specific content area (whether it is science, social studies, English, or math; it could also be teachers of English Language Learners, art or music teachers, etc.), they will learn how to integrate other content areas within their curriculum, making it a stronger lesson. For instance, if I am a social studies teacher, how can I integrate art, music, or physical education/movement into my lesson? This book will explain and provide examples of how to do just that. For those already teaching in their field, the book will also enhance instruction by covering topics of special education, differentiation, multiple intelligence, behavior management, and edTPA.

This book is a practical book—a "how to" sort of text—that will enable both public and private teachers and teachers-to-be to write a full year of curriculum with various levels of integration. It is the hope that those using this textbook will be able to implement strategies for accommodating multiple intelligences and differentiation, working in Inclusive classrooms (special education), and handling behavioral issues that will surely arise.

One of the main problems observed by previewing other textbooks is that the other texts focus on general education only. This book offers a significant contribution because in our schools of today, with the reauthorized IDEA, it is required by federal law that educators instruct students with disabilities in their least restrictive environment. Because of this law, general education teachers are encountering students with exceptionalities and do not know how to work with them in the classroom.

The book will address several of the key components that new(er) teachers face. Part I will focus on Curriculum Fundamentals, which is more of the "what is" portion of Curriculum, while Part II will focus on Curriculum Integration, which is the "how to" portion of Curriculum.

ACKNOWLEDGMENTS

This project could not be accomplished without the support of so many individuals. To a wonderful group of friends, colleagues, and teachers, I offer my sincere thanks for your support throughout this process. A special "thank you" for my fabulous student workers, Gabriel Waters and Allison Garvey, who jumped in with a moment's notice to help with other assignments so I could focus on this project. I would also like to thank the pre-candidate teachers who contributed to this book, including Becca Shephard, Jadon Smith, and Andrew Johnson (SS), Sarah Doughty and Kayla Stevens (TESL).

Finally, an endeavor such as this would not be complete without the encouragement of my wonderful family who I adore profusely. To each of you, I am forever grateful and would like to especially thank my husband, Allen Hackmann, and my dad, George Patterson, for never tiring of the unending stories and progress shared each and every day. Thank you for allowing me to constantly brainstorm ideas while consistently appearing interested.

ABOUT THE AUTHOR

Andrea P. Beam, EdD, is a Professor in the School of Education at Liberty University where she serves as the Chair of Secondary Education. For the last 24 years, she served in a variety of positions, including a teacher of special education, an administrator at both the elementary and secondary level, and, most recently, a full professor in higher education. Presently, she teaches courses in secondary curriculum, special education, and school law. Her numerous research efforts and publications keep her on the cutting edge in the field of education where she has published on the topics of inclusion, Multiple Intelligence, differentiation, Brain Gym, school law, and business programs for special education students. She holds degrees from George Washington University, Norfolk State University, and Old Dominion University.

PART 1

Curriculum Fundamentals

CHAPTER 1

Curriculum

WHAT IS CURRICULUM?

Curriculum is a huge concept to consider. While some might propose that curriculum is developed from theorists and simply "falls" into place after considering various beliefs, others believe that it is far more cumbersome. It is true that curriculum has evolved from past theory, but it also includes the compilation of books, materials, technology, experiences, interactions, and relationships of all involved in the classroom. For the purposes of this text, curriculum exemplifies that which is used to lead a classroom from the first day of school to the last day of school. It includes every lesson, integration, activity, and reinforcement to support a well-run environment. It is the teacher's best resource that will enable him/her survival for the school year.

BACKGROUND OF CURRICULUM

Historically, curriculum development has been shaped not only by society, but educational standards, alike. The Clare Boothe Luce Policy Institute (2015), explained that the first educational ruling came in 1642 with the Massachusetts General Court requiring parents to ensure that their children were able to read the Bible and the laws of the Commonwealth. Most early educational laws were focused on attendance and basic literacy competency. It was not until the early 1900s that formal curriculum planning and decisions began to take shape (Beam & Pinkie, 2015).

Fast-forward to the 1990s and educators were bombarded with more than a dozen varied syllabi and guidelines of which to follow. Not only was the material content-specific in some instances, but some contained assorted aspects of subjects, like handwriting. The format, nonetheless, varied incredibly with regard to language, year levels, and written format (Crown, 2018). Today, curriculum has continued to evolve and is now comprehensive and multifaceted. Teachers now have state and national standards to guide their planning, which aids in the requirements to be taught at each grade level and with individual students.

TYPES OF CURRICULUM

There are several types of curriculum to consider when designing one's own plan for the year. In this section, six types will be discussed: Planned, Implemented, Hidden, Traditional, Individualized, and Open or Free Curriculum. Each of these, while unique, may very well find their way into a preferred plan which is completely acceptable. Some might find that one takes precedence, while others might decide to integrate several of these approaches simultaneously. Nonetheless, curriculum is something that *should* be exclusive to the teacher and his or her style or approach so experimenting is encouraged.

The first type of curriculum is **Planned Curriculum**, which is exactly as it is stated—the curriculum that is actually planned and written into lesson plans, block plans, and curriculum plans. It is the written goal of the teacher for the day, which leads to the week, month, and year. Planned curriculum is different from **Implemented Curriculum**, which is that which is actually carried out from the written plans. Some teachers will write lesson plans but it is quite possible that some information does not get covered within the time period specified. The Implemented Curriculum includes the activities, technology integration, games, and other strategies that have been formally written into plans and are actually carried out within the time frame set aside from a particular lesson.

Hidden Curriculum is the third type to mention. This is the curriculum that just comes about from typical classroom interactions. These could include the discussions that arise from a lesson during small group or whole class conversations. Hidden Curriculum could also include additional reinforcement that is injected on a whim by the teacher. This is anything that is not written into the plan but just arises from the spur-of-the-moment or conversation.

Aside from the typical curriculum such as those mentioned above, there are also methods of developing curriculum. For instance, some teachers and/or schools follow traditional modes, and others follow a more specialized approach like Individualized or Open/Free Curriculum. **Traditional Curriculum** can flow from a top-down approach or a bottom-up approach. Either way, it is really preference of the school (division or teacher). Some school systems believe that one must decide what their students must accomplish upon graduation and work their way down through curriculum to ensure that all learning has taken place as they move down through the grade levels. This is also referred to as Understanding by Design (ASCD, 2018). Developed with seven key points in mind, Wiggins and McTighe (2011) lay out the framework for UbD in an easily accessible format:

1. Learning is enhanced when teachers think purposefully about curricular planning. The UbD framework helps this process without offering a rigid process or prescriptive recipe.

2. The UbD framework helps focus curriculum and teaching on the development and deepening of student understanding and transfer of learning (i.e., the ability to effectively use content knowledge and skill).

3. Understanding is revealed when students autonomously make sense of and transfer their learning through authentic performance. Six facets of understanding—the capacity to explain, interpret, apply, shift perspective, empathize, and self-assess—can serve as indicators of understanding.

4. Effective curriculum is planned backward from long-term, desired results through a three-stage design process (Desired Results, Evidence, and Learning Plan). This process helps avoid the common problems of treating the textbook as the curriculum rather than a resource, and activity-oriented teaching in which no clear priorities and purposes are apparent.

5. Teachers are coaches of understanding, not mere purveyors of content knowledge, skill, or activity. They focus on ensuring that learning happens, not just teaching (and assuming that what was taught was learned); they always aim and check for successful meaning making and transfer by the learner.

6. Regularly reviewing units and curriculum against design standards enhances curricular quality and effectiveness, and provides engaging and professional discussions.

7. The UbD framework reflects a continual improvement approach to student achievement and teacher craft. The results of our designs—student performance—inform needed adjustments in curriculum as well as instruction so that student learning is maximized.

On the other hand, other schools believe that students start at the basic level (kindergarten) and slowly build upon learning each year until graduation. There is neither a right nor wrong way regarding a traditional approach; it is simply preference. As teacher candidates, or new teachers, begin thinking about securing a teaching position after coursework and licensure requirements are met, consideration must be granted on position location. The reason is simple: some school divisions will have a curriculum plan already in place (i.e., larger school divisions), but others (i.e., smaller/rural, overseas, or private locations) may have nothing in place at the school level and depend on the new hire to formulate a plan for the school year. It is important to understand the types of curriculum so one might develop an effective program conducive to student learning in alignment with personal style.

The next approach to curriculum design is called **Individualized Curriculum**. It might also be referred to as Open or Free Curriculum. Both types of curriculum deal with self-discovery. Teachers who implement this type of curriculum focus on the individual student needs, allowing the student to select his/her area of interest. It is similar to Montessori, in which students decide what is learned depending on their interest. Individualized Curriculum allows a student to work at a self-paced, self-directed rate. Students are typically preselected for this type of instruction and the lessons are teacher directed (American Montessori Society, 2018). Teacher candidates and new teachers might find that many students with disabilities prefer this approach. Another type, the final type, which is quite similar to Individualized Curriculum is **Open or Free Curriculum**. Like Individualized, Open or Free Curriculum allows students to be self-directed and self-paced. Additionally, there is free discovery on the student's part. Teachers might set up the students to discover an answer, but it is up to the student to find a solution at their own pace (ISTE, 2018).

Earlier, it was mentioned that some school divisions might have curriculum already in place, while others might rely on their staff to design their plan. There are other approaches that schools take into account during the development of this daunting task. Some choose to hire an external team which is considered *external development*. The external team is a group of experts hired by the school division to review the school demographics, history of the school, and so forth and develop curriculum specific for that school or division. The team provides curriculum to the school and the school (teachers) follow that which is written. Teachers, for this strategy, are not invested, as they are simply following a plan handed down by the experts; however, the teachers should be onboard for any program to be successful. The "buy in" is an important factor which must be considered.

The other approach to curriculum development is *internal development*. This one involves teachers at multiple grade levels and different content areas to meet for common planning and development. The teachers using this approach will plan together across grade levels and across content areas to meet the needs of their unique student population. For this method, the teachers are responsible for what happens in the classroom, considering the planned and implemented curriculum (Beam & Pinkie, 2015).

DEVELOPING THE SCOPE AND SEQUENCE

When beginning to develop curriculum, it is essential that much is considered. Curriculum follows a pattern and is never-ending. After planning and developing the curriculum for the year, teachers need to actually carry through with the plans. Sometimes the plans are flawless and no adjustments are needed. Other times, however, teachers realize that some changes are necessary after they complete their cycle of instruction. It is crucial to evaluate any plan to determine its effectiveness before moving forward. This could be done on a daily basis, a yearly basis, or anything in-between. In short, reflections are important for any growth and changes are inevitable. The cycle, as discussed, resembles a flowchart (see Figure 1) in which curriculum development is never-ending; tweaks and other adjustments are necessary and an understandable need for effective development of a program or course.

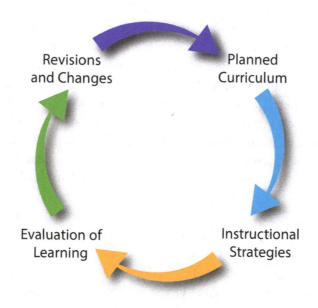

FIGURE 1   The Cycle of Curriculum Progression

As a teacher begins to develop his or her own curriculum, the starting point should derive from his or her own personal philosophy. What is your philosophy? What do you believe? Do you believe all children can learn? Do you believe there are multiple ways to teach students and be effective or do you think there is only one way to educate children? Do you enjoy noise in the classroom with desks spread about, or do you prefer a lecture-style with desks in a row facing the board? Whatever the preference, this begins one's personal philosophy of education. It is important to consider the philosophy, because this leads into the mission statement.

The mission statement is "the 'how-to' statements or action plans that help schools achieve their vision" (Beam & Pinkie, 2015, p. 5). It is the intent of the school or of the department. Any large business, corporation, school, or church will have a mission statement. It is what drives the institution to greatness in meeting its goals. Within the mission statement are specific goals of the school or department, which lead to specific objectives which guide the teacher's instruction. This can be viewed as a progression as seen in Figure 2.

FIGURE 2 Progression of Objective Writing

Once the mission statement is established, the teacher candidate or new teacher (here on out referred to as "teacher") can begin developing the sequence of instruction for the school year. Scope and sequence are terms that parallel with curriculum writing. The material that is taught over the course of the school year is referred to as the scope. It is the horizontal curriculum and should flow in written format with consideration to holidays, teacher workdays, exam schedules, or any other developmental needs of the school. Sequence, on the other hand, is "the order in which the curriculum is presented"; this is the vertical curriculum (Beam & Pinkie, 2015). When writing curriculum, the scope and sequence should spiral, continually raising the level of difficulty, proficiency, and the skill level expected for each grade or learning level.

It is not uncommon for teachers to find resources, supplementals, or other printed material to build a curriculum plan; however, it does become more overwhelming when trying to maximize learning for all students, including those who require specialized instruction. Oftentimes, when teachers are seeking state licensure, they fail to understand that consideration must be provided not only to their general education population, but to their special education population and their gifted education population, as well. As a result, it is important that curriculum development span the entire planned curriculum, even when the selected textbooks do not cover the topic.

The term "curriculum" covers various areas of focus, which might also be referred to as endorsement or content areas. Some areas of which teachers will gain licensure are the traditional Mathematics, Social Studies, Science, English, or Language Arts, but there are other areas equally important. The elective courses that also need curriculum design might include Fine Arts, Music, Business Education, Health and Physical Education, or Foreign Language. Regardless of the endorsement area, the integration of other content areas is essential to building a well-rounded year-long plan for students in a particular grade level. Consideration must be granted to lesson plans, units, and evaluation within each curriculum plan. Additionally, teachers need to ensure that they understand state standards, so they can confirm that students are learning what they need to know for state standardized assessments. Evaluation, then, allows the teacher to reflect on the plan and make changes as necessary. This is inevitable and should be encouraged.

To begin writing curriculum, teachers should begin with a scope and sequence chart which will allow a clear visual of the progression of learning. Figure 3 shows one example of a template that could be used; this template is the framework for curriculum development and should align horizontally and vertically with a nice, even flow of content and activity integration.

TEACHER CANDIDATE'S NAME:
CONTENT SUBJECT AREA:
GRADE LEVEL:
TEXTBOOK NAME WITH PUBLICATION INFORMATION:

Mission Statement:

INCLUDE YOUR MISSION STATEMENT HERE: *The Mission Statement states the school's or department's rationale for teaching this content area. It is a philosophy statement explaining why it is important for students to learn the knowledge, skills, and dispositions taught. The statement should clarify your priorities and give direction to others who might use this curriculum guide to teach.* **LENGTH: 2–3 sentences (clear, direct, and precise).**

AFTER READING AND APPLYING THESE DIRECTIONS, PLEASE DELETE THEM: *Column widths may be adjusted as necessary. All boxes are to be completed in every column. Within reason, you may include field trips, standardized achievement test days, and so forth. Information need not be as detailed as a lesson plan would be; however, it should be clear enough for another teacher to develop lesson plans easily from this curriculum guide. Here are some tips for each section:*

- *CONTENT/OBJECTIVE: You must write complete, measurable objectives for each daily lesson. Some objectives may carry over multiple days.*
- *STANDARDS: It is sufficient to include just the standard numbers for each day. Include state and national standards.*
- *RESOURCES/MATERIALS: Be specific and ensure that you include a variety of different types of resources and technology integration.*
- *LEARNING ACTIVITIES/ASSESSMENTS: This is where you'll need to be specific enough so that another teacher will know what should actually be done to carry out the lesson. Briefly explain what the instructor and learners will do from the opening of class to the end of the class session. Remember that the codes should be inserted throughout the guide and the day numbers where those codes appear should be listed at the top of the chart beside the legend for the code (See Examples in Part II of text).*

Identify units from one another somehow; you may shade unit sections or use color/bolded/highlighted text such as **"UNIT #1 (3 weeks long): ANCIENT ROMAN EMPIRE."**

DAY #	OBJECTIVE	STANDARDS	RESOURCES/MATERIALS	LEARNING ACTIVITIES/ASSESSMENTS
	• The Learner • The Performance • The Task • The Measure	• State Standards • National Standards	*Include (1) resources to assist the teacher in planning and implementing lessons and (2) materials students need to participate.* • Books • Technology • Supplies • Community organizations • Guest speakers • Websites	*After each code below, list the day #'s in which the element is present. Codes are not required in every day's lesson but should be distributed appropriately throughout. You may create other codes if necessary to reflect special considerations not listed here.* *Simply listing the code is not sufficient. A brief explanation is needed to describe what the legend is referring to. For example, instead of just listing "CE," describe what character trait is being taught and how it relates to the lesson. Instead of just listing "ACT," describe how the students will be engaged in active learning.*

DAY #	OBJECTIVE	STANDARDS	RESOURCES/MATERIALS	LEARNING ACTIVITIES/ASSESSMENTS
				ACTIVITY LEGEND (*All of the Activity Codes are **required** to be integrated at least once each week. It's important to show a variety of the legends distributed throughout the project.*)**:** ACT = active learning – Day #: ASSESS = assessment activity – Day #: COLL = There are different types of collaboration: (1) teacher with community members/organizations or other educators and (2) students with other students or community members – Day #: CE = character education – Day #: CT = critical thinking activity – Day #: DIV = diversity consideration – Day #: T = technology – Day#: **INTEGRATION LEGEND** (*A variety of interdisciplinary integrations should be included at least once per 9 weeks. **Not all are necessary**, only those that can reasonably be integrated into your subject area. If a code is not used at all, enter N/A after "Day #'s" for that code.*)**:** A = art – Day #: D = dance – Day #: H = health – Day #: L = language arts – Day #: M = math – Day #: MUS = music – Day #: P = physical education/movement – Day #: S = science – Day #: SS = social science – Day #: TH = Theatre – Day #:
Days 1–180 (use a separate line for each day for a total of 180 lines)	See sample plans for complete curriculum plans in Part II			

FIGURE 3 Curriculum Template, Adapted From the School of Education, Liberty University

BEGINNING TO WRITE CURRICULUM

When beginning to write curriculum, there are several factors to keep in mind. First, one must form a team. In the previous section, external and internal teams were discussed. Within the internal teams, schools can form multiple grade level teams (i.e., grades K, 1, and 2 planning together) or multiple disciplinary teams (English, Math, and Social Studies teachers planning together). Both multigrade and multidisciplinary teams require groups to work together for common decision-making.

Second, once the teams are formed, the teachers need to determine specific roles (i.e., who is responsible for teaching varied content), unless they were preassigned by their administration. For instance, the mathematics teacher might decide to teach 9th grade Algebra I. If this teacher were working on a multidisciplinary team, he or she would work with the other 9th grade teachers for the core subjects in planning 9th grade curriculum to cross-integrate learning. If this teacher, on the other hand, were working on a multigrade team, he or she would work with the 8th grade pre-algebra and 10th grade teacher, as well.

For purposes of writing this curriculum plan, teachers will consider *both* multigrade and multi-disciplinary teams in the formation of this plan. It is important to consider multiple grade levels in writing curriculum to accommodate for the different learners in the classroom. Due to the implementation of the Every Student Succeeds Act (2015) and Individuals with Disabilities Education Act (IDEA), teachers are now required to teach students with disabilities in the general education classroom (i.e., least restrictive environment [LRE]), so it is helpful to consider a grade level beneath the target content area and one above to accommodate for the students with disabilities and the gifted learners.

Philosophy and Mission Statement

Next, reflect on your philosophy. What do you believe is the cornerstone of education? When reflecting on your personal philosophy, you can easily form a mission statement. This should be the first sentence in your curriculum plan and should guide all instruction for the school year (i.e., 180 school days). Remember, the mission statement is a clear and concise statement which describes your school or your department's goal or vision. Typically, it is one to two short sentences. Anything longer would inhibit students to know, learn, or memorize this vision. In reading sample mission statements (Quotescape, 2018), try to determine the focal point of each.

Sample School-Wide Mission Statements:

1. **Princeton* Academy of the Sacred Heart (Private, elementary–middle school):** "Our mission is to develop young men with active and creative minds, a sense of understanding and compassion for others, and the courage to act on their beliefs. We stress the total development of each child: spiritual, moral, intellectual, social, emotional, and physical."

2. **Any Community School (Public, elementary)** Any Community School understands that all children are individuals; they are creative; and they need to succeed in order to be productive members of society. Therefore, Any Community School respects the individual needs of children; fosters an environment of caring and creativity; and emphasizes the social, emotional, physical, intellectual development of each child.

3. **Liberty School (Private, secondary)** The mission of Liberty School is to encourage a rigorous curriculum so all young minds may flourish creatively, intellectually, and spiritually to contribute wisdom, compassion, and leadership to a global society. We provide an academic program through which educators may lead students to self-evaluate and take responsibility for learning.

4. **Corporate High School (Public, secondary)** Corporate High School strives for excellence to instill a community of lifelong learners so all members may not only reach their highest potential but care for others along the way. We are committed to nourishing our environment through diversity and personal experiences and bringing parents alongside to promote a collaborative environment for all learners to succeed.

It is important to receive input from all colleagues in creating a school's mission plan because the "buy in" is so very important. From the mission statement, schools or departments can develop goals, as stated earlier. It is also not unheard of to research other mission statements when creating one for the first time to see what other schools and businesses currently utilize.

Sample Content Specific Mission Statements:

1. The mission of the math department is to provide a solid foundation for continued learning and critical thinking skills pertaining to math and its application in society. In pursuing this mission, the department seeks to be able to provide an environment that promotes individual and group success in the classroom that can be applied to their education as life-long learners.

2. In our mission of science education, we make it our goal to enlighten, involve, and inform our students in a creative and relevant way about the natural world and the beauty and order of life on earth. We encourage students to build off of previous knowledge and explore the study of life by using observation and critical thinking skills.

3. "The mission of the English Department at North Dakota State University is to cultivate understanding, knowledge, and appreciation of the English language, its speakers and writers, and its literatures and cultures, such that students and department members use the language creatively, critically, and effectively to participate ethically in civic and professional life" (NDSU, 2013).*

Bloom's Taxonomy

Now that the mission statement is understood, it is important to begin focusing on objectives and activities to include in the curriculum plan. The first factor is to consider the grade level and subject area of which the plan will be written; next think about Bloom's Taxonomy. Within Bloom's Taxonomy, there are several levels, grade/ability-specific that would guarantee appropriateness for learning (Bloom, Engelhart, Furst, Hill, & Krathwohl, 1956). "Bloom's Taxonomy, as revised by Anderson et al. (2001), consists of six major levels of learning: remembering, understanding, applying, analyzing, evaluating, and creating" (Kidwell, Fisher, Braun, & Swanson, 2013).

The levels are:

1. **Knowledge**, which would typically be used for lower level learners, includes rote memory skills, such as facts, terms, procedures, and classification. While this may be used for older students, it would normally be used for young students. Knowledge is basic information in which students would have to recall, identify, associate, memorize, recite, recognize, or label. When writing activities for the curriculum plan, keep those verbs in mind. Additionally, the objective should mention one of these verbs so it is evident that the objective for the day will focus on the "knowledge" level. The activities will, in turn, correspond. A sample objective at this level could be, "Given ten statements, the student will identify which statements contain historically accurate information with 100% accuracy." I know by reading this objective that the learner is working at the knowledge level. The objective also includes measurement, so I can easily gauge if the student mastered this objective by the evaluation that will be given in alignment with the task.

2. **Comprehension**, which is still used for the younger or lower level learner, includes the ability to translate, paraphrase, interpret, or extrapolate material. This level would be used for elementary-aged students primarily, but secondary could also benefit. Comprehension is understanding something, so the verbs used in the objective and/or activities at this level would be to restate, define, describe, select, determine, or summarize. Any of these verbs would show that the student is being evaluated at the "comprehension" level.

3. **Application** could be used for older elementary-aged or middle school students. This level allows the capacity to transfer knowledge from one setting to another. For example, a learner at this level would be able to use what he or she already knows and apply it in a different manner, like using a learned spelling word in a new sentence, or solving a mathematical problem using a learned method. Verbs to use for the "application" level could be solve, apply, implement, translate, or generate. A sample objective at the application level could be, "Given a list of ten vocabulary words, each student will generate a sentence for each word, applying the correct context, with 100% accuracy."

Each of the three levels mentioned thus far are considered to be lower level thinking skills. The next three levels are considered to be higher level thinking skills. As educators, it is important to move students from the lower levels to the higher levels of learning. Failure to do so would be a disservice to our students who need high expectations and variety of learning in order to succeed.

4. **Analysis**, more of a secondary appropriate level, includes the ability to discover and differentiate the component parts of a larger whole. An example would be, "When given the structure of a sentence, each student assesses the mood of the verb 4–5 times." Sample verbs to consider when writing curriculum could be determine, classify, compare, or analyze.

5. **Synthesis**, definitely a secondary-level appropriate skill, includes the ability to weave component parts into a cohesive part, such as planning, designing, creating, or building something. It is taking many parts and coming up with something new. When developing curriculum at this level, consider verbs such as generate, design, summarize, predict, conclude, or hypothesize.

6. **Evaluation**, the last and highest level of thinking, is the ability to judge the value or use of information using a set of standards. This is choosing, determining, prioritizing, ranking, justifying, or selecting the best alternative or solution to something.

Bloom's Taxonomy could be viewed as a tiered system that increases in difficulty as children/ students mature and learn. Think of it as a visual representation (Figure 4) where as one increases his or her learning ability, he or she is able to move to the next level of learning capable of higher level thinking:

HS	Evaluation
HS	Synthesis
HS/MS	Analysis
MS	Application
MS/ES	Comprehension
ES	Knowledge

FIGURE 4   Tiered Level of Learning From Bloom's Taxonomy

The level of learning is not set firm for a particular grade level, for it is one that really depends on the student and their ability to learn and retain information. It is important to remember that as curriculum is written for older grade levels that higher level thinking skills are also required.

After learning levels are understood, it is time to begin writing the document. Teachers need to be sensitive to budget issues and not incorporate activities that might cost more than a typical teacher or school could afford. For instance, do not plan a field trip to Europe because you are studying the Renaissance. This is not a realistic field trip or activity. Also, consider the time of year that the curriculum is being written. Students, when they return from summer vacation, are very different learners than they are at the end of the school year. For this, it is important to consider timing, in addition to activities and engagement.

Arranging 180 Days of Curriculum

Each time span of the school year has different activities and areas of focus, so curriculum needs to be arranged according to typical student behaviors. If planning is prepared for a full school year, the typical number of days to write is for 180 school days. Within the school year, however, there are events that also should be considered, like semester testing, field trips, half days/teacher work days, and so forth. Be sure to include days for those special events because that will make your curriculum more realistic. Additionally, some schools are on a bell schedule (typical 45 minutes of instruction after accounting for transitions) or a block schedule (95 minutes of instruction). The curriculum activities must cover enough material for the day or more. It is better to overplan than underplan to avoid opportunities for behavioral problems.

When students return from summer vacation (August or September), they are excited and ready to return to school. Because of their energy, it is easy to take time to review rules and expectations, review from the previous school year, and take care of the pretests to evaluate their level of retention. New material can also be integrated, staggering the easy with more difficult, because momentum is strong at the start of a new year.

In October, the "honeymoon" phase might still be lingering but other students might be getting tired and show signs of fatigue. During this month, again, stagger intensity and take advantage of student energy, begin to fall into a routine, and take advantage of the weather. Outdoor activities are always a hit with adolescents so take them outside for appropriate lessons.

In November and December, rules and expectations will probably have to be reviewed because during this time, students are starting to feel the holiday buzz and become anxious—ready for a break. Maintenance skills should be implemented with short, concise units of learning. Take advantage of the learning up to this point and review what has been studied. During this month, you might also be getting ready for semester testing, so be sure to work those days into the curriculum with some fun activities or review games.

January and February calls for special attention because this is when schools begin to have weather delays, restrictions, and student illnesses. Attend to light learning during this time, if you are able, to account for fatigue and flu season. After the holidays, the time seems to creep by because there are not many holidays or breaks, so the days become long and steady. For this, attend to the learner and consider his or her energy level. Now is probably not the best time to integrate the hardest objectives.

With March and April comes a renewed sense of vigor. The weather is turning beautiful and students are getting antsy because they would rather be outside. The weather is beautiful during this time, and spring fever is in full effect so take some time to reel the students back in and work activities into the curriculum that allow for focus. During these months, it is important to implement intense lessons and review because the testing window for state assessments is right around the corner.

Finally, in May and June students are tested, sometimes for as much as a week, so be sure to include a testing window into your curriculum with various aspects of review. A really good activity is to include released items from the previous year of state testing into the lesson. This will enable students to practice actual assessments used previously and familiarize themselves with format. After the testing window, there is usually very little formal learning happening. While unfortunate, this would be an opportune time to integrate field trips into the plan, reinforcing objectives and standards.

After the entire curriculum plan is written for the year, it does not mean it is time to sit back and relax. This is a perfect time to review the program and make any necessary adjustments. Oftentimes, teachers write lesson plans and teach those same plans year after year. While this is good in one sense (i.e., little to no planning time is required because the plans are already written), it is also a bad practice to follow (i.e., little to no planning time is required because the plans are already written—THERE IS NO GROWTH!). Every year, the curriculum should be reviewed to determine what worked and what did not work and "tweak" for minor changes that would allow a more successful program the following year.

Writing the Curriculum

Using the template mentioned in the previous section, be sure to consider the curriculum content. You should create your daily block plans around the state and national standards for your endorsement area. Also, you need to display "*integration*" or the use of an "interdisciplinary" technique.

This means that you should show how the various content areas relate to each other. This can easily be accomplished by using the legend on the right side of the template. The *legend* is a "symbol list" of the many parts that should make up the curriculum which include activities and other content integration. For example, if you are teaching grids and how to plot points in mathematics, you could teach map skills (using longitude and latitude) by incorporating Social Studies standards. On the legend, the "M" stands for "Math" and the "SS" stands for "Social Studies," so you would list the day that this activity is taught in the legend (see samples in Part II of the text). This would be an appropriate example of content integration. Moreover, if you are teaching poetry in English or Language Arts, you could introduce your history lesson with a poem such as "O Captain, My Captain" by Walt Whitman (an homage to Abraham Lincoln after his assassination following the Civil War). This would cover integration for both LA and SS. Finally, if you are teaching the water cycle in Science and a "Rain Dance" from the Native American culture in SS, you are integrating three subjects (i.e., S, SS, and D, or Science, Social Studies, and Dance). You can also integrate content with activities. For example, if you are teaching how to read and create historical timelines in Social Science class, you could have your students create a timeline using Power Point. This would ensure that integration is being met through Social Studies (SS) and Technology (T).

Aside from activity and content integration, it is also your responsibility to consider how other areas of integration can be met. Areas of diversity and accommodations, critical thinking, and active learning will all allow for a more meaningful, multifaceted curriculum. Diversity not only includes a multicultural component, but it also includes differences in learning such as exceptionalities and modalities. For your curriculum plan, it is important to identify how learners of different cultures, modes, and abilities will be addressed. Also, with active learning, this entails anything that keeps the student engaged and active, such as station teaching, group work, or team building.

CURRICULUM RESOURCES

Resources are extremely important as you begin writing curriculum. One textbook used for an entire school year would limit your learners and give them a one-dimensional avenue of learning. For this, you should consult many resources when writing your charts, such as textbooks, curriculum books, idea books, websites, videos, and any other resource that would facilitate the design of a rich program. Within your "Block plan" charts (the template), there is a section for resources. In this column, you will informally cite any resources used to teach a particular daily lesson. For some days, you might only use the textbook, but other days might require the textbook, YouTube, or PowerPoint games for reinforcement. For example, if you gain an idea from consulting a website, simply paste the website address within the block plan and that will be sufficient. This will allow you to keep the site handy.

ADDITIONAL RESOURCES

- For ideas on developing a mission statement, visit: http://www.educationworld.com/a_admin/admin/admin229.shtml
- For information on Bloom's Taxonomy, visit: http://www.nwlink.com/~donclark/hrd/bloom.html

CHAPTER 2

Multiple Intelligences and Differentiation

WHAT IS MULTIPLE INTELLIGENCE?

Multiple Intelligence is when we take the human cognitive competence and describe it "in terms of a set of abilities, talents, or mental skills," which we then refer to as intelligences (Gardner, 2006, p. 6).

As you begin to consider different modalities, it is important to assess your students in class. This could be performed in class during the first week of instruction—the first week of your written curriculum. It is important to evaluate your students so you know how to modify instruction for your students and accommodate for their diverse learning and modalities. By searching the World Wide Web, there are several "Multiple Intelligence Tests" available. You can choose any as they are all fairly consistent. Some are paper-based, while others are computerized. There are also varieties based on the level of learners. This would be a good opener for the new school year to review and discuss while you are also discussing rules and expectations. A web-based test that I like to use can be found by googling "Multiple Intelligence Test." Once there, take any of the preferred tests and discuss as a whole group. This will allow you to group students accordingly and adjust your lessons to meet every need.

All learners are kinesthetic learners when they begin to learn in formal instruction because the early learners need the experiences of concrete activities before they are able to learn abstractly (Education.com, 2018). However, as they continue growing, they will also be able to handle a variety of learning strategies and materials, so it is imperative that teachers prepare lessons with different learning needs in mind, and incorporate the interest of the student into the learning model. For example, if a student enjoys baseball, why not have the student read baseball cards or statistics to facilitate learning? If a student enjoys pop culture, as long as it is appropriate material, try to include magazines into the reading lessons. If teachers can make learning fun and keep students engaged, they will learn. This is where differentiating by modalities, or Multiple Intelligence, comes to mind.

Types of Multiple Intelligence/Strategies for Use

Howard Gardner, the expert of Multiple Intelligence, distinguishes nine different types of learning modalities; they include:

1. **Linguistic Intelligence**: These students have the capacity to use language for expression. They also have the ability to understand (auditory learning) other people to a great extent. This type of learner focuses on his or her ears as the most efficient learning tool. Writers, orators, speakers, lawyers, and other professions who use language as a primary means for work all have great linguistic intelligence. Students with this strength of learning modality think in words, love to read, write, and tell stories. They learn best through books, tapes/compact discs, or debates.

2. **Logical/Mathematical Intelligence**: Students with this strength have the capacity to understand the underlying principles of some kind of causal system, the way a scientist or a logician does. They might also be proficient in the manipulation of numbers, quantities, and operations, the way a mathematician does. They learn best by reasoning and love to experiment, question, or work puzzles. They need manipulatives or trips to planetarium/museum to be successful.

3. **Musical Rhythmic Intelligence**: These students think by use of music; they are able to hear patterns, recognize them, and perhaps manipulate them. People who have strong musical intelligence do not just remember music easily, but they cannot get it out of their mind. They are able to take a concept and implement a beat or rhythm for learning. Obviously, then, they think by rhythm and melodies and love singing, whistling, or humming; they learn best through sing-along time and music playing.

4. **Bodily/Kinesthetic Intelligence**: Students with this modality of learning use his or her whole body or parts of the body (hands, fingers, arms) to solve a problem, make something, or put on some kind of production. Brain-based learning would be extremely effective with this type of learning (Spaulding, Mostert, & Beam, 2010). The most evident examples of bodily/kinesthetic learners are people in athletics or the performing arts, particularly dancing or acting. These students think through somatic sensations and love dancing, running, and jumping; they learn best through role-play, movement, or any other hands-on activity.

5. **Spatial Intelligence**: The ability to represent the spatial world internally in one's mind—the way a sailor or airplane pilot navigates the large spatial world, or the way a chess player or sculptor represents a more circumscribed spatial world. Spatial intelligence (visual learning) can be used in the arts or in the sciences; these students think in images and pictures. Their eyes are the most efficient learning tool. The best strategies to use for these students would be anything where they need to design, draw, or visualize something. They enjoy art, videos, and movies for activity inclusion.

6. **Naturalist Intelligence**: The ability to discriminate among living things, such as plants or animals, and sensitivity to other features of the natural world, such as clouds or rock configurations. This ability was clearly of value in our evolutionary past as hunters, gatherers, and farmers; and it continues to be central in such roles as botanist or chef.

7. **Intrapersonal Intelligence**: Having an *understanding of oneself*—knowing who you are, what you can do, what you want to do, how you react to things, which things to avoid, and which things to gravitate toward. Those with intrapersonal intelligence have a good understanding

FIGURE 5   Learning Activities That Connect With Multiple Intelligences (Connell, D., 2005).

For more information, click here:

https://www.scholastic.com/teachers/articles/teaching-content/clip-save-
checklist-learning-activities-connect-multiple-intelligences/

8. **Interpersonal Intelligence,** on the other hand, is the ability to *understand other people*. It is an ability we all need, but is especially important for those who deal with other people to a great extent, such as teachers, clinicians, salespersons, or politicians.

9. **Existential Intelligence:** The ability and tendency to pose and ponder questions about life, death, and ultimate realities. Although Existential is positioned to be identified as an intelligence, at this time Gardner believes that there is not any neurological evidence of a separately functioning biological existential ability (Gardner, 2014).

Figure 5 illustrates different activities that would be beneficial to include in the curriculum plan where learning modalities are considered. Unfortunately, the ninth intelligence, Existential, has not been included in current images. Additionally, it is a good idea to cite the activities by using the legend in the curriculum template by including the "DIV" acronym (i.e., diversity).

WHAT IS DIFFERENTIATION?

Carol Ann Tomlinson (2013), the expert of differentiated instruction, defines differentiation as the ability to "accommodate the different ways that students learn" (para. 1). She continues to share that it is "an approach to teaching that advocates active planning for student differences in classrooms" (para. 1). Differentiation, then, can be described as the ability to consider differences in academic ability and learning styles, culture, and motivation and is integrated in the curriculum plan by use of the acronym DIV. By utilizing multiple modes of instruction and assessment to meet learning needs, teachers are able to differentiate learning. Differentiation is taking an assignment or evaluation, and changing that assignment or evaluation to meet the specific needs of diverse learners, taking into account their unique learning needs. For example, if I am an English teacher and I assign a novel for students to read, I need to ensure that each student can exhibit learning with consideration of their learning strength. My activity and assessment might be for the students to read and analyze a specific book. Because I teach learners of diversity (i.e., exceptionalities and modalities), I must consider how each student learns best. Some students will read the same novel and express themselves differently when it comes time for evaluation. It is my duty to ensure that all students learn and can demonstrate mastery so I must provide learner appropriate activities and assessment to get a true sense of their knowledge. Using the assignment of reading and analyzing a novel, I might require my linguistic learners to write a synopsis of the book. Conversely, I might require a musical learner to make a song or rap to encapsulate the meaning and outcome of the novel. Still, other students might benefit from discussing the events of the novel. With all three examples of differentiation, I have ensured that learning and mastery has taken place. In your curriculum plan, it is important to include differentiation under the DIV acronym to account for differences in learning.

While differentiation is changing the actual activity or assessment for a particular assignment, Universal Design for Learning (UDL) is incorporating different activities to reach the learners across all activities. It can be defined as "a set of principles for curriculum development that give all individuals equal opportunities to learn" providing a "blueprint for creating instructional goals, methods, materials, and assessments that work for everyone—not a single, one-size-fits-all solution but rather flexible approaches that can be customized and adjusted for individual needs" (CAST, 2012, para. 1). It is similar to differentiation in that instructors teach the same material to reach different learners, but it goes a step further by adding other activities for a specific assignment. For example, if a math teacher was instructing students how to solve basic addition and subtraction problems—a teacher using UDL would use a variety of activities to reach across learning types, like PowerPoint to teach the concept for the visual learners, hands-on activities or manipulatives for kinesthetic learners, or listening to the teacher lecture the procedure for auditory learners. The UDL teacher would use all of the mentioned activities to reach all learners (i.e., all students are exposed to the same activities at the same time), but the differentiated teacher would teach a concept and allow individual students to choose their method of mastery. If we use the same example used previously of an English teacher assigning students to read a novel and analyze the book, the differentiated teacher might share a "menu" of sorts which includes a selection of books for the student to choose from (differentiation), instead of assigning *one* book to analyze (UDL).

Teachers can differentiate any classroom by scaffolding the material for their learners, which is actually extremely beneficial in reaching all levels of students (i.e., high, low, and those who fall in the middle). Some of the scaffolding (differentiated) activities could be independent study, tiered activities, flexible grouping, or alternative assessment. The following section will reveal additional classroom strategies that any teacher can incorporate which would allow for differentiated instruction based off of learning modalities (i.e., Multiple Intelligence).

HOW DOES DIFFERENTIATION ALIGN WITH MULTIPLE INTELLIGENCE?

As discussed, there is a wealth of information available which allows teachers to differentiate material by use of Multiple Intelligences. Carol Ann Tomlinson was fantastic in providing such examples. Some differentiated classroom strategies that would benefit the **linguistic** learner could be lecture or debates, whole or small group discussions, books, worksheets, or manuals, brainstorming, different writing activities, word games, sharing time, storytelling, speeches, reading to the class or choral reading, individual reading, books on tape or compact disc (CD), memorizing linguistic facts, using technology to record one's own words, using technology to publish something (i.e., creating a class newspaper or other assignment), or journal keeping. These are just a few strategies and examples that the linguistic learner would appreciate.

Those students strong in the **logical-mathematical** intelligence, on the other hand, might prefer solving mathematical problems on the board, Socratic questioning, scientific demonstrations, logical problem-solving exercises, creating codes, logical puzzles and games, classifications and categorizations, quantifications and calculations, computer programming, logical-sequential presentation of subject matter, or cognitive thinking exercises.

Spatial learners enjoy visuals and visual learning, so any strategies dealing with charts, graphs, diagrams, and maps would be right up their alley. Also, visual learners might enjoy assignments dealing with photography, videos, slides, and movies; visual puzzles and mazes; 3-D construction kits; art or picture metaphors, imaginative storytelling; creative daydreaming; painting, putting together collages, visual arts, or idea sketching. Finally, any visual thinking exercise would be preferred, along with using mind maps or other graphic organizers, computer graphics software, optical illusions, color cues, telescopes, microscopes, and binoculars; draw-and-paint exercise, computer-assisted design software, or picture literacy experiences.

Most learners would classify themselves as **bodily-kinesthetic** learners to some extent, and to some extent, I think a lot of students encompass this modality. These learners love anything where they are up and out of their seat, moving and learning. They might enjoy creative movement or miming, hands-on thinking and activities, field trips, competitive and cooperative games, physical awareness and relaxation exercises, crafts, or use of kinesthetic imagery/movement. Bodily-kinesthetic learners also enjoy cooking, gardening, and other "messy" activities, using manipulatives, virtual reality software, kinesthetic concepts, physical education activities, communicating with body language and hand signals (i.e., brain-based learning), and using tactile materials and experiences.

The **musical** intelligence is quite easy to incorporate into an integrated lesson. Teachers can simply play music from a particular era (SS) in the background while students work on an assignment and this would be integration of "MUS" (Music) into a "SS" (Social Studies) curriculum. Other strategies that could be used to reach this learning modality could be singing, humming, whistling, playing music (as mentioned), using instruments in class, group singing, mood music, music appreciation, rhythms, songs, raps, or other chants. This is always a fun activity to assign students; teachers could assign an era (again, as mentioned) and differentiate by having some students create a song or rap to explain the era and hardships of that time, while other students might choose to write a paper. The final outcome to be assessed might be for students to understand a particular era (SS) but the way they show mastery is differentiated.

Another "intelligence" is **interpersonal intelligence**. Students strong in this modality appreciate cooperative groups, interpersonal interaction, conflict mediation, peer teaching, board games, cross-age tutoring, group brainstorming activities, peer sharing, community involvement, or apprenticeships because they enjoy working with *others*. They might also like being involved in academic clubs or planning social gatherings or parties as a context for learning. **Intrapersonal intelligence**, on the other hand, are folks who would rather work by themselves. They might actually seek opportunities for independent study, self-paced instruction, individualized projects and games, private spaces for study, interest centers/stations, or other individualized options for homework or classwork. These students would do well with choice time (differentiation), self-teaching instruction (perhaps online learning), self-esteem activities, journal writing, or goal setting sessions.

Naturalistic intelligence can also be referred to as "nature smart." It is no surprise that this intelligence refers to one's personal interest within the environment or with nature. A student strong in naturalistic intelligence is one who enjoys the beauty of the outdoor surroundings and is passionate about protecting against pollution or caring for plants, animals, and rocks (Connell, 2005). Naturalistic-strong students might enjoy collecting feathers, leaves, flowers, and so forth or organizing collections. They might also enjoy using scientific gadgets, like the telescope or microscope. This intelligence would be integrated easily with the Science curriculum. Other activities teachers may employ are anything environment related, such as recycling or creating a better environment for society. Field trips are positive activities that, as already stated, should be embedded into your curriculum at the end of the school year (see Chapter 1), so visiting various natural locations and places where students can mingle with nature (including farms) would be a wonderful addition to the curriculum plan (Parentree, 2018).

The ninth intelligence is the newest, referred to as **Existential Intelligence** or "cosmic smarts." Students who are cosmic smart have the "ability to be sensitive to, or have the capacity for, conceptualizing or tackling deeper or larger questions about human existence" (Wilson, 2008, para. 1). These students might also contemplate the bigger meaning of life or the philosophical ideals of existence, such as "why are we born, why do we die, what is consciousness, or how did we get here?" (Wilson, 2018, para. 1). Students high in existential intelligence are humanitarians, in a sense, and would enjoy projects like planning charity events, focusing on humanitarian events, or reading romantic poetry.

ADDITIONAL RESOURCES

There are an abundance of resources that can be found on the topics of differentiation and multiple intelligence. Carol Ann Tomlinson has published numerous books, journal articles, and chapters on the topic of differentiation and classroom strategies, and Howard Gardner has done the same as it relates to Multiple Intelligence.

For Howard Gardner's professional website, visit https://howardgardner.com/

For Carol Ann Tomlinson's professional website, visit http://caroltomlinson.com/

CHAPTER 3

Inclusion, Co-Teaching, and Collaboration

COMMUNICATION

Communication is the basis of all endeavors, especially those in relation to education. Without proper communication, it is nearly impossible to hold a productive conversation with parents, other teachers, supervisors, or students. It is also quite necessary for teachers to become effective in communication as they lead their students, because without this interactive skill, it is difficult to assess student understanding—a task imperative in our 21st-century schools. Several devices can be sought on how to effectively communicate; however, there are some simple remedies that prove helpful in any situation, even those where de-escalation is necessary.

In order to effectively communicate, teachers should be mindful of their perception as well as the receiver's perception. Active listening is always a great strategy to employ. It allows the communicator to demonstrate understanding of the conversation by use of verbal and non-verbal cues. Some examples of active listening could be a simple head-nod, a smile, a person leaning into the conversation, or a repeat-back/summary of the discussion. All of these strategies show that the conversation is heard and understood. A really good task to assess personal communicative skills could be to evaluate yourself as you engage in a discussion with someone (i.e., spouse, co-worker, friend), and jot down typical habits that you find yourself repeating. When someone is talking to you, for instance, do you lean in, nod, smile at inopportune times, look at your watch, ask a lot of questions, or interrupt? If you find yourself performing any of these actions, it could open the door to recognizing your personal skills and provide work for growth.

Another strategy that is very helpful in becoming an effective communicator is the ability to depersonalize situations. Teachers and other staff members must converse with many individuals, but at the top of the list are students and their parents. In speaking with students and their parents, there will be many pleasant, productive conversations; however, on rare occasions, there may also be unpleasant conversations. Either way, it is quite effective to avoid any negative comments or personal attacks that may interrupt the discussion. Take a neutral stance, and do not take anything personal.

Teachers might also find that, when meeting with one or more counterparts, it is useful to have a purpose for the meeting. Never go into a meeting "blind" without an agenda—keep all meetings focused, timed, and paced. In addition to active listening and depersonalizing situations, find the main purpose for the meeting, find common goals, brainstorm solutions, and follow up to ensure that the goals, in fact, are productive. By following simple strategies, teachers can diminish potential problems that may arise.

STATUS OF THE CLASSROOM

Classrooms of today are not what they used to be 20 years ago. No longer do teachers stand at the front of the classroom lecturing students who sit quietly in their rows of chairs (Beam, Yocum, & Pinkie, 2016). Today, our schools look and feel differently because they *are* different. Federal legislation, such as the Individuals with Disabilities Education Act (IDEA), has dictated that students with disabilities (SWD) be educated along with their non-disabled peers in the least restrictive environment, so as not to take away from their or anyone else's learning experience (Beam et al.). Doing so allows SWD to be offered the same opportunities as their age-appropriate peers and enables them to advance not only academically, but socially as well.

"The primary objective is to provide the disabled child an opportunity to interact, socialize and 'learn' with regular students, thus minimizing the tendency to become stigmatized and isolated from the school's regular program" (Essex, 2012, p. 105).

UNDERSTANDING SPECIAL EDUCATION

Many teachers leave the university level with their new state credentials and venture into their own classroom to instruct students without proper preparation surrounding special education topics. The unfortunate fact of the matter is these teachers, who might be very well prepared to teach their content area, might be extremely unprepared in working with the K–12 students. Our schools and classrooms are not all the same. Our schools "look" different and our students are very different. Within one World Geography class, a teacher might have five different types of students of which to work: gifted, special education, limited English proficient, attention deficit, and the standard student. It is important for new teachers to understand the challenges that are to come, and prepare him or herself as much as possible leading into his or her first position.

This section will surround the topic of special education from a general educator's perspective. As a general educator, the requirements in understanding special education is very different than that of a special educator, so this section will focus on the requirements that a general educator must consider and be aware of when working with students of diversity.

First and foremost, it is important to understand that when a teacher begins teaching at any level (i.e., elementary, middle, or high school), all of the students will not be age-appropriate in the classroom. The IDEA mandates that students who are identified and receive services for special education be allowed to attend the public school from ages 3 to 21 (and sometimes 22 depending on the age in which the student begins school for a particular school year). This means that a new teacher, who is fresh out of college, could have a student in his or her secondary classroom who is only a year or two younger. It is your responsibility to understand this law and be prepared to educate all students. As a general educator, there are several people who can make a recommendation for services (if you think a student might have a disability). You, as the general educator, can make a recommendation, the parent of the student, another teacher who works with the student, or the administrator can make a recommendation. If anyone suspects that a child has a disability or would benefit from receiving special services, they are required to report this information to the child study team in the school for testing and discussion (Individuals with Disabilities Education Act, 2004).

Once a student is identified as having a disability and is found to need special services, he or she will qualify for 1 of 13 possible IDEA categories, any of which could be in your classroom:

1. **Autism** (AUT)—One of the most astounding disabilities because of the "spectrum." Students with AUT "look" very different from one another and react differently to various stimuli.

2. **Brain Injury/Traumatic Brain Injury** (TBI)—Perhaps one of the saddest disabilities. For this, anyone can get a TBI at any time. While some students are born with a TBI, others are caught in unfortunate life circumstances and develop this disability. A person could acquire a TBI by walking down the street and getting hit by a car. For most, TBI students "look," speak, and interact appropriately, but short-term memory could be a factor. Accommodations,* again, are probably warranted in the classroom for this disability.

3. **Deaf-Blindness**—These students have a combination of being both deaf and blind.

4. **Deafness**—The student who is deaf cannot hear, even with accommodations.* For these students, they typically benefit from a sign language interpreter.

5. **Emotional Disturbance/Emotional Disability/Emotional Behavioral Disability** (ED/EBD)—Students who are ED may or may not find themselves into your classroom, depending on their behaviors and if it takes away from learning. However, if they are in your classroom, there will more than likely be accommodations* you will be required to follow.

6. **Hearing Impairments** (HI)—Students with an HI have trouble hearing various tones in the classroom, which could include pitch or level of voice. You could have HI students in your classroom, but they will require accommodations.*

7. **Intellectual Disabilities** (ID)—This disability is previously referred to as Mental Retardation. These students have a very low IQ and will, more than likely, be included in the general curriculum by use of electives or other lower level courses, some of which might require the support of a teacher assistant/paraprofessional.

8. **Learning Disabilities** (LD) or **Specific Learning Disabilities** (SLD)—This is one of the most common disabilities that can be found in the general education classes. These students, for the most part, learn differently in one aspect of their education, such as reading or math. For these students, they require accommodations* but can be extremely successful in the general education classes.

9. **Multiple Disabilities** (MD)—Students with MD have more than one primary disability that affects his or her daily activities. An MD student could be one who is a cerebral pelagic who also has a learning disability but they are both pervasive.

10. **Orthopedic Impairments** (OI)—Students who have orthopedic needs, or who are in a wheelchair, might qualify for services under this category.

11. **Other Health Impairments** (OHI)—This seems to be the "catchall" of disabilities; if teachers do not know what is going on with a particular student, but it is evident that there are some delays, the student is oftentimes classified as OHI. It could also be for students who have Attention Deficit (Hyperactive) Disorder. As ADD/ADHD is not an IDEA recognized category, schools and their staff will label these students under OHI so they may receive services.

---

*Accommodations will be discussed in a later section.
**IEPs will be discussed in a later section.

12. **Speech or Language Impairment** (SLI)—This could be a separately labeled disability or it could be a related service for some students. It includes students who have trouble forming words or enunciating. If the disability impacts his or her education, a student might qualify to receive speech services. However, if the student has a speech impediment but is progressing in the curriculum, it is unlikely that services will be warranted.

13. **Visual Impairment** (VI, including blindness)—Students considered to have a VI could be completely blind or have limited vision. For the classroom, accommodations* are necessary for progression in the curriculum and are probably mandated through the student's Individualized Education Plan** (U.S. Department of Education, 2015).

As mentioned previously, anyone can refer a student for special education services. When deciding if a student would qualify, there is a team that is formed, of which you could be involved. The required committee members for a special education team include a general education teacher (you), a special education teacher, the local education agency (LRE) who is usually the administrator overseeing special education or the special education department chair, the parent(s) and the student, depending on his or her age. Other members may attend, if necessary, and include the school psychologist, the nurse, counselors, advocates or attorneys, or any other related personnel as deemed suitable. For the secondary instructor, you must be aware that your presence at special education meetings (i.e., IEPs, Triennials, and Modifications—to be discussed in the following sections) is required by law.

In attending Individual Education Plan (IEP) meetings, you should also be aware of your rights as the general educator representative. Anything written into the IEP is a requirement for all teachers of the student to follow; failure to do so would be a violation of their rights and could result in litigation. For this reason, it is imperative that you have a voice at the meetings and share what is and is not realistic in the classroom. Once the IEP is signed, it must be followed by all as it is written.

You might be wondering, "What is an IEP and what does it mean to me?" There has been a lot of talk about this document but how is it followed so a lawsuit can be avoided? An IEP is a document that is written and reviewed on an annual basis for any student who qualifies and receives special education services. It is the special educator's responsibility to develop this document and share the required components with all individuals who work with the particular student. It includes several aspects, including:

1. A statement detailing the child's present level of academic achievement and functional performance (PLAAFP);

2. A statement of annual goals, as well as short-term instructional objectives;

3. A description of specific educational services to be provided and a determination as to whether the child is able to participate in regular educational programs;

4. A description of transitional services to be rendered if the child is a junior or senior in high school, to ensure that necessary services are provided when the child leaves the regular school environment;

5. A description of services to be provided and a timetable for providing these services;

6. An explanation of relevant criteria and procedures to be employed annually to determine if instructional objectives are or have been achieved (Virginia Department of Education, 2018).

---

*Accommodations will be discussed in a later section.
**IEPs will be discussed in a later section.

Since most general education teachers have never seen an IEP, one has been included with emphasis placed on the relevant sections. Below, you will note that the following IEP (Figure 6) was taken from the Virginia Department of Education's website. While the format might vary across states, the information does not, and will be consistent no matter where a teacher is employed. Be sure to pay special attention to the colored boxes, as they will explain *your* responsibility in the meeting.

FIGURE 6   VDOE Sample IEP

Virginia Department of Education's Sample Elementary IEP Form
(Virginia Department of Education, 2018)

For Use with Students up to Age Twelve, as Appropriate

Student Name _____

Student ID Number _____

> This is the demographics page, which includes basic contact information.

DOB ____ / ____ / ____ Age _____ Disability(ies) _____

Parent Name _____

Home Address _____ Phone # (H) (____) _____

_____ Phone # (W) (____) _____

Date of IEP meeting _____

Date parent notified of IEP meeting _____

This IEP will be reviewed no later than _____

Most recent eligibility date _____

> The "dates" sections are a reminder for the special education teacher to hold the annual and triennial meetings before they expire. Your only concern is to attend, if you are invited.

Next re-evaluation, including eligibility, must occur before _____ ____ / ____ / ____

Copy of IEP given to parent (Name) _____ On (Date) ____ / ____ / ____

IEP Teacher/Manager _____ Phone # (____) _____

The Individualized Education Plan (IEP) that accompanies this document is meant to support the positive process and team approach. The IEP is a working document that outlines the student's vision for the future, strengths, and needs. The IEP is not written in isolation. The intent of an IEP is to bring together a team of people who understand and support the student in order to come to consensus on a plan and an appropriate and effective education for the student. No two teams are alike and each team will arrive at different answers, ideas, and supports and services to address the student's unique needs. The student and his/her family members are vital participants, as well as teachers, assistants, specialists, outside service providers, and the principal. When all team members are present, the valuable information shared supports the development of a rich student profile and education plan.

PARTICIPANTS INVOLVED:

The list below indicates that the individual participated in the development of this IEP and the placement decision; it does not authorize consent. Parent consent is indicated on the "Prior Notice" page.

NAME OF PARTICIPANT   **POSITION**

For EVERY special education meeting (IEP, Triennial, Modification), a general education teacher is REQUIRED to attend. You may be invited and, by law, MUST attend.

ELEMENTARY INDIVIDUALIZED EDUCATION PROGRAM

Student Name _____ Date _____ Page _____ of _____

Student ID Number _____

During the IEP meeting, the following factors must be considered by the IEP team. Best practice suggests that the IEP team document that the factors were considered and any decision made relative to each. The factors are addressed in other sections of the IEP if not documented on this page (for example: see Present Level of Academic Achievement and Functional Performance).

1. Results of the initial or most recent evaluation of the student:

   _____

   _____

2. The strengths of the student:

   _____

   _____

3. The academic, developmental, and functional needs of the student:

   _____

   _____

4. The concerns of the parent(s) for enhancing the education of their child:

   _____

   _____

5. The communication needs of the student:

   _____

   _____

6. The student's needs for benchmarks or short-term objectives:

   _____

   _____

7. Whether the student requires assistive technology devices and services:

   _____

   _____

8. In the case of a **student whose behavior impedes his or her learning or that of others**, consider the use of positive behavioral interventions, strategies, and supports to address that behavior:

    _____

    _____

9. In the case of a **student with limited English proficiency**, consider the language needs of the student as those needs relate to the student's IEP:

    _____

    _____

10. In the case of a **student who is blind or is visually impaired**, provide for instruction in Braille and the use of Braille unless the IEP team determines after an evaluation of the student's reading and writing skills, needs, and appropriate reading and writing media, including an evaluation of the student's future needs for instruction in Braille or the use of Braille, that instruction in Braille or the use of Braille is not appropriate for the student. When considering that Braille is not appropriate for the child the IEP team may use the <u>Functional Vision and Learning Media Assessment for Students who are Pre-Academic or Academic and Visually Impaired in Grades K–12</u> (FVLMA) or similar instrument; and

    _____

    _____

11. In the case of a **student who is deaf or hard of hearing**, consider the student's language and communication needs, opportunities for direct communications with peers and professional personnel in the student's language and communication mode, academic level, and full range of needs, including opportunities for direct instruction in the student's language and communication mode. The IEP team may use the Virginia Communication Plan when considering the student's language and communication needs and supports that may be needed.

    _____

    _____

ELEMENTARY INDIVIDUALIZED EDUCATION PROGRAM

PRESENT LEVEL OF ACADEMIC ACHIEVEMENT AND FUNCTIONAL PERFORMANCE

Student Name _____ Date _____ Page _____ of _____

Student ID Number _____

The Present Level of Academic Achievement and Functional Performance summarizes the results of assessments that identify the student's interests, preferences, strengths, and areas of need. It also describes the effect of the student's disability on his or her involvement and progress in the general education curriculum, and for preschool children, as appropriate, how the disability affects the student's participation in appropriate activities. This includes the student's performance and achievement in academic areas such as writing, reading, math, science, and history/social sciences. It also includes the student's performance in functional areas, such as self-determination, social competence, communication, behavior, and personal management. Test scores, if included, should be self-explanatory or an explanation should be included, and the Present Level of Academic Achievement and Functional Performance should be written in objective measurable terms, to the extent possible. There should be a direct relationship among the desired goals, the Present Level of Academic Achievement and Functional Performance, and all other components of the IEP.

_____

_____

This section might be helpful for you to read as it will provide an overview of the student and his or her needs. It will include information on academics, social needs, behavioral needs, transition services, etc.

ELEMENTARY INDIVIDUALIZED EDUCATION PROGRAM (IEP)

PRESENT LEVEL OF ACADEMIC ACHIEVEMENT AND FUNCTIONAL PERFORMANCE (continued)

Student Name _____ Date _____ Page _____ of _____

Student ID Number _____

ELEMENTARY INDIVIDUALIZED EDUCATION PROGRAM (IEP)

MEASURABLE ANNUAL GOALS, PROGRESS REPORT

Student Name _____ Date _____ Page _____ of _____

Student ID Number _____ Area of Need _____

 # _____ MEASURABLE ANNUAL GOAL:

> This is a section you might be asked to help develop. Depending on the student's disability, he or she might need specific content goals that you can help incorporate into the plan. Every goal listed in the IEP must be measurable.

The IEP team considered the need for short-term objectives/benchmarks.

☐ **Short-term objectives/benchmarks are included for this goal.** (Required for students participating in the VAAP)

☐ **Short-term objectives/benchmarks are not included for this goal.**

How will progress toward this annual goal be measured? (check all that apply)		
_____ Classroom Participation _____ Checklist _____ Classwork _____ Homework	_____ Observation _____ Special Projects _____ Tests and Quizzes _____ Written Reports	_____ Criterion-referenced test: _____ _____ Norm-referenced test: _____ _____ Other: _____

Progress on this goal will be reported to the parent or adult student using the following codes. Attach comments using progress report comment form located in section two.

Anticipated Date of Progress Report*							
Actual Date of Progress Report							
Progress Code							

SP—The student is making **S**ufficient **P**rogress to achieve this annual goal within the duration of this IEP.

ES—The student demonstrates **E**merging **S**kill but may not achieve this goal within the duration of this IEP.

M—The student has **M**astered this annual goal.

IP—The student has demonstrated **I**nsufficient **P**rogress to meet this annual goal and may not achieve this goal within the duration of this IEP.

NI—The student has **N**ot been provided **I**nstruction on this goal.

* Progress reports will be provided at least as often as parents are informed of the progress of their children without disabilities.

ELEMENTARY INDIVIDUALIZED EDUCATION PROGRAM (IEP)

SERVICES—LEAST RESTRICTIVE ENVIRONMENT—PLACEMENT

ACCOMMODATIONS/MODIFICATIONS

Student Name _____ Date _____ Page _____ of _____

Student ID Number _____ Area of Need _____

This student will be provided access to general education classes, special education classes, other school services, and activities including nonacademic activities and extracurricular activities, and education related settings:

___ with no accommodations/modifications

___ with the following accommodations/modifications

Accommodations/modifications provided as part of the instructional and testing/assessment process will allow the student equal opportunity to access the curriculum and demonstrate achievement. Accommodations/modifications also provide access to nonacademic and extracurricular activities and educationally related settings. Accommodations/modifications based solely on the potential to enhance performance beyond providing equal access are inappropriate.

Accommodations may be in, but not limited to, the areas of time, scheduling, setting, presentation and response. The impact of any modifications listed should be discussed.

ACCOMMODATIONS/MODIFICATIONS (list, as appropriate)

Accommodation(s)/ Modification(s)	Frequency	Location (name of school*)	Instructional Setting	Duration m/d/y to m/d/y

> This is probably one of the main sections you will need to focus upon. These are the accommodations for the student that are to be followed by every person who works with him or her. You MUST follow the accommodations as written.

* IEP teams are required to identify the specific school site (public or private) when the parent expresses concerns about the location of the services or refuses the proposed site. A listing of more than one anticipated location is permissible, if the parents do not indicate that they will object to any particular school or state that the team should identify a single school.

Supports for School Personnel: (Describe supports such as equipment, consultation, or training for school staff to meet the unique needs for the student) _____

_____

_____

_____

_____

_____

_____

_____

ELEMENTARY INDIVIDUALIZED EDUCATION PROGRAM (IEP)

SERVICES—LEAST RESTRICTIVE ENVIRONMENT—PLACEMENT, Continued

PARTICIPATION IN THE STATE AND DIVISION-WIDE ACCOUNTABILITY/ASSESSMENT SYSTEM

Student Name _____ Date _____ Page _____ of _____

Student ID Number _____

This student's participation in state and division-wide assessments must be discussed annually. During the duration of this IEP:

Will the student be at a grade level for which the student must participate in a state- and/or division-wide assessment? *If yes, continue to next question.*	☐Yes ☐No
Based on the Present Level of Academic Achievement and Functional Performance, is this student being considered for participation in the Virginia Alternate Assessment Program (VAAP), which is based on Aligned Standards of Learning? *If yes, complete the "VAAP Participation Criteria."*	☐Yes ☐No
Does the student meet the VAAP participation criteria? *If yes, refer to the Aligned Standards of Learning for development of annual goals and short-term objectives or benchmarks.*	☐Yes ☐No
Based on the Present Level of Academic Achievement and Functional Performance, is this student being considered for participation in the Virginia Grade Level Alternative (VGLA)? *If yes, complete the "VGLA Participation Criteria" for each content considered and attach justification statement.*	☐Yes ☐No
Does the student meet the VGLA participation criteria? *If yes, determine for specific content area.*	☐Yes ☐No
Based on the Present Level of Academic Achievement and Functional Performance, is this student being considered for participation in the Virginia Modified Achievement Standards Test (VMAST)? *If yes, complete the "VMAST Participation Criteria" for each content considered.*	☐Yes ☐No
Does the student meet the VMAST participation criteria? *If yes, determine for specific content area.* **Note:** *VMAST will be available as an assessment option beginning in Spring 2012 in mathematics.*	☐Yes ☐No

If "yes" to any of the above, check the assessment(s) chosen and attach (or maintain in student's educational record) the assessment page(s), which will document how the student will participate in Virginia's accountability system and any needed accommodations and/or modifications.

State Assessments:
_____ SOL Assessments and retake (SOL) ☐ Reading ☐ Math ☐ Science ☐ History/Social Science ☐ Writing
_____ Virginia Grade Level Alternative* (VGLA) ☐ Reading ☐ Math ☐ Science ☐ History/Social Science ☐ Writing
_____ Virginia Modified Achievement Standards Test* (VMAST) ☐ Math (beginning Spring 2012)
_____ Virginia Alternate Assessment Program** (VAAP)
_____ Other State Approved Substitute(s): _____

Division-Wide Assessment (list):

_____

_____

_____

_____

_____

_____

* Refer to Procedures for Determining Participation in the Assessment Component of Virginia's Accountability System and the Implementation Manual for VGLA and/or VMAST. <u>Note: VGLA in Math will no longer be available as an assessment option after the Spring 2011 test administration.</u>

** Refer to Virginia Alternate Assessment Program (VAAP) Participation Criteria and Implementation Manual.

ELEMENTARY INDIVIDUALIZED EDUCATION PROGRAM (IEP)

PARTICIPATION IN THE STATE- AND DIVISION-WIDE ACCOUNTABILITY/ASSESSMENT SYSTEM (continued)

Student Name _____ Date _____ Page _____ of _____

Student ID Number _____

PARTICIPATION IN STATEWIDE ASSESSMENTS

Test	Assessment Type* (SOL, VGLA, VMAST,[1] VAAP, or Board of Education Approved Substitute)	Accommodations**	If yes, list accommodation(s)
Reading	☐ _____ ☐ Not Assessed at this Grade Level	☐Yes ☐No	
Math	☐ _____ ☐ Not Assessed at this Grade Level	☐Yes ☐No	
Science	☐ _____ ☐ Not Assessed at this Grade Level	☐Yes ☐No	
History/SS	☐ _____ ☐ Not Assessed at this Grade Level	☐Yes ☐No	
Writing	☐ _____ ☐ Not Assessed at this Grade Level	☐Yes ☐No	

(i)

* An IEP team may not exempt a student from participation in a content area assessment, only determine <u>how</u> the student will be assessed.

** Accommodation(s) must be based upon those the student generally uses during classroom instruction and assessment. For the accommodations that may be considered, refer to "Accommodations/Modifications" page of the IEP.

[1] VMAST will be available in mathematics 3–8 and EOC Algebra I beginning with the Spring 2012 test administration.

Division-Wide Assessment (list):

_____

_____

_____

_____

_____

(ii)

(iii) EXPLANATION FOR NON-
       PARTICIPATION IN REGULAR STATE OR
       DIVISION-WIDE ASSESSMENTS

If an IEP team determines that a student must take an alternate assessment instead of a regular state assessment, explain in the space below why the student cannot participate in this regular assessment; why the particular assessment selected is appropriate for the student, including that the student meets the criteria for the alternate assessment; and how the student's nonparticipation in the regular assessment will impact the child's promotion; or other matters. Refer to the VDOE's <u>Procedures for Participation of Students with Disabilities in Virginia's Accountability System</u> for guidance.

☐ Alternate/Alternative Participation Criteria is attached or maintained in the student's educational record

_____

_____

_____

_____

_____

_____

ELEMENTARY INDIVIDUALIZED EDUCATION PROGRAM (IEP)
SERVICES—LEAST RESTRICTIVE ENVIRONMENT—PLACEMENT, Continued

Student Name _____ Date _____ Page _____ of _____

Student ID Number _____

Least Restrictive Environment (LRE)

When discussing the least restrictive environment and placement options, the following must be considered:

- To the maximum extent appropriate, the student is educated with children without disabilities.

- Special classes, separate schooling, or other removal of the student from the regular educational environment occurs only when the nature or severity of the disability is such that education in regular classes with the use of supplementary aids and services cannot be achieved satisfactorily.

- The student's placement should be as close as possible to the child's home and unless the IEP of the student with a disability requires some other arrangement, the student is educated in the school that he or she would attend if he or she did not have a disability.

- In selecting the LRE, consideration is given to any potential harmful effect on the student or on the quality of services that he/she needs.

- The student with a disability shall be served in a program with age-appropriate peers unless it can be shown that for a particular student with a disability, the alternative placement is appropriate as documented by the IEP.

Free Appropriate Public Education (FAPE)

When discussing FAPE for this student, it is important for the IEP team to remember that FAPE may include, as appropriate:

- Educational Programs and Services
- Proper Functioning of Hearing Aids
- Assistive Technology
- Transportation
- Nonacademic and Extracurricular Services and Activities
- Physical Education
- Extended School Year Services
- Length of School Day

SERVICES: Identify the service(s), including frequency, duration and location, that will be provided to or on behalf of the student in order for the student to receive a free appropriate public education. These services are the special education services and as necessary, the related services, supplementary aids and services based on peer-reviewed research to the extent practicable, assistive technology, supports for personnel,* accommodations and/or modifications* and extended school year services* the student will receive that will address area(s) of need as identified by the IEP team. Address any needed transportation and physical education services including accommodations and/or modifications.

Service(s)	Frequency	Location (name of school **)	Instructional Setting	Duration m/d/y to m/d/y

Extended School Year Services: (see attached summary sheet as a means to document discussion)

☐ The IEP team determined that the student needs ESY services.

☐ The IEP team determined that the student does not need ESY services. Describe.

* These services are listed on the "Accommodations/Modifications" page and "Extended School Year Services" page, as needed.

** IEP teams are required to identify the specific school site (public or private) when the parent expresses concerns about the location of the services or refuses the proposed site. A listing of more than one anticipated location is permissible, if the parents do not indicate that they will object to any particular school or state that the team should identify a single school.

ELEMENTARY INDIVIDUALIZED EDUCATION PROGRAM (IEP)

SERVICES—LEAST RESTRICTIVE ENVIRONMENT—PLACEMENT, Continued

Student Name _____ Date _____ Page _____ of _____

Student ID Number _____

PLACEMENT

No single model for the delivery of services to any population or category of children with disabilities is acceptable for meeting the requirement for a continuum of alternative placements. All placement decisions shall be based on the individual needs of each student. The team may consider placement options in conjunction with discussing any needed supplementary aids and services, accommodations/modifications, assistive technology, and supports for school personnel. In considering the placement continuum options, check those the team discussed. Then, describe the placement selected in the **PLACEMENT DECISION** section below. Determination of the Least Restrictive Environment (LRE) and placement may be one or a combination of options along the continuum.

Placement Continuum Options Considered (check all that have been considered):

Services provided in:

   ____ general education class(es)

   ____ special class(es)

   ____ special education day school

   ____ state special education program/school

   ____ residential facility

   ____ home-based

   ____ hospital

   ____ other (describe):

PLACEMENT DECISION: _____

Based upon identified services and the consideration of least restrictive environment (LRE) and placement continuum options, describe in the space below the placement. Additionally, summarize the discussions and decision around LRE and placement. This must include an explanation of why the student **will not** be participating with students without disabilities in the general education class(es), programs, and activities. Attach additional pages as needed.

Explanation of Placement Decision:

ELEMENTARY INDIVIDUALIZED EDUCATION PROGRAM (IEP)

PRIOR NOTICE AND PARENT CONSENT

Student Name _____ Date _____ Page _____ of _____

Student ID Number _____

PRIOR NOTICE

The school division proposes to implement this IEP. This proposed IEP will allow the student to receive a free appropriate public education in the least restrictive environment. This decision is based upon a review of current records, current assessments, and the student's performance as documented in the Present Level of Academic Achievement and Functional Performance. Other options considered, if any, and the reason(s) for rejection is attached, or can be found in the Placement Decision section of this IEP. Additionally, other factors, if any that are relevant to this proposal are attached. Parent and adult student rights are explained in the Procedural Safeguards. If you, the parent(s) and adult student, need another copy of the Procedural Safeguards or need assistance in understanding this information please contact _____ at (_____) _____ or email _____ or _____ at (_____) _____ or email _____ .

_____ Parent(s) initials here indicate that the parent(s) has read the above prior notice and attachments, if any, before giving permission to implement this IEP.

PARENT/ADULT STUDENT CONSENT: Indicate your response by checking the appropriate space and sign below.

_____ I <u>give</u> permission to implement this IEP.

_____ I <u>do not give</u> permission to implement this IEP.

_____ _____ / _____ / _____

Parent Signature   Date

Meetings

Now that you are a bit more familiar with what an IEP looks like and what your role with the document entails, it is time to delve a little deeper into your responsibilities as the general education teacher. As mentioned, you are required BY LAW to attend any IEP meeting, Triennial meeting, or modification meeting, if invited. IDEA requires that *at least one* general education teacher attend any of the special education meetings, so be prepared to give up some of your "free" time to attend.

If you remember on the IEP sample, there was a section of "participants." Some participants are required, while others are invited. Those required to attend all meetings include the local education agency (LEA), general education teacher, special education teacher, parent, student (depending on age), and several others are invited, such as the counselor, nurse, speech/language interpreter, occupational therapist, physical therapist, and so forth, as applicable for the meeting.

Each IEP, to reiterate, must be reviewed and revised annually, at a minimum, to ensure that the continuing needs of the child are met. If changes are contemplated, the child's parent or legal guardian must be notified and a modification meeting can be held. The modification meeting is a meeting that you, as a general education teacher, might also have to attend. This meeting is to make any changes to the IEP, such as services, goals, or accommodations/modifications. If either party (parents or school personnel) objects to the proposed changes, an impartial hearing must be held to resolve the conflict. This is called a mediation meeting. If this process proves unsuccessful, the parent or guardian may appeal to the state agency and subsequently to the courts, also referred to as due process. Rarely do teams have to go to mediation or due process (i.e., "court") but it does happen in some situations when neither party can agree.

Accommodations and Modifications

Students with identified disabilities, who follow an IEP, are allowed any accommodations in the classroom that will help them be academically and/or behaviorally successful, as agreed upon by the team. The University of Washington (2017) was succinct in describing the difference between accommodations and modifications. "The term 'accommodation' may be used to describe an alteration of environment, curriculum format, or equipment that allows an individual with a disability to gain access to content and/or complete assigned tasks. They allow students with disabilities to pursue a regular course of study. Since accommodations do not alter what is being taught, instructors should be able to implement the same grading scale for students with disabilities as they do for students without disabilities" (para. 1). However, modifications, on the other hand, "may be used to describe a change in the curriculum. Modifications are made for students with disabilities who are unable to comprehend all of the content an instructor is teaching. For example, assignments might be reduced in number and modified significantly for an elementary school student with cognitive impairments that limit his/her ability to understand the content in the general education class in which they are included" (para. 3). Unfortunately, there is not a list of approved accommodations or modifications of which teachers choose. To have this would violate the IEP, which is required to be individualized per student. As a result, teachers and teams must determine how to best meet student needs.

There are several accommodations or modifications that could be utilized in the classroom to help students with various needs. For instance, for a student with an auditory processing disorder, the teacher could use short, one-concept phrases, ask shortened questions, use gestures or picture cues, and give appropriate "wait time." Of course, there are several other options that the teacher may allow. For a student with a visual perception or memory disorder, the teacher might find it beneficial to allow the student the use of books on tape/CD, provide instruction through both auditory and visual channels, or provide visual and verbal cues when student is describing or responding orally.

Teachers could also grade differently for students with various disorders or disabilities (i.e., pass/fail, rather than an actual letter/numerical grade), or use proximity for students who tend to get "off task" easily. Finally, other classroom accommodations or modifications that are used readily across grade levels include extended time for assignments, use of peer tutoring, use of weekly or biweekly progress reports, or use of a laptop or other technological device. Still, some other accommodations or modifications that might prove helpful could be to provide peer notetaker, provide a copy of teacher's notes or PowerPoints, preferential seating (which means allowing the student to sit front and center of instruction), allow the use of a behavioral modification chart for self-monitoring, break assignments into smaller segments or chunks, allow short breaks after a specified amount of time (varies by student need), use of a token economy system, or reduce amount of work (such as completing odd or even mathematical problems).

One thing to keep in mind, as a general education teacher, is that when you are teaching students with disabilities (SWD), they may have accommodations or modifications listed on their IEP that you are required to follow and some could extend to the testing environment as well. If SWD have accommodations or modifications listed as testing accommodations, they *must* also be used in the classroom environment, too. For example, a student cannot have a testing accommodation (oral administration, or something similar) that is not used in the classroom. If a student has oral administration as a testing accommodation, he or she is required to use it in the classroom, too. However, a student can have a classroom accommodation that is not used as a testing accommodation.

In addition to oral administration as a testing accommodation, some other common testing accommodations could include oral participation, oral tests, extra test time, allow someone to transcribe test answers, or provide a variety of test items, such as multiple-choice, essay, matching, true-false, or short answer.

Response to Intervention

In 2004, Response to Intervention (RtI) was reintroduced into the school setting through IDEA. This data collection strategy involves a combination of assessment and intervention used to provide early, effective assistance and support to children who are experiencing difficulty learning. Unbeknownst to popular belief, RtI is *not* a program for SWD. It is actually something used to collect data in the general education classroom, beginning in elementary school but quite possibly carrying into the secondary classroom. It is a method of diagnosing learning disabilities with some degree of specificity, hopefully minimizing academic failure because of the early intervention, regular progress reports, and intensive research-based instructional interventions for (general education) children who continue to experience learning difficulty. After collecting data on a specified student for a period of time, the teacher can then use this information to move forward with other interventions, if RtI is ineffective. One program RtI typically leads to is a special education program for a student.

Before a student could be identified for special services, there are steps (tiers, really) that a student progresses through for the data collection. Tier I is the lowest tier, in which all students participate, using targeted adaptations, as needed. Let us use "reading comprehension" as an area of concern for an example. If a teacher generally instructs "reading" for 90 minutes a day, a student who falls under RtI might receive the 90 minutes of instruction, in addition to another 20 minutes under Tier I. If the student begins to progress with reading comprehension, then the teacher continues at that pace, providing the extra reading time. However, if the student is still not progressing, he or she will move to Tier II, which is commonly applied as a type of pre-referral intervention. Students at Tier II will receive the same 90 minutes of reading instruction, plus the additional 20 minutes, but might also receive small group reinforcement before school, after school, or during a break during the school day. Again, if this intervention is successful, the student(s) will remain at this tier receiving the extra support. On the other hand, if this additional reinforcement is still not working, the student(s) will move to Tier III. This tier is even more intensive, and may include a referral for special education services.

Section 504

Another general education program that students might qualify for includes a 504 plan. A 504 was derived from the civil rights laws to prohibit discrimination on the basis of a disability in programs and activities (public and private) that receive federal money. Wright (2018) states that, "Section 504 ensures that the child with a disability has equal **access** to an education. The child may receive accommodations and modifications" (para. 1). A student who receives a 504 plan, almost always, has a medical condition (possibly temporary) that limits his or her progress in the academic curriculum. Any person with a physical or mental impairment that substantially limits one or more major life activities, has a record of impairment, or is regarded as having an impairment could qualify for a 504 (USDOE, 2018, para. 18). Some examples could be a student who has school phobia, irritable bowel syndrome, ADD/ADHD, a broken arm, or a pregnancy, to name a few.

Section 504 applies to both public and private recipients of federal financial assistance. In order for a student to qualify, he or she must either be incapable of performing a designated activity or must be significantly restricted in performing an activity. While 504 applies to both students and adults, for purposes of this text, it will be addressed for the secondary students of whom you will be working.

Students who are on a 504 plan are general education students who have a plan similar to the IEP, but it is significantly less detailed. While the IEP covers a multitude of information, including goals, services, and accommodations or modifications, the student on a 504 will only have the accommodations or modifications section that you, as a general educator, are to follow.

Gifted

The final population of students of whom you might instruct in your classroom is the gifted learner. Gifted education is considered special education, in that you must provide special instruction to meet their individual needs, but these students, as you are aware, are at the other end of the spectrum and require higher level thinking skills and activities to progress through the curriculum. A failure to do so could produce students with behavioral problems because of their boredom. Instructing gifted students does not mean the teacher is to give more problems or more reading—you do not want to punish the students for being bright. Therefore, as a teacher of gifted learners, it is your responsibility to enhance the curriculum and differentiate instruction to allow the critical thinking that this population craves.

One strategy to use with gifted students is compacting the curriculum. Compacting the curriculum can best be defined as, "a technique for differentiating instruction that allows teachers to make adjustments to curriculum for students who have already mastered the material to be learned, replacing content students know with new content, enrichment options, or other activities" (NAGC, 2018, para. 1). It is an instructional technique designed to make adjustments to the curriculum, regardless of the students' age or grade level, and can be used for any content area. Essentially, the procedure involves four steps, as identified by researchers at the University of Connecticut (2018). The steps involve

1. Defining the goals and outcomes of a particular unit or segment of instruction,

2. Determining and documenting which students have already mastered most or all of a specified set of learning outcomes, and

3. Providing replacement strategies for material already mastered through the use of instructional options that enable a more challenging and productive use of the student's time (Reis & Renzulli, 2018, para. 3).

As a teacher who is differentiating his or her lessons for the various learning modalities and exceptionalities, including the spectrum of special education to gifted education, it is important to keep Bloom's Taxonomy at the forefront of instruction because using the levels of learning is extremely effective in working with all learners.

WHAT IS INCLUSION AND CO-TEACHING?

Working with so many different types of students in one classroom can be an overwhelming task, but it can be even more intimidating when instructing all variations single-handedly. With the passing of IDEA, SWD are now required to be instructed in the least restrictive environment (i.e., one in which they are progressing through the curriculum without taking away from their or anyone else's needs). For this, Inclusion was developed. In years past, schools followed a "mainstreamed" method of instruction for SWD. Mainstreaming is similar but essentially different than Inclusion for several reasons. Mainstreaming is when "students with disabilities remain the responsibility of special education and are brought into general education settings if and when the curriculum and instruction are appropriate for individual students" (Beam, 2005, p. 22). It is allowing SWD to take general education classes without the support of the special education teacher. Most classes that are mainstreamed at the secondary level are the electives or physical education. Inclusion, on the other hand, is defined as "special education services [given] to students with special needs in general education classrooms in area schools among age-appropriate peers without disabilities" (Beam, 2005, p. 20). Inclusion is allowing the SWD to take general education classes *with* the support of the special education teacher. For the purposes of this text, Inclusion will be considered co-teaching, in which both the general education and special education teacher team teach a particular content specific lesson (i.e., math, English, science, or social studies) together for all students. It is beneficial because it allows two teachers to work with all students, not just those on a special education teacher's case load. This helps those students who would normally "fall through the cracks" and gives them the support they desperately need to be academically successful (Beam & Pinkie, 2015).

Inclusion is an extension of the traditional concept of mainstreaming with the intent of ensuring, as much as possible and when appropriate, that SWD be placed in regular classrooms along with their non-disabled peers. In situations where certain types of discipline are warranted, an effort must be made to ensure that the punishment does not *materially* and *substantially* interrupt the child's education. Marilyn Friend, the guru of co-teaching, has developed six different models to aid with Inclusion, any of which would be beneficial in all classrooms. The first co-teaching model is "**team teaching,**" also referred to as interactive teaching. By this, teachers share the responsibility and work closely together teaching the lesson(s). They might appear to be seamless in instruction where one teaches and the other adds to the discussion, much like two parents might instruct their children through discussion. The second approach is "**one teach-one drift.**" This approach is often observed when one teacher is leading the direct instruction, usually the general education teacher, and the other is assisting students by circulating during the lesson, usually the special education teacher. With the "**one teach-one observe**" approach, one teacher is responsible for instruction, while the second teacher observes to gather information for analysis. Next is "**station teaching.**" Some teachers might prefer to have smaller groups of students working in the classroom through independent work stations. During this type of method, both teachers will circulate and provide assistance, as needed. "**Parallel teaching**" is when the class is divided into skill or ability groups and both teachers lead a single group. The final strategy is "**alternative teaching**" by which one teacher leads the larger group, usually the general education teacher, and the other teacher provides additional practice or support, usually the special education teacher (Friend, 2007).

BEST PRACTICES FOR INCLUSION

Guidelines of Co-Teaching

One of the most important determinants of inclusion success is the attitude of the general education teacher toward accommodating SWD (Beam et al., 2015). It is difficult for two teachers to understand their unique roles so common planning time, additional training for inclusive teaching, and additional resources is imperative for a smooth transition. Co-teachers must plan together so they can discuss goals and objectives, aligning who will teach what in the classroom. It is also helpful if they both inform the parents of the arrangement, so they are not caught off guard with the changes.

There are numerous benefits to co-teaching, such as improved instruction, sharing the load of grading and instruction, reaching all learners of various needs, and more opportunities to generalize learned skills to the general education environment. There are also challenges to Inclusion for some. A large concern is the financial obligation of the program. The school district is paying for two teachers, essentially, instead of one, so it is more costly, but the two teachers do not necessarily stay together throughout the entire school day, so the special education teacher can accommodate different SWD at different grade levels, ensuring to meet their IEP service needs. If there is no common planning time, this could be a huge concern; the teachers need to know what their individual roles are within the classroom so the instruction is flawless. If there is any lack of cooperation or personality conflicts, this could be a concern, too. The administration should be on board with the program, which will, hopefully, trickle down to the classroom.

Collaborating With Others

Aside from collaborating with a co-teacher in an Inclusive environment, the general education teacher must collaborate with a number of other constituents. In order to effectively work with others, teachers must cooperate with individual needs, be able to effectively communicate and voice concerns as they arise, and share in problem-solving and finding solutions.

Some of the individuals the general education teacher will collaborate with include other colleagues, families, and community members, including doctors, psychologists, counselors, and so forth. While collaborating with others, effective communication is imperative. Teachers must be sensitive to the family structure of their students and understand the environment of which they are being raised. They should also build a positive rapport early on, preferably before the school year begins, so teachers and parents have open communication and are able to resolve potential problems before they become problematic.

ROLES FOR INCLUSIONARY TEACHERS

Inclusionary teachers should begin the habit of weekly planning time at the start of the school year. By engaging in common planning, they can discuss instruction strategies, co-teacher roles, student concerns, or personality concerns. It is best to address concerns early on so they do not escalate into larger problems. In addition to sharing the teaching load, they should also share in grading procedures. Both teachers should show that they are equal partners within the classroom. Some ways to exhibit their equality is by having both teachers' names on the board, having two desks in the classroom, having both teachers grade assignments so students can see each teacher's handwriting on assignments and both attending parent/teacher conferences, showing a united front (Friend, 2015).

COLLABORATION-AT-A-GLANCE

Co-teachers are, essentially, partners, much like a husband and wife. They should be viewed by the students as equal "parents," both having shared load and discipline in the classroom. Ultimately, they should be a cohesive unit that the students cannot undermine. Throughout several years of teaching, one acronym has always seemed to surface without author acknowledgment. It is the explicit acronym of PARTNERS, which is the epitome of collaboration at a glance:

Plan together weekly
Address classroom concerns proactively
Receive active and ongoing administrative support
Thrive on challenges and opportunities for growth
Nurture a sense of classroom community
Evaluate student performance systematically
Reflect on their practice and strive to improve their performance
Support each other professionally

(author unknown)

ADDITIONAL RESOURCES

- For additional information on Curriculum Compacting, visit the research conducted by University of Connecticut students at https://gifted.uconn.edu/schoolwide-enrichment-model/curriculum_compacting/
- For more information on Inclusion and co-teaching, visit Marilyn Friend's Co-Teaching Connection at http://www.marilynfriend.com/friendbio.htm

CHAPTER 4

Assessment

INTRODUCTION

Assessments are an inevitable part of education, for without some type of evaluative tool, it would be impossible to assess student learning. As teachers move into their first year in the classroom, it is imperative that consideration be given to the various styles of assessment. Many teachers are familiar, and use, traditional assessments, but what about other forms of evaluation, such as activity- (problem) or project-based assessment? When differentiating student learning, it is also acceptable to differentiate the assessments provided. For instance, how would a project or essay be evaluated? An answer key would not suffice for this type of assessment but, instead, the use of a rubric would. As teachers develop and become familiar with the varying kinds of evaluative tools, they should check to ensure that the directions are clear, that point values are understood (by section, if necessary), and that there are no "tricky" questions. The goal of evaluating students is not to "trick" them, but to really demonstrate if understanding of a previously learned topic has occurred.

TYPES OF ASSESSMENTS

There is a variety of terminology when discussing assessment. There are pretests; formal and informal assessments; formative and summative assessments; tests and quizzes; and traditional and product/ activity-based assessments. **Pretests** allow teachers to see the degrees of proficiency students have with the material and are typically provided at the beginning of a lesson to gain baseline data of student understanding of a particular topic; it is the starting point to investigate what students are actually coming into class already knowing about a topic (Kelly, 2017). Select examples could include any activity, assignment, or game. **Formal assessments** "have data which support the conclusions made from the test" (Weaver, 2018, para. 1). They, like pretests, might include **traditional** (i.e., multiple-choice, true-false, fill-in-the-blank, short answer, essay, or matching) assessments or **problem/ project-based** assessments. A problem- or project-based assessment, also known as a performance assessment, is "a student centered approach to learning which uses an interdisciplinary approach to solve an ill-structured problem" (Ferguson-Joseph, 2018). These are assessments that would require students to develop, design, or make something, such as a portfolio, poster, pamphlet, or presentation.

The teacher, in this scenario, acts more as a facilitator. **Informal** assessments, on the other hand, are not as data-driven, but more content- or performance-driven (Kelly, 2017). Examples include open discussion during class to see if students understand the material, exit tickets, or interaction through a class game, like Jeopardy or Who Wants to Be a Millionaire.

Most people understand the difference between a test and a quiz. A **quiz** typically covers a smaller "chunk" of information like a chapter in a unit. A **test,** however, covers much broader information, like a unit. When integrating tests, teachers can assign formative or summative tests. The **formative** assessments are a series of assessments that gauge and monitor learning throughout instruction. They typically have no point value and are "low stakes," while the **summative** assessment evaluates learning at the end of a unit. This type of assessment is typically considered "high stakes" and carries a high point value (CMU, 2016). Formative Assessments can be formal or informal assessments that, much like a pretest, might include tests, quizzes, activities, or games that would allow the teacher to check for understanding throughout each lesson. Summative assessments, then, could also be formal or informal assessments that cover a larger span of material. An example of a traditional summative assessment might comprise of a 30-item test that includes multiple-choice, true-false, matching, fill-in-the-blank, short answer, and essay, which of course would be evaluated using an answer key (and rubric for short answer and essay). An example of a problem- or project-based assessment, though, might require students to perform or display a skill developed from one or more of the curriculum content objectives such as the development of a portfolio, poster, pamphlet, or presentation.

The ASSESS acronym from the Curriculum Template (Chapter 1) could be used as often as every day because the assessment *could* be formal or informal. The informal assessments may not even be graded but it will give the teacher an idea of how students are progressing in the curriculum. When assessing the students, teachers should absolutely consider the testing format and ensure that the proportion of the tested items match the proportion of the insructional time spent on the lesson. Additionally, as teachers quiz students on various materials, they use that information to compile tests, which includes information that will be used for exams.

IMPLEMENTING ASSESSMENTS

As teachers continue to develop curriculum for the school year, it is important to space out the traditional assessments (i.e., tests and quizzes) throughout. As a rule of thumb, but not immutable, teachers could assess students with a quiz every 5–7 days, or after each chapter or concept in a lesson. Tests, then, could be every 7–10 days, or after each unit. Finally, exams, which would cover the most amount of cumulative material, could be delivered every quarter or semester, which could include all of the information learned during that time span.

Oftentimes, teachers develop curriculum off of one main textbook, and this would be encouraged. However, teachers should not build curriculum from one textbook, alone; teachers should adopt many resources (i.e., other books, textbooks, videos, or other supplementary material) to strengthen their subject area. As publishers' testing banks or teacher-made assessments are utilized, the common factor to consider is that students have clear directions listed at all times. By doing this, students will be able to understand exactly what is expected for each testing item. They will also understand how many points would be awarded for each section. It is probably not a bad idea to include a sample item for those who might have difficulties following directions. Furthermore, directions should include simple language, maintain consistency, and include a point value or other grading criteria. If teachers are assessing students with a product- or activity-based tool, rubrics should be included which also include specific instructions and grading criteria.

The goal of evaluation, as previously stated, is not to "trick" students, but to assess student mastery. As a result, when developing multiple-choice items, for instance, teachers should be mindful about the choices, such as opposite answers, choosing the best answer, or choosing possible answers. This type of option might be confusing which could warrant inaccurate results, so should be avoided. Moreover, teachers should be mindful with grammar connections, like ending sentences or options with an article ("a" or "an") as this will "give away" the correct answer. Instead, teachers would be more effective if they used complete statements.

When designing traditional tests that include "matching" items, teachers should limit the numbers to sets of 7 to 10 so as not to overwhelm the students. Tests can be reformatted quite nicely to separate testing items and including an extra blank space in-between items can make a huge difference for visual learners. Another helpful suggestion is to ensure that all matching items fit on one page, keep relationships (such as terms to definitions, items to functions, cause to effect, problem to solution, or item to function) consistent within the testing set (Beam & Pinkie, 2015).

True-False tests, in comparison, should also include complete sentences and should be free from any trivia items as this could be viewed as a "tricky" test strategy. Finally, when including essay items, teachers should have clearly established and stated directions with a specific question posed. They should contain enough information in the question that the student can accurately address in a complete manner and, again, should be assessed using a rubric. Grading rubrics for a short answer or essay can be developed to assess multiple areas such as grammatical errors, relationship concepts, or clarity of concept. A wonderful rubric-making tool that is available for free can be found at www. rubistar.com and includes an array of assessment items for short answer, essay, or oral presentation.

GOALS OF ASSESSMENT

As stated, the goal of evaluation is to ensure student mastery of previously taught material. It should also be used to assess the effectiveness of instructional techniques; if all students missed the same question on a test, for instance, the teacher might consider removing that test item from grading as it might be a "bad" question. Furthermore, in considering teaching practices, educators can evaluate what information should be retaught, possibly in a different manner to ensure that all students are learning pertinent information. A final goal of evaluation is to ensure that teachers are testing what they are teaching and that the material has been covered adequately in the curriculum. Otherwise, changes to the curriculum should be adjusted.

"TEST-TAKING" STRATEGIES

Students are not always aware of the best strategies to apply when taking tests or quizzes, so it would be helpful for the teacher to review effective test-taking strategies that would benefit all students in any class of which they are enrolled. Some of the strategies are quite simplistic, such as confirming that the students check test items for accuracy and that no missing answers have been included on the test. Students should also form strong habits of following all directions and reading all test options before selecting an answer. Sometimes, an answer might seem as if it is the correct answer, but after reviewing other choices, another answer might be more fitting to the question. This is a strategy that should be taught and reiterated often. One approach that seems to be quite helpful is for students to eliminate obviously incorrect answers. For example, if a student is taking a multiple-choice test and there are four answers, one of which is clearly inaccurate, the student should eliminate that option so as not to have unnecessary selections. They should also be cautious of key words that are commonly found in tests, such as "always" or "never," which are typically also incorrect choices. If all else fails, guessing is a useful strategy as it is better than leaving an answer blank. The last strategy that may prove helpful is to skip questions that might waste time, especially if there is a time limit, and then return to that question after the rest of the test has been completed. Again, however, it is important for students to habitually check over the testing items before they submit to the teacher to ensure that there are no blank spaces on their answer sheet.

GRADING PROCEDURES

Because there are several evaluative options that a teacher may impose on his or her students, it should be understood that there is not and should not be a "one size fits all" mentality with regard to grading. Some tests or quizzes, such as the traditional tests, will have an answer key provided. Answer keys are more objective because there is a "correct" or "incorrect" answer in most situations. Rubrics, however, often used with problem- or project-based assessments, are more subjective because there is no concrete "yes" or "no," "right" or "wrong," "black" or "white" answer, but yet a range of point values dependent upon the final product. When evaluating SWD, in contrast, teachers must follow their IEP as it is written, especially if there are grading options included. If students do not have a disability, teachers may grade by choice; they may use numerical grades, pass or fail approach, double-standard for various students, or no grade at all. It is completely in the power of the teacher to make that decision.

In considering all that was learned, thus far, regarding assessments, ideas seem to be well-defined with the inclusion of samples. In the next section, 9th grade English Curriculum assessments have been inserted to show the variations of a pretest, formative, and summative assessment. Figure 7 on page 58 includes a sample pretest assessment.

SAMPLE ASSESSMENTS

English: 9th Grade

Unit: Short Stories

Pretest/Diagnostic Assessment:

- *Diagnostic Assessment:* Literary Elements Spider Web Activity
  - Objective: Given a pre-assessment activity on literary elements, students will identify different uses of plot, setting, characterization, point of view, symbolism and irony, with each student identifying at least one use for every element.

Formative Assessments:

- *Formative Assessment #1:* Pop Quiz on "Da-Duh" and Point of View
  - Objective: Given instruction on point of view and a reading of the short story "Da-Duh," the students complete a pop quiz in class, scoring at least 16/20 correct.

- *Formative Assessment #2:* "Your Ring to Rule Them All" Activity
  - Objective: Given instruction on symbolism and movie clips from the trilogy *The Lord of the Rings*, students will identify and define four different uses of the ring of power as a symbol in the story.

Summative Assessments:

- *Traditional Summative Assessment:* Short Story Unit Exam
  - Objective: Given a 2-week unit on short stories, students will complete a unit exam, scoring at least a 75% or higher.

- *Product Summative Assessment:* Original Short Story
  - Objective: Given a 2-week unit on short stories, students will write their own original, fictional short story, fulfilling all the components set forth on the rubric and scoring at least an 80/105.

FIGURE 7   Pretest/Diagnostic Sample Assessment

Literary Elements Spider Web Activity

1. Begin activity by having students push back their chairs and desks and form a circle sitting on the floor. Lay out a large sheet of butcher paper and draw a spider diagram on it, similar to the one pictured below:

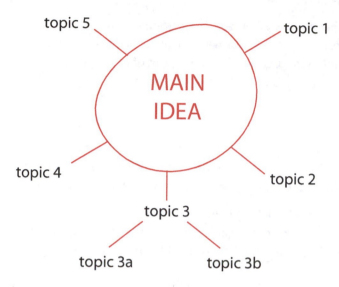

2. Scatter Sharpies on the floor and write "Literary Elements" in the circle. In corresponding stems from the circle, write the six different elements to be studied in the unit: plot, setting, characterization, point of view, symbolism, and irony. Ask students to brainstorm about the different components and contemplate their understanding of each: what do the terms mean to you? Are you familiar with them? Can you think of stories/movies that use these elements in a unique way? And so forth. On the branches of the stems, ask students to each write/draw at least one idea per element that expresses their basic understanding of it. They may draw pictures, write down titles of works/characters/stories, write personal experiences, and so forth. Each student should write their initials in small letters next to each of their ideas for assessment purposes.

3. After each student has written at least one idea per element, open up class time to discussion. Have each student take a turn sharing their understanding of these elements.

FIGURE 8   Formative Sample Assessment #1

"Da-Duh" and Point of View Quiz

Name: _____

Date: _____   Class: _____

There are 10 questions; each question is worth 2 points, totaling 20 possible points.

1.   What do the narrator and Da-Duh keep discussing/debating throughout the story?

   A.   Religion
   B.   Politics
   C.   Their Hometowns
   D.   Skin color

2.   What city is the narrator from? _____

   Answer: New York City

3.   Where does the narrator travel to? *(may answer with city or country)*: _____

   Answer: St. Thomas; Barbados

4.   Why does the narrator's mother *apologetically* present her daughter to Da-Duh?_____

   Answer (Any of the following are correct): She knows Da-Duh will disapprove of her skin color; Her skin is darker than the rest of the family's; The daughter is willful and bold

5.   *(Creative Response)* Provide one adjective that describes Da-Duh [think about her characterization].

   Possible Answers: Snarky, dry-humored, critical, insightful, perceptive, analytical, sharp, bold, brazen, and so forth.

6.   By the time the narrator has sent a postcard of the Empire State Building, what has happened to Da-Duh?

   A.   She has moved away
   B.   She has died
   C.   She is blind and cannot read/see the postcard
   D.   Her husband has died

7.   What happens on the last day of the narrator's trip?

   Answer: A huge storm blows up

8.   "'But Adry,' she said to my mother and her laugh was cracked, thin, <u>apprehensive</u>. 'Where did you get this one here with this fierce look?'" Define *apprehensive*.

   Answer: feeling alarm; afraid, anxious, or worried

9.   This story is told in which point of view?

   A.   First Person
   B.   Second Person
   C.   Third Person Omniscient
   D.   Third Person Limited

10.   True or False: The narrator uses the pronoun "I" frequently throughout the story.

   Answer: True

FIGURE 9   Formative Sample Assessment #2

"Your Ring to Rule Them All" Activity

Name: _____

Date: _____   Class: _____

Directions: Fill in each segment of the Ring of Power with examples from *The Lord of the Rings* that helps make the ring such a potent symbol. You may draw or write about each example. You may also draw/write reasons why the ring is an ironic symbol in the story. Below the ring, write at least one sentence for why you chose each of your four drawings/descriptions.

Arcady/Shutterstock.com

Label each of your four sections on the ring chart. Now explain why you chose the particular representations above.

#1: *Possible Answer:* **War**: *The ring symbolizes war because many groups of people in Middle Earth have fought over it for centuries. Many men have lost their lives over it, and it is the object that ruins peace and causes people to turn people against each other.*

#2: *Possible Answer:* **Power**: *The ring symbolizes power because of how many men desire to obtain it in order to exercise dominion over their enemies. The characters use powerful, potent language to describe the ring and actually refer to it as the "Ring of Power."*

#3: *Possible Answer:* **Evil**: *The ring symbolizes evil because of its negative influence on almost all who obtain it. Gollum is the perfect embodiment of this. Although the ring may prolong life or give the ring bearer power, it comes at a high cost of evil influence. Also, because the ring was made by the Dark Lord and consequently the most evil man in Middle Earth, its meaning and symbolism is inherently evil in nature.*

#4: *Possible Answer:* **Obsession**: *The ring symbolizes obsession because of its enticement and power over individuals; it does not only symbolize political war power because it potently affects women as well.*

FIGURE 10   Traditional Summative Sample Assessment

FICTIONAL SHORT STORIES
EXAM

Name: _____

Date: _____   Class: _____

PART I—Graphing and Labels

Directions: Label the graph with the different parts of plot. Provide a descriptive phrase of what each part means. *(Worth 4 points each [2 points per blank, 2 points per description]; total of 20 possible points)*

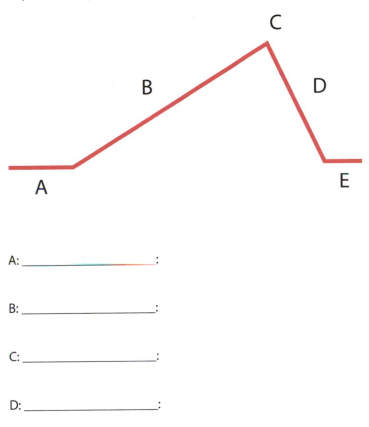

A: _____:

B: _____:

C: _____:

D: _____:

E: _____:

PART II—Multiple-Choice

Directions: Answer each multiple-choice question with the answer that *best* fits. *(Worth 4 points each; total of 40 possible points)*

1. An *inference* is _____ .

    A) A visual description of a character
    B) A logical assumption readers can make about a character
    C) A part of the plot where the story comes to a conclusion
    D) The way one distinguishes between the protagonist and the antagonist

2. In relation to symbols, "red rose is to _____, as a skull and crossbones is to _____."

    A) passion; anger
    B) comfort; poison
    C) beauty; fury
    D) love; death

3. Which story is the character Madame Loisel from?

    A) "The Necklace"
    B) *The House on Mango Street*
    C) "The Lottery"
    D) *Angela's Ashes*

4. In class, we continually talked about how irony brings _____ to a story.

    A) Depth
    B) Horror
    C) Humor
    D) Passion

5. "Even cannibals wouldn't live in such a Godforsaken place. But it's gotten into sailor lore, somehow. Didn't you notice that the crew's nerves seemed a bit jumpy today?" This excerpt from "The Most Dangerous Game" is an example of setting used as _____.

    A) An inference
    B) Irony
    C) Foreshadowing
    D) Symbolism

6. We read the short story, "Thank You, M'am," by Langston Hughes as a prime example of _____ in writing.

    A) Passive sentences
    B) An effective use of Point of View
    C) Unique voice
    D) Characterization

7. J. M. Barrie's creation of the character Peter Pan has become a _____ of eternal childhood.

    A) Inherited symbol
    B) Invented symbol
    C) Ironic representation
    D) False symbol

8. Which of the following is NOT one of the ways from which we draw character inferences from a text?

    A) Through thoughts, like stream of consciousness
    B) Through other characters' reactions, like dialogue
    C) By studying static versus dynamic characters
    D) A character's actions

9. In what stage of plot is characterization of the main characters most likely to take place?

    A) Exposition
    B) Falling Action
    C) Rising Action
    D) None of the Above

10. In Third Person Omniscient point of view, the narrator . . .

    A) Tells the story using pronouns like I, we, and us
    B) Is an actual character in the story
    C) Often refers to himself/herself directly
    D) Can tell readers what every character thinks/feels

PART III—Matching

Directions: Choose a word from the word bank below that best matches/describes each sentence. *(Worth 4 points each; total of 20 possible points)*

Passive Sentence	**Active Sentence**	
Figurative language	**Antagonist**	**Conflict**

1. The terms "Mam," "Cod," and "Souper" are all examples of this element in stories. _____

2. Marcelle took the book from the shelf and perused it in the library. _____

3. This is central to every story's plot. _____

4. The book was taken from the shelf and was perused by Marcelle in the library. _____

5. Often coined as "the bad guy" of the story. _____

PART IV—Short Answer

Directions: Respond to the two short response questions with mini paragraphs. You may write in complete sentences or simply list your points, but each answer should be thorough and explanative. You will be graded on the accuracy with which you answered the question, the depth/thoroughness of your answer, and your ability to clearly and concisely convey your answer. *(Worth 5 points each; total of 10 possible points)*

1.   Choose one round character from one of the short stories that we read in this unit. Briefly explain how that character was characterized so that we as readers could draw inferences about them. (Hint: Think of the five methods of making inferences)

2.   Recall our class discussion about *La Clairvoyance* by Rene Magritte. Discuss at least one element in this painting that represents either <u>symbolism</u> or <u>irony</u>.

PART V—Matching

Directions: Match each term to its definition and each character or setting to its correct story. *(Worth 1 point each; total of 10 possible points)*

1.	New York versus Barbados	A.	"The Most Dangerous Game"
2.	Static Character	B.	"The Necklace"
3.	Mrs. Hutchison	C.	"Peter and Rosa"
4.	Forestier	D.	*The House on Mango Street*
5.	Dynamic Character	E.	Does not change in story
6.	Elenita	F.	"To Da-Duh"
7.	Ship-Trap Island	G.	*Angela's Ashes*
8.	The ship's figurehead	H.	"The Lottery"
9.	Irish Immigrant Family	I.	Changes/grows in story
10.	Ring symbolism	J.	*The Lord of the Rings*

1.   _____

2.   _____

3.   _____

4.   _____

5.   _____

6.   _____

7.   _____

8.   _____

9.   _____

10.   _____

FICTIONAL SHORT STORIES
EXAM ANSWER KEY

Part I:

A: <u>Exposition</u>: introduction material of a story
B: <u>Rising Action</u>: the problem/conflict(s) are introduced; tension builds
C: <u>Climax</u>: the "height" of the book
D: <u>Falling Action</u>: the effects of the climax
E: <u>Resolution</u>: how the book ends; the conclusion

Part II:

1. B
2. D
3. A
4. A
5. C

6. D
7. B
8. C
9. A
10. D

Part III:

1. Figurative Language
2. Active Sentence
3. Conflict
4. Passive Sentence
5. Antagonist

Part IV:

1. Grade individually. Students should draw from the five ways: thoughts, appearance, other characters' reactions, words, and actions. Students should accurately represent the character they choose to discuss.

2. Grade individually. Students' answers might discuss the subject versus the actual painting, the relationship between the bird and the egg and what that signifies, where the man's eyes are directed, his facial expression, and so forth.

Part V:

1. F
2. E
3. H
4. B
5. I

6. D
7. A
8. C
9. G
10. J

FIGURE 11   Product Summative Sample Assessment:

Original, Fictional Short Story

Explanation: Throughout the unit, students have learned about fictional short stories and seven primary literary elements that are present components in almost every story. In writing their own story, students must creatively apply what they have learned by creating their own story and implementing all seven of the literary elements in their own unique work.

Grading: Students will be graded according to the rubric. With 7 categories at 5 points each, there is a total of 105 possible points.

RUBRIC:

CATEGORY	4 Excellent	3 Good	2 Satisfactory	1 Unsatisfactory
Length	Paper is typed, double-spaced, and 3–6 pages long.	Paper is typed, double-spaced, but slightly under or over page length (2 1/2 pages or 7 pages long).	Paper is typed. Spacing may be incorrect. Paper is 2 pages in length or >8.	Paper is not typed nor double-spaced. Paper clearly does not meet length requirements: under 2 pages.
Grammar and Mechanics	Paper is excellently written and is void of glaring errors. The paper is void of grammatical and spelling errors and void of all misplaced or missing punctuation.	Paper reads well. Relatively good grammar and punctuation, with less than 5 errors in grammar, spelling, and punctuation.	Paper is relatively coherent. Contains more than 1 glaring error and/or has 5–8 mistakes in grammar, spelling, and punctuation.	Paper is poorly written, with multiple glaring errors and >10 mistakes in grammar and punctuation.
Setting	Many vivid, descriptive words are used to tell when and where the story took place.	Some vivid, descriptive words are used to tell the audience when and where the story took place.	The reader can figure out when and where the story took place, but the author didn't supply much detail.	The reader has trouble figuring out when and where the story took place.
Active/ Passive Voice	Several action verbs (active voice) are used to describe what is happening in the story. The story seems exciting!	Several action verbs are used to describe what is happening in the story, but the word choice doesn't make the story as exciting as it could be.	A variety of verbs (passive voice) are used and describe the action accurately but not in a very exciting way.	Little variety seen in the verbs that are used. The story seems a little boring.

CATEGORY	4 Excellent	3 Good	2 Satisfactory	1 Unsatisfactory
Plot	It is very easy for the reader to understand the problem the main characters face and why it is a problem. The parts of the plot can be clearly identified (on plot graph).	It is fairly easy for the reader to understand the plot and problem the main characters face and why it is a problem. The parts of the plot can be identified (on plot graph).	It is fairly easy for the reader to understand the problem the main characters face but it is not clear why it is a problem. It is difficult to identify the parts of the plot (on plot graph).	It is not clear what problem the main characters face. It is not possible to identify the specific parts of the plot (on plot graph).
Characters	The main characters are named and clearly described in text as well as pictures. Most readers could describe the characters accurately.	The main characters are named and described. Most readers would have some idea of what the characters looked like.	The main characters are named. The reader knows very little about the characters.	It is hard to tell who the main characters are.
Title	Title is creative, sparks interest, and is related to the story and topic.	Title is related to the story and topic.	Title is present, but does not appear to be related to the story and topic.	No title.
Point of View	The chosen point of view is appropriate to the style/content of the story. Student maintains consistent point of view.	The student stays relatively within the chosen point of view and does not change perspective.	The point of view that was chosen is not clearly identified; student may use more than one point of view.	No definite point of view is evident.
Symbolism	Student uses one or more symbol(s) in his/her story and incorporates irony into the plot and/or symbolism.	Student uses at least one symbol effectively in the story.	Student uses one symbol, but it is hard to identify and textual details supporting the symbol are not clear.	Student uses no symbolism in the story.

SPECIAL EDUCATION TESTING ADAPTATIONS

As discussed several times in various chapters, general education teachers will, more than likely, have SWD learning alongside their non-disabled peers in the classroom. As a result, it is essential that teachers, whether working in an inclusive environment or not, understand how to modify assessments. Below are several strategies that may be useful for general education teachers in working with students of varying needs: assign a peer tutor to facilitate with note-taking, teach test-taking strategies, use a variety of testing formats, enlarge printed material, reduce number of items assigned or provide fewer choices for tests/quizzes, read aloud or oral administration, use of transcribe, allow partial credit for graded assignments, remove time restrictions, and simplify language of assignments. The Pacer Center (2015) also shared several examples for testing accommodations and testing modifications that might also prove beneficial:

Tests: Accommodations

- Go over directions orally
- Permit extended time to complete tests
- Allow test to be taken in a room with few distractions
- Have materials read to the student and allow oral responses (for tests that don't measure reading or writing)
- Divide tests into small sections of similar questions and problems
- Allow the student to complete an independent project as an alternative test
- Provide study guides and study questions that directly relate to tests
- Provide a sample or practice test

Tests: Modifications

- Use recognition tests (true-false, multiple-choice, or matching) instead of essays
- Grade spelling separately from content
- Provide the first letter of the missing word
- Allow take-home or open-book tests
- Provide a vocabulary list with definitions
- Provide possible answers for fill-in-the-blank sections

While this list is not comprehensive, it does allow a starting point for teachers to adapt curriculum for SWD.

ADDITIONAL RESOURCES

- For a great rubric making tool, visit www.rubistar.com. This tool will allow teachers to create a plethora of rubrics and pull from already built-in assessment criteria.
- A wonderful site to visit that helps with test-taking strategies, study skills, and relieving anxiety can be found at https://www.testtakingtips.com/
- For additional ideas in working with SWD, this site shares examples of textbook and curriculum, classroom, and instruction accommodations and modifications: http://www.pacer.org/parent/php/PHP-c49a.pdf

CHAPTER 5

Writing Lesson Plans

LESSON VS. SESSION

Writing lesson plans is a skill that all teachers will master during their professional career. One of the first things that teachers will learn as teacher candidates is the difference between a lesson and a session. Lessons, which cover a period of instruction, begin with an objective and end with an evaluation. It is the material learned from start to finish when mastering objectives. Sessions, in comparison, cover a specific period of time in which students are focused upon learning, leaving time for reflection and practice. Sessions of learning occur within lessons, so there could be multiple sessions. When developing curriculum, teachers should be mindful that each session could last as long as one instructional period for one day, but could also carry over to multiple sessions (i.e., days) within each lesson. For this, the objectives should also carry over for each day that the sessions/lessons are planned. After teachers and students complete the lesson for a particular objective, the teacher should then summarize the learning that has taken place and evaluate using formative or summative (informal or formal) assessments to gauge mastery of the material. For SWD, more frequent review might be necessary for retention.

TEMPLATE

All schools and/or districts will develop a particular template which teachers should follow when writing daily lesson plans. Daily lesson plans are more detailed than are the block plans and are primarily used for beginning teachers. Block plans, then, are typically used for curriculum writing, such as those that would be written in the curriculum template (Chapter 1). The lesson plan template, however, provides similar information, regardless of the format in which it is written. Originally developed by Madeline Hunter (1982), a simple lesson plan template, emphasizing masterly teaching and learning, can be found in Figure 12.

FIGURE 12 Template for Sample Lesson Plan

I. Subject and Grade Level:
II. Topic:

III. Standards:
     A. (Insert State) Standards of Learning:
     B. National Standards of Learning:

IV. Objective:
V. Materials:
VI. Technology Connection:
VII. Character Education Principle:
VIII. Pre-Assessment/Anticipatory Set:

IX. Procedures:
     A. Set
     B. Developmental Activities:
         1. Instruction:
             a.
             b.
             c.
         2. Guided Practice:
 	
         3. Independent Practice:
     C. Closure:

X. Diversity/Differentiation for Exceptionalities:
     A. Learning Styles (***modalities/multiple intelligences***):
         1.
         2.
         3.
     B. Exceptionalities:
         1. Gifted
         2. LEP/ESL
         3. LD/ED/etc.
     C. Multicultural Connections:

XI. Evaluation/Assessment:

Adapted from School of Education, Liberty University. (2015).

SUBJECT/GRADE LEVEL

For the Subject/Grade level section, teachers write the subject of the lesson and the grade level for which the lesson is taught. An example would be 11th grade U.S. History.

TOPIC

The topic of the lesson is the specific area of which learning will focus; it is the topic within the subject area. For instance, for 11th grade U.S. History, the topic within the subject area of Social Studies could be Manifest Destiny.

STANDARDS

The standards should include both state and national standards for each curriculum plan and are required to be included into the daily lesson plans and block plans. If the lesson were written in the state of Virginia, the standards would be listed as such:

Virginia Standards of Learning: *VUS.6.b*—identifying the economic, political, and geographic factors that led to territorial expansion and its impact on the American Indians.

National Standards of Learning: *NSS-USH.5-12.4L*—The institutions and practices of government created during the Revolution and how they were revised between 1787 and 1815 to create the foundation of the American political system based on the U.S. Constitution and the Bill of Rights.

There are several websites that will facilitate finding state standards, particular to a teacher's locality, in addition to the national standards. Each student should search their state department of education for their specific state standards. For example, in Virginia, the student would search "VDOE" for the state standards of learning (SOLs). He or she should then refine the search by grade level and content area, to retrieve specific state content standards. Many states choose to use Common Core Standards and only nine have not adopted the standards. For a complete list of the English/Language Arts and Math standards, please visit www.corestandards.org.

Searching national standards is a little different. The links for national standards, by content area, are listed below for reference:

English	NCTE	www.ncte.org
Foreign Language	ACTFL	www.actfl.org
Mathematics	NCTM	www.nctm.org
Music	MTNA	www.mtna.org
Reading	IRA	www.reading.org
Science	NSTA	www.nsta.org
Social Studies	NCSS	www.ncss.org
TESL	WIDA	www.wida.us/

OBJECTIVE

An objective is typically one sentence that summarizes what the student should be able to do at the end of the lesson. The sentence should be a simple statement that is specific in nature, measurable, and purposefully communicates the evaluation. It should include four parts: the **condition** (the circumstances under which a task will be performed), the **learner** (who is responsible for learning), the **task** (states what the learner will be able to do at the end of the lesson, and the **measure** (to what extent the task shows mastery; it could include a percentage or a number of accuracy). When developing curriculum objectives, the level of learning is clearly communicated by the verbs used in the condition, according to Bloom's Taxonomy.

> **Reminder:** The higher the grade level, the higher the level of Bloom's Taxonomy verbs that are to be inserted into the objectives (condition).

Using the same subject, grade level, and topic as used previously, an example of an appropriate objective, which includes all four parts could be the following:

> **Objective**: Given the information about traveling to the west, the students will map out the trails to the west with 4/4 correct answers.

Without a doubt, when inserting comprehensive objectives into the daily lesson plans and curriculum, teachers are able to easily determine exactly what they are or should be teaching and how to assess mastery of learning as it provides guidance to students of what they should be learning and how they will prove that learning has taken place. Arreola (1998) shares the three key ingredients in developing a solid objective:

1.　A description of what the student will be able to do;

2.　The conditions under which the student will perform the task; and

3.　The criteria for evaluating student performance

MATERIALS

Materials are an important component of any lesson as it prepares the teacher for the day ahead. It is imperative to include not only the text materials, but also to include any websites, technology, or other supplementary material that is necessary to carry out the lesson. Failure to be prepared makes a teacher appear unprepared and, sometimes, ignorant of the lesson. Planning a curriculum means that all student needs must be addressed (DIV—differentiation) and understand that not all students learn the same way with the same materials, so variety is key with teaching approach and materials. Using the same example as a guide, there are several materials that would ensure a productive lesson:

> **Materials**: PowerPoint, textbook, map of the United States, markers, color pencils, paper, pencil

TECHNOLOGY INTEGRATION

The next section of a lesson plan is technology integration. This includes *any* form of technology that will be used to follow through with the lesson, including that which will be used to present the lesson, that which will enable the students to be engaged, or that which facilitates the activities. Some ideas of technology integration are Prezi, PowerPoint, or PowToons to present the lesson; and Smartboard, Prometheus, Elmo, Wikis, iPads, Twitter, Poll Everywhere, Kahoot.it, Quia, or Webquests to facilitate student engagement.

CHARACTER EDUCATION INTEGRATION

Character Education (which falls under the acronym CE on the template), while not a typical part of lesson plans, is something that should certainly be implemented and considered when working with youth of any age. The Character Education Partnership (CEP) is "a nonprofit, nonpartisan and nonsectarian organization that supports and promotes social, emotional and ethical development in youth defines character education as 'the deliberate effort by schools, families, and communities to help young people understand, care about, and act upon core ethical values'" (1999, para. 1). This principle (sometimes called moral education) when molded successfully, "fosters ethical, responsible, and caring young people by modeling and teaching good character through an emphasis on universal values that we all share. It is the intentional, proactive effort by schools, districts, and states to instill in their students important core, ethical values such as respect for self and others, responsibility, integrity, and self-discipline" (CEP, para. 2).

As teachers, we are constantly striving to help students be more successful academically, emotionally, morally, and ethically. For this, along with the decline of societal values, the concept of Character Education is finding its way into public and private schools alike. By enacting a CE program into the classroom, teachers are finding that there is a stronger, positive, classroom environment, which in turn, helps with classroom management (Beam & Pinkie, 2015).

Concepts of Character Education

The concepts of CE, which transpire in all facets of life include many of the "common sense" ideals that one would consider when envisioning the definition of CE. Some of the pillars of CE are trustworthiness, respect, responsibility, fairness, caring, and citizenship. Any of these would enable a student to learn to be a productive member of society and the qualities would benefit him or her throughout their lives. Additional doctrines which are of utmost importance to develop are the character principles of having a positive attitude, self-discipline, conflict resolution, or caring. As a teacher who is investing in the lives of his or her students, teaching the CE principles is setting the students up for success in *life*, not just the school environment. It is something that can be integrated quite successfully in any content area and allows the teacher to tie in values (often found in children's literature books), historical concepts from the past (from social studies content), or consequences (may be found in cause and effect discussions from science curriculum). Movie clips are also a great way to integrate CE principles by use of values. Teachers, as stated, are able to positively influence the lives of their students through modeling various CE principles, some of which will be discussed below (Beam & Pinkie, 2015, p. 52):

1. **Consideration of Others**—Encompasses several values, such as compassion (being able to share and respond to the needs of others, providing assistance to comfort them), conflict resolution (being able to handle uncomfortable situations without offending oneself or the other person), cooperativeness (being able to work together, as a team player), courtesy (inclusive traits of politeness, manners and kindness), forgiveness (being able to remove resentment and anger toward someone who has wronged us), gratitude (being appreciative for kindness, admiration, or love toward us from another), loyalty (commitment to a person or group of persons), reliability (the ability to depend on someone), or tolerance (being able to respect differences in nature, beliefs, or standards between parties). All of these values have one common thing—*others*!

2. **Truth**—Incorporates values of honesty (absence of fraud, deceit, lying, or stealing), integrity (being able to live honestly, truthfully, and sincerely in all aspects of life), or justice (respect and concern for others, peace).

3. **Consideration of Self**—Includes the values of discipline (being able to practice restraint over one's emotions and behaviors), perseverance (continued effort toward achieving success, even in the face of opposition), sacrifice (being able to give up something valuable for the sake of others), self-control (being able to exercise restraint over one's impulses, emotions, or desires), and self-esteem (exercising the belief in one's self and potential as a productive contributor of society).

4. **Responsibility**—Contains the values of citizenship (working, voting, paying taxes), courage (being able to face obstacles, danger, and determination), stewardship (taking care of something, especially something of perceived value), equality (equal rights, opportunities, and status), respect for authority (being able to accept the direction of leaders or supervisors in different circumstances with a balance of obligation and acceptance), respect for environment (taking care of the world around us), and work ethic (understanding that diligence in all aspects of work is honorable and will be rewarded with personal satisfaction, the sense of accomplishment, and possibly, material prosperity).

Using the same example from the Social Studies lesson as a guide, here is how a teacher can integrate Character Education into the lesson:

Character Education Principle: Using the example from the 11th grade U.S. History: Manifest Destiny lesson, an appropriate principle could be:

Perseverance—it was America's idea that we should have all of the land so they kept moving west until one day America would acquire all 50 states.

PRE-ASSESSMENT

The pre-assessment was discussed in-depth in the previous chapter. This is an important component of any lesson plan as it creates baseline data for the teacher to better prepare activities.

PROCEDURES

The Procedures section of the lesson plan is the "meat" of the plan as it discusses the "set," the "instruction" that the teacher will deliver; the "guided practice" that is the teacher-led instruction, aligned with practice opportunities; the "independent practice," which is the time allotted for students to work by themselves for reinforcement; and the "closure," which is a formal or informal evaluation to gauge student mastery over the set objective. A more detailed description follows.

Set

This section is the anticipatory set but could also be considered the pretest. It allows the teacher to provide an opportunity of collecting baseline data on the student's previous knowledge of a particular topic to see what the students are coming to the class already knowing about the upcoming lesson. It also will identify areas the teacher may need to strengthen or reinforce with some students (DIV). The set is usually an interactive or, otherwise, fun way of getting the students involved and engaged in the learning to follow.

(Example) **Set**: The students will watch a brief rap video about Manifest Destiny.

Instruction

The instruction is the initiation of a new topic and should be delivered at the knowledge or comprehension level of Bloom's Taxonomy. Different instructional strategies will keep the students involved at different rates, so it is important to determine and understand the class as a whole and deliver the material appropriately. Some methods to use for direct instruction are lecture or whole or small group discussion. The instruction should be very detailed and allow any person to come into the classroom and be able to teach the lesson (i.e., substitute teacher) so as much detail should be listed as possible. An example of instruction for the Manifest Destiny lesson is:

Instruction: The first thing that I will talk about is the reasons why Americans wanted to go west. These reasons are for religion and for new land at a cheap price. Then I will move on to the definition of Manifest Destiny and how John O'Sullivan coined this term in 1846 in the newspaper *Democratic Review*. Though it was coined Manifest Destiny, James K. Polk talked about America's right to move west in his Inaugural Speech. Then I will talk about how squatters were claiming land before it was settled and then congress passed the Preemption Act of 1830 which allowed people to claim land before the government surveyed it. They were allowed to claim as much as 160 acres at the price of 1.25 an acre. Then I will go on to talking about the land of Oregon. At the time, the United States and Great Britain occupied the land jointly. Then I will talk about the response Great Britain gave the United States after James K. Polk was inaugurated. Then I will talk about the American Missionaries that headed to Oregon to convert Native Americans. On their trip they find that Oregon is beautiful and they tell all of their east coast friends that they need to go see it. I will then talk about settling California. Mexico became independent from Spain in 1821. Though few people lived there in 1839 the governor gave John Sutter 50,000 acres. These acres became Sutter's forge. This is a place people would come when they first arrived in California, it was a trading post and a cattle ranch. By 1845 there were only 200 Americans living in California. Then I will talk about how the trails were founded. Mountain men became familiar by the routes with the help of Native Americans and eventually there was the Oregon trail, the California trail, and the Santa Fe trail. Then I will talk about the Donnor Party and how they got stuck in the Sierra Nevada and how that resulted in cannibalism. Then I will talk about the preparation the people had to go through before they left to go west. Then I will talk about the roles of men and women while they traveled west. The last thing that I will talk about is Native Americans and how they helped the Overlanders on their way out west. As the traffic increased the Native Americans began to worry about the buffalo. The United States and 8 tribes came together and created the Treaty of Fort Larafie in 1851. This plotted out specific territories that the tribes owned and it was promised to them forever. The last movement I will talk about is the Mormons moving west. I will talk about how Joseph Smith was murdered and then Brigham Young became the leader. The Mormons were facing religious persecution and so they decided to skip town and move west to Utah.

Guided Practice

Guided practice is not the same as direct instruction, also referred to as modeling, where the students are able to see what they are learning as the teacher demonstrates the process or lesson (Hunter, 1987). Guided practice is more teacher-dominated rather than student-dominated and allows the students to practice the new learning under teacher supervision. For this, the teacher guides the learning process and works through problem-solving with the students collaboratively. After the instructional time, the guided practice allows the teacher to work with a small group of students or work with individual students. Once the teacher believes the class understands the information, he or she moves on to the "independent practice section." The guided practice portion should be at the application or analysis level of Bloom's Taxonomy. In continuing with the 11th grade History lesson, the guided practice for Manifest Destiny might appear similar to this:

> **Guided Practice**: As the instruction goes on the students will be asked to draw on their United States maps the trails that I will be talking about. By the end of the lesson they should have four trails drawn on their map and they will also label the states that the trails went through.

Independent Practice

Independent Practice is the portion of the "procedures" in the lesson plan that allows the students to transition from group work to independent work. The teacher does not remove him or herself from facilitating learning; however, he or she might take a step back and allow the student to make mistakes, guiding them to find their errors by pointing out necessary corrections. Independent Practice should be at the application or analysis level of Bloom's Taxonomy. Using the same lesson from Manifest Destiny, an example of Independent Practice could be:

> **Independent Practice**: After hearing about the different trails and the life of moving west, the students have the option of drawing what it may have looked like or students may write a descriptive piece on life moving west.

Closure

Closure is the final piece of the "procedures" portion of the lesson plan. For this, the teacher should be able to wrap up the learning and develop some sort of assessment to assess student learning. The assessment, as previously mentioned, could be informal or formal assessment and should be at the synthesis and evaluation level of Bloom's Taxonomy. An example of an appropriate closure for the 11th grade lesson is:

> **Closure**: After the students have finished their writing or drawing I will ask the students to volunteer and read or describe what is in their writing or drawing. They will then point out the difficulties of moving west and how they portrayed them.

DIVERSITY/DIFFERENTIATION

Differentiation (which falls under the acronym DIV on the template) has been discussed in depth during Chapter 2. The discussion from Chapter 2 discusses how to differentiate and how to account for diversity by learning styles/modalities, exceptionalities, and multicultural experiences. Teachers are strongly encouraged to review this chapter when developing the Diversity portion of the lesson plan as it may provide more guidance and suggestion.

Learning Styles—Multiple Intelligence

A thorough discussion of learning styles and modalities can be found in Chapter 2. Please refer to this chapter when developing this section of any lesson plan. An additional example, taken from the Manifest Destiny lesson plan is as follows:

> **Learning Styles** (*modalities/multiple intelligences*)—*Visual*—There will be a PowerPoint with lots of pictures, which will facilitate for UDL. We will also be watching a short video at the beginning of class to accommodate the UDL for visual learners. *Kinesthetic*—To accommodate for UDL, we will be drawing trails on the U.S. map and we will also be drawing pictures of the hardships of life moving west. To individually differentiate, students may choose if they participate in that activity or build a model to display the trails. *Auditory*—For UDL, the students will listen to the lecture and also hear the rap in the video. To individually differentiate, students may make their own rap or poem. *Linguistic*—The students will have the option of descriptive writing portraying what life was like while going west or drawing what it might have looked like during that time period.

Learning Preferences

Learning Preferences is also another way to show DIV in the template. Sometimes, something as simple as changing the learning environment can make the world of difference for various learners. Teachers may choose to group students differently (small group, whole group, individual, pairs, etc.) or change the lighting in the classroom (natural lighting of opening the windows or shades, turning on lamps, or having the fluorescent lights on during instruction). Teachers might also accommodate for student preferences by changing where students sit. Sometimes, it might be appropriate to hold class in the classroom, but other times, if the weather is nice, to go outside and sit on the lawn to work. Changing seating arrangements from time to time can keep increased motivation levels, too. Another way to accommodate differences is the temperature in the classroom. Sometimes having it too hot will make students sleepy, while having it too cold will hinder learning. A good balance is necessary at all times.

Gifted Education

Gifted education was previously discussed, as well (see Chapter 3). An example could be the following:

> **Gifted**—The students will be asked to put in their descriptive writing all of the elements that were part of moving west.

Limited English Proficiency

While several types of students have been previously discussed, such as gifted and SWD, those students with limited English proficiency (LEP) have yet to be shared. Students with LEP are similar to special education, in that they may require accommodations to progress in the general education curriculum, but they are *not* SWD. Students with LEP may range from a level 1 ("entering"—WIDA, 2012) to a level 5 ("bridging"—WIDA, 2012), but the level 4s and 5s are those who will, most likely, be more successful in the general education classroom because those are the students who are better able to speak and understand the English language. An example of accommodating the LEP students in a lesson plan could be:

> **LEP**—In the lesson I will provide many visual aids, and a few words on the Power-Point, so that the students with Limited English Proficiency will be able to follow along with the lesson.

Special Education

This topic has been discussed at length in Chapter 3, so as teachers prepare for the DIV section of lessons, special attention should be directed to the appropriate section in this chapter. To differentiate for SWD, here is an example:

> **LD, ED, ADD**—For the *learning disabled*, I will print off the PowerPoint and also provide additional notes before class starts. This way the students can focus on the notes and what I am saying and not trying to write down their own notes. For the *emotionally disturbed*, I will place students by a person they feel comfortable beside. I will also place the student at the end of the row for easy access. For the students with *Attention Deficit Disorder* (while this is not an IDEA identified disability, it is one that I will accommodate for in the classroom), I will not hand out the worksheet until I am about to begin the assignment. This will make sure that the students are focused on the lesson and not the additional materials. These students will be placed in the front of the classroom so I can easily regain their attention.

Multicultural Connections

It is always a good practice to differentiate by multicultural connections as well, if possible, in the classroom. Any time a teacher can tie his or her student's heritage into the lesson, it is a good way to make the material relevant and personal. Some examples are to discuss the variations of ethnicity and/ or religion in a particular lesson, or to have students bring in food from that time period or culture to immerse themselves and others in learning (Beam & Pinkie, 2015).

ASSESSMENT/EVALUATION

This is the final section of the lesson plan that teachers should complete so attention should be focused on Chapter 4, since it discusses assessment and evaluation in great detail and also provides samples of alternative assessments. Special attention to Chapter 4 should be sought if additional support is preferred while writing the "assessment/evaluation" section of the lesson plan. For teachers to be effective in their subject matter and confirm that learning has taken place, he or she should be sure to seek and implement different types of tests, be aware of the purpose the test serves, consider how the test can be used, and understand how to interpret the results. Students, as stated in Chapter 4, need to be tested on the learned material and practice different testing options and strategies. Following is an example of different types of assessment that could be used for our lesson:

> **Assessment**: (Informal)—informal discussion of questioning and asking the class to tell what they heard during the lesson. (Formal)—this could be a test or a quiz on the material learned.

WRITING BLOCK PLANS

Block plans are similar to lesson plans, in that they both plan out what the teacher will teach their students for the day. However, block plans are different from lesson plans because they do not go into the same amount of detail as do formal lesson plans. Earlier in this chapter, teachers learned the required sections of a lesson plan; these parts should always be included on a daily basis. When teachers are completing their teacher licensure programs and student teaching, they oftentimes follow a traditional lesson plan format. Conversely, after student teaching is completed and a teaching position is secured, teachers tend to follow a block plan. Sometimes, private schools or schools located overseas do not have curriculum plans already in place for teachers to follow. Because of that, teachers may be responsible for writing curriculum for an entire school year. In that event, they will use the template (Chapter 1), or something similar, to write block plans, enabling a more manageable and realistic approach to daily lessons.

A block plan focuses on the objective, activities, and assessment that will be covered for a daily lesson. Instead of writing out every detail of the lesson (i.e., the standard, objective, materials, technology connection, character trait connections, the set, instruction/teacher modeling, guided instruction, independent practice, diversity and differentiation alternatives, closure, and evaluation—lesson plan format), the teacher simplifies the lesson into bullet points or numbered points of what exactly will be covered (i.e., page numbers in the book, worksheets, general guidelines of instruction—block plan format). The detailed lesson plan would typically be written out in detailed form and probably be as long as two to three typed pages, but the block plan will take just a small "block" of time in the template.

For the purposes of this curriculum project, teachers will complete the template using block plans only. To otherwise follow a lesson plan format for 180 days would be an unrealistic expectation. Consider yourself a curriculum planner who is providing an "overview" of what would be involved in each lesson. Therefore, create the block plan using the template; this will enable you to then use this overview to create a detailed daily lesson plan.

The block plans (template) should include a measurable daily learning objective, the state and national content standards covered for the lesson, any materials or other resources required to carry out the lesson, and the learning activities and assessments (using the legend from the template) clearly denoted which would account for the amount of class time utilized for each lesson. In addition, each block plan should exhibit an adequate amount of time for instruction as well as learning activities (i.e., planned experiences should sufficiently fill the allotted instruction time of 45 minutes for a bell schedule or 95 minutes for a block schedule). The lessons should be creative, engaging, hands-on, and include age-appropriate learning activities and assignments (be sure to complete the legend for each activity assessment—see samples in Part II of the text). Finally, although in block plan form, instructional plans and activities should be thorough enough to understand concepts and experiences.

ADDITIONAL RESOURCES

Madeline Hunter, the originator of appropriate and effective lesson plan writing, has shared countless ideas on how to write a lesson plan containing all of the required sections. This resource breaks down the lesson plan in a step-by-step format and allows the candidate to develop age-appropriate, measurable lesson plans: https://www.doe.in.gov/sites/default/files/turnaround-principles/8-steps-effective-lesson-plan-design-madeline-hunter.pdf

Writing daily lesson plans vary tremendously from writing block plans, and there are several formats that are acceptable. For a few examples in writing block plans, go to Chapters 8 and 9 to see how candidates formatted their plans. The block plans should be detailed enough and include a measurable objective, the materials, and a step-by-step skeleton plan of the daily work.

CHAPTER 6

edTPA

WHAT IS EDTPA?

With new initiatives constantly on the horizon, edTPA is no different. Developed by Stanford University faculty and staff at the Stanford Center for Assessment, Learning, and Equity (SCALE), edTPA appears to be the "new" normal with regard to teacher preparation programs. This program, owned with exclusive rights to Stanford University, required countless hours of collaboration from teachers, teacher educators, and national subject-matter organizations such as the National Council of Teachers of Mathematics, the National Council of Teachers of English, and the National Science Teachers Association, to name a few (SCALE, 2018).

The question that often arises is, "What is edTPA?" edTPA is the acronym for Educative Teacher Performance Assessment and is a "performance-based, subject-specific assessment and support system used by teacher preparation programs throughout the United States to emphasize, measure and support the skills and knowledge that all teachers need from Day 1 in the classroom" (SCALE, 2018, para. 3). In short, it is a way to measure teacher effectiveness in the classroom with regard to planning, instruction, and assessment. The electronic portfolio is constructed by the teacher candidate to validate their ability to deliver high quality instruction to a differentiated audience through effective lesson plans (i.e., learning segment). Once the plans are developed, the candidate must then video and self-assess actual periods of instruction from the lesson plans, and compile student work samples, pre- and posttest assessments, and student data to analyze assessments directly aligned with the learning segment (IFLTE, 2013).

Each content area of instruction has its own edTPA handbook which includes specific details on how to display mastery. To date, there are 27 different handbooks which drive the instruction in elementary education, special education, and all content areas of secondary education (e.g., math, science, social studies, art, music, business, etc.).

Teacher candidates are now required in over 35 states to prepare a portfolio during their student teaching semester to gain state licensure. "edTPA requires aspiring teachers to demonstrate readiness to teach through lesson plans designed to support their students' strengths and needs; engage real students in ambitious learning; analyze whether their students are learning, and adjust their instruction to become more effective. Teacher candidates submit unedited video recordings of themselves at work in a real classroom as part of a portfolio that is scored by highly trained educators" (SCALE,

2018, para. 4). These requirements are also referred to as separate tasks (i.e., Task 1, Task 2, and Task 3), which will be explained in further detail a little later in the chapter.

Because our schools are charged by the Every Student Succeeds Act (ESSA), formally referred to as No Child Left Behind (NCLB), it is now the responsibility of the teacher preparation programs of various colleges and universities to ensure that our candidates are prepared to meet the various academic needs to all learners. Teachers must now come equipped with not only content knowledge, but skills to support learning needs, modalities, and differentiated strategies (AACTE, 2018). Evaluated by Pearson, this is the first standards-based assessment to become nationally available in the United States and could be compared to other licensing exams required in other professions (i.e., medical licensing, architecture exam, or the bar exam in law) (AACTE).

The assessment is not requiring candidates to do anything more than what they are already doing in their student teaching experience, but it does require additional proof of their abilities. For example, instead of a teacher candidate writing various strategies and objectives into a daily lesson plan, he or she must include research of best practices to demonstrate *why* various aspects are included in the plans. The theory is equally tied to the practice and student performance with edTPA. Designed to focus on three aspects (e.g., Planning, Instruction, and Assessment), successful teachers, according to IFLTE (2013), should be able to:

- Develop knowledge of subject matter, content standards, and subject-specific pedagogy
- Develop and apply knowledge of students' varied needs
- Consider research and theory about how students learn
- Reflect on and analyze evidence of the effects of instruction on student learning (para. 2)

As identified in Figure 13, every aspect and content in education has its own unique edTPA handbook of which candidates may refer to while compiling documentation (Liberty University, 2018). Students seeking initial licensure in Liberty University's education preparation program submit specific content endorsed material to their electronic portfolio by using the following codes:

FIGURE 13   edTPA Endorsement Codes *(Initial Licensure Only)*

- ELE Elementary Education *(preK–6)*
- SPE Special Education *(K–12)*

Secondary *(6-12) *preK–12 programs*

- BUS   Business Education
- EAL*   English as an Additional Language *(TESL)*
- FCS   Family and Consumer Science
- PED*   Physical Education *(with Health)*
- PFA*   K–12 Performing Arts *(Music-Instrumental/Vocal, Theatre Arts)*
- SEH   Secondary History/Social Studies
- SEL   Secondary English Language Arts
- SEM   Secondary Mathematics
- SES   Secondary Science *(Biology, Chemistry)*
- TED   Technology and Engineering Education *(Computer Science)*
- VSA*   Visual Arts
- WLA*   World Language *(Spanish)*

Middle *(6–8) (MAT only)*

- MCE   Middle Childhood English Language Arts
- MCH   Middle Childhood History/Social Studies
- MCM   Middle Childhood Mathematics
- MCS   Middle Childhood Science

Other Codes

- AGR   Agricultural Education
- CLA   Classical Languages
- ECH   Early Childhood (add-on)
- ELL   Elementary Literacy
- ELM   Elementary Mathematics
- ETS   Educational Technology Specialist
- HED   Health Education (only with PE)
- LBS   Library Specialist
- LSP   Literacy Specialist

It is each candidate's responsibility to ensure that they read and understand their own subject-endorsed edTPA handbook as they begin to build their portfolio for Pearson submission.

EDTPA STATE PARTICIPATION

As noted in Figure 14, more than 40 states including the District of Columbia (and 771 Educator Preparation Programs) have formally adopted edTPA or are considering edTPA for state license renewal (AACTE, 2018). Some states have policies in place while others are still in an "exploratory phase." The states coded "white" are not yet participating in edTPA initiatives, while those in "red" have a current policy in place. "Blue" represents the states that are taking steps toward implementation, and the "tan" include the states that are participating in edTPA (AACTE).

FIGURE 14 [AU: ADD TITLE]

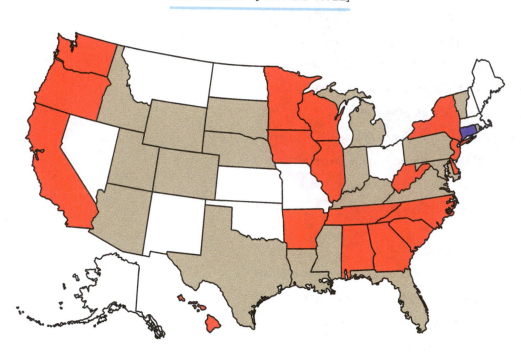

Image © Ad_hominem/Shutterstock.com

Data source: http://edtpa.aacte.org/state-policy

☐ **Not yet participating in edTPA**

🟥 **Policy in Place**
In general, these states have statewide policies in place requiring a state-approved performance assessment as part of program completion or for state licensure and/or state program accreditation/review. In these states, edTPA also has been approved as a performance assessment for these purposes.

🟦 **Taking Steps Toward Implementation**
A performance assessment and/or edTPA are being considered at the state level for program completion or as a licensure requirement.

🟫 **State Participating in edTPA**
At least one provider of teacher preparation—either traditional or alternative—is exploring or trying out edTPA.

Additional information on state participation can be found on the edTPA website.

TASKS DEFINED

As discussed previously, there are three tasks associated with the completion of edTPA. The first task surrounds the topic of Planning (intended teaching), while the second task deals with Instruction (enacted teaching). Task 3, then, includes the assessment aspect (impact of instruction on student learning). Figure 15 (IFLTE, 2013) encompasses a visual of edTPA.

FIGURE 15   edTPA Cycle of Tasks

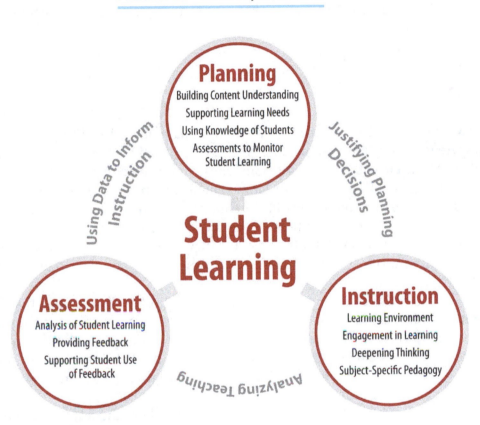

With student learning at the forefront of edTPA, the evidence of the three tasks provides a cyclical framework. Teacher candidates, in their prospective educator preparation programs, must reflect and analyze the relationship that each task addresses with the focus, again, on learning needs (AACTE, 2018).

The first task, Task 1, envelopes the planning aspect. This includes the daily lesson plans and the units, also referred to as "learning segments." A learning segment is a mini unit comprised of three to five daily lesson plans that build upon one another from one day to the next. In this planning phase, teacher candidates build their content knowledge, support learning needs, use knowledge of students to further develop plans, and include assessments that monitor student learning. The planning piece contains the typical instructional piece of instruction, including direct instruction, guided practice, and independent practice. It then, however, goes a step further to include differentiation, prior knowledge, and language demands. When teacher candidates submit their edTPA portfolio to Pearson for evaluation, they are assessed on four components, which include Planning, Instruction, Assessment, and the Analysis of their Teaching (AACTE, 2018).

The second task of edTPA focuses on effective teaching and the ability for candidates to evaluate their instruction. The preferred method of this analysis is through video capture. Candidates may use a video camera, cell phone, or laptop computer to record an actual lesson. Within the video recording, candidates should ensure that the learning environment is visible to display engagement in the learning, a deepening concept of thinking, and subject-specific pedagogy. This task is heavily focused on the teacher candidate's ability to instruct a solid, content specific, lesson (AACTE, 2018).

The final task is Task 3, which includes the assessment portion of edTPA. The assessment submission should include an analysis of student learning, evidence of teacher feedback, and support the use of student feedback. By review of student learning through assessment, candidates can modify their lessons in Task 1 to ensure that all students are learning the presented material at their highest potential (AACTE, 2018).

TASK 1 (PLANNING)

As previously noted, Task 1 completes the "planning" phase of edTPA. This task requires students to display competence in designing research-based lessons that elicit higher level thinking and evaluation for different learners within one classroom. The planning piece contains the typical instructional piece of instruction, including direct instruction, guided practice, and independent practice. It then, however, goes a step further to include differentiation, prior knowledge, and language demands (see Figure 16). To reiterate, teacher candidates who are seeking employment in an edTPA-participating state must submit their portfolio to Pearson for evaluation and confirm that the required four components are present (i.e., Planning, Instruction, Assessment, and the Analysis of their Teaching) (AACTE, 2018).

Task 1 not only includes the learning segment (i.e., three to five lessons that build upon one another), but there are other required components that candidates must incorporate to show analysis of their submitted learning segment. The first component of Task 1 is the "Context for Learning." This piece of documentation includes the demographics of the school/classroom from which the learning segment is being written. The Context for Learning is at least three pages, and should not exceed four pages (Liberty University, 2018).

The first part of the Context for Learning is information about the *school*. Candidates completing this section should include information on the type of school (e.g., elementary, middle, high, etc.), the description of the school (e.g., city, suburban, rural, etc.), any special features of the school (e.g., charter school, magnet school, Inclusive school, bilingual school, etc.), and requirements or expectations that might affect the planning or delivery of instruction in this school.

The second part of the Context for Learning surrounds the actual *classroom* where the learning segment will be delivered. Information such as the title of the course/subject, the length of the course (e.g., one semester, one year, etc.), or any ability grouping or tracking being used in the class. Candidates should also include the textbook or instructional materials being used for the learning segment.

The third, and final, aspect of the Context for Learning to include covers information about the *students* within the classroom where the learning segment will be delivered. Such information as the grade level, the number of students (including number of each gender), the number of students who have an IEP or 504 (see Chapter 3) or other specific learning needs (i.e., ELL or "At Risk" learners) is also discussed.

Now that the Context for Learning (part 1 of Task 1) and the Learning Segment (part II of Task 1) has been discussed, it is time to discuss the final part of Task 1—the Planning Commentary. The Planning Commentary is the analysis piece of the culminating edTPA Task 1 and also requires that specific information be addressed. As Part I and Part II are analyzed, the Commentary should be at least six pages in length but not exceed nine pages (AACTE, 2018). It should describe the central focus or purpose of the learning segment and include how the objectives and standards address conceptual understanding, technical skills, and problem-solving strategies. A step further, this analysis will require the candidate to further explain how the plans build upon each other to make connections between those skills.

Secondly, the Commentary should address how the knowledge of students has or will inform or adjust instruction. Candidates are required to describe what is known about the students within the classroom with respect to the central focus of the learning segment (part II of Task 1). They must consider academic learning and show evidence of what students currently know, what they are able to accomplish, and what they are still learning to accomplish. It is similar to the previously used K-W-L Charts that preparation programs used in previous years (i.e., What do students **K**now, What do students **W**ant to know, and What did students **L**earn). The second part of the Commentary will require candidates to consider personal, cultural, and community experiences as they relate to the learning segment.

They must also show justification of how they were able to support their students' learning in the classroom using research-based practices and/or theories. Explicit attention to the academic and personal learning needs should show a connection and justification of why the candidate incorporated specific strategies and other planned supports in the learning segment.

A fourth aspect to ponder shows how the candidate developed instruction through language. Students' language needs are completely addressed in this section of the Commentary and should identify the language function, such as the student's ability to analyze, argue, explain, interpret, or summarize. Other language demands are also included and include vocabulary, symbols, syntax, or discourse.

Finally, as with any analysis, monitoring student learning and success is paramount. By completing the fifth section of the Commentary analysis, candidates will describe how the planned formal and informal assessments used in the learning segment provide direct evidence of student understanding, technical skills, and problem-solving strategies throughout the segment. Candidates finish the commentary by explaining how adaptations necessary for students with other learning needs have been addressed (see part III of the Context for Learning) in their learning.

The completion of all three parts encapsulates Task 1: Planning for edTPA. Figure 16 shows the template used and adapted by the Liberty University School of Education leadership team for candidates to practice this task.

FIGURE 16 Daily edTPA Lesson Plan Template

Preliminary Information	
Created by:	**Date developed:**
Subject/Topic:	**Date of lesson:**
Grade Level: **Number of students:**	**Learning Segment Theme:**
Where in the learning segment does this lesson occur? (Beginning, middle, or end?):	**Structure(s) or grouping for the lesson** (Select all that apply) Whole class, small group, 1:1: Other (specify):

Any other information that you know about the context, including diversity among the students:
Resources and materials required for the lesson (e.g., textbook(s), module, equipment, technology, art materials):

1.   **What are your goals for student learning and why are they appropriate for these students at this time?**
Big Idea or Concept Being Taught—CENTRAL FOCUS
Rationale/Context for Learning—JUSTIFICATION FOR YOUR PLANS (Why this lesson at this time, for this group of learners? How does it connect to previous learning or succeeding lessons?)
Prior Knowledge and Conceptions (What knowledge, skills, and/or academic language must students already know to be successful with this lesson?)
Prior knowledge: **Prior skills:**   **Prior academic language:**
Content Standards State National
State: National:

Learning Objective(s)
(These must be behavioral & measurable.) **STATEMENTS OF WHAT STUDENTS WILL <u>KNOW</u>, <u>UNDERSTAND</u>, AND <u>BE ABLE TO DO</u> AT THE END OF THE LESSON** (consider all three domains)—Include condition, performance, criterion

Academic Language Demands Identify the language demand(s)— Identify language support(s)
Language Demands:
Language Supports:

LU SOE Specific Lesson Requirements
Character Education:
TCA Alignment:

2. How will you know and document students' progress toward meeting your learning objectives?
Evidence and Assessment of Student Learning (How will you know whether students are meeting your learning objectives? What tools will you use to measure their progress? How will you provide feedback to promote student learning?)
Diagnostic/pre-assessment(s):
Formative assessment(s)/feedback to learners:
Summative assessment(s):

Expectations for Student Learning—STANDARDS & CRITERIA
(Describe in detail the following levels of student performance. What will students' work look like when it exceeds expectations? When it meets expectations? When it falls below expectations? How will you communicate these expectations to students? Provide any rubrics you will use.)
Exceeds expectations:
Meets expectations:
Below expectations:

3. How will you support students to meet your goals? Describe EXPLICITLY what you will do!
BEGINNING: Launch/Hook/Anticipatory Set (How will you get the lesson started? What questions, texts, inquiry, modeling, and/or other techniques will you use to engage students?)

MIDDLE: Instructional Strategies to Facilitate Student Learning
(For example: How will you engage students with ideas/texts to develop understandings? What questions will you ask? How will you promote question generation/discussion? What activities will you use to engage students in learning . . . for individuals, small groups, or the whole class? How will you incorporate technology? How will you address the academic language demands? **Detail your plan.** Note: For math lesson plans, please write or attach every task/problem students will solve during the lesson—with the correct answers.)
Instruction/Modeling:
Guided Practice:
Independent Practice:

END: Closure (How will you end the lesson in a way that promotes student learning and retention?)

Differentiation/Extension (How will you provide successful access to the key concepts by all the students at their ability levels?
Supporting students with special needs (this includes an explicit and specific description of how you will implement accommodations/modifications required by IEPs/504 Plans and other ways that you will address diverse student needs): **Challenging above-average students:** **Facilitating a classroom environment that supports student learning:** **Extension:**

What Ifs (Be proactive—Consider what might not go as planned with the lesson. What will you do about it?
What if students . . . **What if students cannot . . .**

References (Cite all sources used in the development of this lesson including URLs or other references)

TASK 2 (INSTRUCTION)

While Task 1 shows mastery over Planning, Task 2 allows candidates to visually assess their own teaching practices and complete an analysis on the effectiveness of their lesson. Candidates who wish to show evidence of effective instruction are required to record a lesson pulled from their learning segment (i.e., Task 1) and analyze for student mastery. The video recording will, more than likely, have to be compressed for viewing, and is then uploaded into each candidate's electronic portfolio for easy retrieval. Within the video recording, candidates should ensure that there is evidence of instruction and student engagement.

After the video has been compressed, candidates will review the video and analyze the instruction by completing the Instruction Commentary. The Commentary, as does the Task 1 Commentary, directs candidates to address certain criteria. The first item to include is the specific topic or lesson that is shown in the video. Candidates must then review the video to distinguish a positive learning environment (e.g., demonstration of mutual respect, rapport, and responsiveness to student needs and backgrounds). Student engagement is a critical area of analysis for Task 2, and this entails the development of skills, inquiry, interpretation, or analysis as it relates to instruction. The fourth component addressed in the Commentary is support for deepening student learning during the learning segment. Candidates must explain and provide examples of how they elicited and built upon student responses to support their arguments or conclusions from the engagement. Finally, a summary of the instructional analysis should be included in the commentary. By this, candidates can refer back to the video to identify changes or adjustments that they would make for the whole group instruction, or specific learning challenges. The Commentary should be approximately four single-spaced pages, not to exceed six pages. However, for Special Education, their Commentary should range from five to eight pages.

For the completion of Task 2, candidates will record a lesson, review the recording, and complete the Instruction Commentary to analyze their recording. Pearson uses a rubric to evaluate this task and specifically looks for proficient or advanced performance in various areas. The first evaluates the learning environment (e.g., rapport, respect, challenge and alternative perspectives); the second focuses on student engagement (e.g., subject-specific task development, connections from previous to current material, and connections to lived experiences); the third requires evidence of deepening student learning (e.g., questioning strategies that prompt higher level thinking, interactions among students, and student self-evaluation). The fourth component that is evaluated is the proof of subject-specific pedagogy (e.g., ensuring that students use evidence from various sources to interpret, analyze, and build solid arguments or conclusions based on their content); and the final portion of the rubric analyzes effective instruction (e.g., addresses gaps in whole class learning, re-engages student learning, uses grounded theory or research to address learning).

TASK 3 (ASSESSMENT)

The final task to be completed for edTPA submission is Task 3, Assessment. The assessment submission should include an analysis of student learning, evidence of teacher feedback, and support the use of student feedback. In considering both Task 1 (Planning) and Task 2 (Instruction), candidates will compile all components along with the assessment aspect to assess student learning, Task 3.

As the candidates begin compiling assessment data, such as pre- and posttests, student data, student work samples, and whole class analyses, they must complete the edTPA Task 3 analysis, Assessment Commentary. The Commentary, as does the Tasks 1 and 2 Commentaries, directs candidates to address certain criteria. The first item to include is the analysis of student development of English language proficiency through content-based instruction. Candidates will identify the specific learning objectives from the assessment portion of the learning segment (Task 1). They are also encouraged to provide a graphic or table that summarizes whole class student learning from three student work samples (one of which who is either a SWD, an English Language Learner, or an "at risk" student). If the video from Task 2 shows the candidate working with one of the three students, he or she should clearly identify the student to the Pearson evaluator by whatever means possible.

The second item to address in the analysis is feedback used to guide further instruction. Candidates should refer to evidence included from the three student work samples and identify the feedback that was provided, explain how the feedback was provided addressing strengths and needs, and describe recommendations that are needed to support the identified students.

Third, candidates are required to provide evidence of language understanding and use in the content area. Pearson prefers that candidates provide concrete examples from student work samples and explain how the students used or struggled to use selected language, vocabulary or key phrases, and grammatical, discourse, or pragmatic competence to develop content understanding. All of this evidence provided thus far leads to the final component of Commentary, which is using the assessment to guide instruction. Based on the analysis of student learning provided in the previous sections of the Commentary, candidates should describe the next steps to be used to impact student learning for the whole class and for the three identified students used in the sample. Candidates should also explain how the "next steps" are derived from theory or best practices ensuring that researched-based analyses are thoroughly discussed. The Commentary should be at least seven single-spaced pages, not to exceed ten pages. However, for Special Education, their Commentary should range from five to eight pages.

For the completion of Task 3, candidates gather all of their assessment evidence, along with the student work samples, and organize the material for edTPA submission, if that is the chosen path. Pearson, again, uses a rubric to evaluate this task and specifically looks for proficient or advanced performance in various areas. The first area of evaluation in the assessment rubric analyzes students' development of English language proficiency through content-based instruction (Tasks 1 and 2). Candidates must show evidence in the assessments that lists correct and incorrect answers, lists areas where the whole class excelled or struggled, and shows learning trends.

The second portion of the rubric allows the candidate to provide feedback to guide student development of English language instruction (e.g., specific feedback connected to language proficiency or content, specific feedback addresses strengths and needs connected to English language proficiency and content, and displays how at least one student receives feedback to connect to previous learning). Next, candidates identify student understanding and use of the feedback provided by including a clear description of how one or more focus students understand the feedback to improve their work or deepen their understanding of the content.

Next, candidates analyze students' language use and content understanding by explaining or providing evidence of students' language use and providing examples of their use through their language demands (i.e., vocabulary, key phrases, grammatical, discourse, or metalinguistic competence). Providing evidence for students with various needs would strengthen this section. Finally, candidates should use the assessment piece to guide instruction of English language with specific content. For this evidence, candidates can explain the "next steps" that would/should be taken for whole class language proficiency and content learning, and provide theory and research-based initiatives to support the English Language Learners.

After candidates align their Task 1, 2, and 3 for a specific content area, they may choose to submit to Pearson for evaluation. If there is a possibility that the teaching candidate will be moving to one of the participating edTPA states, he or she should review the process to submit their portfolio for scoring (SCALE, 2018).

ADDITIONAL RESOURCES

There are several resources that may prove useful in the review and implementation of edTPA. Below are some websites that include an abundance of useful information:

- To learn more about edTPA, visit: http://www.edtpa.com/PageView.aspx?f=GEN_AboutEdTPA.html

- For an overview of edTPA, visit: http://edtpa.aacte.org/about-edtpa#Overview-0

- For specific information about the edTPA as it relates to Foreign Language, visit: http://www.flte.illinois.edu/edtpa/

- For general information, including frequently asked questions, visit: http://edtpa.aacte.org/faq.

- For submission requirements, visit: http://www.edtpa.com/PageView.aspx?f=HTML_FRAG/GENRB_FAQ_Candidates.html

- For edTPA resources, visit:

www.edtpa.com
http://edtpa.aacte.org/
https://scale.stanford.edu/

CHAPTER 7

Behavior Management

CONTEXT OF BEHAVIOR

Student behavior is, quite possibly, one of the most difficult tasks for a first year or new teacher to manage. Once under control, however, students directly involved and those in the near environment will perform better on tasks, both academically and emotionally (Beam & Pinkie, 2015). New teachers should understand that their behavior and the way they react to various situations is very often a response to their environment, which could include interaction with teachers, peers, other personnel, or their physical environment (Ackerman, 2007). There is not a "one size fits all" reason or response to student behavior, but it is important to know that when they do "act out," there is a function. Some reasons could include power, revenge, attention, or avoidance (Ackerman). Sometimes, power-seeking students attempt to provoke teachers into a struggle of wills, also referred to as a "power struggle." It is a good practice to avoid these types of situations and, instead, direct attention to other students within the classroom.

Students who have behavioral issues might also be performing such actions because of revenge or they might be seeking attention. Attention-seeking students prefer being punished, admonished, or criticized over being ignored, so they will do anything to get a reaction from whomever the attention is sought. Teachers should provide attention to the student when he or she is on task and cooperating and following directions. By this, it will allow them to retrain their attention-seeking behavior from negative to positive—kind of like the "catch 'em being good" concept—and they gain positive attention. Sometimes, students might also misbehave because they are trying to avoid a situation or they might just want to be left alone. If a student is academically weak in a particular area, say math, he or she might begin to disobey so as to redirect attention off of their shortcomings. A lot of times teachers, rather than dealing with the real issue, send students out of the classroom, which saves the embarrassment that the student would feel if he or she had to actually mathematically perform, but this does not resolve the true issue.

Teachers who have a well-managed classroom will find that students tend to have more fun while learning, as they appreciate the structure of the classroom. They might also be able to cover more material than those with poor management skills. In order to begin to have a smooth-running classroom, free from constant behavioral disruptions, teachers need to establish positive relationships with their students. When students know that their teacher cares (dare I say "loves"?) them, they will work harder because they know that the teacher is coming from a good place. On the other hand, when a teacher reports to work on a daily basis and has no meaningful interaction with the students or just acts like he or she would rather be elsewhere, the dynamic of the class shifts from what could be a positive learning experience, to an "I don't care" feel. Many misbehaviors exhibited by students are responses to a behavior exhibited by the teacher (Wong & Wong, 2009), so the relationship component of teaching is crucial to first year success. Also, teachers should never tolerate undesirable behavior, no matter what the excuse (Ackerman, 2007). This does not mean that the teacher cannot be sensitive to situations that might be causing the misbehavior, but there are always consequences for behavior (good or bad), so the ground rules must be established on day one of a new school year. The relationship component, remember, will carry far in managing classroom issues that will certainly arise. For that, try to understand the *why* factor, as this will allow the teacher to effectively deal with that behavior.

DEFINING BEHAVIOR

When students misbehave, teachers are constantly wondering why it has occurred, and how to reduce the occurrences. Sometimes, they might think that a student just has a "bad attitude" or is "lazy." This is never okay in the educational realm; everything a teacher does or says should be backed up with facts, and not "feelings." The data collection, and yes—it is all data collection when you step foot into a classroom—is what is relevant in parent/teacher conferences, teacher-teacher meetings, or in the event of "due process," which is a term used for going to court at the school level. Individuals at the various levels never want to hear that a student has a bad attitude. Instead, define what that means in terminology that everyone can understand (this is where the data collection begins). For example, instead of saying, "Sara never gets anything done in class," say "She doesn't complete her classwork in 4 out of 5 days per week." Perhaps there is an unidentified learning disability or some other circumstances that are keeping her from completing her work, rather than her just being "lazy." The factual data will allow teams to brainstorm possible solutions to overcome the classroom issues that Sara is facing in class.

When students misbehave in class, there is something to help with easy retrieval—referred to as the ABCs of behavior. As teachers begin to learn additional strategies in overcoming behavioral obstacles, they should always consider first the Antecedent (i.e., What happened immediately before the behavior? Will environmental changes set the student up for success or failure?); then the Behavior (i.e., What is the actual behavior being observed?); and lastly the Consequence (i.e., What happened following the behavior and why did the student act out in such a manner?) (Webster, 2018). By considering the reasons behind the action will allow the teacher(s) to try different strategies to help replace the misbehavior with a positive reaction. It might be helpful for you to make a chart of student behavior, similar to the sample in Figure 17. Candidates can also track student behavior to see how often a particular behavior occurs. By collecting and disaggregating the data, candidates can develop an effective behavior management plan that should deter and eliminate behavioral problems.

FIGURE 17   Student Behavior Chart

Student Name	Behavior: Talking to Other Students	Behavior: Refusing to Stay on Task	Behavior: Sleeping in Class	Behavior: Talking Back
Monday	XXX		XX	X
Tuesday	XX	XXX	X	
Wednesday		XXXX	X	XX
Thursday	XX		XX	
Friday	XXXX		X	X

MOTIVATION

The motivation behind student behavior is difficult to determine, oftentimes. However, it is imperative to find the root of behavior. In determining what makes students "tick," teachers should try to establish a supportive, organized classroom that is elusive for peer support and help to be motivational, themselves. Also, if teachers remain positive and even-keeled in their position, it will certainly benefit those of whom he or she works. Try to use statements of acceptance of all students and be careful not to show favoritism. While we are all human, this is very important for the students in the classroom. Another method to try in keeping the atmosphere positive is to ensure that all materials are appropriate for different learners (i.e., remember "differentiation"?). If students are working at a pace that is too easy, they might become bored and, in turn, begin to act out in a negative manner. Alternatively, if the material is too difficult, some students might "shut down" rather than feel like a failure. The balance of classwork and presentation for different learners is a craft certainly gained more effectively with experience. At any time, it is appropriate to reward positive behavior, but you must know your students. Some students will embarrass easily, so public attention is not the best strategy. Others, on the other hand, might appreciate public acknowledgment, so a quick, "good job" or "nice going" will go a long way. As a new teacher, though, be careful with overuse of compliments or praise. When overused, praise tends to lose its effect.

STRATEGIES

Some strategies have been addressed vaguely, but this section will provide an overview of other approaches to employ. First, for students who are exhibiting behavioral difficulties, teachers should model how to set goals and monitor the progress. With anything, students and teachers alike might find it helpful to set and reach their potential with assigned tasks. Ensuring that the goals are realistic will allow mastery and confidence, providing an avenue to push to other, more difficult tasks, perhaps. As a former teacher, I found it helpful to encourage family members to also participate. If the parents followed similar practices and reinforcement at home, it made for a smoother transition at school. Additionally, another strategy could be to include these students in the decision-making procedures and tasks. All students should feel important, so be sure to include those with less desirable behavior, too. For example, if a student has trouble sitting in his or her seat, ask him or her to help pass out papers or run errands for you.

Setting classroom rules on the first day of class is a necessity. Depending on the age of the students will determine how many classroom rules should be established. Regardless, all classroom rules should be explained clearly in a manner that the students can understand and should be modeled, if the students are younger. Some find it helpful to have the students help make the classroom rules because it shows "buy-in," but this is an individual preference.

Next, which might sound extremely simple, is to make the classroom environment FUN! By planning thoughtful, engaging lessons, teachers can minimize behavioral issues by extraordinary measures. When working on your curriculum plan, using the given template (Chapter 1), there are several opportunities to integrate different content areas and strategies—all of which will help reduce misbehavior. The goal is to keep a fast-paced lesson, but not too fast where you "lose" students. Transitions are an important component of planning, so (again, depending on the students' age) teachers should plan for different activities several times throughout the lesson. For younger students, they need more transitions than do the older students as they cannot sit still for extremely long periods of time. The older the student, the fewer transitions that are needed. Not only do the tasks vary in a lesson, but the manner of teaching will vary, too. You might begin your lesson with lecture, then open up with a whole group discussion, move into smaller groups or partner activities, and then come together with the whole group again. There are so many options but the bottom line is this: the pace and activities should move during the period of time students are learning a particular lesson. In addition to having variety in the engaging lesson, teachers can be fun by their demeanor. Your students will know if you are passionate about your craft by *your* display of energy. Always try to be positive, energetic, and enthusiastic about learning—it is contagious!

Some other strategies can be found in Dr. Beth Ackerman's (2007) book, entitled, *P.R.A.I.S.E.* She discusses the importance of other factors such as being positive, using humor, being structured, being consistent, utilizing on-task behavior, maximizing on-task behavior, maximizing on-task teacher behavior, effectively setting limits, and being fair. All of these strategies are useful in any classroom, but especially useful with those who have behavioral problems.

Another strategy is to set up a successful behavior modification program. The first step in making this successful, however, is to find out that which the student(s) is/are willing to work. If a teacher uses a fancy pencil as a reward, and the student cares less about a pencil, it will be ineffective. On the other hand, if a student enjoys listening to music, use that as a reward. To begin the modification program, the teacher must first target and define the behavior that is exhibited by the student. If the student is disrespectful, explain that the student talked back to the teacher 3 out of 5 days—keep the behavior factual and measurable. By this, the teacher can begin collecting data to find baseline (i.e., the starting point) data, and then be able to reduce the occurrences over time. During the data collection, the teacher might choose to ignore the behavior (unless it is positive), redirect the individual, reward appropriate behavior, and continue to reinforce positive behavior. Teachers should also keep tasks interesting (making sure the rewards are meaningful to the student), be enthusiastic and sincere with praise (not overusing praise), be patient when expecting change (change takes time), continue to collect data, be consistent, be orderly, set behavioral standards, keep students engaged and motivated, model appropriate behavior, be positive, control emotions, maintain discipline, take corrective action as needed, and solicit the cooperation of parents (Beam & Pinkie, 2015). A wonderful resource that might help with case scenarios, modules, and video vignettes can be found through Vanderbilt Peabody College (2018). See additional information at the end of this chapter.

REINFORCEMENT

As mentioned previously, there are two different types of reinforcement: positive and negative. It is important to understand your students and which strategy works best for their personality. Some students love positive reinforcement and flourish, while others might only respond to negative reinforcement. The following sections will describe each.

Positive Reinforcement

Positive reinforcement is "a very powerful and effective tool to help shape and change behavior. It works by presenting a motivating item to the person after the desired behavior is exhibited, making the behavior more likely to happen in the future" (North Shore Pediatric Therapy, 2011, para. 3). It includes the components of praise and rewards. Praise, when given, should be specific, highly motivating, sincere, and—at times—delivered publicly. The rewards tied to positive reinforcement should be used to reinforce student success. Overuse of rewards, though, will prove to be ineffective, so they should be used sparingly and meaningfully. Sometimes, teachers might misunderstand the term of "reward" and believe it be to "bribe." Students must learn that each action does not warrant a reward, and that, over time, the rewards should reduce in number. Bribes, conversely, are used to get students to act because they are promised a reward. When using rewards, the conditions should be arranged with criteria for meeting each condition clarified. Both tangible and intangible rewards are options for students but fairness is essential. It is also important to know that fairness does not mean equality, as the two are not synonymous. When designing a reward system for a student or students, be sure to always start with the least restrictive reward and move to more tangible rewards. This is also important when developing a Behavioral Intervention Plan (BIP) (see example later in this chapter). Some rewards are simple praise, phone calls home, behavioral contracts, or token economy systems. Token systems can be used with individual students or whole classrooms and may be intertwined with BIPs or contracts. When developing a token system, teachers should ensure to target one or two behaviors to change, select the token (reward) to use, and use a chart to track behavior (see Figure 18). Some sample rewards to use at school that have been especially helpful are to allow the student to be a class monitor, line up first, have "free" time, extra recess, help correct or pass out papers, play games in class, listen to music, make something for the bulletin board, earn stickers, earn a grab bag, earn a certificate or award, earn a colorful pencil, or earn a homework pass. These tokens can be anything that would be rewarding for students—something they would like to work toward. Likewise, parents can also implement rewards at home. Some sample *home* rewards to use are extra TV time, later bedtime, playing a game with mom or dad, going out for pizza, help make dinner, have a friend stay overnight, being read to, food treat, earn grab bag, earn small toy, earn new book, or earn new clothes. For example, I use a token economy system at home with both my 4-year-old and my 15-year-old. The first task was to determine what they both wanted to work toward. My 4-year-old loves to stay up past her bedtime and read books, so I made her a sticker chart. The sticker chart includes tasks I would like her to begin and complete on her own, so I created her chart to resemble that goal. For each day that she completes each task, she would earn a sticker. For example, it could be quite possible for her to earn six stickers in one day. It looks like the Figure 18 on the following page.

FIGURE 18   Sample Token Reward System

AM	Monday	Tuesday	Wednesday	Thursday	Friday
Brush Teeth on Own					
Get Dressed/Hair on Own					
Follow Directions					
PM	**Monday**	**Tuesday**	**Wednesday**	**Thursday**	**Friday**
Eat Dinner					
Clean Up After Self					
Follow Directions					

6 Stickers = 8:15 pm bedtime and (2) stories

5 Stickers = 8:00 pm bedtime and (2) stories

4 Stickers = 7:30 pm and (2) stories OR 8:00 pm and (1) story

3 Stickers = 7:30 pm and (1) story

2 Stickers = 7:30 pm

1 Sticker = Nothing

Temper Tantrum or Time Out = Loss of (1) Sticker

My 15-year-old, on the other hand, enjoys "free days" out of school or getting money, so she is assessed on her grades. She is rewarded quarterly, as this is when report cards are issued through her school district, and her chart might resemble something closer to this:

4.0 GPA or higher = (1) free day out of school
3.5–3.9 GPA = ½ day out of school
Lower than 3.5 GPA = No free time out of school

Pay $5 for each A
Pay $3 for each B
Lose $3 for each C
Straight As = $50

For the "free" time out of school, our arrangement is that we will do anything that we are able to fit into that time frame, such as going to the movies, going out to lunch, getting a pedicure, and so forth. We will do anything she would like to do for the day as her reward. For the money reward, which is in conjunction with the "free" time, she is also paid for her grades. My belief is that when my children are in school, their "job" is to do well. In effect, they are not able to hold a job outside of school, so they get paid for their grades (i.e., paycheck). For any report card that is not straight As, and whatever monies have been earned for the total "payday," half of the money must go into her savings account and the other half is hers to spend. Her incentive then, is to earn straight As, because with those grades, she is paid $50 and is allowed to keep all of her money.

Parents are able to reinforce behaviors at home just as easily as can the teachers; they just need to form the rewards and consequences appropriate to their child's interests so the chart is effective.

Negative Reinforcement

While some students respond well to positive reinforcement, other students do not and may only respond to negative consequences. Negative reinforcement occurs "when a certain stimulus/item is removed after a particular behavior is exhibited. The likelihood of the particular behavior occurring again in the future is increased because of removing/avoiding the negative stimuli" (North Shore Pediatric Therapy, 2011, para. 5). Still, other students might respond to a combination of the two effects. For negative reinforcement to be instilled, teachers should always start with the least restrictive consequence and work toward a more intrusive response in a tiered manner. Some of the less obtrusive reactions of which a teacher might begin may include a "look," a verbal warning, or proximity control. As the behaviors increase, and the teacher must move up the tier of infractions, other consequences could be implanted, such as a note home to the parent, a phone call home to the parent, time out, detention, or, in more serious situations, a referral to the office to see the principal. For students who might respond more appropriately to negative reinforcement, a chart could also be used, similar to those shared above. The teacher needs to be especially mindful of the rewards and consequences to extinguish the unfavorable actions of the student. Figure 19 is an example of how a tiered system of behavior might flow in a BIP format for a student with emotional disturbance (ED), showing the tiered system of both positive and negative reinforcement.

FIGURE 19 Sample BIP

Cover page

Basic Information

Include the:

- Student Name: Desmond Simms

- School: Hereford Elementary School

- Grade: 5th grade

- Date of Development: 9/26/2018

- **Social Interaction:** Desmond is an outgoing student who loves to talk and dislikes quiet activities. Desmond is friendly toward his classmates, but his outbursts often disrupt the class. Occasionally his outbursts include profanity, screaming, and often involve distracting other students. Peers often invite him to play with them but tend to avoid him inside the classroom.

- **Academic Performance:** Desmond's behavior has begun to interfere with his academic achievement as he has begun to act out and not complete any individual work. He enjoys math class and participating in math games like Speedy Sam and Around the World. He is active in P.E. class and enjoys playing baseball on the weekend. English class is when Desmond has the most outbursts. He finds it difficult to read to himself or listen patiently as others read aloud.

Philosophy

Each student deserves free and appropriate education whoever and wherever they are. Students have various strengths and weaknesses which cannot be put into one standard category. The knowledge a student acquires goes beyond the words on a page and provides a foundation for the life skills to come. Desmond is a strong boy who is capable of many accomplishments but is limited due to his behavior outbursts. Although he struggles with anger management, Desmond will not be given up on and he will be pushed academically but given space when overwhelmed. Just because a student has a limitation, teachers should be persistent and not give up on them.

Baseline Data Results

Desmond's disruptive behavior escalates from interrupting and calling out to screaming and cussing with an average total disruptive time of 1.5–2 hours daily. His disruptions occur on average 37 times a day and generally occur in his core classes during individual work.

Attachment 1

- Baseline Data

	Interrupting	Screaming	Cussing	Disrupting others	Calling out
11/1/18	XXXXXXX—14 minutes	XXX—6 minutes	XXXXXXXXX—9 minutes	XXXXXXXXXXXX—24 minutes	XXXX—12 minutes
11/2/18	XXXXXXXXXXX—20 minutes	XXXX—8 minutes	XXXXXXXXXXXX—12 minutes	XXXXXXXXX—26 minutes	XXXXXXX—21 minutes
11/3/18	XXXXX—10 minutes	XXXXX—12 minutes	XX—2 minutes	XXXXXXXXXX—28 minutes	XXXXXXXXXXXXX—34 minutes
11/4/18	XXXXXXXXXXXXXXXXX—34 minutes	XX—4 minutes	XXXXXXX—7 minutes	XXXXX—25 minutes	XXXX—12 minutes
11/5/18	XXX—6 minutes	XX—4 minutes	XXX—3 minutes	XXXXXXX—27 minutes	XXX—9 minutes
11/8/18	XXXXXXXXXXXXXX—30 minutes	XXXXXXXX—16 minutes	XXXXX—5 minutes	XXXXXXX—27 minutes	XXXXXXX—21 minutes
11/9/18	XXXX—8 minutes	XXXXXX—14 minutes	XX—2 minutes	XXXXXXXXXX—28 minutes	XXXX—12 minutes
11/10/18	XXXXX—10 minutes	XXX—6 minutes	XXXXXXXXXXX—15 minutes	XXXXXX—23 minutes	XXXXXXXXX—26 minutes
11/11/18	XXXXXXXXXXX—24 minutes	XX—4 minutes	XXXXXXX—7 minutes	XXX—10 minutes	XXXXXXXX—24 minutes
11/12/18	XXXXXXXXXXXXXX—30 minutes	XXXXXXXX—16 minutes	XX—2 minutes	XXXXX—23 minutes	XXXX—12 minutes
Occurrence	3–17x/day	2–8x/day	2–12x/day	3–11x/day	3–13x/day
Duration	15–18 minutes average	11–14 minutes average	15–17 minutes average	21–25 minutes average	24–27 minutes average
Intensity	Mildly disruptive	Extremely disruptive	Extremely disruptive	Very disruptive	Mildly disruptive

Hypothesis Statement

Desmond's disruptive behavior during individual work is a cause of frustration and anxiety as he is given work he is afraid he will not understand and will not be able to figure out on his own. When he is given individual work he becomes irritated and disruptive.

Desmond's behavior is an attempt to avoid undesired tasks that he must work on by himself and will have a hard time comprehending. This behavior occurs during each class when the students are given individual work they must complete. On average, his behavior escalates from interrupting and calling out to cussing and screaming in 5 minutes and lasts an average of 15 minutes.

His behavior stems from the feeling that he will not understand his work on his own and will ultimately be unable to do the work his peers can do. He gets frustrated when this feeling comes and angry that he does not seem to be at the same level as his peers. Desmond's disruptive behavior comes from a fear that he will be unsuccessful and embarrassed.

Desmond shows little disruptive behavior when working with a group that can help him. He enjoys being with other students and having people to bring the pressure of the work off of him. He does well in math as this is a strong subject of his as well as gym where he is able to run around and get his energy out. Desmond still does not like to do the work assigned to the group, but is less frustrated and angry than when he must try to do the work on his own.

Behavior Description

Target Behavior

This Behavior Intervention Plan will target Desmond's behavior of calling out during class, interrupting other students and teachers, and occasionally swearing.

Behavior Defined

During Transition Time, Desmond consistently calls out which includes screaming, incessantly interrupting others, and occasionally swearing. This negative behavior occurs 80% of the transition and instruction time throughout a school day. Each occasion of calling out can last between 1 to 5 minutes. Desmond's outbursts begin with a small interruption and increase throughout the day into screaming and cursing. The occurrence of this negative behavior has been increasing to the point where it has started to affect other students.

Intervention Goal

During daily transition and instruction time, Desmond will reduce the amount of times that he calls out to occurring no more than three times a day and only lasting less than 1 minute for no more than 30% of the day for 8 weeks (2 months).

Intervention Plan

STRATEGY 1

Verbal Praise/Warning

Desmond will receive verbal praise every time that he raises his hand instead of calling out in class. Verbal praise will come from the teacher. He will also receive verbal praise for every subject that he does not interrupt another student or the teacher.

If Desmond calls out in class and interrupts the teacher or another student he will receive a verbal warning from the teacher. This verbal warning will state that Desmond needs to raise his hand if he would like to talk and that another outburst will result in the switching of his car moving from green to yellow.

There is a classroom behavior management system which is the traffic light system. All students begin on green. If students begin to misbehave, the teacher gives a warning and if they begin to continue to misbehave, the student moves to yellow. Once the student moves to yellow, they will stay there until the rest of the day and the student will get minutes off of their recess time. If the student continues to misbehave throughout the day, the students will be moved to red. If a student moves to red, a note will be sent to their parents or the teacher will give their parent a phone call to talk about why the student was moved to red.

STRATEGY 2

Reward System

Desmond will have a sticker chart inside of his school folder. This chart will have traffic lights on them. The teacher of each of his classes will be able to put a sticker or signature on his daily behavior sheets every day and every class period. Every time that Desmond goes 15–20 minutes without calling out, interrupting, or disrupting the class he may receive a sticker from his teacher. Also, Desmond will have a copy of his behavior contract in his folder. This behavior contract is an agreement between Desmond and his teachers about his reward system. If he does not comply with the contract, Desmond knows that there will be consequences for his actions.

*The sticker chart will be continued in Strategy 5 and allow Desmond to trade his stickers for prizes from the treasure box.

If Desmond continues to call out, interrupt, or disrupt other students and the classroom his card will be changed from green to yellow. The yellow indicates that he needs to control his outbursts and he will lose minutes from his recess time due to moving to yellow.

Attachment 2

DESMOND'S DAILY BEHAVIOR CHART

Homeroom Math English

Social Studies Art Science

Gym Lunch Library

STRATEGY 3

Quiet Game

Desmond and his classmates will participate in a "Quiet game." Before students begin or while they do their independent work, students will be able to talk for 5–10 minutes. After their talk time is up, the students will have to be quiet for the remaining time. At the end of the game, students who stayed quiet the whole time or for the longest time will receive a prize at the end of the game. This strategy is for the classroom, but is very helpful for Desmond. This game allows Desmond to talk for a certain amount of time (calling out as much as he wants, but for a limited amount of time). This allows the teacher to effectively time Desmond to see how long he can go without calling out after the talk time period ends.

If Desmond has at least three calling out or outbursts after talk time is over, Desmond will get a warning for the second outburst (the first time he will be out of the game—which is expected since it is a game; therefore, there is no reason for a warning). The third time he calls out or has an outburst, his teacher will direct him to home base to reorganize and regather himself.

STRATEGY 4

Home Base

There will be a home base in every classroom that Desmond attends. Desmond's teacher will direct Desmond to home base or Desmond can go to home base when he feels the need to. Desmond will use home base when he is calling out or having too many outbursts too often within a certain amount of time (such as back-to-back calling out within 10–15 minutes). Desmond's teacher will direct Desmond to home base where he will have to complete three strategies. These strategies will be in the form of a stop light. The strategies are as follows:

Red: STOP!

Yellow: Calm Down and Think

Green: Do and GO!

Desmond will stand in front of each color. Before he can move to the next color, he must complete the given command or strategy. Once Desmond has completed each strategy, his teacher will come and talk to Desmond about what he is going to do now that he has recovered from his outburst. If Desmond cannot think of a new way to do something his teacher can think of one for him or he can use the strategy from the poster beside the "Do and GO!"

If Desmond shows that he cannot control his calling out and outbursts after using home base, Desmond's car will move to red. Since he will move to red, his parents will receive a note or a phone call from his teacher explaining Desmond's behavior for the day.

Attachment 3

On Your Mark! Get Set! GO!

"Do and GO!" Strategies

1. Raise your hand.
2. Wait for your turn to talk.
3. Listen carefully while others are talking.
4. Use kind and gentle words.
5. Let your cue cards do all the talking.
6. Apologize for interrupting.
7. Think before speaking.
8. Ask a buddy.
9. Write your question or comment down.
10. Share questions and comments when the time is given to do so.

Attachment 4

Red Light Note

- Name: _____ Date: _____
- Dear Mom and Dad,
- I was moved to red light today because: _____

_____

_____

- I can do better or make better choices by: _____

_____

_____

_____

_____

- Student signature: _____
- Parent signature: _____
- Teacher signature: _____

STRATEGY 5

Staying After School and Suspension

If Desmond is able to receive at least 30 stickers on green of his daily behavior chart over the course of the week for good behavior (no cursing, outbursts, limited calling out), Desmond will be able to make a trip to the treasure box. The treasure box contains candy, pencils, erasers, snacks, little toys, gum, and so forth.

If Desmond receives at least 25 stickers and/or cannot control his calling out and outbursts after a call or note from his parents, Desmond will have to stay after school with at least one of his teachers. His teacher will try to implement and practice some of the "Do and GO!" strategies with Desmond to reduce his talking out and outbursts.

If Desmond shows or demonstrates that he cannot control his talking out and outbursts which is causing his classmates to be distracted and unable to learn for long periods of time, Desmond will be suspended. The period of time will be calculated by Desmond's teacher with the recording record (baseline sheet) to know if his talking out and outbursts exceed 1½ hours. Desmond will have in-school suspension for 1 day. By suspending Desmond for 1 day, the goal is for Desmond to realize that his behavior is not acceptable in the classroom and around his classmates. Desmond will need to take responsibility for his actions.

After 5 days of in-school suspension, a team meeting will be held to discuss further action.

Other Details

Implementation Logistics

The plan will occur in all of Desmond's classes. This plan will begin immediately.

Next Steps

If the plan is successful or if Desmond reaches his goal within the 8-week time span, Desmond will continue his plan until his next reevaluation. If the plan is unsuccessful or Desmond does not reach his goal, the team members will reconvene and plan for further actions to help Desmond achieve his goal or they will set a new goal for Desmond.

POSITIVE BEHAVIOR INTERVENTION SYSTEM

Positive Behavior Intervention Systems (PBIS) are often used in the schools for school-wide implementation. They vary from school to school, based on behavioral need but are quite effective if integrated realistically. The advantages of a PBIS are that the same rules are enforced throughout the school, enabling consistency among teachers of varying grade levels and student expectations. An example is shown in Figure 20, but there are many more examples online and available by grade level. A disadvantage of PBIS, conversely, is that some students may not respond to the PBIS because it is not individualized to their specific needs. When developing a PBIS, there are seven core principles that might prove useful for the application:

1.   We can effectively teach appropriate behavior to all children;

2.   Intervene early;

3.   Use of a multi-tier model of service delivery;

4.   Use research-based, scientifically validated interventions to the extent available;

5.   Monitor student progress to inform interventions;

6.   Use data to make decisions;

7.   Use assessment for three different purposes (PBIS, 2018).

FIGURE 20   PBIS Sample

EAGLES	Classroom	Cafeteria	Restroom	Playground	Hallway	Bus
S SAFE	Be a good listener	Keep your hands and feet to yourself	Wash hands thoroughly	Be a problem-solver	Walk at all times	Listen to the driver
	Always try your best	Eat your own food	Keep your hands and feet to yourself	Play with everyone	Keep your hands and feet to yourself	Stay in assigned seat
	Be an active participant	Keep your food in the cafeteria	Use an "inside" voice	Take care of yourself	Follow directions	Follow bus rules
O ORGANIZED	Arrive on time for class	Use an "inside" voice	Properly dispose of trash	Resolve conflicts	Use a hall pass if not with the class	Keep bus clean
	Stay on task	Wait calmly for your turn	Use a bathroom pass from your teacher	Use appropriate language	Go directly to your location noted on your hall pass	Polite conversations
	Respect differences	Do not cut in front of others in line	Be sure to flush the toilet	Agree on rules before a game	Report problems and injuries to nearest adult	Keep hands and feet to yourself
A ACCOUNTABLE	Follow directions	Clean up your area	Return to class promptly	Learn new games and activities	Maintain personal space	Be on time
	Raise your hand	Dispose of trash properly	Use only the supplies that you need	Line up at first signal from teacher	Use an "inside" voice	Take accountability for your actions at all times
	Be honest	Return trays to the appropriate area	Take turns using the sink	Make good choices	Be honest at all times when questioned in the hall way	Be honest with the bus driver at all times
R RESPECTFUL	Maintain personal space	Use good table manners	Be respectful of others' privacy	Enter the building quietly	Do not cut in front of others in line	Have polite conversations with your peers
	Have all supplies	Say "please" and "thank you"	Line up in assigned area	Be kind	Follow the directions of all adults	Say "please" and "thank you"
	Use an "inside" voice	Make healthy choices		Put away equipment when finished	Use good manners with your classmates	Use good manners with your bus partner and those in close proximity

ADDITIONAL RESOURCES

- A wonderful behavior management resource that includes case scenarios, modules, and video vignettes can be found through Vanderbilt Peabody College (2018) at: https://iris.peabody.vanderbilt.edu/.

- Also, more information for developing a PBIS can be found at: http://www.pbis.org/.

PART 2

Curriculum Integration Examples

CHAPTER 8

Example #1—Social Studies

IDEAS FOR INTEGRATION

If social studies is your endorsement area of which you are gaining state licensure, your curriculum will focus, of course, on social studies, but you will integrate other areas within your content, such as science, English, mathematics, active learning, and so forth. Use the acronym key on the template for areas of integration. You can easily integrate other content as follows:

Objective

Given the lesson discussing the thriving exploration and scientific advancements of the Chinese, students will formulate a brief one-paragraph analyses that contains at least three reasons why the Chinese reverted to an isolationist policy under the Ming Dynasty, with 3/3 reasons accurately identified.

Content Integration

ASSESS: Students will complete a 10-question, short answer Pretest on Chinese history prior to beginning the unit. This is an ungraded assignment intended to help the teacher assess the student's prior knowledge.

SCIENCE/MATH (S/M): Students will understand how China's scientific understanding of wind and the sea led to early exploration that even exceeded European systems. (Discuss nautical systems and math involved.)

TECHNOLOGY (T): Students will analyze, using Google Earth, the vast exploration movement in the Ming Dynasty even predating the European Age of Exploration.

CRITICAL THINKING (CT): Given the lesson discussing the thriving exploration and scientific advancements of the Chinese, students will formulate a brief one-paragraph analyses that contains at least three reasons why the Chinese reverted to an isolationist policy, with 3/3 reasons accurately identified. This will be completed in the journals.

DIVERSITY/COLLABORATION/ACTIVE LEARNING (DIV/COLL/ACT): Students will be placed into groups of four to begin filling in a wall-size chart differentiating between English culture and Chinese culture. This will continue through the Qing lecture.

CHARACTER EDUCATION (CE): Students will discuss Confucius' ideas and recognize positive themes and detrimental themes that kept the common man oppressed by the upper echelon of Chinese Society. Confucius was canonized as a religion in Chinese culture.

LANGUAGE ARTS (L): Students will understand how regional differences (Terrain barriers) in China caused differing languages and dialects.

ADDITIONAL RESOURCES

Below are three lists for your reference:

1.   National Standards by Content Area

2.   Common Core Standards (adopted by most states)

3.   State Content Standards (those who did not adopt Common Core)

National Standards

English	National Council of Teachers of English (NCTE)	www.ncte.org
Reading	International Reading Association (IRA)	www.reading.org
Fine arts	National Art Educational Association (NAEA)	www.naea.org
Foreign language	American Council on the Teaching of Foreign Languages	www.actfl.org
Math	National Council of Teachers of Math (NCTM)	www.nctm.org
Science	National Science Teachers Association (NSTA)	www.nsta.org
Social Science	National Council for the Social Sciences (NCSS)	www.nscc.org
TESL	WIDA English Language Development (ELD) Standards	www.wida.us

Common Core Standards: (adopted by 41 states)   http://www.corestandards.org/

State Standards: (Common Core not adopted)

Alaska Department of Education	https://education.alaska.gov/
Florida Department of Education	http://www.fldoe.org/
Indiana Department of Education	https://www.doe.in.gov/
Minnesota Department of Education	https://education.mn.gov/mde/index.html
Nebraska Department of Education	http://www.education.ne.gov/
Oklahoma Department of Education	http://sde.ok.gov/sde/
Puerto Rico Department of Education	http://www.de.gobierno.pr/
South Carolina Department of Education	https://www.ed.sc.gov/
Texas Department of Education	https://tea.texas.gov/Home/
Virginia Department of Education	http://www.doe.virginia.gov/

SAMPLE CURRICULUM

TEACHER CANDIDATE'S NAME:
CONTENT SUBJECT AREA: World History II
GRADE LEVEL: 10th
TEXTBOOK NAME WITH PUBLICATION INFORMATION: World History: The Human Journey.
Carrington, Laurel; Colins, Mattie P. (2005). *World History: The Human Journey*. Austin: Holt, Rinehart, and Wineston.

Mission Statement:

The World History Department strives to equip students to be critical thinkers that can evaluate the credibility of sources, recognize historical themes, patterns, and influences, and formulate a coherent worldview. Our department's goal is to produce active citizens with an historical appreciation and continue to grow academically and as contributing members of society.

Unit Sections

Unit #1: Aqua Blue, "REFORMATION YEARS"
Unit #2: Yellow, "AGE OF DISCOVERY AND COLONIZATION"
Unit #3: Dark Green, "EASTERN EMPIRES AND THE MERCANTILE SYSTEM"
Unit #4: Red, "SCIENTIFIC REVOLUTION AND THE AGE OF ABSOLUTISM"
Unit #5: Pink, "ENLIGHTENMENT AND REVOLUTION YEARS"
Unit #6: Purple, "FALL OF THE *ANCIEN REGIME*"
Unit #7: Gray, "INDUSTRIAL REVOLUTION"
Unit #8: Orange, "WORLD WAR I AND THE DEPRESSION"
Unit #9: Brown, "WORLD WAR II"
Unit #10: Dark Blue, "THE COLD WAR"
Unit #11: Moss Green, "THE COLD WAR SPREADS GLOBALLY"
Unit #12: Gold, "MODERN TIMES, MODERN DANGERS"

DAY #	CONTENT/OBJECTIVE	STANDARDS	RESOURCES/MATERIALS	LEARNING ACTIVITIES/ASSESSMENTS
DAY #	• Skills • Knowledge • Dispositions • Concepts • Themes • Values	• VA SOLs • National Standards • TCAs	Include (1) resources to assist the teacher in planning and implementing lessons and (2) materials students need to participate. • Books • Technology • Supplies • Community organizations • Guest speakers • Websites	ACT = active learning—Day #: 2, 3, 5, 6, 7, 9, 11, 18, 20, 21, 22, 23, 24, 30, 33, 34, 35, 39, 40, 45, 48, 53, 54, 59, 61, 63, 70, 73, 79, 84, 86, 91, 96, 101, 102, 107, 109, 111, 113, 117, 119, 121, 123, 125, 131, 135, 137, 139, 140, 144, 154, 158, 162, 168, 170, 173, 177 ASSESS = assessment activity—Day #: 1, 2, 7, 10, 14, 16, 19, 20, 23, 27, 34, 43, 44, 46, 47, 49, 55, 60, 62, 67, 73, 74, 79, 81, 85, 89, 92, 97, 101, 102, 108, 118, 120, 121, 123, 125, 127, 129, 132, 133, 135, 141, 147, 148, 150, 153, 155, 159, 162, 170, 176, 178, 179 COLL = There are different types of collaboration: (1) teacher with community members/organizations or other educators and (2) students with other students or community members—Day #: 2, 3, 4, 5, 6, 7, 12, 16, 20, 21, 22, 23, 24, 25, 28, 29, 30, 31, 32, 33, 34, 35, 36, 37, 38, 41, 45, 51, 55, 58, 60, 63, 64, 65, 67, 69, 70, 71, 72, 73, 74, 77, 78, 86, 89, 90, 91, 92, 94, 97, 98, 101, 102, 103, 106, 109, 111, 113, 114, 115, 117, 121, 122, 123, 124, 125, 126, 127, 128, 129, 133, 134, 136, 137, 138, 139, 140, 143, 144, 145, 146, 149, 152, 154, 158, 159, 165, 167, 170, 175

DAY #	CONTENT/OBJECTIVE	STANDARDS	RESOURCES/MATERIALS	LEARNING ACTIVITIES/ASSESSMENTS
				CE = character education—Day #: 1, 3, 4, 5, 6, 8, 12, 17, 20, 27, 33, 44, 48, 52, 57, 58, 65, 74, 75, 82, 89, 90, 95, 99, 104, 110, 114, 115, 116, 125, 129, 132, 135, 141, 145, 147, 153, 158, 164, 168, 169, 171, 172, 174
				CT = critical thinking activity—Day #: 1, 3, 5, 6, 8, 12, 16, 17, 20, 23, 25, 27, 29, 32, 33, 40, 42, 46, 47, 48, 51, 52, 56, 58, 63, 64, 66, 67, 68, 71, 72, 73, 76, 77, 78, 80, 81, 82, 83, 86, 88, 89, 90, 93, 98, 99, 100, 101, 102, 104, 106, 109, 111, 112, 114, 116, 117, 122, 123, 125, 126, 127, 128, 129, 131, 133, 134, 135, 136, 137, 138, 139, 142, 143, 144, 145, 146, 147, 149, 150, 151, 154, 155, 157, 158, 159, 161, 164, 165, 166, 167, 169, 172, 174, 175, 176, 180
				DIV = 2, 3, 5, 6, 8, 11, 13, 17, 20, 21, 24, 25, 29, 30, 33, 44, 47, 48, 51, 52, 59, 63, 64, 68, 69, 72, 74, 75, 76, 78, 80, 83, 87, 90, 91, 93, 94, 95, 98, 104, 109, 113, 116, 117, 121, 122, 123, 124, 128, 130, 136, 141, 146, 148, 152, 155, 158, 159, 161, 164, 166, 167, 173
				T = technology—Day #: 2, 3, 4, 6, 8, 9, 13, 14, 16, 20, 21, 25, 27, 28, 31, 32, 34, 35, 36, 37, 41, 43, 47, 53, 55, 56, 57, 60, 61, 65, 68, 69, 70, 71, 72, 78, 80, 84, 86, 87, 88, 89, 92, 94, 100, 103, 105, 106, 107, 110, 112, 113, 116, 118, 120, 122, 123, 125, 126, 127, 128, 133, 141, 142, 143, 145, 146, 147, 151, 153, 157, 158, 161, 162, 169, 171, 174, 180
				INTEGRATION LEGEND
				A = art—Day #: 3, 6, 8, 11, 25, 31, 33, 40, 46, 47, 58, 71, 77, 79, 101, 102, 110, 111, 121, 138, 142, 163, 165, 173
				B = Biblical principles—Day #: 3, 4, 5, 12, 17, 22, 25, 42, 70, 87, 89, 90, 105, 110, 125, 130, 147, 151, 157, 163
				D = dance—Day #: 35, 37, 110
				H = health—Day #: 6, 28, 86, 110, 112, 114, 126, 131, 134
				L = language arts—Day #: 2, 5, 6, 8, 12, 18, 20, 23, 29, 42, 43, 58, 65, 70, 76, 90, 91, 95, 99, 101, 102, 122, 130, 142, 144, 163
				M = math—Day #: 2, 3, 11, 20, 26, 88, 124, 139
				MUS = music—Day #: 6, 23, 34, 35, 37, 71, 89, 90, 110, 113, 122, 143, 145, 149
				P = physical education/movement—Day #: 3, 4, 6, 9, 22, 33, 35, 73, 86, 96
				S = science—Day #: 4, 7, 20, 26, 33, 40, 41, 88, 94, 110, 114, 124, 126, 130, 131, 134, 139, 140, 170, 173, 174
				SS = social science—Day #: Every day
				TH = Theatre—Day #: 5, 24, 30, 45, 54, 75, 91, 135

DAY #	CONTENT/OBJECTIVE	STANDARDS	RESOURCES/MATERIALS	LEARNING ACTIVITIES/ASSESSMENTS
1	**Introduction of Class, Overview of Class (Syllabus), Pre-Assessment** Given prior classes on the Middle Ages and the Renaissance, students will take a 20-question comprehensive exam on these units with 12/20 accuracy. This will not be a graded assignment.	Era 6 The Emergence of the First Global Age, 1450–1770: Standard 2: How European society experienced political, economic, and cultural transformations in an age of global intercommunication, 1450–1750 WHII.2 The student will demonstrate an understanding of the political, cultural, geographic, and economic conditions in the world about 1500 A.D. (C.E.) by a) locating major states and empires; b) describing artistic, literary, and intellectual ideas of the Renaissance; TCA: 1.1	Technology: Google Earth, projector, computer Paper slips with fake indulgences Homework worksheet (T-Chart listing plights against the Catholic Church on one side and how the Protestant Reformation responded to those on the other) Textbook: *World History: The Human Journey*	ASSESS: Given prior classes on the Middle Ages and the Renaissance, students will take a 20-question comprehensive exam on these units with 12/20 accuracy. This will not be a graded assignment. CT/CE: Students will be required to write a brief paragraph on why they think history is important. They must apply how they can use history to be more active participants in government and society. It will demonstrate how history can enrich their lives.

DAY #	CONTENT/OBJECTIVE	STANDARDS	RESOURCES/MATERIALS	LEARNING ACTIVITIES/ASSESSMENTS
2	**Using Maps and Sources** Given the unit on basic map skills and geographic features, students will distinguish between countries, continents, oceans, bays, harbors, isthmuses, latitudes, and longitudes by identifying examples of them using Google Earth to navigate to the points, with 6/8 accuracy.	Era 6, Standard 1, 6 WHII.1: a, b, c TCA: 1.1, 1.3, 1.6, 1.9, 1.10	Video clip from *Luther* (2003 Independent film) (clip deals with Diet of Worms and Augsburg Confession) Technology: PowerPoint, computer Blank timeline Excerpt from the Treaty of Westphalia 1648 Textbook: *World History: The Human Journey*	T: Using Google Earth and a projector, the students will understand political and geographical aspects pertaining to the course; highlighting key locations that will be discussed. DIV: Students will recognize how various geographical regions have diverse cultures and languages. ACT: Students will navigate the globe via Google Earth using a SMARTboard. COLL: Students will be teaching each other using the technology. In addition, they will be communicating with the instructor that they understand the content through participation in the activities and discussion. L: Students will use the map to recognize different language groups. M: Students will use basic math to determine latitude and longitude as well as a basic understanding of legends. ASSESS: Given the unit on basic map skills and geographic features, students will distinguish between countries, continents, oceans, bays, harbors, isthmuses, latitudes, and longitudes by identifying examples of them using Google Earth to navigate to the points, with 6/8 accuracy. For example, if a student is asked for an example of a continent, they would find Africa (seven total options) on Google Earth and then justify their choice. In keeping with the example, "I chose Africa because it is a large, continuous, discrete mass of land separated by expanses of water." S: The activity will discuss the effect tectonic plates have in causing natural disasters, currents, etc.

DAY #	CONTENT/OBJECTIVE	STANDARDS	RESOURCES/MATERIALS	LEARNING ACTIVITIES/ASSESSMENTS
3	**Protestant Reformation and Europe in the 1500s** Given the lesson on the early stages of the Protestant Reformation, students will list two political and three theological complaints against the Catholic Church that triggered the Protestant Reformation with a sentence to summarize each point, with 4/5 accuracy.	Era 6, Standard 2, 6 WHII.2 a, b, c WHII.3 a, b TCA 1.1, 1.3, 1.5, 1.6, 1.8, 1.9, 1.10	Primary source documents from Catholic Church, Martin Luther, and John Calvin Technology: PowerPoint, computer Journals Timeline continued Textbook: *World History: The Human Journey*	T: Using Google Earth students will recognize that despite the vast regional differences, the Catholic Church still held sway with all European powers prior to 1517 (will zoom in on various locations such as Vatican City, Spain, etc.). DIV: Students will recognize the fragmented structure of Germany culturally and how the Protestant Reformation served to unite them and lay the basis for what eventually would become unified Germany in 1871. A: Discuss the large-scale art and architecture projects undertaken by the Catholic Church which necessitated the sale of indulgences to compensate for the payments (i.e., St. Peter's Basilica). B: Students will understand the concept of salvation by faith alone articulated by Martin Luther. M/COLL/ACT/P: Students will participate in an activity to illustrate the sale of indulgences using fake homework passes and free test grades for sale. (Goal is to make students believe that the instructor actually has the power to sell grades, shows corruptness and how much money people were willing to spend.) This will involve the instructor and open classroom discussion at the end. CE: Students will value the importance of standing up for what they believe in like Martin Luther did. ASSESS: Given the lesson on the early stages of the Protestant Reformation, students will list two political and three theological complaints against the Catholic Church that triggered the Protestant Reformation with a sentence to summarize each point, with 4/5 accuracy. This will be a homework assignment forcing the students to recall and think about what was taught in class (every point was covered in the class period).

DAY #	CONTENT/OBJECTIVE	STANDARDS	RESOURCES/MATERIALS	LEARNING ACTIVITIES/ASSESSMENTS
4	**Luther's Excommunication and Results of the Protestant Reformation** Given an excerpt from the Treaty of Westphalia, students will identify the three agreements the Holy Roman Empire consented to and predict how these agreements would change the political makeup of Europe in a concise one-paragraph response with 3/3 agreements accurately identified.	Era 6, Standard 2, 6 WHII.3 a, b, c TCA 1.1, 1.3, 1.5, 1.6, 1.8, 1.9, 1.10	YouTube clip "King Henry VIII (1491–1547)–Pt 1/3" (Show only first 4 minutes) http://www.youtube.com/watch?v=1xW7BhEBeEA Sound clip by Henry VIII "If Love Now Reigned" (1540) http://www.youtube.com/watch?v=xw59KAcObFl Technology: PowerPoint, computer Timeline continued Journals Textbook: *World History: The Human Journey*	T: Following the lecture on Luther's excommunication and the Diet of Worms, students will watch a 6:18 clip from the film, *Luther*, in which Martin Luther is offered a pardon by the Holy Roman Emperor, Charles V, at the Diet of Worms in 1521 but Luther defiantly refuses to recant. Following the clip, lecture will continue and another clip from the movie will be shown (2:33 clip) illustrating the Augsburg Confession in 1555. B: Students will recognize the Biblical doctrine in which Martin Luther clung to. CE/S: Students will value the importance of standing up for what they believe in. Luther and the German princes at Augsburg were both offered reconciliation but refused in favor of their convictions (Not always the easy road, but the right one). This will be compared with Galileo who recanted his theories of Earth rotation. COLL: Students will participate in classroom discussion to fill out the timeline participating both with the instructor and each other. CT: Given an excerpt from the Treaty of Westphalia, students will identify the three agreements the Holy Roman Empire consented to and predict how these agreements would change the political makeup of Europe in a concise one-paragraph response with 3/3 agreements accurately identified.

DAY #	CONTENT/OBJECTIVE	STANDARDS	RESOURCES/MATERIALS	LEARNING ACTIVITIES/ASSESSMENTS
5	**Protestant Reformation Goes Global** Given the lesson differentiating Calvinism, Lutheranism, and Catholicism, students will analyze primary source documents from these three theological camps and summarize, articulate, and be able to justify their stances on the two topics discussed in the primary source documents with 2/2 accuracy (they will prepare like they would for a debate).	Era 6, Standard 2, 3, 6 WHII.3 a, b, c TCA 1.1, 1.3, 1.5, 1.6, 1.8, 1.9, 1.10	Timeline continued Technology: PowerPoint, computer Textbook: *World History: The Human Journey*	CT: Students will begin class by journaling for 8 minutes about how the Protestant Reformation challenged the authority of the church, not only religiously but politically. CT/DIV: Students will continue to fill in the timeline from session #4 and draw conclusions of how actions in one geographic area influenced ideas in others (for instance, Martin Luther's movement in Germany and John Calvin's in Switzerland). In short, students will recognize and draw conclusions of how the Protestant Reformation affected other parts of the globe (comparing dates and possible causations). L: Students will understand the importance of language; discussing the Catholic Church's refusal to translate the bible from Latin, Martin Luther's translated vernacular bible, and the Gutenberg printing press. B: Students will differentiate between Calvin's views and Luther's views of salvation (TULIP, etc.). COLL/TH/ACT: Students will be placed into three groups (Catholic, Protestant, and Calvinist). They will be then given a primary source from their group's founder (i.e., Calvinists study a piece from John Calvin). Students then will conduct a debate embracing the ideas of their founder (Arguing from their religious denomination's perspective). Topics will include "What is the proper relationship between church and government" and "role of the individual (lay man) in faith processes." The instructor will be the mediator and students will debate in panel format. CE: Students will value the importance of understanding what they believe and why.

DAY #	CONTENT/OBJECTIVE	STANDARDS	RESOURCES/MATERIALS	LEARNING ACTIVITIES/ASSESSMENTS
6	**Reformation in Jolly Ole England** Given the lesson on England's split from the Catholic Church under Henry VIII, students will complete a worksheet for homework composed of 15 multiple-choice questions and an essay that requires them to summarize the split of England and the Catholic Church with 14/16 accuracy.	Era 6, Standard 2, 6 WHII.3 a, b, c TCA 1.1, 1.2, 1.3, 1.5, 1.6, 1.9, 1.10	Technology: PowerPoint, computer, Google Earth Textbook: *World History: The Human Journey*	T: Show video clip displaying the controversial historical legacy of Henry VIII. CT/COLL/P: Students will use their journals to argue their opinion of whether Henry VIII was an idealist with true convictions or merely a drunk womanizer chasing his own ambitions. This will trigger quite a bit of debate so immediately after journaling, students will organize into teams based on their opinions (the various positions will stand on opposite sides of the room) and a debate will be conducted. The instructor will mediate and guide the debate. MUS: As students are journaling they will listen to the song clip written by Henry VIII. A: In addition to Henry VIII's passion for music, he loved art. Students will be able to view several pieces of his work throughout the lecture. L/DIV: Students will understand the critical role that language and culture played in further alienating England from the Roman Catholic Church. CE: This one will primarily be aimed at the males in the room but it will deal with the value of treating people with decency and respect. Henry VIII was a very immoral individual that had two of his wives beheaded just so he could move on to the next wife. H: Students will understand the importance of health through a discussion of Henry VIII, who was morbidly obese and a drunkard. He was so overweight that a special hoisting mechanism had to be designed just to get him on his horse.

DAY #	CONTENT/OBJECTIVE	STANDARDS	RESOURCES/MATERIALS	LEARNING ACTIVITIES/ASSESSMENTS
7	**Catholic Counter-Reformation** Given the lesson on the Council of Trent, students will identify and list the five major plights against the Catholic Church and how the Catholic Counter Reformation responded to these plights with 5/5 accuracy.	Era 6, Standard 2 WHII.3 a, b, c TCA 1.1, 1.2, 1.3, 1.5, 1.6, 1.9, 1.10	YouTube clip, "Horrible Histories: The Spanish Armada" https://www.youtube.com/watch?v=w6_UkLHcdJk Wood supplies and cloth for building miniature warships A vat of water and a fan Journal Textbook: *World History: The Human Journey*	ASSESS: Students will take a brief quiz to begin class covering textbook readings and topics on the Protestant Reformation covered in class. This will also assist in reviewing for the lecture. It is a 20-question multiple-choice quiz so it will not be exuberantly time-consuming. S: Discuss Newton's Third Law: "For every action, there is an equal and opposite reaction" (relate this concept to the Reformation and then Counter-Reformation). ACT/COLL: The classroom will be organized in a round pattern much like the design at the Council of Trent in 1545. Students will select the head bishop with a vote prior to the activity. Students will then be given a list of plights against the Catholic Church from the Protestant Reformation and debate and create solutions to these problems. At the end of the debate, the instructor will reveal how close the mock Council of Trent was to the actual solutions taken between 1545–1563. (This will occur prior to the lecture) (This will take up almost all the class period, a very brief lecture of what actually happened will follow). CT: Students will reflect on their timelines and write a brief paragraph for homework analyzing three unique aspects of how certain dates correlate (For instance, establishment of the Church of England in 1534 and the Counter-Reformation in 1545).
8	**Catholic Counter-Reformation (continued)** Given the lesson on the Catholic Counter-Reformation, students will analyze three pieces of art from this period and speculate what the artist is trying to convey about Catholicism, justifying their speculation in one in three sentences per piece of art using content discussed in the lecture, with 2/3 accuracy.	Era 6, Standard 2, 6 WHII.3 a, b, c TCA 1.1, 1.2, 1.3, 1.5, 1.6, 1.9, 1.10	Multiple-Choice/Short Answer Exam	T, L, DIV: Students will use Google Earth to find the various locations of the Reformers in order to greater understand their impact in the culturally diverse areas they served. It will demonstrate that despite cultural and language barriers, the reforms from the Protestant Reformation found an appeal throughout Europe. A/CT: Students will analyze art generated from the Catholic Counter-Reformation and write down for each of the three images the message it is conveying or the value of Catholicism being represented. COLL: Given the lesson on the Catholic Counter-Reformation, students will analyze three pieces of art from this period and speculate what the artist is trying to convey about Catholicism, justifying their speculation in one to three sentences per piece of art using content discussed in the lecture, with 2/3 accuracy. CE: Display to the students the importance of helping others. All of the reformers discussed in this lecture took an invested interest in the physical needs of others before they tended directly to their spiritual needs.

DAY #	CONTENT/OBJECTIVE	STANDARDS	RESOURCES/MATERIALS	LEARNING ACTIVITIES/ASSESSMENTS
9	**Elizabeth I, the Not So "Virgin Queen"** Given the lesson on Elizabeth I's reign of England, students will identify her 4 greatest accomplishment and then draw an illustration that symbolizes each accomplishment with 4/4 accuracy.	Era 6, Standard 2, 6 WHII.3 a, b, c TCA 1.1, 1.2, 1.3, 1.5, 1.6, 1.9, 1.10	YouTube clip, "Horrible Histories: The Spanish Armada" Wood supplies and cloth for building miniature warships A vat of water and a fan Journal Textbook: *World History: The Human Journey*	T: Show "Horrible Histories: The Spanish Armada" to introduce the conflict with Spain. ACT/P: Students will design small vessels following the teacher's instructions and will draw either a British or Spanish symbol on their sail (made of cloth). Using a fan, the defeat of the Spanish Armada will be illustrated in the vat of water. It will simulate the harsh weather and how the British used it to their advantage. COLL: Students will participate in class discussion on Elizabeth I's accomplishments and how this contributed to the prominence of England in years to come. ASSESS: Given the lesson on Elizabeth I's reign of England, students will identify her four greatest accomplishments and then draw an illustration that symbolizes each accomplishment with 4/4 accuracy. This is a non-graded assignment and is intended to help the student associate an image with an answer. It will help them on the test.
10	**Test Day** Given the units on the Protestant Reformation, the Catholic Counter-Reformation, and the spread of their ideas, students will complete a 30-question multiple-choice and short answer test on this content with 27/30 accuracy.	Era 6, Standard 2, 6 WHII.3 a, b, c TCA 1.1, 1.2, 1.3, 1.5, 1.6, 1.9, 1.10	Written exam with an essay question, short answer, and multiple-choice	ASSESS: Given the units on the Protestant Reformation, the Catholic Counter-Reformation, and the spread of their ideas, students will complete a 30-question multiple-choice and short answer test on this content with 27/30 accuracy.

DAY #	CONTENT/OBJECTIVE	STANDARDS	RESOURCES/MATERIALS	LEARNING ACTIVITIES/ASSESSMENTS
11	**Introduction to the European Age of Discovery** —Given a world map and a lesson students will identify how the various continents were connected via the trading routes with 10/10 correct. —Given a map, activity, and lecture, students will identify the economic benefits from trading with other continents with 1/1 correct.	Era 6, Standard 1, 2, 6 WHII.4 a TCA 1.1 ,1.7, 1.9	Textbook: *World History: The Human Journey* Map and instructions for activity Colored pencils/crayons	ACT/A: Students will be given a map of Europe and Asia and will be required to map out the various trade routes including where they begin, stop, and end. They will map out routes over land and sea. M: Students will be required to figure the mark-up of certain items. For example, the mark-up of Indian Pepper is 32,000 times higher when it reaches Europe. DIV: Students with ADHD will not be given the map until absolutely necessary to avoid distraction.
12	**Motivations for Settling New Lands** —Given a lecture, students will determine the different motivations for explorers to go to distant lands with 10/10 correct. —Given the text of *White Man's Burden*, students will analyze why various Europeans would go to foreign lands for religious purposes with 9/10 correct.	Era 6, Standard 1, 4, 6 WHII.4 a, b TCA 1.1, 1.3, 1.4, 1.9	Textbook: *World History: The Human Journey* Text of *White Man's Burden* Journal	CT/COLL/L: Students will read *White Man's Burden* and describe what Kipling was trying to communicate. The students will discuss this in small groups first and then engage in a larger class discussion. CT/CE/B: Students will be asked if they would be willing to travel to a foreign nation to promote their religion or set of beliefs. They will write their response in a journal book as either affirmative or negative.

DAY #	CONTENT/OBJECTIVE	STANDARDS	RESOURCES/MATERIALS	LEARNING ACTIVITIES/ASSESSMENTS
13	**Colonization** —Given a lecture supplemented with Google Earth, students will locate where migration and settlement patterns occurred across the map with 5/5 correct. —Given scholarly Internet sources, students will identify the various challenges settlers experienced with 12/12 correct.	Era 6, Standard 2, 3 WHII.4 c TCA: 1.1, 1.2, 1.3, 1.9	Textbook: *World History: The Human Journey* Computer with Internet Access and Google Earth	T: Using Google Earth students will locate the various areas that were colonized by Europeans. This will be broken down into three sections: Americas, Asia, and Africa. DIV/T: Using scholarly Internet sources students will make a list of the challenges settlers would have in regard to the location where they settled. These challenges should range from climate to interaction with natives.
14	**Colonization (Continued)** Given two videos and a discussion, students will determine the social classes in the colonized areas and continue expanding their knowledge base in cultural diffusion by taking notes during class and during the video with 9/10 correct.	Era 6, Standard 2, 3 WHII.4 a, c TCA: 1.1, 1.2, 1.3, 1.9	Textbook: *World History: The Human Journey* YouTube videos: https://www.youtube.com/watch?v=uXcj0ZEyIY8 https://www.youtube.com/watch?v=zRLXH8EE5bA Projector Computer with Internet access	T: Students will watch two videos on colonization. The movies will be stopped midway through their entirety and the class will participate in a discussion of the content of the videos. ASSESS: Students will be given a quiz based off the videos they watch on colonization.

DAY #	CONTENT/OBJECTIVE	STANDARDS	RESOURCES/MATERIALS	LEARNING ACTIVITIES/ASSESSMENTS
15	**Columbian Exchange** —Given a lecture and Internet sources, students will recognize the impact the Columbian Exchange had on native populations with 9/10 correct. —Given scholarly sources, students will be able to identify the different products that crossed the ocean with 19/20 correct.	Era 6, Standard 4, 6 WHII.4 d TCA: 1.7, 1.9	Textbook: *World History: The Human Journey* Computer with Internet access	COLL: Students will be put into groups of four and will be assigned a country/location and a product. They will then have to research their country/location during class and create a short PowerPoint outlining how this new product impacted the country/location. The students will present the PowerPoint during the next class. The speech that accompanies the PowerPoint should be approximately 10 minutes long. Ex. How the horse changed the Native Americans' way of life.
16	**Columbian Exchange (Continued)** —Given scholarly resources, students will recognize the impact the Columbian Exchange had on native populations with 5/5 correct. —Given PowerPoint lectures, students will be able to identify the different products that crossed the ocean with 90% accuracy.	Era 6, Standard 4, 6 WHII.4 d TCA: 1.3, 1.7, 1.9	Textbook: *World History: The Human Journey* Computer and projector	ASSESS/T: Students will give their PowerPoint presentations to the class and will be graded based upon if they have met the required criteria outlined in a rubric. CT: After the presentations are completed the class will be asked which product that was brought over was the most important.

DAY #	CONTENT/OBJECTIVE	STANDARDS	RESOURCES/MATERIALS	LEARNING ACTIVITIES/ASSESSMENTS
17	**The Triangular Trade and Precious Metals to America** —Given a lecture and a writing assignment, students will be able to correctly articulate the triangular trade with 2/2 correct. —Given a lecture, students will recognize the significance of precious metal exports from the Americas with 10/10 correct.	Era 6, Standard 1, 4, 6 WHII.4 e, f TCA: 1.1, 1.3, 1.7	Textbook: *World History: The Human Journey* Computer with Internet access	DIV/CT/CE/L: Students will be asked to write, in-class, a letter justifying why the slave trade was good. They will need to list several reasons based on the day's lecture. This activity asks the students to take a counter-perspective. This will help the students understand why the slave trade was so prosperous. However, it should reinforce their beliefs of why slavery is inherently wrong. It is wrong to own a person. CT: Students will discuss the significance of metal exports from the Americas in a class discussion.
18	**Test Review** Given a test review on the latest material, students will demonstrate their knowledge of the subject by playing a review game with 48/50 correct.	Era 6, Standard 1, 2, 3, 5, 6 WHII.4 a, b, c, d, e, f TCA: 1.1, 1.3, 1.4, 1.5, 1.7, 1.8, 1.9	Textbook: *World History: The Human Journey*	ACT: Students will be playing a game to help them review for the test. This game will be Family Feud-style where the class is broken into two teams and will send one representative up for each team to compete.
19	**Test Day** Given a test on the latest material, students will demonstrate their knowledge of the subject by taking a test with 90% accuracy.	Era 6, Standard 1, 2, 3, 5, 6 WHII.4 a, b, c, d, e, f TCA: 1.1, 1.3, 1.4, 1.5, 1.7, 1.8, 1.9	Written exam with an essay question, short answer, and multiple-choice	ASSESS: Students will be given a comprehensive exam on the European Age of Discovery and expansion into the Americas, Africa, and Asia.

DAY #	CONTENT/OBJECTIVE	STANDARDS	RESOURCES/MATERIALS	LEARNING ACTIVITIES/ASSESSMENTS
20	**Ming Dynasty: Formation and Fall** Given the lesson discussing the thriving exploration and scientific advancements of the Chinese, students will formulate a brief one-paragraph analyses that contains at least three reasons why the Chinese reverted to an isolationist policy under the Ming Dynasty with 3/3 reasons accurately identified.	Era 6, Standard 1, 2, 3, 5, 6 WHII.5 c TCA: 1.1, 1.3, 1.4, 1.5, 1.7, 1.8, 1.9	Technology: Google Earth, PowerPoint Journals Textbook: *World History: The Human Journey*	ASSESS: Students will complete a 10-question, short answer Pretest on Chinese history prior to beginning the unit. This is an ungraded assignment intended to help the teacher assess the student's prior knowledge. S/M: Students will understand how China's scientific understanding of wind and the sea led to early exploration that even exceeded European systems. (Discuss nautical systems and math involved.) T: Students will analyze, using Google Earth, the vast exploration movement in the Ming Dynasty even predating the European Age of Exploration. CT: Given the lesson discussing the thriving exploration and scientific advancements of the Chinese, students will formulate a brief one-paragraph analyses that contains at least three reasons why the Chinese reverted to an isolationist policy with 3/3 reasons accurately identified. This will be completed in the journals. DIV/COLL/ACT: Students will be placed into groups of four to begin filling in a wall-size chart differentiating between English culture and Chinese culture. This will continue through the Qing lecture. CE: Students will discuss Confucius' ideas and recognize positive themes and detrimental themes that kept the common man oppressed by the upper echelon of Chinese Society. Confucius was canonized as a religion in Chinese culture. L: Students will understand how regional differences (Terrain barriers) in China caused differing languages and dialects.

DAY #	CONTENT/OBJECTIVE	STANDARDS	RESOURCES/MATERIALS	LEARNING ACTIVITIES/ASSESSMENTS
21	**Qing Dynasty: Formation and Fall** Given the lesson on the Qing Dynasty, students will complete a 10-item terms list which will require them to use the textbook to define the terms and then require them to make a one-sentence assertion about how it affected Chinese culture or politics with 9/10 accuracy.	Era 6, Standard 1, 2, 3, 5, 6 WHII.5 c TCA: 1.1, 1.3, 1.4, 1.5, 1.7, 1.8, 1.9	YouTube clip: (on Taoism) http://www.youtube.com/watch?v=LbN5PSJ_6jo (clip time 3:45) Textbook: *World History: The Human Journey*	DIV/COLL/ACT: Students will continue to work on their wall charts. This class period, the Qing Dynasty will be added. It will be compared and contrasted to the other dynasties. T/DIV: Students will watch the YouTube clip on Taoism in order to understand how it complimented and how it challenged certain aspects of Confucianism. CT: Given the lesson on the Qing Dynasty, students will complete a 10-item terms list which will require them to use the textbook to define the terms and then require them to make a one-sentence assertion about how it affected Chinese culture or politics with 9/10 accuracy.
22	**China and the Europeans** Given the lesson on the European powers trade with China, students will complete a 15-question, short answer worksheet that reviews the content discussed in class with 14/15 accuracy.	Era 6, Standard 1, 2, 3, 5, 6 WHII.5 c, e TCA: 1.1, 1.3, 1.4, 1.5, 1.7, 1.8, 1.9	Items of value from home ranging from 50 cents to $100 Textbook: *World History: The Human Journey*	COLL/ACT/P: Students will participate in an activity to illustrate the British concept for Free trade which they pressed on the Chinese. Students will be instructed the class before to bring an item of value between 50 cents to $100. Students will then have 10 minutes to trade their items around the room (Agreement must be mutual). Students will recognize very quickly that the student with the most expensive item (such as iPhone, laptop, etc.) will be less willing to trade because they perceive that they have the most valuable item and that to open trade with another student would ultimately lead to what they consider a loss. (Items will be returned.) Ideas will demonstrate the Chinese's concept of self-sufficiency which was the basis of their isolationist policy. B: Students will understand why the Portuguese Jesuits' message was well received by Chinese culture and then ultimately resented. ASSESS: Given the lesson on the European powers trade with China, students will complete a 15-question, short answer worksheet that reviews the content discussed in class with 14/15 accuracy.

DAY #	CONTENT/OBJECTIVE	STANDARDS	RESOURCES/MATERIALS	LEARNING ACTIVITIES/ASSESSMENTS
23	**Tokugawa Shogun in Japan** Given the lesson and activities covering the distinct social groups in Japan, students will summarize in their journals what life would be like for their assigned social class (i.e., Warrior Class, Peasant, etc.) and use at least two terms or concepts discussed in class to support their summaries with 2/2 accuracy.	Era 6, Standard 1, 2, 3, 5, 6 WHII.5 c TCA: 1.1, 1.3, 1.4, 1.5, 1.7, 1.8, 1.9	Textbook: *World History: The Human Journey*	ACT/COLL: Students will be organized into the social structure created in Japan (Warrior Class, Daimyo, artisans/merchants, and peasants). Desks will be organized in the room into groups of four to represent the various social groups. This will personalize the lecture. (For instance, "Matt as a peasant in Tokugawa, Japan"...) It will enable the instructor to assign roles to each individual in the class and is just a unique way to present the material. Allows the student to put themselves "in the shoes" of someone from that time frame (understand their power, their responsibilities, their social limitations, etc.). CT: Given the lesson and activities covering the distinct social groups in Japan, students will summarize in their journal what life would be like for their assigned social class (i.e., Warrior Class, Peasant, etc.) and use at least two terms or concepts discussed in class to support their summaries with 2/2 accuracy. There is no length requirement, but responses should adequately summarize their social group. Issues to be addressed should include power, responsibilities, duties, and social limitations. MUS: Students will listen to music from the Tokugawa period in Japan while they journal. L: Students will recognize Japanese symbols and their meanings.
24	**Contact With Japan and the End of Its Isolation** Given the activity on opening China to trade, students will identify the major goals of their assigned country and formulate a plan that will persuade China to accept their terms, citing at least two key goals of their country based on their primary source document with 2/2 accuracy.	Era 6, Standard 1, 2, 3, 5, 6 WHII.5 c TCA: 1.1, 1.3, 1.4, 1.5, 1.7, 1.8, 1.9	Primary source documents Textbook: *World History: The Human Journey*	ACT/COLL/TH/DIV: Students will form into four groups (Japanese, American, British, and Portuguese). Using primary source documents groups will pick out the concerns and desires of each nation in wanting to open up trade with Japan. Japan will list their concerns they have in opening up trade. Each group will then take turns approaching the Japanese council to convince them to open up their borders to trade. Proper customs and greetings will be followed (bowing, greetings, respectful, formal dialogue, etc.). This will happen in three 2-minute rounds in which each group will propose an agreement trying to persuade the Japanese, and the Japanese will list the reasons they cannot accept. Groups will then regroup and amend their proposals to draw the appeal of the Japanese. Students are limited in offering only things that their country historically offered. Japan will then choose who to select in the end.

DAY #	CONTENT/OBJECTIVE	STANDARDS	RESOURCES/MATERIALS	LEARNING ACTIVITIES/ASSESSMENTS
25	**The Rise of the Ottoman Empire** Given the lesson on the rise of the Ottoman Empire, students will design baseball cards with a picture on one side of either Osman or Suleiman and then with their basic info (i.e., hometown, date of birth, etc.), stats (length of rule, lands conquered, etc.), and then an awards section where the students will list three major accomplishments with 3/3 accuracy.	Era 6, Standard 1, 2, 3, 5, 6 WHII.5 a TCA: 1.1, 1.3, 1.4, 1.5, 1.7, 1.8, 1.9	YouTube clip: http://www.youtube.com/watch?v=phGqXgVLn14&list=PLL3z2uy3jLQ52uFsarCh-mnYO2CAkV5zL (5:34) Flashcards Textbook: *World History: The Human Journey*	A: Students will view art from the period illustrating the great campaigns of Suleiman "The Magnificent." DIV/B: Islamic religion will be compared and contrasted with other major world religions. Also, the way the Ottomans treated Christians in the millet system will be analyzed ("People of the Book"). CT/ COLL: Students will analyze a map that illustrates the expansion of the Ottoman empire through the years (textbook, p.241). They will participate in a class discussion of how this threatened European control as the Ottomans moved west. T: Students will watch a brief video on Suleiman "The Magnificent" and his accomplishments. (Time: 5:34) A: Given the lesson on the rise of the Ottoman Empire, students will design baseball cards with a picture on one side of either Osman or Suleiman and then on the flip side with their basic info (i.e., hometown, date of birth, etc.), stats (length of rule, lands conquered, etc.), and then an awards section where the students will list three major accomplishments with 3/3 accuracy. Flashcards will be used.
26	**Culture and Achievements of the Ottoman Empire** Given the lesson on Ottoman artwork and innovations, students will design and make pottery that reflects elements of Ottoman culture with one-sentence justifications for why the design is uniquely Ottoman in accordance with the rubric provided.	Era 6, Standard 1, 2, 3, 5, 6 WHII.5 a TCA: 1.1, 1.3, 1.4, 1.5, 1.7, 1.8, 1.9	Images of Ottoman Art Art or Home Education Room Pottery Assignment Rubric Clay Textbook: *World History: The Human Journey*	S/M: Students will recognize the radical innovations in math and science of the Ottoman empire. Achievements that even exceeded Western Europe's development. Ideas would be shared through culture and war. T: Students will study images of various Ottoman art and develop certain themes. A: Given the lesson on Ottoman artwork and innovations, students will design and make pottery that reflects elements of Ottoman culture with one-sentence justifications for why the design is uniquely Ottoman in accordance with the rubric provided. Students will proceed to an empty art room or home education room (whatever is available) to practice pottery-making using clay. Art should reflect an aspect or style from the Ottoman Empire.

DAY #	CONTENT/OBJECTIVE	STANDARDS	RESOURCES/MATERIALS	LEARNING ACTIVITIES/ASSESSMENTS
27	**Computer Lab/Technology Day** Given access to the Web, students will research a Sultan from the Ottoman Empire and formulate a well-written persuasive essay that proposes three clearly stated reasons with justification as to why their leader was a good leader or a poor leader with 3/3 accuracy and in accordance with the rubric provided.	Era 6, Standard 1, 2, 3, 5, 6 WHII.5 a TCA: 1.1, 1.3, 1.4, 1.5, 1.7, 1.8, 1.9	Computer (in the Computer Lab or mobile computer lab) Sultan opinion Essay Rubric Textbook: *World History: The Human Journey*	T/CT/ASSESS/CE: Students will be assigned a Sultan from the Ottoman Empire. They will then proceed during class time to gather information and write a persuasive essay (one full page, single-spaced, Times New Roman, 12-point font) with a three-point thesis arguing why their character in Ottoman history was a good leader or a bad leader (opinion essay at its core). Students will recognize characteristics of leadership that are beneficial or harmful. Whatever is not finished in class will be assigned for homework and due by Class #29, it will be a graded assignment based on quality and effort. Rubric will be provided.
28	**The Mughal Empire in India** Given the video on the dominance of the Rajput in early Indian history, students will outline the six main reasons why the Mughal Empire was able to consolidate power in spite of the Rajput's established control of India with 5/6 accuracy.	Era 6, Standard 1, 2, 3, 5, 6 WHII.5 b TCA: 1.1, 1.3, 1.4, 1.5, 1.7, 1.8, 1.9	"The Deadliest Warrior" on Spike TV ("Rajput Warrior") Textbook: *World History: The Human Journey*	T: Students will watch "The Deadliest Warrior" episode on the Rajput warrior. It will display how vicious a warrior they were and how they controlled the early history of India, intimidating sultans. It is a 20-minute clip so it will take the majority of class. It is a fun way that covers the majority of early Indian history. It is not your typical informational history video. H: Students will learn about the value the Rajput placed on physical fitness. The video goes into details of how they did so and how it made them healthier and stronger than their foes. COLL: Students will participate in a lecture and discussion period on how India was consolidated under Mughal control.

DAY #	CONTENT/OBJECTIVE	STANDARDS	RESOURCES/MATERIALS	LEARNING ACTIVITIES/ASSESSMENTS
29	**Growth of the Mughal Empire** Given the lesson on the blending of religions under Mughal rule, students will shade in various regions of India according to their dominant religion (i.e., NE India is Muslim so it might be green on the color key) and predict how the intermingling of these religions would affect India's history with 5/7 accuracy.	Era 6, Standard 1, 2, 3, 5, 6 WHII.5 b TCA: 1.1, 1.3, 1.4, 1.5, 1.7, 1.8, 1.9	Blank map Textbook: *World History: The Human Journey*	DIV: The Mughal empire was able to grow because it blended cultures and ideas from various regions, even religion. This blending, while causing it to grow, would later cause its demise and even lead to the split of India with portions becoming Muslim Pakistan. Students will be able to identify how decisions made in the past affect India today. CT/COLL/L: Using notes from the lecture and their textbook, students will shade in a blank map of India. The shading will be a representation of the various religious and political factions within India. For instance, the Muslims would be in the region of the NE in India so it would be colored green. This will allow the students to understand and predict how these groups will clash and intermingle. After this is completed, the class will discuss the maps and evaluate each other's predictions. Languages will also clearly be affected by these groupings on the map so it will be discussed as well.
30	**Religion and Religious Strife** Given the lesson on religions in India, students will create a three-circle Venn diagram comparing and contrasting Islam, Sikhism, and Hinduism with at least one item in each circle with 7/7 accuracy.	Era 6, Standard 1, 2, 3, 5, 6 WHII.5 b TCA: 1.1, 1.3, 1.4, 1.5, 1.7, 1.8, 1.9	Blank Venn Diagram Textbook: *World History: The Human Journey*	DIV: Students will understand how Sikhism sought to blend the two very diverse religions of Hinduism and Islam into one religion. Students will analyze how these religions could coexist together and what are some of the conflicting doctrine between the two. TH/COLL/ACT: Students will organize into groups of four following the lecture and develop a skit that illustrates the elements of Hinduism (Dharma, Karma, and reincarnation). The skit can be introduced in any context or scenario so long as it clearly reflects the principles. CT: Given the lesson on religions in India, students will create a three-circle Venn diagram comparing and contrasting Islam, Sikhism, and Hinduism with at least one items in each circle with 7/7 accuracy.
31	**Art and Architecture of the Mughals** Given the lesson on Mughal art and architecture, students will construct a model Taj Mahal and identify two aspects of the design that was uniquely Mughal with 2/2 accuracy.	Era 6, Standard 1, 2, 3, 5, 6 WHII.5 b TCA: 1.1, 1.3, 1.4, 1.5, 1.7, 1.8, 1.9	Model Taj Mahal materials: toothpicks, Styrofoam, scissors Images of Mughal Art Textbook: *World History: The Human Journey*	A: Students will construct a model Taj Mahal in groups of four. At the end of the assignment students will explain to the class two aspects of the Taj Mahal architecture that was unique to Mughal culture at the time (i.e., the dome, minarets, etc.). T/COLL: Students will analyze Mughal art and identify elements of the artwork that are a reflection of other cultures (i.e., Persian). This will be guided by the instructor.

DAY #	CONTENT/OBJECTIVE	STANDARDS	RESOURCES/MATERIALS	LEARNING ACTIVITIES/ASSESSMENTS
32	**Computer Lab/ Technology Day** Given the WebQuest on the Hindu Caste system, students will compose a two-paragraph response that cites at least four reasons that the system still can be seen to this day with 3/4 accuracy.	Era 6, Standard 1, 2, 3, 5, 6 WHII.5 b TCA: 1.1, 1.3, 1.4, 1.5, 1.7, 1.8, 1.9	Computer lab or mobile computer lab WebQuest Textbook: *World History: The Human Journey*	T/COLL/CT: Students will work in groups of two to complete a WebQuest. The WebQuest will require students to view several media links (images and video clips) that analyze the plights of the lowest class ("untouchables") in the Hindi Caste system. They will then briefly write down these plights and then go onto the next series of media links which reveal that elements of the Hindu Caste system exist to this day. Students will then work individually to compose a two-paragraph argument based on the video of why it still lingers in Indian society to this day. This will show students the impact history has on modern times.
33	**Dissent and Rebellion in the Mughal Empire** Given the lesson on the turmoil in India under the reign of Aurangzeb, students will summarize why his rule failed; citing at least one political, one religious, and one economic reason and then re-teaching this to a fellow classmate with 3/3 accuracy.	Era 6, Standard 1, 2, 3, 5, 6 WHII.5 b TCA: 1.1, 1.3, 1.4, 1.5, 1.7, 1.8, 1.9	Image from textbook of Aurangzeb painting (page 251) Textbook: *World History: The Human Journey*	CE/DIV: Aurangzeb was intolerant of all other religious groups other than Sunni Islam. As a result he vehemently suppressed and persecuted Hindus which consequently led to countless rebellions and civil unrest. If he had dealt with the Hindus with respect and given them the courtesy of his predecessors then he could have avoided much of the turmoil his reign had. Teach students that beliefs cannot be forced on others; beliefs are convictions of the heart and mind. A/CT/ACT/COLL/P: Painting of Aurangzeb majestically mounted on a horse purging the "impurities" in India. The painting is covered with Muslim artifacts and symbols. Students will write down five themes that they believe the artist is trying to depict and then discuss those with the class. For the discussion, all students will stand with their five themes and remain standing. Starting on the left side of the room students will list one of the five themes they picked and tell that one to the class and why they chose that. Students will then cross off the list the themes already said by other students that they have. If all five of their themes are called they must sit down. The last one standing will get five points extra on their unit test. This is to make it more competitive and fun. COLL: Given the lesson on the turmoil in India under the reign of Aurangzeb, students will summarize why his rule failed; citing at least one political, one religious, and one economic reason and then re-teaching this to a fellow classmate with 3/3 accuracy.

DAY #	CONTENT/OBJECTIVE	STANDARDS	RESOURCES/MATERIALS	LEARNING ACTIVITIES/ASSESSMENTS
34	**Europe's Mercantile System** Given the lesson on the Mercantile system, students will identify and label on a map where the main countries involved in the Mercantile race were (i.e., England, Spain, France, etc.) with 6/9 accuracy.	Era 6, Standard 1, 2, 3, 5, 6 WHII.5 e TCA: 1.1, 1.3, 1.4, 1.5, 1.7, 1.8, 1.9	YouTube video: "Mercantile Rap" http://www.youtube.com/watch?v=BxmB2DB10Ts (3:35) Textbook: *World History: The Human Journey*	COLL/ACT/ASSESS: The term "Mercantilism" will be written on the center of the board at the beginning of class. Students will have 5 minutes for everyone to write as many descriptive, one-word terms as they can about Mercantilism (i.e., greed, gold, power, etc.). This will be a competition between class periods to see what class can generate the most thought. It will also be an informal assessment which will enable the teacher to evaluate student's prior knowledge. T/MUS: Students will watch the YouTube clip in order to preview the project they will be working on during next class. Instructions for this are listed under day 35. Given the lesson on the Mercantile system, students will identify and label on a map where the main countries involved in the Mercantile race were (i.e., England, Spain, France, etc.) with 6/9 accuracy. This will demonstrate just how much of a global phenomenon this system was. It was not strictly mainland Europe.
35	**Work Day: Mercantilism Rap Battle** Given the lesson on Mercantilism and the example video from the previous class, students will compose a rap music video which dictates at least five reasons as to why their assigned country thought they were superior to the others with 5/5 accuracy.	Era 6, Standard 1, 2, 3, 5, 6 WHII.5 c, e TCA: 1.1, 1.3, 1.4, 1.5, 1.7, 1.8, 1.9	A means for recording their music video Rubric for Mercantile Rap Assignment Textbook: *World History: The Human Journey*	T/COLL/ACT/P/MUS: Students will be divided into groups of four. They will then be assigned a country that participated in the Mercantile period actively (i.e., England, Spain, Portugal, etc.). Instructions for their assignment are as follows: They are to construct a rap music video that focuses on why their country is better than the others (this will draw on material from the past and present), why they pursue mercantilism, and the areas that they colonized (Africa, America, etc.). This assignment will require the students to self-teach the unit on Commercialization in Europe and how Europe interacted economically and politically with the rest of the globe (especial attention to Africa). A rubric will be provided and whatever is not finished in class will be due by day 37. It is key to remember that it is a rap battle so music videos can take shots at the other countries. Strict school policy will be in place with language and content. D: Dance is optional although it would be a clever touch to add to their videos.

DAY #	CONTENT/OBJECTIVE	STANDARDS	RESOURCES/MATERIALS	LEARNING ACTIVITIES/ASSESSMENTS
36	**Europe Becomes Interested in Africa** Given the lesson on the colonization of Africa, students will identify three reasons why African tribes/empires generally succumbed to European colonization with 3/3 accuracy.	Era 6, Standard 1, 2, 3, 5, 6 WHII.5 c, e TCA: 1.1, 1.3, 1.4, 1.5, 1.7, 1.8, 1.9	Google Earth Textbook: *World History: The Human Journey*	T: Students will experience an interactive map tour on Google Earth displaying how topography influenced political hegemony in Africa. COLL: Students will participate in a lecture and discussion that traces the history of major African countries and empires and how it relates to colonization and global trade. This will not be a heavy lecture because the students have already been covering this material with their music videos. ASSESS: Given the lesson on the colonization of Africa, students will identify three reasons why African tribes/empires generally succumbed to European colonization with 3/3 accuracy. This will be used by the instructor to evaluate student comprehension of the content. It will not be a graded assignment.
37	**Presentation Day for "Mercantile System Rap Battle" (Started Day 35)** Given their peers' music videos, students will identify three historical events summarized in their peers' videos and express the significance of these events with 3/3 accuracy.	Era 6, Standard 1, 2, 3, 5, 6 WHII.5 c, e TCA: 1.1, 1.3, 1.4, 1.5, 1.7, 1.8, 1.9	Completed Music Videos Textbook: *World History: The Human Journey*	T.MUS/D: Students will present their music videos to the class and at the end students will write their favorite video group on a note and slip it into the ballot box. Group with the most votes will be declared the winner. COLL: Students will have an opportunity to ask one another questions about their video content. ASSESS: Given their peers' music videos, students will identify three historical events summarized in their peers' videos and express the significance of these events with 3/3 accuracy. This will be collected for a class work grade.
38	**Test Review** Given the unit notes on the growth of government in China, India, Turkey, and competition among European nations, students will participate in a game of Jeopardy in which they will identify the correct answer with 40/50 accuracy.	Era 6, Standard 1, 2, 3, 5, 6 WHII.5 a, b, c, d, e TCA: 1.1, 1.3, 1.4, 1.5, 1.7, 1.8, 1.9	Textbook: *World History: The Human Journey*	COLL/ASSESS: Students will participate in a brief review of lecture notes and then play a game of Jeopardy. A review sheet with key terms and concepts will be given. This will be used to gauge where students are at in preparation for the exam and help students that are struggling in specific areas.

DAY #	CONTENT/OBJECTIVE	STANDARDS	RESOURCES/MATERIALS	LEARNING ACTIVITIES/ASSESSMENTS
39	**Test** Given the unit on China, India, the Ottomans, and Mercantilism, students will take a comprehensive exam composed of an essay portion and 30 multiple-choice questions with 27/31 accuracy.	Era 6, Standard 1, 2, 3, 5, 6 WHII.5 a, b, c, d, e TCA: 1.1, 1.3, 1.4, 1.5, 1.7, 1.8, 1.9	Written exam with an essay question, short answer, and multiple-choice	ASSESS: Students will be given a comprehensive exam composed of an essay portion and 30 multiple-choice questions. The content will cover the unit on China to European Mercantilism.
40	**Scientific Revolution** Given a lecture and chart, students will list the factors that contributed to the Scientific Revolution with 10/10 correct.	Era 6, Standard 2 WHII.6 a TCA: 1.2, 1.8	Textbook: *World History: The Human Journey* Paper and pencil	ACT/A/S: Students will create a chain-of-events chart organizing the factors that contributed to the Scientific Revolution. CT: Students will participate in a class discussion following the day's lecture and will be asked what scientific contribution was the most important. They will then be asked what recent scientific discoveries are important.
41	**Scientific Revolution (Continued)** Given a lecture and an assignment, students will identify various important characters who contributed to the Scientific Revolution with 9/10 correct.	Era 6, Standard 2 WHII.6 a TCA: 1.2, 1.8	Textbook: *World History: The Human Journey* Computer with Internet access	COLL/T/S: Students will be placed into groups of four and be asked to create a Facebook page for one of the various scientists discussed in the lecture. This assignment will be completed in class and should take the entire period. The assignment must include a picture, accomplishments from the individual, and other information as appropriate. DIV: ESL students will find this use of technology easier than textbook material.

DAY #	CONTENT/OBJECTIVE	STANDARDS	RESOURCES/MATERIALS	LEARNING ACTIVITIES/ASSESSMENTS
42	**Age of Absolutism** —Given a writing assignment, students will be able to give an account of Louis XIV's monarchy with 9/10 correct. —Given a lecture, students will identify who the Huguenots were with 5/5 correct.	Era 6, Standard 4 WHII.6 b TCA: 1.3, 1.6, 1.10	Textbook: *World History: The Human Journey* Paper and pencil	ASSESS/CT/L: Students will be given an in-class writing assignment in which they must decide if they would rather live under an absolute government or a democracy. CT: Students will create a T-chart in class to recognize differences between a democracy and an absolute government. They should draw comparisons using Louis XIV's rule as an example. B: Students will create a list of important facts about the Huguenots' beliefs.
43	**Age of Absolutism (Continued)** Given a lecture and a video on absolutism, students will be able to give an account of Peter the Great's rule in Russia with 15/17 correct.	Era 6, Standard 4 WHII.6 b TCA: 1.3, 1.6, 1.10	Textbook: *World History: The Human Journey* YouTube video: https://www.youtube.com/watch?v=eNfKBY1MazE	T/L: Students will take notes on the video shown in class. The video should cover roughly the entire class time. Several times throughout the class the video will be stopped and the students will be asked questions on what has been seen.
44	**Age of Absolutism (Continued)** Given a lecture and creating a chart, students will be able to give an account of Peter the Great's and Catherine the Great's rule in Russia with 10/10 correct.	Era 6, Standard 4 WHII.6 b TCA: 1.3, 1.6, 1.10	Textbook: *World History: The Human Journey* Quiz	ASSESS: Students will be given a quiz on the Scientific Revolution as well as the monarchies of Louis XIV and Peter the Great. DIV/CE: Students will be asked to identify by creating a chart of the difficulties Catherine the Great would have as a female ruler. This conversation will then continue into whether female leaders still have the same difficulties as male leaders throughout all time in history.

DAY #	CONTENT/OBJECTIVE	STANDARDS	RESOURCES/MATERIALS	LEARNING ACTIVITIES/ASSESSMENTS
45	**Age of Absolutism (Continued)** —Given a lecture and a game, students will be asked to explain how the Habsburgs gained and held power and how the Hohenzollerns rose to power with 3/3 correct. —Given a game show and lecture, students will be able to identify the factors that contributed to conflicts between Prussia and Austria with 5/5 correct.	Era 6, Standard 4 WHII.6 b TCA: 1.3, 1.6, 1.10	Textbook: *World History: The Human Journey* Paper and pencil	ACT/COLL/TH: Students will be placed into groups to create a talk show called "Who's the Greatest?" The show's guests are Frederick William I and Frederick II. Students will compose questions to be asked by the interviewer and responses for Frederick William I, Frederick II, and an interviewer. Elect students to be Frederick William I, Frederick II, and an interviewer.
46	**England** Given a lecture, a chart, and an art assignment, students will be able to explain the English Monarchy leading up to the English Civil War with 90% accuracy.	Era 6, Standard 2, 6 WHII.6 c TCA: 1.1, 1.2, 1.6, 1.10	Textbook: *World History: The Human Journey* Poster board, markers, crayons	COLL/CT: Students will work in groups to make a T-chart of bullet points showing the differences between Mary Tudor and Elizabeth I. COLL/ASSESS/A: Students will work in groups of four to construct a family tree to help them better understand the Tudor family. This will be done on a large piece of poster board. These group projects will be graded as well. They must accurately display the Tudor family, and they must be aesthetically pleasing.
47	**England (Continued)** Given a video and lecture, students will be able to articulate how the English Civil War led to Cromwell's Commonwealth with 7/10 correct.	Era 6, Standard 2, 6 WHII.6 c TCA: 1.1, 1.2, 1.6, 1.10	Textbook: *World History: The Human Journey* YouTube video: https://www.youtube.com/watch?v=3FyQnEDt7eA	T/A: Students will create a cluster diagram identifying the causes of the English Civil War using their textbook and the YouTube video as sources. CT/COLL: Students will be asked to discuss in groups the differences in the Instrument of Government and the U.S. Constitution. A/DIV: Students will make a chart highlighting the weaknesses and strengths of the Commonwealth.

DAY #	CONTENT/OBJECTIVE	STANDARDS	RESOURCES/MATERIALS	LEARNING ACTIVITIES/ASSESSMENTS
48	**England (Continued)** —Given a lecture and a discussion, students will be able to describe the reduced power of the British monarchy under the Glorious Revolution with 90% accuracy. —Given a lecture, students will be able to identify the principal features of Britain's limited constitutional monarchy with 9/10 correct. —Given a lecture, students will be able to identify the two political parties with 10/10 correct.	Era 6, Standard 2, 6 WHII.6 c TCA: 1.1, 1.2, 1.6, 1.10	Textbook: *World History: The Human Journey*	CE: Students will be asked to identify in a class discussion why the English Bill of Rights was so critical a change in English Government. Students will relate many of the major ideas in the English Bill of Rights to the United States Constitution, Declaration of Independence, and Bill of Rights. DIV/CT: Students will compare the Whigs and Tories in a class discussion. The students will be required to make a chart that will list the differences between the Whigs and Tories. ACT: Students will all come up to the board, creating a T-chart highlighting how the British monarchy's power was reduced by the Glorious Revolution.
49	**Test Review** Given a test review on the latest material, students will demonstrate their knowledge of the subject by playing a review game with 48/50 correct.	Era 6, Standard 2, 4, 6 WHII.6 a, b, c TCA: 1.1, 1.2, 1.3, 1.6, 1.8, 1.10	Textbook: *World History: The Human Journey*	ACT: Students will be playing a game to help them review for the test. This game will be Family Feud-style where the class is broken into two teams and will send one representative up for each team to compete.
50	**Test Day** Given a test on the latest material, students will demonstrate their knowledge of the subject by taking a test with 90% accuracy.	Era 6, Standard 2, 4, 6 WHII.6 a, b, c TCA: 1.1, 1.2, 1.3, 1.6, 1.8, 1.10	Written exam with an essay question, short answer, and multiple-choice	ASSESS: Students will be given an exam covering the Scientific Revolution and the various monarchs in Europe.

DAY #	CONTENT/OBJECTIVE	STANDARDS	RESOURCES/MATERIALS	LEARNING ACTIVITIES/ASSESSMENTS
51	**Enlightenment** —Given a lecture and chart, students will identify the principal characteristics of Enlightenment thinking with 90% correct. —Given a lecture, students will be able to explain the political, religious, and social ideas of the Enlightenment with 10/10 correct.	Era 7, Standard 1 WHII.6 d, f TCA: 1.2, 1.4	Textbook: *World History: The Human Journey* Paper and pencil	CT/DIV: Students will construct a chart to list the characteristics and achievements of various philosophes. CT/COLL: Students will work together in groups to create a list of questions they would ask a specific Enlightenment thinker in an interview. DIV: Students with an LD (ex. dyslexia) will be placed in groups with students that can help accommodate their needs.
52	**Enlightenment (Continued)** —Given a lecture, students will analyze the impact of the Enlightenment with 19/20 correct. —Given the Declaration of Independence students will identify the causes of the American Revolution with 90% accuracy.	Era 7, Standard 1 WHII.6 d TCA: 1.2, 1.4	Textbook: *World History: The Human Journey*	CT/CE: Students will each be given a copy of the Declaration of Independence and then will be asked to list the demands the colonies made to England. Afterward, there will be a class discussion on why these were the rights listed. DIV: Students who are ESL learners will be allowed to work in a group if they need assistance.
53	**French Revolution** Given a lecture, students will analyze the discontent that began to grow in Europe in the mid-1700s with 19/20 correct.	Era 6, Standard 2, 3, 6; Era 7, Standard 1 WHII.6 e, f TCA: 1.1, 1.2, 1.4, 1.8	Textbook: *World History: The Human Journey* Computer with Microsoft Word Projector	ACT/T: Students will use a computer and projector to create a pie chart of the three estates showing the population distribution. This should help the student understand how hilariously outnumbered the clergy and nobles were compared to the commoners. T: Using Google Earth, students will view the palace of Versailles and observe how magnificent it is and how much it cost to build. Following this the class will engage in a brief discussion as to why this giant palace was built. Some key events that took place here will also be mentioned.

DAY #	CONTENT/OBJECTIVE	STANDARDS	RESOURCES/MATERIALS	LEARNING ACTIVITIES/ASSESSMENTS
54	**French Revolution (Continued)** Given a lecture and an activity, students will explain why and how the French Revolution spread with 95% accuracy.	Era 6, Standard 2, 3, 6; Era 7, Standard 1 WHII.6 e TCA: 1.1, 1.2, 1.4, 1.8	Textbook: *World History: The Human Journey*	ACT/TH: Students will act out the storming of the Bastille to better understand the symbolic purpose of the takeover. The teacher will act as a rebel-rouser, and the students will be the horde that follows. This will probably have to take place outside. Afterward the students will analyze the things the teacher said during the mock takeover to see what the people were demanding.
55	**French Revolution (Continued)** Given a lecture and video, students will compare the French Revolution with American Revolution with 10/10 correct.	Era 6, Standard 2, 3, 6; Era 7, Standard 1 WHII.6 e TCA: 1.1, 1.2, 1.4, 1.8	Textbook: *World History: The Human Journey* YouTube video: https://www.youtube.com/watch?v=lTTvKwCylFY Paper to take a quiz	T: Students will watch a video on the French and American Revolutions. CT/COLL: Students will work in groups and will list the similarities and differences in the French and American Revolution. This will be brought together in a larger group discussion. ASSESS: Students will be given a short informal quiz at the end of class on the French Revolution.
56	**French Revolution (Continued)** —Given a lecture, students will identify key characters present in the French Revolution with 10/10 correct. —Given an activity, students will be able to describe how the French Revolution eventually led to the Reign of Terror with 9/10 correct.	Era 6, Standard 2, 3, 6; Era 7, Standard 1 WHII.6 e TCA: 1.1, 1.2, 1.4, 1.8	Textbook: *World History: The Human Journey* YouTube video: https://www.youtube.com/watch?v=PyZsLYxaIuM	CT/COLL: Students will all be placed in a faction as either the Jacobins or Girondins. The students will then, using their book, work together to make a list of policies their group would advocate. After they have been given a chance to work together they will present their policies to the rest of the class. T: Students will watch a short YouTube video on the Reign of Terror to supplement the lecture.
57	**French Revolution (Continued)** Given a video, lecture, and assignment, students will analyze how Napoleon came to power with 15/15 correct.	Era 6, Standard 2, 3, 6; Era 7, Standard 1 WHII.6 e TCA: 1.1, 1.2, 1.4, 1.8	Textbook: *World History: The Human Journey* YouTube: https://www.youtube.com/watch?v=MrbiSUgZEbg	T: Students will watch a video on Napoleon and take notes. They will be expected to write down 15 facts about Napoleon from the film as an assignment. CE: Students will be asked to write a short paper giving reasons why they would or would not support Napoleon and will discuss them in class.

DAY #	CONTENT/OBJECTIVE	STANDARDS	RESOURCES/MATERIALS	LEARNING ACTIVITIES/ASSESSMENTS
58	**French Revolution (Continued)** Given a lecture and an activity, students will be able to explain the campaigns of Napoleon with 90% correct.	Era 6, Standard 2, 3, 6; Era 7, Standard 1 WHII.6 e TCA: 1.1, 1.2, 1.4, 1.8	Textbook: *World History: The Human Journey* Chalk and a sunny day	ACT/DIV: Students will go out into the parking lot where a map of the world will be drawn in chalk. The students will all be assigned a certain country and will stand in that country mark by chalk. The students who are France will then begin conquering the other countries in the same pattern that Napoleon conquered.
59	**French Revolution (Continued)** Given a lecture and assignment, students will be able to explain the campaigns of Napoleon with 5/5 correct.	Era 6, Standard 2, 3, 6; Era 7, Standard 1 WHII.6 e TCA: 1.1, 1.2, 1.4, 1.8	Textbook: *World History: The Human Journey* Computer with Microsoft PowerPoint and Internet access	ASSESS/T/COLL: Students will be placed into groups of four for this class and will be required to create a PowerPoint using their books, Internet, and lessons on Napoleon's conquests. The students will present the PowerPoints to the class next period.
60	**Art, Philosophy, Literature, and New Technology** Given a lecture and text of Swift and Warren, students will be able to explain how art, philosophy, and literature changed during the 16th, 17th, and 18th century with 17/18 correct.	Era 6, Standard 2, 6 WHII.6 e TCA: 1.1, 1.2, 1.4, 1.8	Textbook: *World History: The Human Journey* Text of Swift and Warren to hand out to the class Paintings of Napoleon	ASSESS/T: Students will present their PowerPoints to the class. They should cover all of Napoleon's major conquests, up to the 100 days. COLL/CT/CE/L: Students will be asked to analyze political satire of the time by reading Swift and Warren. They will then be put into groups of three and asked if they think satire was effective then, and if it is still effective today. A: Students will compare paintings of Napoleon to see how different artists portrayed him.
61	**Test Review** Given a test review on the latest material, students will demonstrate their knowledge of the subject by playing a review game with 48/50 correct.	Era 6, Standard 2, 3, 6; Era 7, Standard 1 WHII.6 d, e, f TCA: 1.1, 1.2, 1.4, 1.8	Textbook: *World History: The Human Journey*	ACT/T: Students will be playing a game to help them review for the test. This game will be Family Feud-style where the class is broken into two teams and will send one representative up for each team to compete.

DAY #	CONTENT/OBJECTIVE	STANDARDS	RESOURCES/MATERIALS	LEARNING ACTIVITIES/ASSESSMENTS
62	**Test Day** Given a test on the latest material, students will demonstrate their knowledge of the subject by taking a test with 90% accuracy.	Era 6, Standard 2, 6 WHII.6 d,e,f TCA: 1.1, 1.2, 1.4, 1.8	Written exam with an essay question, short answer, and multiple-choice questions	ASSESS: Students will be given an exam covering the Enlightenment and French Revolution.
63	**Colonial Society in Latin America** Given the unit on the social division in Latin America and the population pie graph, students will coordinate with a partner to verbally answer why the Amerindians remained suppressed despite having the largest population and make assertions as to why the Creoles were considered the most dangerous element of Latin Society with 2/2 accuracy.	Era 7, Standard 1, 4, 6 WHII.7 a TCA: 1.1, 1.2, 1.3, 1.4, 1.6, 1.10	Pie graph on page 247 of McDougal Littel's *Modern World History: Patterns of Interaction*	CT/COLL: Students will study the pie graph after the lecture. The graph shows the population percentages of the various social divisions (i.e., Mullato, Peninsulares, Amerindians). They will then discuss with a partner how this vast majority of Amerindians remained suppressed by the other groups, especially the Peninsulares. Students will also speculate as to why the Creoles were considered the most dangerous part of society. DIV/COLL/ACT: The Instructor will draw a large blank pyramid on the board and then have students come up and draw in the next social class (go top to bottom; meaning Peninsular to Indian). At each point teachers will discuss the obstacles that prevented social maneuverability in Latin American society.

DAY #	CONTENT/OBJECTIVE	STANDARDS	RESOURCES/MATERIALS	LEARNING ACTIVITIES/ASSESSMENTS
64	**Revolutionary Sentiments in Latin America** Given the primary source analysis of the Declaration of Independence and the French Constitution of 1791, students will compare and contrast the documents and extract four themes that would have an especially strong appeal in Latin American culture, with 3/4 accuracy.	Era 7, Standard 1, 4, 6 WHII.7 a, b TCA: 1.1, 1.2, 1.3, 1.4, 1.6, 1.10	Primary sources: Declaration of Independence and the French Constitution of 1791 Textbook: *World History: The Human Journey*	COLL: Instructor will cipher through the Declaration of Independence and the French Constitution of 1791 with the class drawing out key themes of both. CT: Given the primary source analysis of the Declaration of Independence and the French Constitution of 1791, students will compare and contrast the documents and extract four themes that would have an especially strong appeal in Latin American culture, with 3/4 accuracy. DIV: Compare and Contrast of the American Revolution and French Revolution (should be review).
65	**Revolution in Haiti** Given the lecture notes on the Haitian Revolution, students will summarize the revolution in Haiti to a peer in less than 5 minutes (re-teach) citing the major causes, course of events, and conclusion with 5/5 accuracy.	Era 7, Standard 1, 4, 6 WHII.7 a, c TCA: 1.1, 1.2, 1.3, 1.4, 1.6, 1.10	Google Earth Textbook: *World History: The Human Journey*	T: Students will study the geography of Haiti and recognize why the Europeans were drawn to it (economic and strategic advantages). CE: Toussaint L'Ouverture led a revolution against the French based on his convictions of the evils of slavery. He would not back down until it was abolished. L: Students will understand the significance of the change of the name from Saint Domingue to Haiti following the revolution. "Haiti" in the native language of the Arawak means "mountainous land." COLL: Given the lecture notes on the Haitian Revolution, students will summarize the revolution in Haiti to a peer in less than 5 minutes (re-teach) citing the major causes, course of events, and conclusion with 5/5 accuracy.

DAY #	CONTENT/OBJECTIVE	STANDARDS	RESOURCES/MATERIALS	LEARNING ACTIVITIES/ASSESSMENTS
66	**Reading Day** Given the text from *All Souls Rising* and what has been covered in lecture, students will construct a declaration of independence for the Haitian people in accordance with the rubric provided.	Era 7, Standard 1, 4, 6 WHII.7 a, c TCA: 1.1, 1.2, 1.3, 1.4, 1.6, 1.10	Letterhead paper with the Haitian flag on it Project Rubric for Declaration assignment Students will be assigned a lengthy excerpt from the novel, *All Souls Rising* (novel about the revolution in Haiti). Textbook: *World History: The Human Journey*	CT: Students will work individually to read the excerpt, *All Souls Rising* (pp. 145–159). As they read they will pick out key themes and expectations from the Haitian Revolution. This reading and note-taking will take the majority of the class period. For homework, they will then write a one-page Declaration of Independence for Haiti on the given letterhead. Students are expected to draw from the document, specifically taking into account Haitian plights, concerns, and ideal of its leaders (especially L'Ouverture and Dessalines). A rubric will be provided and declarations will be read aloud to the class on Day 67.
67	**Declaration Day** Given their peer's presentation of their declaration, students will identify common themes that reflect the needs of the Haitian people with 6/8 correct.	Era 7, Standard 1, 4, 6 WHII.7 a, c TCA: 1.1, 1.2, 1.3, 1.4, 1.6, 1.10	Declaration Assignment and Rubric Textbook: *World History: The Human Journey*	COLL: Students will present their declarations to the class and at the end the instructor will clarify the major points and evaluate which declarations most accurately embodied the spirit of the Haitian Revolution. ASSESS: Students will have their declaration assignment graded according to the given rubric.
68	**Creole Led Independence** Given the lecture and discussion on Simon Bolivar and Jose de San Martin, students will compare and contrast in a one-paragraph response the two leaders and their revolutions, citing a minimum of two differences and two similarities with 4/4 accuracy.	Era 7, Standard 1, 4, 6 WHII.7 a, c TCA: 1.1, 1.2, 1.3, 1.4, 1.6, 1.10	YouTube clip on Simon Bolivar (1:53): http://www.youtube.com/watch?v=8HFISUjEzVs Textbook: *World History: The Human Journey*	CT: Given the lecture and discussion on Simon Bolivar and Jose de San Martin, students will compare and contrast in a one-paragraph response the two leaders and their revolutions, citing a minimum of two differences and two similarities with 4/4 accuracy. DIV: Students will compare the revolutions of Bolivar and San Martin in class discussion with a focus on determining factors that contributed to their eventual revolutionary alliance to push the Spanish out of several Latin American colonies. T: YouTube clip discussing the background and impact of Bolivar.

DAY #	CONTENT/OBJECTIVE	STANDARDS	RESOURCES/MATERIALS	LEARNING ACTIVITIES/ASSESSMENTS
69	**Creole Led Independence (Continued)** Given a blank map of South America, students will label the major battles of Bolivar and San Martin's revolutionary campaigns with 5/5 accuracy.	Era 7, Standard 1, 4, 6 WHII.7 a, c TCA: 1.1, 1.2, 1.3, 1.4, 1.6, 1.10	Google Earth Painting of the Battle of Ayacucho Textbook: *World History: The Human Journey*	COLL/T: Students will participate in a class discussion studying the revolutionary movements of Bolivar and San Martin. Using Google Earth, students will discuss how geography affected the military campaign. A: Students will analyze a painting of the Battle of Ayacucho and detect the revolutionary symbolism within it. DIV: Students will understand how the Gran Columbia created by Bolivar with assistance of San Martin eventually crumbled into several different nations in 1831 due to the various regional needs and culture not being satisfied under a unified government.
70	**Mexican Independence** Given the lecture and video, students will list the three characteristics that differentiated the Mexican Revolution from other Spanish colonies with 3/3 accuracy.	Era 7, Standard 1, 4, 6 WHII.7 a, b TCA: 1.1, 1.2, 1.3, 1.4, 1.6, 1.9, 1.10	YouTube video clip (1:17) of Miguel Hidalgo's "Grito de Delores" speech: http://www.youtube.com/watch?v=BzSnAvVhzE0 Textbook: *World History: The Human Journey*	L: Students will understand what "Grito de Delores" ("Cry of Delores") means in Spanish and its impacting call for revolution. T/COLL/ACT: Students will listen to Father Hidalgo's Grito de Delores speech that rallied the Indians and Mestizos for revolution in Mexico (Important, revolution in Mexico was not through the Creoles). Students will then discuss in groups of four how this speech may have appealed to the lower classes and not the Creole and Peninsulares (special focus on Hidalgo's endorsement of Enlightenment ideas). After writing down four appeals on paper, all students at once will come up to the board and write down one of their group's ideas and they will be discussed as a whole once posted on the board. B: Students will see the ways in which Father Hidalgo used Biblical principles to endorse revolution against Spain.
71	**Conclusion to Mexican Independence** Given the lecture notes and class discussion, students will create a timeline that illustrates the six critical events of the Mexican Revolution that led to Mexican Independence along with a one-sentence description of each with 5/6 accuracy.	Era 7, Standard 1, 4, 6 WHII.7 a, b TCA: 1.1, 1.2, 1.3, 1.4, 1.6, 1.10	Empty Timeline Handout YouTube clip of a Mexican Revolution song with image slide show (2:37) http://www.youtube.com/watch?v=jYJxpWF25OI Paintings from the Mexican Revolution on PowerPoint Textbook: *World History: The Human Journey*	COLL: Given the lecture notes and class discussion, students will form into groups of four to create a timeline that illustrates the six critical events of the Mexican Revolution that led to Mexican Independence along with a one-sentence description of each with 6/6 accuracy. A: Students will discuss artwork that symbolized major events from the Mexican Revolution. MUS/T: Students will listen to music describing the Mexican Revolution (in Spanish, lyrics will be provided) as well as watch a picture slideshow with the YouTube clip. CT: At the end of class, students will be given an assignment for homework. The assignment will require them to gather at least three credible sources on the revolution and general colonial history of Brazil and study them thoroughly.

DAY #	CONTENT/OBJECTIVE	STANDARDS	RESOURCES/MATERIALS	LEARNING ACTIVITIES/ASSESSMENTS
72	**Brazilian Revolution** Given the three credible sources researched for homework, students will compose a four-paragraph essay with a three-point thesis on why the revolution in Brazil was relatively bloodless in comparison to other Latin American revolutions. Students will follow guidelines set in the provided rubric.	Era 7, Standard 1, 4, 6 WHII.7 a, b TCA: 1.1, 1.2, 1.3, 1.4, 1.6, 1.10	Mobile Computer lab Prompt/rubric instruction Textbook: *World History: The Human Journey*	CT/COLL/DIV/T: Students will be given the class period to begin working on their very short essay described in the objective. During this time, the instructor will be at the student's aid assisting in constructing a higher level paper with a clear thesis. The paper will be collected on Day 74. The mobile computer lab will be at the student's disposal. The main purpose is to self-research the material and work on writing skills to prepare them for college-level writing.
73	**Monroe Doctrine** Given the lecture notes and taking into account Latin American Revolutions, students will list the three purposes of the Monroe doctrine as well as summarize its effect on European powers in a brief two-sentence reply with 4/4 accuracy.	Era 7, Standard 1, 4, 6 WHII.7 a, b TCA: 1.1, 1.2, 1.3, 1.4, 1.6, 1.10	Primary source document of the Monroe Doctrine (1823) Textbook: *World History: The Human Journey*	ASSESS: Essays on Brazil's "bloodless" revolution will be collected and graded according to the rubric. CT: Students will analyze the Monroe doctrine and pick out all the provisions of it and what this meant for the Americas. COLL/ACT/P: Students will compete in an "Around the World" game in which everyone stands. Students will play a one-on-one matchup with other students in which the instructor asks the question and tries to "go around the world" of the classroom. This assignment is in preparation for Day 74 quiz on the Latin American Revolution Unit and will contain topics and even some direct questions from the quiz.
74	**Quiz Day on Latin American Revolution Unit** Given the unit on Latin American Revolutions, students will answer 20/25 correctly on a multiple-choice quiz styled along SOL test standards.	Era 7, Standard 1, 4, 6 WHII.7 a, b, c, d TCA: 1.1, 1.2, 1.3, 1.4, 1.6, 1.10	Textbook: *World History: The Human Journey*	ASSESS: Given the unit on Latin American Revolutions, students will answer 20/25 correctly on a multiple-choice quiz styled along SOL test standards. DIV: Students will get to sample some Latin American food brought by the instructor. A reward for their hard work during the unit and a fun way to teach a different culture. COLL/CE: As students eat their meal AFTER their quiz, they will casually discuss characteristics of the revolutionary leaders that allowed them to be so impactful (leadership skills).

DAY #	CONTENT/OBJECTIVE	STANDARDS	RESOURCES/MATERIALS	LEARNING ACTIVITIES/ASSESSMENTS
75	**Congress of Vienna** —Given a lecture, students will describe how the Congress of Vienna attempted to restore stability to Europe with 10/10 correct. —Students will identify the role of various politicians present at the Congress of Vienna with 15/15 correct.	Era 7, Standard 1 WHII.8 a TCA: 1.2	Textbook: *World History: The Human Journey* Paper for letter	CT/L: Students will pretend to be a representative of a country that was present at the Congress of Vienna. They will then write a short journal entry explaining what they hope to gain for their country at the Congress. Following this assignment the students will be asked to share what is it is their county wanted. This will lead to a short class discussion on how the Congress attempted to restore stability and mention several of the more prominent politicians in attendance. DIV/TH: Pretending to be a politician from another country will help the students better understand cultural differences. They will see a new perspective.
76	**Changes in Europe** Given a lesson, students will identify the reforms that took place in England with, specifically, the education reform with 10/10 accuracy.	Era 7, Standard 1, 4, 5 WHII.8 b TCA: 1.2, 1.6, 1.10	Textbook: *World History: The Human Journey*	CT/CE/DIV: Students will write an essay on how expansion of public education accompanied expansion of suffrage in Great Britain. They must also ask if a well-educated populace is essential to the long-term success of a democratic government. This paper will probably take most of the class to write.
77	**Unification of Italy** —Given a lecture, students will describe the events that led to nationalistic movements for unification in Italy with 10/10 correct. —Given an activity, students will identify the important leaders in the fight for the unification of Italy with 10/10 correct.	Era 7, Standard 1, 4, 5 WHII.8 c TCA: 1.1, 1.2, 1.5, 1.6, 1.9, 1.10	Textbook: *World History: The Human Journey* Paper and crayons/colored pencils	COLL/A: Students will work in pairs to make visual representations of the events leading to Italian unification (Ex.: Stair-steps with a step toward unification on every stair). CT: Students will engage in a class discussion on the leaders in Italian unification. They will then be asked who they believe was the most important person to help unify Italy. Students will be expected to back up their answers with sound logic.

DAY #	CONTENT/OBJECTIVE	STANDARDS	RESOURCES/MATERIALS	LEARNING ACTIVITIES/ASSESSMENTS
78	**Unification of Italy (Continued)** Given an activity, students will explain the problems Italy faced after unification with 9/10 correct.	Era 7, Standard 1, 4, 5 WHII.8 c TCA: 1.1, 1.2, 1.5, 1.6, 1.9, 1.10	Textbook: *World History: The Human Journey*	COLL/CT/T/DIV: Students will be divided in groups and then research an area that has recently experienced conflict due to national or cultural alliances. They will create a PowerPoint on the project and present it in class the next day.
79	**Unification of Germany** Given a PowerPoint assignment, students will explain how Prussia replaced Austria as the leading German state in Europe with 10/10 correct.	Era 7, Standard 1, 4, 5 WHII.8 d TCA: 1.1, 1.2, 1.5, 1.6, 1.9, 1.10	Textbook: *World History: The Human Journey* Sunny day and chalk	ASSESS: Students will present their PowerPoints from yesterday's class. Their PowerPoints must accurately convey the information of their chosen topics to receive full credit. A: Students will create a timeline of Germany's unification identifying major events. ACT: Students will be given a random German state and the teacher will play as Prussia. The various students, playing as the German state, then have to agree if they will join Prussia based on the teacher's dialogue.
80	**Unification of Germany (Continued)** Given a lesson, students will identify the major gains for Germany during wars for unification with 9/10 correct.	Era 7, Standard 1, 4, 5 WHII.8 d TCA: 1.1, 1.2, 1.5, 1.6, 1.9, 1.10	Textbook: *World History: The Human Journey* YouTube video: https://www.youtube.com/watch?v=1TVp9SaJi-4	T: Using maps, students will be able to see how Germany was divided into many different states and how they progressively became more united through the German unification wars. CT: In a class discussion, students will be asked what factors would help and what would deter Germany from unifying. DIV: Students with ADHD will not be given their maps until necessary to avoid any distractions.
81	**Unification of Germany (Continued)** Given a lesson, students will understand the differences in German and Italian unification with 5/5 correct.	Era 7, Standard 1, 4, 5 WHII.8 c, d TCA: 1.1, 1.2, 1.5, 1.6, 1.9, 1.10	Textbook: *World History: The Human Journey* Quiz	CT: Students will create a chart to compare and contrast nationalism and unification in Italy and Germany. This will lead to a class discussion to identify what were the key differences in German and Italian unification. The discussion will end with a "so what" question, and then the teacher will communicate how the unification of these countries would have major repercussions in the near future. ASSESS: Students will be given a quiz on Italian and German unification.

DAY #	CONTENT/OBJECTIVE	STANDARDS	RESOURCES/MATERIALS	LEARNING ACTIVITIES/ASSESSMENTS
82	**Unification of Germany (Continued)** Given a lesson, students will understand the central role of Bismarck in the unification of Germany with 19/20 correct.	Era 7, Standard 1, 4, 5 WHII.8 d TCA: 1.1, 1.2, 1.5, 1.6, 1.9, 1.10	Textbook: *World History: The Human Journey*	CE/CT: Students will be asked to evaluate Bismarck as a leader by writing in class a one-page paper on how he managed to unify Germany. Students must include various aspects about his character and whether or not his actions were just or questionable. This should take most of the period.
83	**Germany After Unification** —Given an activity, students will explain the problems Bismarck faced as chancellor with 5/5 correct. —Given an activity, students will describe how Germany became industrialized under Bismarck's leadership with 9/10 correct.	Era 7, Standard 1, 4, 5 WHII.8 d TCA: 1.1, 1.2, 1.5, 1.6, 1.9, 1.10	Textbook: *World History: The Human Journey*	CT: Students will be given verbally a list of Bismarck's problems he faced as chancellor, and then they will be asked to present their own solution to these problems. After this they will be given the actual solution Bismarck came up with. CT: Students will participate in a class discussion on the industrialization of Germany and how Bismarck contributed to it. DIV: Students with ADHD will be given lecture notes to help them remember what was discussed in class and to keep them focused on the assignment.
84	**Test Review** Given a test review on the latest material, students will demonstrate their knowledge of the subject by playing a review game with 48/50 correct.	Era 7, Standard 1, 4, 5 WHII.8 a, b, c, d TCA: 1.1, 1.2, 1.3, 1.5, 1.6, 1.9, 1.10	Textbook: *World History: The Human Journey* PowerPoint, computer, projector	ACT/T: Students will be playing a game to help them review for the test. This game will be Family Feud-style where the class is broken into two teams and will send one representative up for each team to compete.
85	**Test Day** Given a test on the latest material, students will demonstrate their knowledge of the subject by taking a test with 90% accuracy.	Era 7, Standard 1, 4, 5 WHII.8 a, b, c, d TCA: 1.1, 1.2, 1.3, 1.5, 1.6, 1.9, 1.10	Written exam with an essay question, short answer, and multiple-choice	ASSESS: Students will be assessed on changes in Europe, failed revolutions, and Italian and German Unification.

DAY #	CONTENT/OBJECTIVE	STANDARDS	RESOURCES/MATERIALS	LEARNING ACTIVITIES/ASSESSMENTS
86	**Industrial Revolution: The Factory System (Working Conditions, Rise in Urbanization, the Growing Pains of Industrialization)** Given the lecture and video clip, students will list the three major social groups afflicted in the Industrial system and at least three plights/concerns for each group with 6/6 accuracy.	Era 7, Standard 2, 4, 5, 6 WHII.9 a, c TCA: 1.1, 1.2, 1.3, 1.6, 1.7, 1.8, 1.9, 1.10	YouTube clip: "Turning Points in History—Industrial Revolution" (3:30) Textbook: *World History: The Human Journey*	T: YouTube clip to introduce the factory system and special accounts about the abuses of child labor. CT: Given the lecture and video clip on the abuses of child labor, students will list the three major groups afflicted in the Industrial system and at least three plights/concerns for each group with 6/6 accuracy. H/P: Students will understand how the harshness of some factories and rapid growth of urbanization was detrimental to worker's health and why. COLL/ACT/P: Students will participate in an activity to demonstrate how a factory system works. In the activity students will form two lines (two teams, even split of the classroom) and be supplied multiple slips of paper in order to mass-assemble paper airplanes (not existent during Industrial Revolution, but origami would take too long to teach). Students will only be permitted to fold each plane once (i.e., fold one wing) and must construct a plane that will allow them to mass-assemble the airplane faster than the other line. The instructor will act like a boss/overseer with a whistle and create a hostile work environment. This activity will serve as the set.
87	**Industrial Revolution Spreads Globally** Given the brief lecture on development of Industrialization in France, Germany, Russia, and the prior lesson on England, students will distinguish a minimum of three characteristics that differentiated the experience (or lack of experience) in these various countries from one another with 11/12 correct.	Era 7, Standard 2, 4, 5, 6 WHII.9 a, d TCA: 1.1, 1.2, 1.3, 1.6, 1.7, 1.8, 1.9, 1.10	Google Earth Textbook: *World History: The Human Journey*	B: Students will understand how Industrialization in certain countries threatened their heritage and even their religion, like in the Southern United States, especially Virginia. The farmer was, according to Thomas Jefferson, "God's chosen people." DIV: Given the brief lecture on development of Industrialization in France, Germany, Russia, and the prior lesson on England, students will distinguish a minimum of three characteristics that differentiated the experience (or lack of experience) in these various countries from one another. T: Students will take a Google Earth tour in order to understand just how the Industrial Revolution spread and affected each individual country.

DAY #	CONTENT/OBJECTIVE	STANDARDS	RESOURCES/MATERIALS	LEARNING ACTIVITIES/ASSESSMENTS
88	**Transportation Revolution** Given the various transportation inventions of the Industrial Revolution, students will compose a one-paragraph Persuasive essay on a transportation invention of their choosing and justify why it was most beneficial, pointing out at least three advantages listed in class with 3/3 accuracy.	Era 7, Standard 2, 4, 5, 6 WHII.9 a TCA: 1.1, 1.2, 1.3, 1.6, 1.7, 1.8, 1.9, 1.10	Textbook: *World History: The Human Journey*	T/S/M: Students will be explaining how a train and a steam engine works. (Will include physics as well as chemistry.) Mathematical formulas will be used to explain various chemical reactions and speed formulas. CT: Given the various transportation inventions of the Industrial Revolution, students will compose a one-paragraph Persuasive essay on a transportation invention of their choosing and justify why it was most beneficial, pointing out at least three advantages listed in class with 3/3 accuracy.
89	**Capitalism, Socialism, and Communism** Given the lecture differentiating capitalism, socialism, and communism, students will complete a 15-question worksheet that will force the students to match the schools of thought to their famous thinkers, summarize the school of thought's basic beliefs, and contrast the schools of thought from one another with 12/15 accuracy.	Era 7, Standard 2, 4, 5, 6 WHII.9 a, b, d TCA: 1.1, 1.2, 1.3, 1.6, 1.7, 1.8, 1.9, 1.10	YouTube clip: "Soviet Revolutionary Song, Capitalism Oppresses Us" (1:55) Textbook: *World History: The Human Journey*	CE: Students will truly understand how ideas have consequences (i.e., Marxism and the abuses of the Soviet Union). T/MUS/CT/COLL: Students will listen to a song (the YouTube clip) with subtitles of the USSR national choir condemning Capitalism and promoting Communism. (Freaky stuff being said, shows the influence of Marx.) This will get students thinking because at the surface, Communism/Socialism sounds beneficial but most do not realize its consequences and its impracticality. Students will participate in class discussion after. B: How at its core, socialism and communism violate Biblical principles of stewardship and private property. (Important because Christianity is still the dominant world religion at the time.) ASSESS: An informal assessment of the worksheet describing the objective will be given.

DAY #	CONTENT/OBJECTIVE	STANDARDS	RESOURCES/MATERIALS	LEARNING ACTIVITIES/ASSESSMENTS
90	**Revamped Colonization With Industrialization Movement (The Scramble for Africa)** Given a map of Africa in 1878 (in which only 10% of Africa was colonized) and the map of 1913 (in which 96% was colonized), students will list five reasons as to why this rapid change occurred with 5/5 accuracy.	Era 7, Standard 2, 4, 5, 6 WHII.9 a, c, d, e TCA: 1.1, 1.2, 1.3, 1.6, 1.7, 1.8, 1.9, 1.10	T: YouTube documentary on "William Wilberforce" (10:56) Video note sheet that highlights key points of the video (breaks it into sections) Textbook: *World History: The Human Journey*	CE/B: The conviction of William Wilberforce and John Newton to see the end of slavery in England. England was no longer involved in the international slave trade. Focus especially on the life of Newton and the story behind "Amazing Grace." MUS: Students will study the background to the lyrics of Newton's "Amazing Grace." This song is widely known, even outside Christian circles. CT/COLL: Students will speculate in class discussion as to why, despite the gradual global abolishment of slavery, forced colonization was justified in European countries. It had racial, political, and economic justifications in the agenda of European nations. L/DIV: Students will study the various language and cultural groups in Africa in the 19th century.
91	**Revamped Colonization With Industrialization Movement (Continued) (The Division of Africa)** Given the activity on the Berlin Conference and brief lecture, students will summarize the four main agreements of the conference with 4/4 accuracy.	Era 7, Standard 2, 4, 5, 6 WHII.9 a, d, e TCA: 1.1, 1.2, 1.3, 1.6, 1.7, 1.8, 1.9, 1.10	Group Country Prompts Handout Textbook: *World History: The Human Journey*	L/DIV: Students will study the various language and cultural groups in Africa in the 19th century. TH/COLL/ACT: Students will participate in a mock Berlin Conference that will require students to formulate into country groups (groups of two) to state their claim for colonization and justification based on the Group Country Prompt provided. At the end of the mock Berlin Conference, the instructor will discuss what occurred historically at the conference and the agreements among the countries at the conference.
92	**Quiz on Industrial Revolution Unit** Given the unit on Industrialization and its consequences, students will complete a 25-question quiz with 22/25 accuracy.	Era 7, Standard 2, 4, 5, 6 WHII.9 a, b, c, d, e TCA: 1.1, 1.2, 1.3, 1.6, 1.7, 1.8, 1.9, 1.10	Unit quiz YouTube clip: "The Scramble for Africa and the Berlin Conference in Plain English" (5:15) Textbook: *World History: The Human Journey*	T: Students will watch a brief YouTube clip that summarizes the growth of imperialism into Africa (Good review). COLL: Students will play Who Wants to Be a Millionaire as a review for their quiz. They will be split into two teams. ASSESS: Given the unit on Industrialization and its consequences, students will complete a 25-question quiz with 22/25 accuracy.

DAY #	CONTENT/OBJECTIVE	STANDARDS	RESOURCES/MATERIALS	LEARNING ACTIVITIES/ASSESSMENTS
93	**The Spark of World War I** —Given a lesson, students will explain why rivalries increased among European nations with 4/5 correct. —Given a lecture and assignment, students will identify the military alliances that existed at the beginning of World War I with 8/8 correct.	Era 8, Standard 1, 2 WHII.10 a TCA: 1.2, 1.3, 1.4	Textbook: *World History: The Human Journey* Paper	CT/DIV: Ask the students in a classroom discussion how nationalism and militarism influenced the coming of World War I. Themes from the previous classes on German unification will be drawn upon. Be sure to note the rivalry among some of the nations. CT: Using a piece of paper, have the students create a "chain of events" demonstrating how the entangling alliances forced the various countries to go to war with each other.
94	**A New Kind of War** —Given a WebQuest, students will identify the advantages that each side had in World War I with 10/10 correct. —Given a WebQuest, students will explain how the fighting was so drastically different in WWI with 9/10 correct.	Era 8, Standard 1, 2 WHII.10 a TCA: 1.2, 1.3, 1.4	Textbook: *World History: The Human Journey* WebQuest: http://zunal.com/webquest.php?w=231339	CT: Students will particpate in class discussion in coordination with the Webquest T: Using the Webquest students will view videos about trench warfare. This will help the students better understand the conditions. COLL/S: Students will be placed into groups to begin work on construction of their model based on trench warfare.
95	**World War I** Given a lecture and assignment, students will explain the conditions of the war with 3/3 correct.	Era 8, Standard 2 WHII.10 a TCA: 1.2, 1.3, 1.4, 1.8	Textbook: *World History: The Human Journey*	CE/DIV/L: Students will write letters as if they were soldiers on the front lines. Then they will exchange letters with each other and write fictional letters of family or friends back to the soldier on the front lines. Students must highlight some of the places they would be in the war, and some of the new weapons that were a part of this war. Some of the letters will be read aloud in class.
96	**World War I (Continued)** Given a lecture and activity, students will identify how the war progressed with 12/12 correct.	Era 8, Standard 2 WHII.10 a TCA: 1.2, 1.3, 1.4	Textbook: *World History: The Human Journey* Sunny day and chalk	ACT/P: Students will be taken outside. Using chalk, a rough map of Europe will be placed on the parking lot. Students will then be assigned countries and the way to war played out will be visualized by the various students, playing countries, conquer others.

DAY #	CONTENT/OBJECTIVE	STANDARDS	RESOURCES/MATERIALS	LEARNING ACTIVITIES/ASSESSMENTS
97	**World War I (Continued)** Given a WebQuest and quiz, students will explain the conditions of the war with 10/10 correct.	Era 8, Standard 2 WHII.10 a TCA: 1.2, 1.3, 1.4	Textbook: *World History: The Human Journey* WebQuest: http://zunal.com/webquest.php?w=231339	ASSESS: Students will be given a quiz on World War I covering the last several days. COLL: Students will be given time to work on their WebQuest group projects. This time should be spent primarily on the model of the trench. The teacher should provide directions or assistance to the groups as needed.
98	**World War I (Continued)** Given a lecture, students will identify the role of the United States and other countries in the war with 8/9 correct.	Era 8, Standard 2 WHII.10 a, b TCA: 1.2, 1.3, 1.4	Textbook: *World History: The Human Journey*	COLL/CT/DIV: Place the students into groups representing a country in the war. Have the groups research how the different powers wanted to end the war, and what they would want for peace. The students must write down a bullet point list what their selected country hoped to obtain if peace was reached.
99	**Treaty of Versailles** —Given a lecture, students will define President Wilson's 14 points with 1/1 correct. —Given a lecture, students will identify the disagreements that the peacemakers faced with 9/10 correct.	Era 8, Standard 2 WHII.10 b TCA: 1.2, 1.3, 1.4	Textbook: *World History: The Human Journey*	CT/CE/L: Students will write a paragraph as to why the other Allied Powers disagreed with Wilson's 14 points. Following their writing the class will engage in a discussion of the difficulties the peacemakers faced. Specifically, the difference between Wilson and the United States should be highlighted. The United States was the country that was going to be the easiest on the Germans, but the other powers would not have it.
100	**Treaty of Versailles** —Given a lecture and video, students will identify the terms of the Treaty of Versailles. —Given a video, students will explain how the League of Nations was structured with 10/10 correct.	Era 8, Standard 2 WHII.10 b TCA: 1.2, 1.3, 1.4	Textbook: *World History: The Human Journey* YouTube video: https://www.youtube.com/watch?v=L8uWgbRd8 Computer and projector	T: Students will take notes on the YouTube video. By naming at least 25 facts on the video they will receive 5 bonus points for their presentations on the WebQuest tomorrow. CT: Students will engage in a discussion as to the function of the League of Nations. Furthermore, the discussion will exhibit how ineffective the League was and how it was replaced eventually by the United Nations.

DAY #	CONTENT/OBJECTIVE	STANDARDS	RESOURCES/MATERIALS	LEARNING ACTIVITIES/ASSESSMENTS
101	**Presentation Day** Given their model, students will present their Webquest projects being grading using the provided rubric.	Era 8, Standard 1, 2 WHII.10 a TCA: 1.2, 1.3, 1.4	Projects of the students http://zunal.com/webquest.php?w=231339	COLL/CT/L/ACT/ASSESS/A: Students will present their Webquest trench warfare projects based upon the rubric.
102	**Presentation Day** Given their model, students will present their Webquest projects being grading using the provided rubric.	Era 8, Standard 1, 2 WHII.10 a TCA: 1.2, 1.3, 1.4	Projects of the students http://zunal.com/webquest.php?w=231339	COLL/CT/L/ACT/ASSESS/A: Students will present their Webquest trench warfare projects based upon the rubric.
103	**Russian Revolution** —Given Google Earth and a lecture, students will identify the events that led to the Russian Revolution with 5/5 correct. —Given an activity, students will identify key figures with 5/5 correct.	Era 8, Standard 1, 2 WHII.10 c TCA: 1.1, 1.2, 1.3, 1.4, 1.5, 1.6, 1.10	Textbook: *World History: The Human Journey* Computer with Internet access and Google Earth	COLL: Students will work in groups of four and will create a diagram that shows the vents leading to the Russian Revolution and the creation of the Communist Party. Beside this diagram the students should also include several of the major leaders and a short sentence describing their role. T: Using Google Earth, the teacher will show the students where the main fighting between the Mensheviks and Bolsheviks took place.
104	**Russian Revolution (Continued)** Given a lecture and the Communist Manifesto, students will explain the key ideas behind communism with 10/10 correct.	Era 8, Standard 1, 2 WHII.10 c TCA: 1.1, 1.2, 1.3, 1.4, 1.5, 1.6, 1.10	Textbook: *World History: The Human Journey* Online text of the Communist Manifesto	CT/CE/DIV: Students will read parts of the Communist Manifesto and will write out what they think Marx meant when he penned the words. This will lead to a classroom discussion of communism, how it took hold in Russia, and why it is a dangerous ideology. The discussion should also move beyond Russia and countries like Cuba and China should be discussed.

DAY #	CONTENT/OBJECTIVE	STANDARDS	RESOURCES/MATERIALS	LEARNING ACTIVITIES/ASSESSMENTS
105	**Russian Revolution (Continued)** Given a video, students will be able to identify the events that led to the Russian Revolution with 19/20 correct.	Era 8, Standard 1, 2 WHII.10 c TCA: 1.1, 1.2, 1.3, 1.4, 1.5, 1.6, 1.10	Textbook: *World History: The Human Journey* YouTube video: https://www.youtube.com/watch?v=LNknAJHNk2I	T/B: Students will take notes on the YouTube video shown in class. Following the video the class will participate in a discussion of the contents of the video. Specifically, the class will discuss the role of Rasputin. If anyone in history was ever demon-possessed it was this man. This will incorporate Biblical perspectives.
106	**Post-World War I** Given a lecture and collaboration, students will explain where Europe and the world stood following the Treaty of Versailles and the conflicts that still were brewing with 18/20 correct.	Era 8, Standard 1, 2 WHII.10 b TCA: 1.1, 1.2, 1.3, 1.4, 1.5, 1.6, 1.10	Textbook: *World History: The Human Journey* Computer and projector	T: Using maps on a projector, students will be shown how different the political map of Europe looked. Special attention will be paid to the new countries and the shrinking of Germany. CT/COLL: The class will be broken into groups of four and will engage in a discussion as to the problems that Germany was going to face following the war. Special attention should be made as to how this made the rise of Hitler possible.
107	**Test Review** Given a test review on the latest material, students will demonstrate their knowledge of the subject by playing a review game with 48/50 correct.	Era 8, Standard 1, 2 WHII.10 a, b, c TCA: 1.1, 1.2, 1.3, 1.4, 1.5, 1.6, 1.8, 1.10	Textbook: *World History: The Human Journey*	ACT/T: Students will be playing a game to help them review for the test. This game will be Family Feud-style where the class is broken into two teams and will send one representative up for each team to compete.
108	**Test Day** Given a test on the latest material, students will demonstrate their knowledge of the subject by taking a test with 90% accuracy.	Era 8, Standard 1, 2 WHII.10 a, b, c TCA: 1.1, 1.2, 1.3, 1.4, 1.5, 1.6, 1.8, 1.10	Written exam with an essay question, short answer, and multiple-choice	ASSESS: Students will be given a comprehensive exam on World War I, the Treaty of Versailles, and the Russian Revolution.

DAY #	CONTENT/OBJECTIVE	STANDARDS	RESOURCES/MATERIALS	LEARNING ACTIVITIES/ASSESSMENTS
109	**League of Nations: Ideals and Weaknesses** Given the lecture on the League of Nations and case studies, students will summarize the two basic powers of the League of Nations and state its three weaknesses discussed in class with 5/5 accuracy.	Era 8, Standard 1, 2, 3, 5 WHII. 11 a TCA: 1.1, 1.2, 1.3, 1.6, 1.9, 1.10	Handout of Wilson's Fourteen Point Justification Handouts for crises dealt with by the League of Nations Textbook: *World History: The Human Journey*	CT: Students will analyze Wilson's Fourteenth Point Justification that led to the creation of the League of Nations and speculate as to why the United States never joined. (Principles of Washington and Jefferson about staying out of European affairs.) DIV: Students will analyze the members of the League of Nations and make assertions how these groups may come into conflict in the future. The vast majority of different needs within the League of Nations was overbearing on the organization. COLL/ACT: Students will be given a handout covering different crises dealt with by the League of Nations following its creation (i.e., Aland islands dispute, Upper Silesia conflict, etc.). Students will be arranged into groups of four but will first read the handout individually and write down what they see as the biggest weaknesses of the League of Nations. They will then discuss this in their group of four and write down their ideas. As a group, with various assigned roles, students will come to the front of the class and summarize their documents and assert what they concluded was the League of Nation's biggest weaknesses. This will set the stage for the League's ultimate failure in the 1930s with Nazi Germany.
110	**Postwar Uncertainty (Post-WWI)** Given the lecture on postwar society, students will identify two emerging cultural movements and validate how it challenged traditional society with 2/2 accuracy.	Era 8, Standard 1, 2, 3, 5 WHII. 11 b TCA: 1.1, 1.2, 1.3, 1.6, 1.8, 1.9, 1.10	Students will watch a YouTube clip on the Rise of the Jazz Age: http://www.youtube.com/watch?v=QjxpYsTjNPk Image of "The Persistence of Memory" by Salvador Dali Textbook: *World History: The Human Journey*	S: Changes in science and society. Students will understand the greater consequences of Einstein's Theory of Relativity (Age of Relativity). H: Students will begin to identify challenges to traditional culture such as women (flappers) beginning to smoke and drink like men. B/CE: Students will comprehend the dangers of the Age of Relativity and how many of their outlooks on life are actually a reflection of their endorsement of this phenomenon that swept over the 20th century. Students will learn that there is absolutes and unchanging truths. A: Students will learn how the Age of Relativity affected art such as "The Persistence of Memory" by Salvador Dali. MUS/D/T: Students will listen to some jazz from the period in a YouTube clip and watch the styles of dance in the Jazz Age.

DAY #	CONTENT/OBJECTIVE	STANDARDS	RESOURCES/MATERIALS	LEARNING ACTIVITIES/ASSESSMENTS
111	**Worldwide Depression Causation** Given the lecture on causes of the worldwide Depression, students will create an illustrated web diagram that points out the causes of the depression using the four main reasons discussed in class with 4/4 accuracy.	Era 8, Standard 1, 2, 3, 5 WHII. 11 b TCA: 1.1, 1.2, 1.3, 1.6, 1.7, 1.9, 1.10	Poster paper for Web diagram Charts illustrating the inflation of currency in England, France, USA, and Germany Textbook: *World History: The Human Journey*	ACT: Students will be called to the front and will participate in an activity with Monopoly money and a candy bar that demonstrates inflation and what the banks did. Inflation charts will be discussed here. COLL/CT/A: Students will create an illustrated web diagram in groups of four that points out the causes of the Depression using the four main reasons discussed in class with 4/4 accuracy.
112	**Depression in the USA** Given the economic crises in the United States, students will compose a one-paragraph essay that analyzes how FDR's New Deal attempted to recover the economy in accordance with the prompt/rubric provided.	Era 8, Standard 1, 2, 3, 5 WHII. 11 b TCA: 1.1, 1.2, 1.3, 1.6, 1.7, 1.9, 1.10	Graphs of the Employment situation from 1929–1933 Images of the Depression YouTube clip: "The Great Depression" (5:44): http://www.youtube.com/watch?v=myEPfcpKCcs Textbook: *World History: The Human Journey*	T: YouTube clip on the Great Depression will be used as the set (5:44). CT: Given the economic crises in the United States, students will compose a one-paragraph essay that analyzes how FDR's New Deal attempted to recover the economy in accordance with the prompt/rubric provided. H: Students will understand what happened with FDR and his polio.
113	**Depression in Germany** Given the description of the economic depression in Germany under the Weimar Republic, students will compile a seven-item list of all the ways in which German citizens were frustrated with their world standing and their government with 7/7 accuracy.	Era 8, Standard 1, 2, 3, 5 WHII. 11 b TCA: 1.1, 1.2, 1.3, 1.6, 1.7, 1.9, 1.10	Images of Germans doing silly things with Reichsmarks Textbook: *World History: The Human Journey*	M/COLL/ACT: Students will work with conversions to understand the severity of inflation in Germany in the 1930s. For instance, the daily wages in 1920 and how much the pay was in 1932. They will come to the board and do the conversions with fake paper money. T: Images of Reichsmarks being made into kites, stacked on wheel barrows, block castles, etc. DIV: Students will compare a few other economic strategies such as France and Scandinavian countries (very briefly).

DAY #	CONTENT/OBJECTIVE	STANDARDS	RESOURCES/MATERIALS	LEARNING ACTIVITIES/ASSESSMENTS
114	**Rise of Nazism: Germany and Adolph Hitler** Given the lecture on the democratic rise to power of the NSDAP (Nazi Party), students will break down the six means in which Nazis successfully subsumed the Weimar Republic legally with 6/6 accuracy.	Era 8, Standard 1, 2, 3, 5 WHII. 11 b, c TCA: 1.1, 1.2, 1.3, 1.6, 1.7, 1.9, 1.10	Handout of Party Platforms for the NSDAP and the Conservatives Textbook: *World History: The Human Journey*	CT/COLL: After the lecture in which the suffering of the German people is highlighted students will read two party platforms in groups of four. Briefly discuss what they are proposing among each other and then hold a secret ballot to see who wins. Unknowingly to the students, they will be analyzing the Nazi Party's platform and the Conservatives platform in Germany (1933). Even more concerning is that in all likelihood the students will elect the Nazi candidate (the genocidal principles will be excluded from the platform). This will display to students how close the platforms of the Conservatives and Nazis were and the appeal the Nazi party had to a crippled Germany. H/S: Talk about Hitler's views and Social Darwinism. The idea of purifying and eliminating the "unhealthy" /"inferior" elements of society (Jews, "feeble-minded," gypsies, babies with deformity). CE: Students will understand the importance of being educated voters.
115	**Ride of Fascism: Italy and Mussolini** Given the lecture on the rise of Fascism under Mussolini in Italy, students will compare and contrast in a Venn diagram Fascism to Nazism with three similarities and three differences with 6/6 accuracy.	Era 8, Standard 1, 2, 3, 5 WHII. 11 c TCA: 1.1, 1.2, 1.3, 1.6, 1.9, 1.10	Blank Venn diagram Textbook: *World History: The Human Journey*	COLL: Students will fill in a blank diagram comparing and contrasting Italian Fascism to German Nazism throughout the lecture. CE: Students will learn the dangers of pridefullness and how it subsumed Mussolini and ultimately led to his humiliating end.
116	**The Red Revolution: Communism in Russia From Lenin to Stalin** Given the lesson on Stalin's rise to power and purge of the Communist party ("Great Purge"), students will compose a three-point thesis statement on how Stalin eliminated political opposition in the USSR with 3/3 accuracy.	Era 8, Standard 1, 2, 3, 5 WHII. 11 c TCA: 1.1, 1.2, 1.3, 1.6, 1.9, 1.10	"Mini Bio: Joseph Stalin" YouTube clip (4:05): http://www.youtube.com/watch?v=e_2of8pmHYU Textbook: *World History: The Human Journey*	T: "Mini Bio: Joseph Stalin" YouTube clip as set. CT/CE: Students will analyze and take notes on the YouTube clip. They will make assertions on how Stalin's harsh childhood affected his leadership as dictator. DIV: Students will differentiate the symbolism Stalin created of Lenin's legacy and the one that Trotsky envisioned. CT: Given the lesson on Stalin's rise to power and purge of the Communist party "Great Purge" (26), students will compose a three-point thesis statement on how Stalin eliminated political opposition in the USSR with 3/3 accuracy.

DAY #	CONTENT/OBJECTIVE	STANDARDS	RESOURCES/MATERIALS	LEARNING ACTIVITIES/ASSESSMENTS
117	**Japan's Leadership: Hirohito and Hideki Tojo (Red Sun Rising)** Given the passage in the textbook students are assigned, students will create a brief lesson that properly summarizes the passage, points out the key aspects, and properly justifies the importance of those aspects.	Era 8, Standard 1, 2, 3, 5 WHII. 11 c TCA: 1.1, 1.2, 1.3, 1.6, 1.9, 1.10	Textbook: *World History: The Human Journey*	COLL/CT/DIV/ACT: Students will be formed into groups of two and assigned a topic from their chapter on Japan. Topics include Basic History of Japan, Hideki Tojo Bio, Hirohito Bio, Japan's War with China, Japan's War with Russia, Japan's Economic Boom, and Japanese Militarism. Students will have 15 minutes to prepare their lesson and then they will reteach their unit to the class (5 minutes each). Students are required to take notes during each others' lessons. In addition to the lesson, students will post on Blackboard five essential questions for quiz preparation purposes (Homework Assignment).
118	**Quiz on Interwar Periods** Given the unit on the interwar periods between WWI and WWII, students will take a 25-question quiz from old SOL test questions with 22/25 accuracy.	Era 8, Standard 1, 2, 3, 5 WHII. 11 a, b, c TCA: 1.1, 1.2, 1.3, 1.6, 1.7, 1.9, 1.10	Unit Quiz YouTube clip, "The Interwar Year: One War Leads to Another" (26:04): https://www.youtube.com/watch?v=ewdea_aWYa8 Textbook: *World History: The Human Journey*	ASSESS: Given the unit on the interwar periods between WWI and WWII, students will take a 25-question quiz from old SOL test questions with 22/25 accuracy. T: YouTube clip, "The Interwar Year: One War Leads to Another" (26:04). Students will watch this film for recapitulation purposes until the class period ends (after the quiz).
119	**Test Review** Given a test review on the latest material, students will demonstrate their knowledge of the subject by playing a review game with 48/50 correct.	Era 8, Standard 1, 2, 3, 5 WHII. 11 a, b, c TCA: 1.1, 1.2, 1.3, 1.6, 1.7, 1.9, 1.10	Textbook: *World History: The Human Journey*	ACT/T: Students will be playing a game to help them review for the test. This game will be Family Feud-style where the class is broken into two teams and will send one representative up for each team to compete.

DAY #	CONTENT/OBJECTIVE	STANDARDS	RESOURCES/MATERIALS	LEARNING ACTIVITIES/ASSESSMENTS
120	**Test Day** Given a test on the latest material, students will demonstrate their knowledge of the subject by taking a test with 90% accuracy.	Era 8, Standard 1, 2, 3, 5 WHII. 11 a, b, c TCA: 1.1, 1.2, 1.3, 1.6, 1.7, 1.9, 1.10	Written exam with an essay question, short answer, and multiple-choice	ASSESS: Students will be given a comprehensive exam on the worldwide depression of the '30s and the major leaders in Japan, Germany, Italy, and the Soviet Union.
121	**Remilitarization and the Rise of Totalitarian Regimes (Colonization)** Given access to the Internet and computers, students will create a poster that identifies their assigned countries' social movements, government, military, and economic systems prior to World War II in this four-person, in-class, group project with 4/4 accuracy.	Era 8, Standard 4, 5 WHII. 11c WHII. 12 a TCA: 1.1, 1.2, 1.3, 1.5, 1.6, 1.7, 1.8, 1.9, 1.10	Mobile Computer Lab Day with printer Markers, posters Textbook: *World History: The Human Journey*	ASSESS: Students will take a brief 10-question multiple-choice Pre-Assessment quiz (not graded) on World War II to assist the instructor in developing content in the World War II unit. COLL/A/ACT/DIV: Students will work in groups of four and be assigned their own country. They will than look up information on their country prior to World War II (the 1930s is the target area) using the computers. The main topics being located are Social Movements, Government, Military, and Economy (four topics are purposeful; each student within the group will work on that one topic). Students must cite their sources on a separate piece of paper. For example, if a student says, "America had 456,000 troops prior to the outbreak of WWII," the student must be able to prove that the source he/she got that from is credible. They will then take whatever information they have gathered and create an aesthetically pleasing poster with relative content. This will be a completion grade; however, the poster's content and appearance is a reflection of their effort. When all the posters are done, they will be hung around the classroom. Unfortunately, there will not be time to present in class. Whatever is not finished in class will be completed for homework. M: Students will have to measure out the appropriate spaces in order to fit everything on the board.

DAY #	CONTENT/OBJECTIVE	STANDARDS	RESOURCES/MATERIALS	LEARNING ACTIVITIES/ASSESSMENTS
122	**Japan on the Eve of World War II** Given the U.S. Navy's video on the psychology of the Japanese people (created during WWII), students will identify three points of propaganda that are not necessarily true about the Japanese people and why the U.S. government targeted these ideas with 3/3 accuracy.	Era 8, Standard 4, 5 WHII. 12 a TCA: 1.1, 1.2, 1.3, 1.5, 1.6, 1.8, 1.9, 1.10	Video created by the U.S. Navy during WWII that discusses the culture and psychology of the Japanese: https://www.youtube.com/watch?v=F1Nxz7a7T5o Textbook: *World History: The Human Journey*	T/CT/DIV/COLL: Given the U.S. Navy's video on the psychology of the Japanese people (created during WWII), students will identify three points of propaganda that are not necessarily true about the Japanese people and why the U.S. government targeted these ideas with 3/3 accuracy. Since it is a very lengthy movie, it will be stopped about every 7 minutes and recapitulated and discussed amongst the class. MUS: Students will identify in the video how the music enhances the sinister persona trying to be created around the Japanese by the U.S. Navy. L: Students will learn about the rich heritage and symbolism of the Japanese language.
123	**Hitler's Appeasement Ordeal/Defies Versailles Treaty** Given a worksheet with a large map following the lesson on Hitler's Appeasement Ordeal, students will put numbers (beginning with #1) in the correct order in which Hitler annexed these territories with a brief two-sentence explanation of why Hitler was permitted to do so by the Western powers with 4/4 accuracy.	Era 8, Standard 4, 5 WHII. 12 a TCA: 1.1, 1.2, 1.3, 1.5, 1.6, 1.8, 1.9, 1.10	Map worksheet Google Earth Textbook: *World History: The Human Journey*	COLL/ACT: To begin class, students will take out a piece of paper and a writing utensil. Given 2 minutes, students will work individually to recall and write down all the provisions of the Versailles Treaty that concluded World War I. Following this, students will participate in a class discussion and come to the board to write down their ideas one by one. Once all the major provisions have been listed, the instructor will guide a class discussion that works down each point of the Versailles Treaty and analyzes in regard to countries "who wins and loses." Students will pick up pretty quickly how Germany got the raw end of the deal. T/CT/DIV: The instructor will guide a lesson on appeasement that implements Google Earth. Students will recognize key geographic/cultural features (i.e., ethnicities, resources proximity to Germany) of countries Hitler annexed in order to explain Hitler's desire for those countries as well as his justification to the Western World. ASSESS: Given a worksheet with a large map following the lesson on Hitler's Appeasement Ordeal, students will put numbers (beginning with #1) in the correct order in which Hitler annexed these territories with a brief two-sentence explanation of why Hitler was permitted to do so by the Western powers with 4/4 accuracy. This is not a graded assignment but will be measured in order to reflect student's grasp of the content.

DAY #	CONTENT/OBJECTIVE	STANDARDS	RESOURCES/MATERIALS	LEARNING ACTIVITIES/ASSESSMENTS
124	**Germany Finally Tips the Scale to War** Given the lecture on the final cause of World War II, students will identify the three provisions of the Nazi-Soviet Nonaggression Pact and how it set the stage for World War II in a concise paragraph with 3/3 accuracy.	Era 8, Standard 4, 5 WHII. 12 a TCA: 1.1, 1.2, 1.3, 1.6, 1.7, 1.8, 1.9, 1.10	Judge's Scale Vector Student Journals Textbook: *World History: The Human Journey*	COLL/M/S: To review the appeasement ordeal from last class, the instructor will bring in a scale vector. Students will recognize it because it symbolizes justice in society. If one side gets too much weight, the scale is tipped. Using medal blocks, the teacher will balance the scale. Each time the class identifies one of the appeasement violations discussed last class, the teacher will add a very small amount of weight to the left arm of the scale. Using the precise amount of weight, the scale will not fully tip but will lean to the left side (discussion of weight, gravity, and the math behind it will be mentioned). At this point the teacher will teach the new unit on the Nazi-Soviet Nonaggression Pact and the invasion of Poland. Once the instructor has discussed the invasion of Poland and how the Western powers responded, a weight will be added once more to the left side completely tipping the scale. DIV: Given the lecture on the final cause of World War II, students will identify the three provisions of the Nazi-Soviet Nonaggression Pact and how it set the stage for World War II in a concise paragraph with 3/3 accuracy. This is a particularly interesting pact in history because the Communists and Nazis hated each other (their ideology opposes each other, Hitler killed the Communists in Germany). Despite their diverse ideologies, they were set aside to embrace a *realpolitik* strategy (Practical over Idealism).
125	**Fall of France and the Battle of Britain** Given the lecture differentiating the quick fall of France and the persistence of the British, students will identify and list five reasons discussed in class that Britain was able to withhold the Germans from invading while France easily succumbed with 5/5 accuracy.	Era 8, Standard 4, 5 WHII. 12 a TCA: 1.1, 1.2, 1.3, 1.5, 1.6, 1.8, 1.9, 1.10	Classroom will be decorated like London during the Battle of Britain (large-scale cardboard cutout, lamps, air raid alarms). Lights will be turned off with six lamps lighting the ceiling. Churchill's "We Shall Never Surrender" Speech: https://www. youtube.com/watch?v=MkTw3_PmKtc Invasion of France through Belgium YouTube clip: https://www.youtube.com/watch?v=Lc56dSho5hs (10:00)	CT/CE/B: Students will journal to answer the following prompt: "Under what circumstances is war justifiable?" Since this is a public school, the name of the bible will not be mentioned but principles from the bible about Just war/Defensive war will. COLL/T/ACT: Students will perform an air raid drill practiced in British schools while Winston Churchill reads his "We will never surrender" speech about the determination of the British People. CE: The courage displayed by Winston Churchill kept Great Britain in the fight. T: Students will watch the YouTube clip which explains the *blitzkrieg* tactics of Germany as they struck through neutral Belgium toward France bypassing the Maginot line. This will be used to sum up the Fall of France and introduce the lecture on France's Vichy government. ASSESS: Given the lecture differentiating the quick fall of France and the persistence of the British, students will identify and list five reasons discussed in class that Britain was able to withhold the Germans from invading while France easily succumbed with 5/5 accuracy. Not graded but will be used to measure students' comprehension of the lesson.

DAY #	CONTENT/OBJECTIVE	STANDARDS	RESOURCES/MATERIALS	LEARNING ACTIVITIES/ASSESSMENTS
126	**Hitler Turns East and the War in Africa (***Lebensraum* **in Russia)** Given a blank map of the world, students will use their textbooks and notes to label Axis-controlled countries and Allied-controlled countries in 1942 (neutral countries will already be labeled) with 26/30 accuracy.	Era 8, Standard 4, 5 WHII. 12 a, b TCA: 1.1, 1.3, 1.5, 1.6, 1.7, 1.8, 1.9, 1.10	Blank map of the world Images of Slavic POWs seized in Operation Barbarossa Excerpt from Hitler's *Mein Kampf* Textbook: *World History: The Human Journey*	CT/COLL: Students will be given an excerpt from Hitler's *Mein Kampf* in which Hitler describes his desire for Russian *Lebensraum* ("land for survival of the strongest race" or "Land for the German *Volk*"). Students will analyze the passage individually and then it will be discussed amongst the class. T/H: Images of the treatment of the Slavic Prisoners of War (censored images because some are so horrific). The Holocaust truly began in the East. Discuss how the Jews were not Hitler's only target (Blacks, Gypsies, Slavs, etc.). Students will see the effect German treatment on Slavic POWs had on their bodies. S: Students will learn about some of the sadistic experiments conducted on captured "sub-humans" (by Nazi standards) in the East. Students will understand the dangers of Social Darwinism. Given a blank map of the world, students will use their textbooks and notes to label Axis controlled countries and Allied controlled countries in 1942 (Neutral countries will already be labeled) with 26/30 accuracy. This activity will demonstrate the shift in global power toward Axis countries in 1942. Students may ask the instructor questions during this time.
127	**U.S.A.'s Role in World War II** Given the lecture discussing the significant involvement of the United States in World War II prior to even military involvement, students will compose a one-paragraph argument theorizing (three-point argument) whether the United States would have joined the war even if Pearl Harbor had never occurred with justifications for all three points, in accordance with the rubric displayed on the PowerPoint.	Era 8, Standard 4, 5 WHII. 12 a, b TCA: 1.1, 1.3, 1.5, 1.6, 1.7, 1.8, 1.9, 1.10	Google Earth George Washington's Farewell Address Textbook: *World History: The Human Journey*	COLL: The class will read the Farewell Address of George Washington and his desire to stay out of European affairs. In the following discussion students will understand how sentiments such as this defined America's neutrality process at the beginning of World War II. COLL/CT: At the beginning of class, the instructor will guide a discussion/argument for whether the United States should enter World War II or not. As ideas are generated they will be put into a "Pros" or "Cons" T-chart on the board. Once they have generated a sufficient argument for both camps, the instructor will continue the lesson. As the lecture continues several more Pros and Cons ideas will come up as new information is revealed. At this point, students will raise their hand and notify the instructor and it will be added to the list. For example, the instructor teaches about the Lend Lease Act. A student may suggest that the profit generated from the Lend Lease Act should be a reason to stay out of the war. Throughout the lecture the T-chart on the board will be updated. T: Students will use Google Earth to identify where the Japanese aircraft carriers were during the attack on Pearl Harbor. They will also recognize why the Japanese chose to attack Pearl Harbor instead of some other naval base. ASSESS: Given the lecture discussing the significant involvement of the United States in World War II prior to even military involvement, students will compose a one-paragraph argument theorizing (three-point argument) whether the United States would have joined the war even if Pearl Harbor had never occurred with justifications for all three points, in accordance with the rubric displayed on the PowerPoint.

DAY #	CONTENT/OBJECTIVE	STANDARDS	RESOURCES/MATERIALS	LEARNING ACTIVITIES/ASSESSMENTS
128	**War Time Economies and the Home Front (Propaganda)** Given the lesson on propaganda and war sentiments in World War II, students will design a propaganda poster that encourages some sort of war effort (whether that be food rationing, women in the workforce, political cartoons of Hitler, etc.) with the audience and purpose explained in a four-sentence description/justification on the back of the poster with 4/4 accuracy.	Era 8, Standard 4, 5 WHII. 12 a TCA: 1.1, 1.2, 1.3, 1.5, 1.6, 1.7, 1.8, 1.9, 1.10	Example Images of Propaganda Colored pencils, markers, printer paper Disney's "Donald Duck Commando: Fighting the Japanese": https://www.youtube.com/watch?v=IWAf3dQxAfQ (6:53) Textbook: *World History: The Human Journey*	T/CT/COLL/DIV: Students will watch the short film created by Disney, "Donald Duck Commando," as a propaganda scheme targeted against the Japanese. The class will discuss and debate what is trying to be said in the film. Answering questions about purpose, audience (cartoons are for young people . . . ?), etc. The video is not a fair reflection of Japan's culture (Diversity). CE: Students will learn about internment camps in the United States that wrongly confined innocent Japanese Americans. Students will see the danger in applying one label to one race (Racial Stereotyping). A/CT: Given the lesson on propaganda and war sentiments in World War II, students will design a propaganda poster that encourages some sort of war effort (whether that be food rationing, women in the workforce, political cartoons of Hitler, etc.) with the audience and purpose explained in a four-sentence description/justification on the back of the poster with 4/4 accuracy. This is a completion grade. Instructions and examples will be left on the PowerPoint screen during the activity.
129	**Battle for the Pacific** Given a map of islands in the Pacific, students will draw arrows illustrating MacArthur's "Island Hopping Strategy" and will correctly label the seven locations discussed in the lecture with 7/7 accuracy.	Era 8, Standard 4, 5 WHII. 12 a TCA: 1.1, 1.2, 1.3, 1.5, 1.6, 1.7, 1.8, 1.9, 1.10	Seven-row blank T-chart Guest Speaker: Edward Towe Textbook: *World History: The Human Journey*	COLL: Throughout the lecture, students will fill out the seven-row T-chart. On the left side of the T-chart is the "Battles" category and the right side is the "Effects" category. Students will organize the Battles and their effect on the campaign in the Pacific. For example, the Battle of Midway turned the tide in the war in the Pacific. ASSESS: Given a map of islands in the Pacific, students will draw arrows illustrating MacArthur's "Island Hopping Strategy" and will correctly label the seven locations discussed in the lecture with 7/7 accuracy. CT/CE: Edward Towe, a veteran of the Battle for Guadalcanal will speak to the class about his experiences and how it has shaped who he is today. Students will work in groups of four before he arrives to generate one thoughtful question to ask him about his experience. This guest speaker will be the last 15 minutes of class.

DAY #	CONTENT/OBJECTIVE	STANDARDS	RESOURCES/MATERIALS	LEARNING ACTIVITIES/ASSESSMENTS
130	**The Holocaust: Anti-Semitism in Germany and Europe as a Whole** Given a 3-circle Venn Diagram, students will compare and contrast the three different kinds of anti-Semitism in Germany with at least two items in each section, with 6/6 accuracy.	Era 8, Standard 4, 5 WHII. 12 a, b TCA: 1.1, 1.2, 1.3, 1.5, 1.6, 1.7, 1.8, 1.9, 1.10	3-Circle Venn Diagram Worksheet Textbook: *World History: The Human Journey*	B/DIV/L: Students will learn about the three forms of anti-Semitism in Germany (Biblical anti-Semite, National/Cultural Anti-Semite, and Economic anti-Semite). Biblical anti-Semites believe the Jews killed Jesus. Nation/Cultural anti-Semites oppose the influence of Jewish culture and language. Economic anti-Semites believe the Jews do not do hard labor because many Jews in Germany were in the arts, lawyers, or bankers (not agriculture like Germans). They will learn how pogroms wished to keep the Jews suppressed in Germany. Given a 3-circle Venn Diagram, students will compare and contrast the three different kinds of anti-Semitism in Germany with at least two items in each section, with 6/6 accuracy. S: Students will understand the role that evolution and Social Darwinism had in Germany; made the Holocaust palatable to German society.
131	**Field Trip to the Holocaust Museum in Washington, D.C.** Given the lives of their assigned Holocaust victim at the Holocaust museum, students will compose a one- page diary that gives a background of their lives, explains their experience in the concentration camps, and how they ultimately died. Students will follow the rubric provided.	Era 8, Standard 4, 5 WHII. 12 a, b TCA: 1.1, 1.2, 1.3, 1.5, 1.6, 1.7, 1.8, 1.9, 1.10	Rubric for "Diary of a Victim" Assignment Textbook: *World History: The Human Journey*	ACT/CT: Students will go on a field trip to the Holocaust museum in Washington, D.C. As part of the tour they assign the student to a historical Holocaust victim in order to understand that these were real people. Students will take detailed notes to assist them with the homework assignment that follows the field trip. Given the lives of their assigned Holocaust victim at the Holocaust museum, students will compose a one-page diary that gives a background of their lives, explains their experience in the concentration camps, and how they ultimately died. Students will follow the rubric provided. H: Students will learn about the health conditions of the Holocaust victims. S: Students will learn about the experiments conducted on the Jews and other groups.

DAY #	CONTENT/OBJECTIVE	STANDARDS	RESOURCES/MATERIALS	LEARNING ACTIVITIES/ASSESSMENTS
132	**Aftermath of the "Final Solution" and Presentation of "Diary of a Victim"** Given the lives of their assigned Holocaust victim at the Holocaust museum, students will compose a one-page diary that gives a background of their lives, explains their experience in the concentration camps, and how they ultimately died. Students will follow the rubric provided.	Era 8, Standard 4, 5 WHII. 12 a, b TCA: 1.1, 1.2, 1.3, 1.5, 1.6, 1.7, 1.8, 1.9, 1.10	Rubric for "Diary of a Victim" Assignment Textbook: *World History: The Human Journey*	ASSESS: Students will read aloud their one-page diary entry to the class. During this time the teacher will be assessing them according to provided rubric. This will allow the student to hear several accounts about the suffering of the Holocaust victims. CE: Students will learn about the hardships endured and the courage that so many showed in the face of evil. Students will be encouraged to join organizations that work to stop mass genocide such as the current genocides in Southern Sudan and Rwanda.
133	**Allied Victory in Europe** Given the lecture on the Allied Victory in Europe, students will be given a 10-question short answer worksheet that requires that they summarize events and compose brief two- to three-sentence answers that adequately respond to each prompt with 8/10 accuracy.	Era 8, Standard 4, 5 WHII. 12 a, c TCA: 1.1, 1.2, 1.3, 1.5, 1.6, 1.7, 1.8, 1.9, 1.10	"Last Survivor of the Bedford Boys": https://www.youtube.com/watch?v=3U506RX495l (1:30) Textbook: *World History: The Human Journey*	T: Students will watch this brief clip about the last survivor of the Bedford Boys. Nineteen Bedford, Virginians were killed within the first 10 minutes of the Battle of Omaha Beach. It is the most deaths from any locality in World War II. COLL: Students will complete a graphic organizer in class during the lecture at certain stopping points. It lists the battles from D-Day to V-Day and their significance/outcome. CT/ASSESS: Given the lecture on the Allied Victory in Europe, students will be given a 10-question short answer worksheet that requires that they summarize events and compose brief two- to three-sentence answers that adequately respond to each prompt with 8/10 accuracy. This is a completion grade to gauge their comprehension of the content.

DAY #	CONTENT/OBJECTIVE	STANDARDS	RESOURCES/MATERIALS	LEARNING ACTIVITIES/ASSESSMENTS
134	**Japanese Surrender: Impact of Atomic Bomb** Given President Truman's decision to use the atomic bomb on Japan as a means of forcing surrender, students will compose an outline that either justifies the decision or criticizes it with three supporting points with 3/3 accuracy.	Era 8, Standard 4, 5 WHII. 12 a, c TCA: 1.1, 1.2, 1.3, 1.6, 1.8, 1.9, 1.10	Textbook: *World History: The Human Journey*	S: Students will learn about the science that causes the atomic bomb to do the damage it does (splitting the atom). This will be demonstrated with formulas. H: Students will understand how the radiation released from the atomic bomb affected the Japanese people's health in the days and years that followed. CT: Students will read the following quote by Robert Oppenheimer, the man who led the team that created the atomic bomb. They will then compose a brief paragraph free-thought response about what the quote means. "In some sort of crude sense, which no vulgarity, no humor, no overstatement can quite extinguish, the physicists have known sin; and this is a knowledge which they cannot lose." CT/COLL: Given President Truman's decision to use the atomic bomb on Japan as a means of forcing surrender, students will compose an outline that either justifies the decision or criticizes it with three supporting points with 3/3 accuracy. Ideas will be shared and debated during the class period. The instructor will note the best points on the board and students will vote on whether they agree with the decision or not at the end of the class.
135	**Nuremberg Trials** Given the unit on World War II and its conclusion, students will take a brief 25-question quiz composed of old SOL test questions with 22/25 accuracy.	Era 8, Standard 4, 5 WHII. 12 a, c TCA: 1.1, 1.2, 1.3, 1.4, 1.6, 1.7, 1.8, 1.9, 1.10	Textbook: *World History: The Human Journey*	ASSESS: Given the unit on World War II and its conclusion, students will take a brief 25-question quiz composed of old SOL test questions with 22/25 accuracy. CT/ACT/TH: Students will participate in a mock Nuremberg Trial in which they will serve as the military tribunal. The instructor will read the defendant's defense speeches and students will debate and ask questions to the defendant that will help them in reaching a verdict. CE: Students will learn about the importance of justice. The Nuremberg trials showed a world committed to opposing war crimes and crimes against humanity. Students will learn never to tolerate acts that steal the nature of what it means to be human like the Nazis and even the Soviets did in World War II.

DAY #	CONTENT/OBJECTIVE	STANDARDS	RESOURCES/MATERIALS	LEARNING ACTIVITIES/ASSESSMENTS
136	**Postwar: Picking up the Pieces** Given the lecture on General Douglas MacArthur's mission to establish a new government in Japan following occupation, students will compare the new Japanese democracy to Great Britain's government system, pointing out in a bulleted list at least six provisions in common with 6/6 accuracy.	Era 8, Standard 4, 5 Era 9, Standard 1 WHII. 12 a, c TCA: 1.1, 1.2, 1.3, 1.5, 1.6, 1.7, 1.8, 1.9, 1.10	Graphic Organizer, "Cost of War: Allies and Axis" Textbook: *World History: The Human Journey*	COLL/CT: Students will study the graphic organizer, "Cost of War: Allies and Axis," which shows financial war cost, military losses, and civilian casualties. Students will then participate in a debate to argue which country suffered the worst in World War II, arguing from a statistical analysis. DIV: Students will learn about how individual countries and cultures healed from World War II. CT: Given the lecture on General Douglas MacArthur's mission to establish a new government in Japan following occupation, students will compare the new Japanese democracy to Great Britain's government system, pointing out in a bulleted list at least six provisions in common with 6/6 accuracy.
137	**Partitioning of Germany: Beginning of the Cold War. Creation of the U.N.** Given the lesson on East and West Germany, students will summarize the general treatment of both East and West Germany in one paragraph each and then provide a two-sentence explanation at the end of each paragraph that connects how Communist and Democratic ideology affected this treatment with 4/4 accuracy.	Era 9, Standard 1, 2, 3 WHII. 12 c TCA: 1.1, 1.2, 1.3, 1.5, 1.6, 1.7, 1.8, 1.9, 1.10	Map illustrating the partitioning of the German *Landers* ("states") Textbook: *World History: The Human Journey*	COLL/ACT: The room will be divided by a wall (wall made by a cable line and sheet across it) with some students contained within "West Germany" and the others within "East Germany." Students in West Germany will be given food and drinks while those in East Germany will be given rationed food (a cracker each). Students in West Germany are also permitted to roam freely so long as they do not enter East Germany. East Germany students will be confined to their desks and will have their food rations taken away if they move. This will be used to illustrate the difference between the U.S. and U.S.S.R.'s treatment of their occupied zones. Students in West Germany will take Hershey Kisses and construct small parachutes and then gently toss them over the wall to East Germany when the instructor comes up to the section on the Berlin Airlift. Students will learn how the newly formed United Nations aided in the effort. CT: Given the lesson on East and West Germany, students will summarize the general treatment of both East and West Germany in one paragraph each and then provide a two-sentence explanation at the end of each paragraph that connects how Communist and Democratic ideology affected this treatment with 4/4 accuracy.

DAY #	CONTENT/OBJECTIVE	STANDARDS	RESOURCES/MATERIALS	LEARNING ACTIVITIES/ASSESSMENTS
138	**The "Iron Curtain" and U.S. Policy** Given two maps of the world (one from 1933 and the other from 1962) students will identify Democratic countries and Communist countries on both maps by shading them in and then compare and contrast the maps in a three-sentence response with 3/3 accuracy.	Era 9, Standard 1, 2, 3 WHII. 12 b, c TCA: 1.1, 1.2, 1.3, 1.5, 1.6, 1.7, 1.8, 1.9, 1.10	Two blank maps of the globe (1933 and 1982) Textbook: *World History: The Human Journey*	CT/COLL: Students will analyze a graph illustrating how the funds from the Marshall Plan were dispersed across nations. They will quickly notice that the countries most aided are France and Great Britain by a substantial number. What is curious is that Yugoslavia broke away from the U.S.S.R. in order to take a piece of the Marshall Plan but did not even receive a tenth of what Great Britain did. The class discussion will be aimed at answering questions such as these as well as analyzing its general impact. A: Given two maps of the world (one from 1933 and the other from 1982), students will identify Democratic countries and Communist countries on both maps by shading them in and then compare and contrast the maps in a three-sentence response with 3/3 accuracy.
139	**The Space Race (U.S. vs. U.S.S.R.)** Given the lecture on the Space Race, student will list the 11 major events of the Space Race and organize them chronologically into a timeline with 11/11 accuracy.	Era 9, Standard 1, 2, 3 WHII. 12 b, c TCA: 1.1, 1.2, 1.3, 1.5, 1.6, 1.7, 1.8, 1.9, 1.10	Blank timeline Rocket kits (will cost the students $2 each) Textbook: *World History: The Human Journey*	COLL/CT: Given the lecture on the Space Race, student will list the 11 major events of the Space Race and organize them chronologically into a timeline with 11/11 accuracy. ACT/S/M/COLL: Students will begin to build a rocket kit within groups of four (most cost-effective and time-effective setup). This rocket will be launched on day #140. The rocket comes with a parachute kit and all the essentials. It is a creative way to teach the struggles that scientists had with launching objects into space. There will be considerable amounts of math and measurements used and physics will be discussed. All in all the kit is very easy to use and can be put together in about 15 minutes. Painting it will be assigned as homework. The instructor will stay after school in the art room so that students have access to necessary tools and help.
140	**The Space Race (Activity Day)** Given their model rockets, students will be evaluating how they performed and will verbally summarize the challenges with 5/5 correct.	Era 9, Standard 1, 2, 3 WHII. 12 c TCA: 1.1, 1.2, 1.3, 1.5, 1.6, 1.7, 1.8, 1.9, 1.10	Rocket kits (will cost the students $2 each) Textbook: *World History: The Human Journey*	S/COLL/ACT: Students will launch their rockets on this day. After all of them have been launched, students will come back into the classroom and discuss the hardest parts of putting together their rocket and evaluate how their rockets performed. Students will see the physics at work and will better understand what the scientists struggled with during the space race.

DAY #	CONTENT/OBJECTIVE	STANDARDS	RESOURCES/MATERIALS	LEARNING ACTIVITIES/ASSESSMENTS
141	**Nationalists vs. Communists in China** Given access to the Web, students will research information on Jiang Jieshi and Mao Zedong and create a fake Facebook page for each individual covering their basic biography, the areas they ruled, what foreign country supported them, their domestic policy, their public support, military support, and their legacy in accordance with the rubric provided.	Era 9, Standard 1, 2, 3 WHII. 12 c TCA: 1.1, 1.2, 1.3, 1.5, 1.6, 1.7, 1.8, 1.9, 1.10	Mobile Computer Lab Day Rubric for Textbook: *World History: The Human Journey*	ASSESS: Given access to the Web, students will research information on Jiang Jieshi and Mao Zedong and create a fake Facebook page for each individual covering their basic biography, the areas they ruled, what foreign country supported them, their domestic policy, their public support, military support, and their legacy in accordance with the rubric provided. Rubric will be left on the PowerPoint screen during the class period. This assignment will take some time but can easily be finished by the end of the class period. It will be collected and graded according to the rubric. DIV: Student research will show the vast differences in culture in China, especially between North and South. T: Mobile lab will be used in this assignment. CE: Students will learn the importance of not idolizing man. The Chinese to this day are wrapped up in a Mao Cult where many overlook the fact that his rule is the top incidence of democide (term coined by R. J. Rummel) in human history yet people worship him like a god.
142	**Communism Takes Power in China** Given the unit on communist ideals in China under Mao Zedong, students will complete a T-chart that contrasts communism in China today from what Mao had envisioned in the mid-20th century with at least the five differences with 5/5 accuracy.	Era 9, Standard 1, 2, 3 WHII. 12 c TCA: 1.1, 1.2, 1.3, 1.5, 1.6, 1.7, 1.8, 1.9, 1.10	YouTube video, "Communists Take Over China" (3:00): https://www.youtube.com/watch?v=ZQ-PbppXLic Images of Chinese artwork influenced by the communists (in PowerPoint slides) Textbook: *World History: The Human Journey*	T: YouTube video, "Communists Take Over China" (3:00) will be used as the set. A: Students will see images illustrating how art in China changed during the "Cultural Revolution." L: Students will recognize Chinese characters that symbolized the Communist Party in China. CT: Given the unit on communist ideals in China under Mao Zedong, students will complete a T-chart that contrasts communism in China today from what Mao had envisioned in the mid-20th century with at least the five differences with 5/5 accuracy.

DAY #	CONTENT/OBJECTIVE	STANDARDS	RESOURCES/MATERIALS	LEARNING ACTIVITIES/ASSESSMENTS
143	**Korean War** Given the quote in which President Harry S. Truman declared that the war in Korea was a "police action," students will either support the United States' perceived responsibility as a global police force or deny the assumed obligation in an outline form with at least three justifications to back up their stance with 3/3 accuracy.	Era 9, Standard 1, 2, 3 WHII. 12 c TCA: 1.1, 1.2, 1.3, 1.5, 1.6, 1.7, 1.8, 1.9, 1.10	Google Earth Video about Bob Hope visiting American troops in Korea: https://www.youtube.com/watch?v=ppA4qYF7ARo (7:00) Textbook: *World History: The Human Journey*	T: Google Earth will be used throughout the lesson to identify locations such as the 38th parallel, Pohang, etc. T/MUS: Students will see Bob Hope perform before American troops in Korea (7:00). CT/COLL: Given the quote in which President Harry S. Truman declared that the war in Korea was a "police action," students will either support the United States' perceived responsibility as a global police force or deny the assumed obligation in an outline form with at least three justifications to back up their stance with 3/3 accuracy. Students will then assemble into two groups based on their stance and a controlled debate will be conducted.
144	**Vietnam War** Given the lecture on the Vietnam War, students will complete a 10-question worksheet in which they are required to match the different political leaders from the Vietnam crisis with their accomplishments or ideas with 8/10 accuracy.	Era 9, Standard 1, 2, 3 WHII. 12 c TCA: 1.1, 1.2, 1.3, 1.5, 1.6, 1.7, 1.8, 1.9, 1.10	Large amount of dominos Textbook: *World History: The Human Journey*	ACT/COLL: As a set, students will come to the front and build a domino maze (give them about 3 minutes). At this point, the instructor will knock over the first domino and students will see how that one domino managed to knock over every single one of the other dominos. This will be used as an illustration to teach the Domino Theory that President Eisenhower developed. He said that the South East Asian countries were like a set of dominos, the fall of one to communism would lead to the fall of their neighbors. L: Students will learn about the importance language can convey. Ho Chi Minh was originally named Nguyen That Thanh but he changed it to Ho Chi Minh because it means "He Who Enlightens." This name better captured his goals as the communist inspiration in Vietnam. CT: Given the lecture on the Vietnam War, students will complete a 10-question worksheet in which they are required to match the different political leaders from the Vietnam crisis with their accomplishments or ideas with 8/10 accuracy.

DAY #	CONTENT/OBJECTIVE	STANDARDS	RESOURCES/MATERIALS	LEARNING ACTIVITIES/ASSESSMENTS
145	**Conclusion of Vietnam War: How Is It Remembered?** Given the lectures on the Vietnam War and the Korean War, students will compare and contrast in a two-circle Venn Diagram the two conflicts with at least three items in each circle with 9/9 accuracy.	Era 9, Standard 1, 2, 3 WHII. 12 c TCA: 1.1, 1.2, 1.3, 1.5, 1.6, 1.7, 1.8, 1.9, 1.10	John Lennon's *Imagine* YouTube clip: http://www.youtube.com/watch?v=yRhq-yO1KN8 (3:14) Textbook: *World History: The Human Journey*	MUS/T/COLL: Students will listen and watch John Lennon's "Imagine" music video and make assertions about what he means and how it related to the Vietnam War. This will be a class discussion. CE: There are several people that look down on soldiers that fought in Vietnam because they did not agree with the war. They disgraced and dishonored American soldiers when they came back from the war. Students will understand that regardless of personal opinion on a war, it is important to support American troops and honor their sacrifices for freedom. CT: Given the lectures on the Vietnam War and the Korean War, students will compare and contrast in a Venn Diagram the two conflicts with at least three items in each circle with 9/9 accuracy.
146	**Cold War Goes Global: Cuban Missile Crisis, Bay of Pigs, and Revolutions in South America** Given the lecture on the global spread of the Cold War, students will identify three major events that almost resulted in direct military engagement between the U.S. and U.S.S.R. with 3/3 accuracy.	Era 9, Standard 1, 2, 3 WHII. 12 b, c TCA: 1.1, 1.2, 1.3, 1.5, 1.6, 1.7, 1.8, 1.9, 1.10	YouTube clip on Fidel Castro's ideals from his own mouth: https://www.youtube.com/watch?v=67ZWBl-66H (5:10) YouTube clip on the Bay of Pigs: https://www.youtube.com/watch?v=8qXZp8bxpNY (5:05) Textbook: *World History: The Human Journey*	T/CT/COLL: Students will watch a short YouTube clip in which a young Fidel Castro expresses his vision for communism in Cuba. Students will work independently to list how this vision differentiates with Russian communism. The list will then be discussed in class. T: Students will watch a short video clip on the blunder at the Bay of Pigs. Video stresses Kennedy's attempt to hide the United States' involvement. DIV: Students will recognize how the revolutions in Nicaragua differed from Cuba's revolution. Students will be able to give reasons for why communism was never fully implemented in Nicaragua (cultural and historic reasons). Given the lecture on the global spread of the Cold War, students will identify and summarize three major events that almost resulted in direct military engagement between the U.S. and U.S.S.R. with 3/3 accuracy.

DAY #	CONTENT/OBJECTIVE	STANDARDS	RESOURCES/MATERIALS	LEARNING ACTIVITIES/ASSESSMENTS
147	**WebQuest on Margaret Thatcher** Given the primary source documents and the videos, students will compose a two-paragraph letter from the perspective of Margaret Thatcher expressing her grievances about the modern government system in Britain in accordance with the rubric.	Era 9, Standard 1, 2, 3 WHII. 12 b, c TCA: 1.1, 1.2, 1.3, 1.5, 1.6, 1.7, 1.8, 1.9, 1.10	Mobile Computer Lab WebQuest Rubric Textbook: *World History: The Human Journey*	ASSESS/T/CT: Students will participate in a WebQuest that will require them to read two primary source documents and watch three videos. The two primary source documents deal with Margaret Thatcher and her starch opposition to communism and socialism (she was dubbed the "Iron Lady" in a Soviet journal). Students will then watch three videos explaining the current government/society of Great Britain and just how far it has deviated from Thatcher's vision (modern British government has a socialist aspect to it that occurred even after the fall of the communist Russia). This will allow students to relate history to today. Given the primary source documents and the videos, students will compose a two-paragraph letter from the perspective of Margaret Thatcher expressing her grievances about the modern government system in Britain in accordance with the rubric. This will be a graded assignment and a rubric will be provided to each student in hard copy and in the WebQuest instructions. B: Students will understand the impact of Thatcher's Christian values on her policies. Her belief in individual faith was one of the main reasons she opposed a society in which the individual is lost in communism. CE: Students will learn about the leadership skills of Margaret Thatcher. They will learn the importance of not only standing for your convictions but actively opposing ideas that are detrimental to those things you value.
148	**Movement Toward Détente With the U.S.S.R.** Given 10 terms directly relating to the Cold War, students will provide a one- to two-sentence summary of their/its impact on the process toward detente with 9/10 accuracy.	Era 9, Standard 1, 2, 3 WHII. 12 b, c TCA: 1.1, 1.2, 1.3, 1.5, 1.6, 1.7, 1.8, 1.9, 1.10	Textbook: *World History: The Human Journey*	DIV: Students will learn about the difficulties the U.S.S.R. had in sustaining its union with so many diverse cultures and languages. This caused splits with the Soviet Union from its satellite states and other communist nations such as China. ASSESS: Given 10 terms directly relating to the Cold War, students will provide a one- to two-sentence summary of their/its impact on the process toward detente with 9/10 accuracy. This will be conducted as informal assessment of students' comprehension of the content.

DAY #	CONTENT/OBJECTIVE	STANDARDS	RESOURCES/MATERIALS	LEARNING ACTIVITIES/ASSESSMENTS
149	**Reagan and Gorbachev: The Fall of the U.S.S.R. Test Review** Given the fall of the Soviet Union, students will formulate a three-point thesis and paper outline that explains and summarizes why the Soviet Union collapsed in 1991 with 3/3 accuracy. Students will not actually be writing the paper (just trying to teach good habits of organization).	Era 9, Standard 1, 2, 3 WHII. 12 b, c TCA: 1.1, 1.2, 1.3, 1.5, 1.6, 1.7, 1.8, 1.9, 1.10	Sound clip of David Hasselhoff singing on the Berlin Wall Textbook: *World History: The Human Journey*	COLL: Students will participate in a lecture that explains the conclusion of the Cold War. MUS: Sound clip of David Hasselhoff singing on the Berlin Wall will be played. CT: Given the fall of the Soviet Union, students will formulate a three-point thesis and paper outline that explains and summarizes why the Soviet Union collapsed in 1991 with 3/3 accuracy. Students will not actually be writing the paper (just trying to teach good habits of organization and paper writing skills). ACT: Any time remaining in the class period will be used to review for the test on day #150. Students will play "Match that Term." On the board will be listed over 35 terms (concepts, people, ideas, and events). Students will be organized into two teams and two students will be called to the board at a time where they will be handed a fly swatter. Students will be turned away from the board and told a definition for one of the terms. When the instructor is done reading the definition, students will spin around and try to find the term as quickly as possible. The students that swats first wins.
150	**Test on the Cold War** Given the unit on the Cold War, students will take a test with 20 multiple-choice questions from old SOL tests and one short essay, achieving 18/21 accuracy.	Era 9, Standard 1, 2, 3 WHII. 12 b, c TCA: 1.1, 1.2, 1.3, 1.5, 1.6, 1.7, 1.8, 1.9, 1.10	Textbook: *World History: The Human Journey*	ASSESS: Given the unit on the Cold War, students will take a test with 20 multiple-choice questions from old SOL tests and one short essay, achieving 18/21 accuracy.
151	**India and Ghandi** Given a lecture and map on British control of India, students will describe the scope of the British Empire and how the people of India pursued independence with 10/10 correct.	Era 9, Standard 1, 2, 3 WHII. 14 a TCA: 1.1, 1.2, 1.3, 1.5, 1.6, 1.10	Textbook: *World History: The Human Journey* Computer, projector	T: Students will be shown a map online of the British empire and will be shown a chart that indicates how many square miles and how many people were under British control. CT: Students will be given quotes from Gandhi and then will be asked to evaluate it in a group class discussion. This discussion should bridge onto Gandhi's accomplishments and his policy of passive rebellion.

DAY #	CONTENT/OBJECTIVE	STANDARDS	RESOURCES/MATERIALS	LEARNING ACTIVITIES/ASSESSMENTS
152	**Indian Independence** Given an activity and lecture on Indian Independence, students will explain the difficulties India faced with 90% correct.	Era 9, Standard 1, 2, 3 WHII. 14 a TCA: 1.1, 1.2, 1.3, 1.5, 1.6, 1.10	Textbook: *World History: The Human Journey*	COLL/CT: Students will be placed into three groups: socialists, free market, and mixed economies. They will then prepare a memo they would present to the new India government suggesting that the new government should adopt this model. CT/DIV: In a class discussion students will speak on the effects of India's huge population. DIV: Students with ESL or ADHD will be placed with students that can help them with their deficiencies as their work on their projects.
153	**Mother Teresa** Given a lecture on Mother Teresa, students will identify why she was revered in India and throughout the world with 5/5 correct.	Era 9, Standard 1, 2, 3 WHII. 14 a TCA: 1.1, 1.2, 1.3, 1.5, 1.6, 1.8, 1.10	Textbook: *World History: The Human Journey* Computer, projector YouTube video: https://www.youtube.com/watch?v=qnhiGtCBc10	T: Students will watch part of a YouTube video on Mother Teresa, there will be class discussion after it finishes on the subject. CE/B: Students will write a short in-class essay to identify why Mother Teresa would invest her life in a poor country like India. These essays will be a completion grade.
154	**Issues With Indian Independence** Given a lecture, students will identify the key problems with the Kashmir Province, the tensions between the Hindus and the Muslims, and the splitting of Bangladesh with 90% correct.	Era 9, Standard 1, 2, 3 WHII. 14 a TCA: 1.1, 1.2, 1.3, 1.5, 1.6, 1.8, 1.10	Textbook: *World History: The Human Journey* Quiz	ACT/COLL: The students will be broken up into two groups, one representing Hindus and the other Muslims. Have the groups meet and then elect a spokesperson to demand the rights they want as Hindus and Muslims (This rights should be specifically religious in nature). If an agreement cannot be met then the students will be allowed to "riot" (Students can pretend to stage protests, refuse to work, riot in the streets.) CT: Following the activity students will engage in a discussion as to the problems facing India today concerning specifically the Kashmir Province, the rivalry with China, as well as religious problems. ASSESS: Students will be given a short quiz on Indian Independence.
155	**African Independence** Given a lecture and activity on African nationalism after WWII, students will be able to identify the factors that led to a rise of African nationalism with 10/10 correct.	Era 9, Standard 1, 2, 3 WHII. 14 b TCA: 1.1, 1.2, 1.3, 1.5, 1.6, 1.8, 1.10	Textbook: *World History: The Human Journey* Internet access	CT/DIV: Students will all be given a separate country in Africa and must explain how it came to be independent. The students will be given some time in class after a lecture to find resources. The students must prepare a short (3–4 minute) speech about their country. The speech must include: • Where the country is located as well as a rough population • Who ruled the country before independence • Prominent leaders • What type of government is ruling the country now • Difficulties the country is facing currently

DAY #	CONTENT/OBJECTIVE	STANDARDS	RESOURCES/MATERIALS	LEARNING ACTIVITIES/ASSESSMENTS
156	**African Independence** Given a lecture and activity on African nationalism after WWII, students will be able to identify the factors that led to a rise of African nationalism with 10/10 correct.	Era 9, Standard 1, 2, 3 WHII. 14 b TCA: 1.1, 1.2, 1.3, 1.5, 1.6, 1.8, 1.10	Textbook: *World History: The Human Journey*	ASSESS: Students will present their projects on African countries and will be graded by the criteria listed above.
157	**Prominent African Leaders** Given a lecture and short video on Jomo Kenyatta and Nelson Mandel, students will be able to identify the specific impacts these men had on their countries with 9/10 correct.	Era 9, Standard 1, 2, 3 WHII. 14 b TCA: 1.1, 1.2, 1.3, 1.5, 1.6, 1.8, 1.10	Textbook: *World History: The Human Journey* YouTube videos: https://www.youtube.com/watch?v=zL0m6yDyCcc https://www.youtube.com/watch?v=LnGeMBNS9ZA	T/CT: Students will watch parts of YouTube videos on Kenyatta and Mandel. These videos should take up at least half of the class time. Afterward the class will engage in a group discussion as to whether they thought the policies of the two men were genuine or corrupt.
158	**The Middle East** Given a lecture and video on European withdrawal from the Middle East and creation of Israel, students will explain how the Middle East experienced change with 95% correct.	Era 9, Standard 1, 2, 3 WHII. 14 c TCA: 1.1, 1.2, 1.3, 1.5, 1.6, 1.8, 1.10	Textbook: *World History: The Human Journey* YouTube video: https://www.youtube.com/watch?v=4X4JCPckWgY Chalk and a sunny day	T: Students will watch this video to help them understand the conflict between Israel and the Middle East. COLL/CT/CE/DIV/B: Students will be split into groups of four to answer the question: If the Holocaust had not occurred would Israel have received its own nation-state? Next, students will be asked to identify if they believe Israel should have gotten its own state. Students will then share what they discussed in their groups with the rest of the class. ACT: To visually demonstrate how small Israel is compared to the rest of the Arab world, the students will be taken outside to the parking lot. The teacher will draw a small circle representing Israel's population and then draw a much larger circle representing the rest of the Arab world. Next, all the students but one will be placed into the big circle and the single student will be placed in the smaller circle indicating the population difference.

DAY #	CONTENT/OBJECTIVE	STANDARDS	RESOURCES/MATERIALS	LEARNING ACTIVITIES/ASSESSMENTS
159	**The Middle East (Continued)** Given an assignment on Middle Eastern countries, students will correctly identify how the various countries came to independence and what government currently controls them with 90% accuracy.	Era 9, Standard 1, 2, 3 WHII. 14 c TCA: 1.1, 1.2, 1.3, 1.5, 1.6, 1.8, 1.10	Textbook: *World History: The Human Journey* Internet access	COLL/CT/DIV: Students will be placed into groups of two, will be given a separate country in the Middle East, and must explain how it came to be independent. The students will be given some time in class after a lecture to find resources. The students must prepare a short (3–4 minute) speech about their country. The speech must include: • Where the country is located as well as a rough population • Who ruled the country before independence • Prominent leaders • What type of government is ruling the country now • Difficulties the country is facing currently
160	**The Middle East (Continued)** Given an assignment on Middle Eastern countries, students will correctly identify how the various countries came to independence and what government currently controls them with 90% accuracy.	Era 9, Standard 1, 2, 3 WHII. 14 c TCA: 1.1, 1.2, 1.3, 1.5, 1.6, 1.8, 1.10	Textbook: *World History: The Human Journey*	ASSESS: Students will present their projects on African countries and will be graded by the criteria: • Where the country is located as well as a rough population • Who ruled the country before independence • Prominent leaders • What type of government is ruling the country now • Difficulties the country is facing currently
161	**Prominent Middle East Leaders** Given a lecture on Golda Meir and Gamal Abdul Nasser students will be able to explain their rise to power as well as their roles in shaping the Middle East with 90% accuracy.	Era 9, Standard 1, 2, 3 WHII. 14 c TCA: 1.1, 1.2, 1.3, 1.5, 1.6, 1.8, 1.10	Textbook: *World History: The Human Journey* YouTube video: https:// www.youtube.com/ watch?v=cU_4PYR50ek	CT/T: Students will analyze an interview with Nasser to find if his comments were true. The students will take notes during the film and then a class discussion will take place on the subject of Nasser's interview. (This interview is on Zionism.) A short lecture before this should supplement the video well. DIV: Any terms that might be confusing to ESL, ADHD, or ELL students will be put on a handout and given to them.

DAY #	CONTENT/OBJECTIVE	STANDARDS	RESOURCES/MATERIALS	LEARNING ACTIVITIES/ASSESSMENTS
162	**Test Review** Given a test review on the latest material, students will demonstrate their knowledge of the subject by playing a review game with 48/50 correct.	Era 9, Standard 1, 2, 3 WHII. 14 a, b, c TCA: 1.1, 1.2, 1.3, 1.5, 1.6, 1.8, 1.10	Textbook: *World History: The Human Journey*	ACT/T: Students will be playing a game to help them review for the test. This game will be Family Feud-style where the class is broken into two teams and will send one representative up for each team to compete.
163	**Test Day** Given a test on the latest material, students will demonstrate their knowledge of the subject by taking a test with 90% accuracy.	Era 9, Standard 1, 2, 3 WHII. 14 a, b, c TCA: 1.1, 1.2, 1.3, 1.5, 1.6, 1.8, 1.10	Written exam with an essay question, short answer, and multiple-choice questions	ASSESS: The exam will cover Indian democracy with emphasis on Gandhi, Africa's independence movement, the Middle-East's independence movement, and will focus on major leaders in some of these countries.
164	**The Five Most Prominent Religions** Given directions and a large assignment on the five most prominent religions, students will complete a portfolio project with 90% accuracy.	Era 9, Standard 1 WHII. 15 a, b TCA: 1.1, 1.2, 1.3, 1.5, 1.6, 1.8, 1.10	Textbook: *World History: The Human Journey*	DIV/CT/CE/A/B/L: Students will be introduced in class to their assignment on the five most prominent religions: Christianity, Islam, Hinduism, Buddhism, and Judaism. The students will be crafting a portfolio about these religions with specific guidelines. These will be turned in several weeks from now. A sample project will be shown and questions about the project should be answered during this day. A short discussion of the religions should take place after the directions are given.
165	**The Six-Day War** Given a lecture on the Six-Day War, students will explain how Arab-Israeli conflicts have shaped recent history with 90% accuracy.	Era 9, Standard 1 WHII. 16 a TCA: 1.1, 1.2, 1.3, 1.5, 1.8	Textbook: *World History: The Human Journey*	CT/COLL: Students will be placed into two groups, one Arab and one Israeli. The groups will collaborate and come up with a list of demands each side would require to live peaceably. Once this is reached, the teacher will ask how radical elements undermine peace (riots, bombings, terrorist acts). The students will then discuss why these radicals do these acts.

DAY #	CONTENT/OBJECTIVE	STANDARDS	RESOURCES/MATERIALS	LEARNING ACTIVITIES/ASSESSMENTS
166	**Oil** Given a lecture and map assignment on oil deposits and the Middle East with a focus on OPEC, students will correctly identify where the oil fields in the Middle East are located with 10/10 correct.	Era 9, Standard 1 WHII. 16 b, c TCA: 1.1, 1.2, 1.3, 1.5, 1.7, 1.8	Textbook: *World History: The Human Journey* Poster board, color pencils/markers	CT/A: Students will create a map using color pencils/markers of the Middle East. The map will have to mark which states have the most oil, if they are a member of OPEC, and where the oil fields are located. DIV: Students will be shown pictures of how many of the Middle East countries use their oil money (Ex. indoor ski slope).
167	**Recent Latin American History** Given an assignment on Latin American countries, students will correctly identify how the various countries came to independence and what government currently controls them with 90% accuracy.	Era 9, Standard 1, 2, 3 WHII. 16 b, c TCA: 1.1, 1.2, 1.3, 1.5, 1.6, 1.8, 1.10	Textbook: *World History: The Human Journey* Internet Access	COLL/CT/DIV: Students will be placed into groups of two, will be given a separate country in Latin America, and must explain how it came to be independent. The students will be given some time in class after a lecture to find resources. The students must prepare a short (3–4 minute) speech about their country. The speech must include: • Where the country is located as well as a rough population • Who ruled the country before independence • Prominent leaders • What type of government is ruling the country now • Difficulties the country is facing currently
168	**Recent Latin American History** Given an assignment on Latin American countries, students will correctly identify how the various countries came to independence and what government currently controls them with 90% accuracy.	Era 9, Standard 1, 2, 3 WHII. 16 b, c TCA: 1.1, 1.2, 1.3, 1.5, 1.6, 1.8, 1.10	Textbook: *World History: The Human Journey*	ASSESS: Students will present their projects on Latin American countries and will be graded by the criteria: • Where the country is located as well as a rough population • Who ruled the country before independence • Prominent leaders • What type of government is ruling the country now • Difficulties the country is facing currently

DAY #	CONTENT/OBJECTIVE	STANDARDS	RESOURCES/MATERIALS	LEARNING ACTIVITIES/ASSESSMENTS
169	**Drug Trade** Given an activity, video, and debate, students will be able to explain the effects of the drug trade on America and abroad with 85% accuracy.	Era 9, Standard 3 WHII. 16 a, b, c TCA: 1.1, 1.2, 1.3, 1.5, 1.6, 1.8, 1.10	Textbook: *World History: The Human Journey* YouTube video: https://www.youtube.com/watch?v=HhbP61íTv8	CT/CE/T: Students will engage in a classroom debate as to whether drugs should be legalized following a viewing of a YouTube video. The debate should draw back to the terrible violence that is being committed in Latin America.
170	**Technology** Given an activity and short lecture, students will be able to describe the most recent technical improvements with 90% accuracy.	Era 9, Standard 3 WHII. 16 a, b, c TCA: 1.1, 1.2, 1.3, 1.5, 1.6, 1.8, 1.10	Textbook: *World History: The Human Journey* Quiz	ASSESS: Students will be given a quiz on oil and drugs before class begins. ACT/COLL/S: Students will be split into groups and then choose something they could invent from free or inexpensive materials. After the students have developed a plan they will try and create their invention (Ex. fishing hooks, thread, and stick equals a rod and reel).
171	**9/11 and Terrorism** Given videos on the 9/11 terror attacks, students will explain the sequence of how the attacks were perpetrated with 100% accuracy.	Era 9, Standard 3 WHII. 16 d TCA: 1.1, 1.2, 1.3, 1.5, 1.6, 1.8, 1.10	Textbook: *World History: The Human Journey* YouTube videos: https://www.youtube.com/watch?v=8tgQ75GxAZk https://www.youtube.com/watch?v=0TqqzOCPmRE	T: Students will watch YouTube videos and then engage in a discussion of the attacks. This discussion should cover the attacks, aftermath, and struggles. CE: As a homework assignment students will be required to ask their parents or an older person about their remembrance of the 9/11 attacks. They will share their story in class the next day.
172	**Terrorism** Given a lecture on the various terrorist groups, students will be able to locate on maps and describe the purposes of the terrorist organizations with 100% accuracy.	Era 9, Standard 3 WHII. 16 d TCA: 1.1, 1.2, 1.3, 1.5, 1.6, 1.8, 1.10	Textbook: *World History: The Human Journey*	CT: Students will create a chart of the various terrorist groups. The chart will include major known leaders, when the group was originated, and in what countries it is most active. CE: Students will share their 9/11 stories and discuss them as appropriate. Students should understand how heartbreaking the attacks were and how they can be prevented in the future.

DAY #	CONTENT/OBJECTIVE	STANDARDS	RESOURCES/MATERIALS	LEARNING ACTIVITIES/ASSESSMENTS
173	**Space** Given a lecture on the continuing progress of space exploration, students will be able to describe the advances in space exploration with 85% accuracy.	Era 9, Standard 3 WHII. 16 a, b, c TCA: 1.1, 1.2, 1.3, 1.5, 1.6, 1.8, 1.10	Textbook: *World History: The Human Journey*	DIV/ACT/S/A: Students will be assigned the task of making a model of either a satellite, space shuttle, rocket, or other spacecraft. This is a take-home project. The model can be made of popsicle sticks, cardboard, paper, metal, anything will work. The students must bring in a picture of what their model is based off of, though. They will be graded based upon the quality of the model.
174	**Scientific Advancement** Given a lecture and discussion on scientific advancement, students will be able to list the new scientific accomplishments with 5/5 correct.	Era 9, Standard 3 WHII. 16 a, b, c TCA: 1.1, 1.2, 1.3, 1.5, 1.6, 1.8, 1.10	Textbook: *World History: The Human Journey* YouTube video: https://www.youtube.com/watch?v=4Qhlp-X3EHA	T: Students will watch a video on the morality of science to supplement the discussion. CE/CT/S: In a classroom discussion, students will discuss the morality of some of the new scientific advancements in the medical field such as gene splicing and baby designing.
175	**Human Rights** Given a lecture, students will list some recent examples of human rights abuses with 10/10 correct.	Era 9, Standard 3 WHII. 16 a, b, c TCA: 1.1, 1.2, 1.3, 1.5, 1.6, 1.8, 1.10	Textbook: *World History: The Human Journey* Computers with Internet access	COLL: Students will be broken into groups and given time to research various human rights abuses on the Internet. They will make a list of these abuses and then they will share them in class. CT: There will be a classroom discussion on why these abuses took place and how they can be prevented in the future.
176	**Spread of Democratic Ideals** Given a lecture and in-class assignment, students will discuss how democratic ideals and practices spread in the late 1900s with 90% accuracy.	Era 9, Standard 3 WHII. 16 a, b, c TCA: 1.1, 1.2, 1.3, 1.5, 1.6, 1.8, 1.10	Textbook: *World History: The Human Journey*	ASSESS: The students' space projects are due today and will be judged based upon the criteria on day 173. CT: Students will create a list of nations that have become more democratic over the last 40 years. Next, students will create a list of nations that are particularly anti-democratic. This will be followed up with a class discussion as to why these nations have resisted democracy and if there is hope for the future.

DAY #	CONTENT/OBJECTIVE	STANDARDS	RESOURCES/MATERIALS	LEARNING ACTIVITIES/ASSESSMENTS
177	**Test Review** Given a test review on the latest material, students will demonstrate their knowledge of the subject by playing a review game with 48/50 correct.	Era 9, Standard 1, 2, 3 WHII. 16 a, b, c TCA: 1.1, 1.2, 1.3, 1.5, 1.6, 1.8, 1.10	Textbook: *World History: The Human Journey* Computer and projector	ACT: Students will be playing a game to help them review for the test. This game will be Family Feud-style where the class is broken into two teams and will send one representative up for each team to compete.
178	**Test Day** Given a test on the latest material, students will demonstrate their knowledge of the subject by taking a test with 90% accuracy.	Era 9, Standard 1, 2, 3 WHII. 16 a, b, c TCA: 1.1, 1.2, 1.3, 1.5, 1.6, 1.8, 1.10	Written exam with an essay question, short answer, and multiple-choice questions	ASSESS: Students will be assessed on all material covered since the last exam. This includes Israel, oil, technology and science advancement, Latin American countries, human rights, and the spread of democratic ideals.
179	**SOL prep** Students will be taking practice tests from older SOL exams to practice for their upcoming SOL tests.	All	SOL practice tests for the students	ASSESS: The students portfolio projects are due today and will be graded by the criteria on day 163.
180	**Party!** Given the movie *October Sky*, students will list how the WV boys overcame challenges as high school students with 10/10 correct.	None directly. We are having a party	Movie: *October Sky* Computer and projector screen	CT: Students will engage in a discussion as to what was their favorite section to study from our class. T: The movie *October Sky* is a film that highlights the determination of four WV boys from a coal mining town. They invent rockets and overcome adversity.

CHAPTER 9

Example #2 — Teaching English as a Second Language (TESL)

IDEAS FOR INTEGRATION

If TESL is your endorsement area of which you are gaining state licensure, your curriculum will focus, of course, on TESL, but you will integrate other areas within your content, such as science, English, mathematics, active learning, and so forth. Use the acronym key on the template for areas of integration. You can easily integrate other content as follows:

Objective

Students will write a five-sentence paragraph describing what they want to be when they grow up with five or less writing errors.

Content Integration

CRITICAL THINKING (CT)—The teacher will ask the class, "What do you want to be when you grow up?" and "Why do you want to be a _____ when you grow up?" "Will you have to work hard to become a _____?"

TECHNOLOGY/PHYSICAL EDUCATION/DANCE/CHARACTER EDUCATION (T/P/D/CE)—The teacher will give a short presentation about different types of jobs using a PowerPoint. The class will also watch the dance video "Let's Go To Work." The students will have the opportunity to dance along with the video. The teacher will highlight the importance of hard work and diligence when it comes to achieving our dream jobs.

COLLABORATION (COLL)—The teacher will ask a doctor to come to the class and share about his profession. The students will be given the opportunity to ask questions about his profession.

ACTIVE LEARNING (ACT)—Students will be split up into five groups to discuss their parents' jobs as well as what they want to be when they grow up.

ASSESSMENT (ASSESS)—Students will write a five-sentence paragraph describing what they want to be when they grow up and why.

ADDITIONAL RESOURCES

Below are three lists for your reference:

1. National Standards by Content Area

2. Common Core Standards (adopted by most states)

3. State Content Standards (those who did not adopt Common Core)

National Standards

English	National Council of Teachers of English (NCTE)	www.ncte.org
Reading	International Reading Association (IRA)	www.reading.org
Fine arts	National Art Educational Association (NAEA)	www.naea.org
Foreign language	American Council on the Teaching of Foreign Languages	www.actfl.org
Math	National Council of Teachers of Math (NCTM)	www.nctm.org
Science	National Science Teachers Association (NSTA)	www.nsta.org
Social Science	National Council for the Social Sciences (NCSS)	www.ncss.org
TESL	WIDA English Language Development (ELD) Standards	www.wida.us

Common Core Standards (adopted by 41 states)   http://www.corestandards.org/

State Standards (Common Core not adopted)

Alaska Department of Education	https://education.alaska.gov/
Florida Department of Education	http://www.fldoe.org/
Indiana Department of Education	https://www.doe.in.gov/
Minnesota Department of Education	https://education.mn.gov/mde/index.html
Nebraska Department of Education	http://www.education.ne.gov/
Oklahoma Department of Education	http://sde.ok.gov/sde/
Puerto Rico Department of Education	http://www.de.gobierno.pr/
South Carolina Department of Education	https://www.ed.sc.gov/
Texas Department of Education	https://tea.texas.gov/Home/
Virginia Department of Education	http://www.doe.virginia.gov/

SAMPLE #1 CURRICULUM

TEACHER CANDIDATE'S NAME:

CONTENT SUBJECT AREA: *Teaching English as a Second Language (TESL)*

GRADE LEVEL: *5th Grade, All Levels*

TEXTBOOK NAME WITH PUBLICATION INFORMATION: Grammar Links 1

Butler, L., Podnecky, J., & Mahke, M. K. (2005). *Grammar links 1: A theme based course for reference and practice.* Boston, MA: Houghton Mifflin Company.

Mission Statement:
Our English as a Second Language curriculum strives to enable students to speak, write, read, and listen to the English language with fluency and competence. Through incorporating vocabulary, grammar, culture, and practical opportunities to use the English language, this curriculum will allow students to grasp all aspects of language learning and attain proficiency. Our curriculum will also be centered on biblical principles in order to glorify God and empower students to attain a biblical worldview.

DAY #	CONTENT/OBJECTIVE	STANDARDS	RESOURCES/MATERIALS	LEARNING ACTIVITIES/ASSESSMENTS
	• Skills • Knowledge • Dispositions • Concepts • Themes • Values	• **VA SOLs** • **National Standards** • **TCAs**	*Include (1) resources to assist the teacher in planning and implementing lessons and (2) materials students need to participate.* • Books • Technology • Supplies • Community organizations • Guest speakers • Websites	*After each code below, list the day #'s in which the element is present. Codes are not required in every day's lesson but should be distributed appropriately throughout. You may create other codes if necessary to reflect special considerations not listed here.* *Simply listing the code is not sufficient. A brief explanation is needed to describe what the legend is referring to. For example, instead of just listing "CE," describe what character trait is being taught and how it relates to the lesson. Instead of just listing "ACT," describe how the students will be engaged in active learning.* **ACTIVITY LEGEND** *(All of the Activity Codes are **required** to be integrated at least once each week. It's important to show a variety of the legends distributed throughout the project.):* ACT = Active Learning—Day #: 8, 11, 14, 15, 16, 18, 20, 21, 23, 24, 38, 39, 41, 49, 51, 56, 59, 61, 63, 70, 73, 74, 77, 79, 84, 85, 91, 94, 96, 101, 104, 108, 109, 111, 116, 117, 121, 123, 128, 129, 131, 133, 134, 136, 139, 141, 143, 144, 146, 148, 153, 158, 161, 164, 168, 174, 180 ASSESS = Assessment Activity—Day #: 1, 2, 3, 5, 7, 10, 12, 17, 18, 20, 21, 22, 25, 27, 29, 30, 33, 35, 36, 38, 42, 45, 47, 56, 59, 60, 62, 67, 68, 71, 75, 77, 87, 83, 89, 90, 92, 93, 95, 97, 101, 102, 107, 109, 110, 111, 112, 119, 123, 127, 128, 130, 131, 136, 139, 140, 147, 148, 149, 151, 152, 153, 154, 155, 157, 161, 162, 165, 166, 167, 168, 173, 174, 175, 176, 177, 179 COLL = There are different types of collaboration: (1) teacher with community members/organizations or other educators and (2) students with other students or community members—Day #: 3, 9, 10, 14, 17, 20, 26, 35, 36, 41, 46, 50, 56, 61, 66, 70, 76, 81, 86, 93, 95, 96, 101, 109, 111,

DAY #	CONTENT/OBJECTIVE	STANDARDS	RESOURCES/MATERIALS	LEARNING ACTIVITIES/ASSESSMENTS
				116, 121, 127, 131, 133, 136, 142, 144, 145, 148, 151, 158, 159, 161, 168, 174, 175, 178
				CE = Character Education—Day #: 1, 6, 13, 17, 21, 26, 33, 39, 41, 46, 51, 56, 61, 66, 72, 77, 83, 86, 95, 97, 101, 106, 111, 117, 122, 126, 127, 132, 136, 145, 151, 159, 161, 169, 171, 180
				CT = Critical Thinking Activity—Day #: 1, 7, 11, 17, 21, 26, 31, 39, 41, 46, 55, 61, 66, 79, 86, 95, 104, 109, 111, 115, 121, 126, 132, 137, 145, 151, 156, 158, 159, 160, 169, 180
				DIV = Diversity Consideration—Day #: 4, 8, 10, 13, 14, 16, 22, 24, 25, 31, 35, 38, 46, 53, 58, 59, 61, 68, 71, 74, 80, 86, 91, 95, 98, 109, 114, 119, 121, 134, 136, 142, 144, 148, 152, 153, 154, 159, 161, 168, 180
				T = Technology—Day #:2, 7, 8, 10, 12, 15, 16, 19, 21, 37, 39, 40, 42, 49, 50, 54, 55, 57, 61, 64, 65, 69, 72, 73, 74, 77, 78, 80, 82, 84, 85, 86, 91, 94, 97, 99, 100, 101, 104, 105, 111, 112, 113, 115, 117, 122, 124, 125, 127, 130, 135, 136, 142, 150, 152, 154, 156, 159, 161, 163, 170, 171, 172
				INTEGRATION LEGEND *(A variety of interdisciplinary integrations should be included at least once per 9 weeks.* **Not all are necessary,** *only those that can reasonably be integrated into your subject area. If a code is not used at all, enter N/A after "Day #'s" for that code.):* A = Art—Day #: 1, 4, 5, 9, 32, 35, 42, 70, 75, 91, 105, 120, 137, 145, 151 B = Biblical principles—Day #: 7, 71, 77, 97, 126, 151, 128, 146, 159 D = Dance—Day #: 16, 25, 39, 42, 49, 54, 111, 143 H = Health—Day #: 26, 56, 86, 96, 156 L = Language Arts—Day #: 2, 7, 12, 17, 22, 27, 32, 37, 42, 47, 52, 57, 62, 65, 70, 72, 77, 82, 87, 92, 97, 102, 107, 112, 117, 120, 122, 127, 132, 137, 142, 147, 151, 152, 157, 160, 161, 162, 167, 172, 177 M = Math—Day #: 3, 8, 13, 18, 23, 28, 33, 38, 43, 48, 53, 58, 63, 68, 73, 78, 83, 88, 93, 98, 103, 108, 113, 118, 123, 128, 133, 138, 143, 148, 153, 158, 163, 168, 173, 178 MUS = Music—Day #: 16, 39, 42, 49, 50, 54, 95, 131, 161 P = Physical Education/Movement—Day #: 8, 11, 13, 14, 15, 16, 18, 23, 25, 38, 39, 42, 49, 54, 111, 143, 146, 168 S = Science—Day #: 4, 9, 14, 19, 24, 29, 34, 39, 44, 49, 54, 59, 64, 69, 74, 79, 84, 89, 94, 99, 104, 109, 114, 119, 124, 129, 134, 139, 144, 149, 154, 159, 164, 169, 174, 179 SS = Social Science—Day #: 5, 10, 15, 20, 25, 30, 35, 40, 45, 50, 55, 60, 65, 70, 75, 80, 85, 90, 95, 100, 105, 110, 115, 120, 125, 130, 135, 140, 145, 150, 155, 160, 165, 170, 175 TH = Theatre—Day #: 6, 7, 22, 27, 32, 36, 41, 86, 120, 146

DAY #	CONTENT/OBJECTIVE	STANDARDS	RESOURCES/MATERIALS	LEARNING ACTIVITIES/ASSESSMENTS
1	**Introductions** Given the four introductory activities, students will actively participate in 4/4.	Standard 1 (Social & Instructional Language) TCAs: 2(2B). Cultural Groups and Identity 2(4I): Language Proficiency Assessment 2(4J): Classroom-Based Assessment for ESL	A globe bulletin board map "Bingo icebreaker game Markers, crayons, and other craft supplies Paper Polaroid camera Pins	Introductions to classmates. Students will use a globe to point out to each other where they are from. The students will also play a Bingo icebreaker game. **CE**—The teacher will explain class rules and expectations. She will also explain the importance of responsibility. **CT**—After the teacher explains the class rules and expectations, she will ask the students, "Why do we have rules and expectations?" The teacher will then give the students the opportunity to think about why the class has rules and share their answer with their neighbor. **A**—Students will make name tags to put on their desks. The teacher will take Polaroid photos of the students and have them pin their pictures onto a bulletin board map showing where they are from. **ASSESS**—The students will take a pre-assessment test to show what level of English speaking they have achieved.
2	**BEGINNING OF UNIT 1: Communication: Speaking, Listening** Give the guided question, "What was the favorite part of your summer?" Students will be able to answer the question with less than five speaking mistakes. Given the listening comprehension worksheet, students will be able to answer 4/5 questions correctly.	Unit 1: Communication: Speaking, listening, media TCAs: 2(3F): Managing and Implementing Standards-Based ESL and Content Instruction 2(3G): Using Resources Effectively in ESL and Content Instruction 2(4J): Classroom-Based Assessment for ESL	Pre-assessment: http://youtu.be/GO9XP_JfeUo Projector	**L/ASSESS**—The students will be given informal pre-assessments regarding speaking and listening. First, the students will be split into groups of three or four. Then, the teacher will present the students with the question "What was the favorite part of your summer?" As the students discuss this question in their small groups for a few minutes, the teacher will walk around the room and take note of each student's ability to speak and contribute to group conversation. After the speaking pre-assessment is given, the teacher will play a short advertisement for Ovaltine. http://youtu.be/GO9XP_JfeUo The teacher will give the students a worksheet with five questions about the advertisement to check the students' listening comprehension and the class will also discuss the nature and purpose of advertisements. **T**—Teacher will play the commercial for the class to watch and listen.

DAY #	CONTENT/OBJECTIVE	STANDARDS	RESOURCES/MATERIALS	LEARNING ACTIVITIES/ASSESSMENTS
3	**BEGINNING OF UNIT 1: Vocabulary of Operations and Algebraic Thinking—Pre-Assessment Day** Given a pre-assessment test, the students will answer 100% of the questions to the best of their ability.	Standard 3 (Language of Mathematics) TCAs: 2(3F): Managing and Implementing Standards-Based ESL and Content Instruction 2(4I): Language Proficiency Assessment	Math pre-assessment test Exit ticket	**M/ASSESS**—The students will take a pre-assessment math test consisting mostly of word problems. As the students take the assessment, the teacher will call them up one at a time and have them read a word problem aloud, asking and recording how much of the problem they understand. Afterward, the students will fill out an exit ticket answering these key questions: 1. Were there any words on the test that you did not understand? 2. What was easy on the test? 3. What was hard on the test? **COLL**—For the pre-assessment, the ESL teacher will ask the 4th grade teacher for one of her final math tests and will select questions from that test in order to hopefully ensure that the students are not being tested over material they never would have had an opportunity to learn.
4	**BEGINNING OF UNIT 1: Vocabulary of Scientific Research and Method—Introduction** Given binders, dividers, notebook paper, art supplies, and the names of the six science units for the year, students will divide their binders into six sections, decorating the dividers, and labeling the sections with each unit's name using spelling that is 100% accurate.	Standard 4 (Language of Science) TCAs: 2(3F): Managing and Implementing Standards-Based ESL and Content Instruction	Binders Dividers Markers, crayons, and colored pencils Notebook paper	**S**—Explain to students that they will be using their science notebooks throughout the school year to write down any words they do not understand during their science lesson and while reading their textbook. Explain that when they come to ESL class, they will write the translation of the word into their native language using a dictionary or pocket translator, and that they will write an English definition of the word and will either draw a picture or diagram or come up with a rhyme or song that helps them to remember the meaning. **A**—The students will put their notebook paper into their binders, dividing them into six sections for the six different units, and will label each of the sections with the name of the unit. Then, they will use the art supplies to decorate the dividers. **DIV**—Allowing students to draw pictures or diagrams or create rhymes or songs in addition to recording the written definition of vocabulary words will meet the needs of learners with diverse learning styles. Assign as homework: Students will record and define words on their own and turn them into the teacher to be assessed on each science day of ESL class (each Thursday).

DAY #	CONTENT/OBJECTIVE	STANDARDS	RESOURCES/MATERIALS	LEARNING ACTIVITIES/ASSESSMENTS
5	**BEGINNING OF UNIT 1: United States Encounter, Colonization, and Devastation (1492–1763)**	Standard 5 (Language of Social Science) TCAs: 2(3F): Managing and Implementing Standards-Based ESL and Content Instruction 2(3G): Using Resources Effectively in ESL and Content Instruction 2(4J): Classroom-Based Assessment for ESL	Craft supplies *John Adams* audiobook Pre-assessment	**A**—As an introductory activity, students will create a vocabulary/ideas binder for the class. The teacher will give the students craft supplies to decorate their binder. As the students decorate their binder, they will begin listening to the audiobook *John Adams*. During craft time during the rest of the semester, the class will continue to listen to *John Adams* in order to increase listening comprehension and their knowledge of US History. **SS/ASSESS**—The teacher will give students a comprehensive 25-question pre-assessment of terms used in history class. The pre-assessment will be used to gauge the students' prior exposure and comprehensions of terms used to be successful within 5th grade history.
6	**The Language of the Classroom** Given five role-playing scenarios, students will respond correctly 5/5 times.	Standard 1 (Social & Instructional Language) TCAs: 2(2c): Nature and Role of Culture 2(3F): Managing and Implementing Standards-Based ESL and Content Instruction	PowerPoint Projector *All Clear Listening and Speaking 1*	**CE**—The teacher will lecture, explaining classroom behaviors expected in America. She will teach them about having good character, telling them that respectfulness toward others is important. She will also give them basic listening comprehension and note-taking strategies to be a good student. The teacher will show a PowerPoint with example questions to ask and possible responses. **TH**—The students will role-play a classroom and proper classroom behavior, with one pretending to be a teacher and the others pretending to be students. At the end, the teacher will give the students a copy of the handout from Appendix E on page 183 of *All Clear Listening and Speaking 1*. The handout is a list of common classroom language.

DAY #	CONTENT/OBJECTIVE	STANDARDS	RESOURCES/MATERIALS	LEARNING ACTIVITIES/ASSESSMENTS
7	**Unit 1: Communication: Speaking, Listening** Students will be able to ask two questions with less than two speaking mistakes. Students will be able to give two responses with less than three speaking mistakes.	Standard 2 (The Language of Language Arts) TCAs: 2(3F): Managing and Implementing Standards-Based ESL and Content Instruction 2(3G): Using Resources Effectively in ESL and Content Instruction 2(4J): Classroom-Based Assessment for ESL	PowerPoint Projector Scenarios A bible	The students will begin working on teaching the students different strategies used when listening and speaking. **CT**—The teacher will ask the students "Why is speaking important?" The students will then have the opportunity to share why speaking is important. **B**—The teacher will read the students the story of the Tower of Babel to illustrate why it is so important for people to be able to communicate with one another. **T**—First, the teacher will instruct students on the different ways we speak using a PowerPoint. The teacher will cover asking questions and making requests. The teacher will also emphasize the importance of listening when someone else is giving an answer. **L/ASSESS**—The students will be split into pairs and each pair will be given guided questions and suggested responses for asking questions. Each student will take two turns asking questions and two turns answering questions. **TH**—After the students have finished, they will be asked to "perform" one question and answer in front of the class.

DAY #	CONTENT/OBJECTIVE	STANDARDS	RESOURCES/MATERIALS	LEARNING ACTIVITIES/ASSESSMENTS
8	**Unit 1: Vocabulary of Operations and Algebraic Thinking— Learning Numbers** Given a ball and a group of classmates in a circle, each student will say the next correct number in a sequence at least two times.	Standard 3 (Language of Mathematics) TCAs: 2(3F): Managing and Implementing Standards-Based ESL and Content Instruction 2(3G): Using Resources Effectively in ESL and Content Instruction	Numbers 1–10 flash cards & games: http://quizlet.com/32458146/ english-numbers-1-10-flash-cards/ http://www.mrprintables.com/ printable-number-flash-cards.html http://www.eslgamesplus.com/ numbers-1-to-10-esl-fun-game-catapult-game/ http://www.eslgamesplus. com/numbers-one-to-ten-esl-vocabulary-croc-board-game/ http://www.eslgamesplus.com/ numbers-1-to-10-esl-vocabulary-interactive-board-game/ Numbers 1–100 flash cards & games: http://quizlet.com/16864532/ flashcards http://www.eslgamesplus.com/ numbers-1-100-vocabulary-and-grammar-interactive-crocodile-board-game/ http://www.eslgamesplus.com/ numbers-1-100-vocabulary-and-grammar-interactive-crocodile-board-game/ http://www.eslgamesplus.com/ numbers-10-to-100-esl-vocabulary-interactive-board-game/	**M**—Students will study the numbers of English. The teacher will break the students into groups based on their level of understanding of English numbers, as demonstrated by the pre-assessment test. **DIV**—Students who are at a lower level will study the numbers 1–10. Students who have a more advanced knowledge of English will study the numbers 1–100. Also, the flash cards have the option of using audio so that the students can not only see the numbers and the words that represent them, but also hear them. This will meet the needs of both auditory and read/write learners. The needs of kinesthetic learners will be met during the active learning time when students bounce a ball and count. **T**—The students will use online flash cards and review games to learn. They will use the school's computer lab to do so. **ACT/P**—After the students have gone through the flash cards and one online game of their choice, the class will go outside and stand in a circle. They will practice shouting the numbers in order as they bounce the ball to pass it around the circle.

DAY #	CONTENT/OBJECTIVE	STANDARDS	RESOURCES/MATERIALS	LEARNING ACTIVITIES/ASSESSMENTS
9	**Unit 1: Vocabulary of Scientific Research and Method—Classification Keys** Given a classification key in table form, students will create a flowchart that displays the information from the chart with 100% accuracy.	Standard 4 (Language of Science) TCAs: 2(3F): Managing and Implementing Standards-Based ESL and Content Instruction 2(3G): Using Resources Effectively in ESL and Content Instruction	Science binders Pencils and drawing tools Classification keys from students' other classes Classification key flowchart example: http://biology-igcse. weebly.com/dichotomous-keys. html Projector	**S**—After ensuring that students understand what a classification key is, show them how to take the table-style classification keys from their science class and turn them into a flowchart like the one at the link listed in resources. **A**—The students will draw pictures to illustrate as many features of their flowcharts as possible. **COLL**—The ESL teacher will gather the classification key tables from the students' teachers in order to make sure the information they are learning correlates with their classes.
10	**Unit 1: United States Encounter, Colonization, and Devastation (1492–1763)** Students will be able to use 20 historical vocabulary words in a sentence with 15/20 accuracy.	Standard 5 (Language of Social Science) TCAs: 2(3F): Managing and Implementing Standards-Based ESL and Content Instruction 2(3G): Using Resources Effectively in ESL and Content Instruction	PowerPoint Projector	**COLL**—This week, the teacher will instruct the students on the terms used within the early history of the United States. The teacher will collaborate with the mainstream 5th grade history teacher to see what vocabulary terms and ideas will be used in the class for the particular unit and the following units. To start off the class about the terms used within the early history of the United States, the teacher will ask the class where they are from. The teacher will emphasize the importance of knowing your personal heritage and then explain why it is important to learn about the history of the United States since that is their new home. **T**—The teacher will present a PowerPoint with 20 common United States Encounter, Colonization, and Devastation terms, and then students will be given the opportunity to find a partner and take turns using these words in a sentence. **DIV**—Students with higher fluency will be paired with a student with lower fluency in order to help them achieve higher fluency. **SS/ASSESS**—The teacher will walk around the room and assess each student's comprehension of the vocabulary terms.

DAY #	CONTENT/OBJECTIVE	STANDARDS	RESOURCES/MATERIALS	LEARNING ACTIVITIES/ASSESSMENTS
11	**Interpersonal Language** Given a casual conversation worksheet, students will answer 9/10 correctly.	Standard 1 (Social & Instructional Language) TCAs: 2(2c): Nature and Role of Culture 2(3F): Managing and Implementing Standards-Based ESL and Content Instruction	A kickball Casual conversation worksheet	**CT**—The teacher will ask students, "What are different types of conversations? Would you talk to a friend differently than you would talk to an adult?" **ACT/P/CE**—The class will then go outside to the playground. The teacher will introduce correct ways to behave in these scenarios: taking turns, asking a friend to do something, having casual conversation vs. polite conversation, knowing when to be loud or quiet. She will explain to the students the importance of having a character that is polite. To practice what they have learned, students will play games, including Quiet Mouse, Still Mouse; Mother May I?; and kickball. After playing, students will go inside and do a matching worksheet, matching correct casual conversation questions with their answers.
12	**Unit 1: Communication: Speaking, Listening, Media** Given the video clips, students will answer 9/10 listening comprehension questions correctly.	Standard 2 (The Language of Language Arts) 2(4J): Classroom-Based Assessment for ESL 2(3G): Using Resources Effectively in ESL and Content Instruction 2(3F): Managing and Implementing Standards-Based ESL and Content Instruction	Computers Headphones Listening comprehension questions	Today, the teacher will give the students an opportunity to increase their listening comprehension. **T**—The students will go to the computer lab and work independently on their listening comprehension through choosing and watching video clips listed on http://www.learnenglishfeelgood.com/eslvideo/ **SS/ASSESS**—After the students have watched each video clip, they will answer the accompanying listening comprehension questions provided on the website.

DAY #	CONTENT/OBJECTIVE	STANDARDS	RESOURCES/MATERIALS	LEARNING ACTIVITIES/ASSESSMENTS
13	**Unit 1: Vocabulary of Operations and Algebraic Thinking—Learning Mathematical Symbols** Given a whiteboard and the names of six math symbols, students will write the symbols on their whiteboards and show the teacher with 6/6 accuracy.	Standard 3 (Language of Mathematics) TCAs: 2(3F): Managing and Implementing Standards-Based ESL and Content Instruction 2(3G): Using Resources Effectively in ESL and Content Instruction	Sets of large foam dice Math symbols flash cards: http://quizlet.com/17725876/math-symbols-used-in-algebra-flash-cards/ Individual whiteboards and markers	**M**—Students will first review their numbers by getting in pairs. Each member of the pair will roll a large foam dice and will call out the number they roll in English. They will then check to make sure the other member of the pair answered correctly. The students will study mathematical symbols (such as +, −, etc.). The teacher will introduce each of the symbols, writing the symbol and its written form (e.g., +, plus) on the board and pronouncing them for the students. Next, the teacher will call out the name of a symbol, and the class will write the symbol on their individual whiteboards. **DIV**—Students with higher levels of English will be paired with students with lower levels of English for the foam-dice review activity at the beginning of class. **ACT/P**—Finally, using the flash cards (to be printed from the link in the resources section), the teacher will lead the students in a game of Around the World. **DIV**—During Around the World, different desks will be labeled with the students' home countries. When the students make it "around the world" and back to their home country, they will win.
14	**Unit 1: Vocabulary of Scientific Research and Method—Metric System** Given a list of terms in English from the metric measuring system, students will define the terms with 100% accuracy.	Standard 4 (Language of Science) TCAs: 2(3F): Managing and Implementing Standards-Based ESL and Content Instruction 2(3G): Using Resources Effectively in ESL and Content Instruction	Science binders Pencils and drawing tools Pocket translators Dictionaries List of metric terms of measurement Instructions for Around the World: http://www.greatgroupgames.com/around-the-world.htm	**S**—The class will focus specifically on defining terms from the metric system. **DIV**—If some students finish before others, the teacher will check their work and then allow them to help other students define terms. **COLL**—The ESL teacher will gather the list of metric terms to use from the students' teachers. **ACT/P**—When students have finished defining all the terms on the list from their teacher, they will play the game Around the World, explained in the link in the resources section. **DIV**—During Around the World, different desks will be labeled with the students' home countries. When the students make it "around the world" and back to their home country, they will win.

DAY #	CONTENT/OBJECTIVE	STANDARDS	RESOURCES/MATERIALS	LEARNING ACTIVITIES/ASSESSMENTS
15	**Unit 1: United States Encounter, Colonization, and Devastation (1492–1763)**	Standard 5 (Language of Social Science) TCAs: 2(3F): Managing and Implementing Standards-Based ESL and Content Instruction 2(3G): Using Resources Effectively in ESL and Content Instruction	Computers Headphones Quizlet: (http://quizlet.com/5484012/us-history-vocab-flash-cards/) SMART Board Wheel of Fortune game	This week, the teacher will work on comprehension of the 20 US History terms covered last week. **T**—Students will take a trip to the computer lab and use Quizlet to review the 20 vocabulary terms learned last week. **ACT/P**—Once students have reviewed the terms using Quizlet, they will play SMART Board Wheel of Fortune. The group will be split into two teams and review the terms they have been practicing.
16	**Days of the Week & Months of the Year** Given a sheet of paper, students will accurately write the names of the seven days of the week.	Standard 2 (The Language of Language Arts) TCAs: 2(3F): Managing and Implementing Standards-Based ESL and Content Instruction 2(3G): Using Resources Effectively in ESL and Content Instruction Standard 1 (Social & Instructional Language)	Days of the Week song: http://www.youtube.com/watch?v=XVN-U-c240I Months of the Year Macarena: http://www.youtube.com/watch?v=lTTrlGx-Ctk Projector	**T/MUS/D/P/ACT**—The teacher will play the days of the week song for the students and they will practice singing it together. Next, they will do the months of the year Macarena together. At the end, the students will practice writing the names of the seven days of the week. **DIV**—Students who are kinesthetic learners will learn through doing the dance, students who are auditory learners will learn through the song, students who are visual learners will learn through seeing the words and pictures.
17	**Unit 1: Communication: Speaking, Listening, Media** Students will be able to name five important things the guest speaker talked about with 100% accuracy.	Standard 2 (The Language of Language Arts) TCAs: 2(3F): Managing and Implementing Standards-Based ESL and Content Instruction 2(3G): Using Resources Effectively in ESL and Content Instruction 2(4J): Classroom-Based Assessment for ESL	Guest speaker	**CT/CE**—The teacher will ask students the questions, "What do you want to be when you grow up?" and "What can you be doing now to help you become what you want to be?" She will guide the class's discussion to teach them the character principles of diligence and hard work. **L/COLL**—The students will have the opportunity to listen to a guest speaker from the community. The guest speaker will be a prominent, successful figure who immigrated to the United States and was even in an ESL classroom setting once. Students will be expected to listen carefully, take notes, and ask the speaker questions. **ASSESS**—After the guest speaker has given his speech, students will be asked to name five important things he talked about during the class.

DAY #	CONTENT/OBJECTIVE	STANDARDS	RESOURCES/MATERIALS	LEARNING ACTIVITIES/ASSESSMENTS
18	**Unit 1: Vocabulary of Operations and Algebraic Thinking—Learning Mathematical Symbols (Continued)** Given individual whiteboards and markers and the names of 10 math symbols, students will write 10/10 correctly.	Standard 3 (Language of Mathematics) TCAs: 2(3F): Managing and Implementing Standards-Based ESL and Content Instruction 2(3G): Using Resources Effectively in ESL and Content Instruction 2(4J): Classroom-Based Assessment for ESL	Advanced Math Symbols flash cards: http://quizlet.com/24420937/5th-grade-common-core-math-vocabulary-flash-cards/ Individual whiteboards and markers Buckets and beanbags to toss for The Bucket Game: http://www.pinterest.com/pin/34340015883267193/	**M**—The teacher will continue to teach math symbols, reviewing the symbols learned in the previous math vocabulary lesson. Then, she will introduce new vocabulary (such as parentheses, etc.). **ACT/P**—The students will play The Bucket Game (explained at the link in the resources section) to review the symbols they've learned. **ASSESS**—Lastly, after the teacher has taught the math symbols, students will be required to write the symbol on their individual whiteboard and hold it up so that the teacher can assess their understanding.
19	**Unit 1: Vocabulary of Scientific Research and Method—The Language of Time** Given a set of time-word flash cards and a time-word list on a picture dictionary, students will play the online ESL games and answer 100% of the questions correctly.	Standard 4 (Language of Science) TCAs: 2(3F): Managing and Implementing Standards-Based ESL and Content Instruction 2(3G): Using Resources Effectively in ESL and Content Instruction	Time flash cards: http://quizlet.com/14401761/esl-time-words-flash-cards/ Time picture dictionary: http://www.anglomaniacy.pl/timeDictionary.htm Time vocabulary games: http://www.eslgamesplus.com/learn-words-and-expressions-of-time-esl-grammar-activity/ http://www.eslgamesplus.com/time-daily-routines-expressions-esl-grammar-sentence-activity/ Time bingo game: http://www.anglomaniacy.pl/timeB.pdf	**S**—In conjunction with learning to estimate time elapsed in their science classes, students will use the online flash cards and picture dictionary listed in the resources section to study time vocabulary. Then, they will play the two online games to review the concepts. Last, if time allows, the class will play Time Bingo all together. **T**—The flash cards and the games used to teach about time are online and will require use of the school's computer lab.

DAY #	CONTENT/OBJECTIVE	STANDARDS	RESOURCES/MATERIALS	LEARNING ACTIVITIES/ASSESSMENTS
20	**Unit 1: United States Encounter, Colonization, and Devastation (1492–1763)** Students will participate in all activities and tell the class their favorite topic from the unit with less than three speaking errors.	Standard 5 (Language of Social Science) TCAs: 2(3F): Managing and Implementing Standards-Based ESL and Content Instruction 2(4J): Classroom-Based Assessment for ESL	Homework from history class	For the first half of class, the teacher will assess the students' needs through allowing them to bring their history homework to class. The teacher will assist students with their homework and assess areas, vocabulary terms, and concepts that students are struggling in. **ACT/COLL**—During the second half of class, students will "think, pair, and share" their favorite topic they've covered during Encounter, Colonization, and Devastation (1492–1763). **SS/ASSESS**—After sharing their favorite topics with a partner, each student will tell the whole class about their favorite topic in two to three sentences.
21	**Signs** Given a matching worksheet with 20 signs and their meanings, they will answer 19/20 correctly.	Standard 1 (Social & Instructional Language) 2(3F): Managing and Implementing Standards-Based ESL and Content Instruction	PowerPoint	**T**—The teacher will give a lesson about common signs using a PowerPoint. The lesson will include traffic signs, pedestrian signs, safety signs, bathroom signs, etc. **CT/CE**—The teacher will ask students "Why is it important to know what signs mean?" and "How do signs help us to be safe?" The teacher will conclude the discussion by teaching students the character principle of obedience, explaining that signs and rules help us and that we should obey them. **ACT**—After learning the different signs, the students will participate in a game to review the different signs. The teacher will put a picture of the sign on the PowerPoint and students will learn a hand motion to represent what the sign means. For instance, the students will stretch forth their hand when the stop sign appears. **ASSESS**—Students will do a matching worksheet with 20 signs and their meanings.

DAY #	CONTENT/OBJECTIVE	STANDARDS	RESOURCES/MATERIALS	LEARNING ACTIVITIES/ASSESSMENTS
22	**Unit 1: Communication: Speaking, Listening** Given five speaking scenarios, students will make less than five speaking errors.	Standard 2 (The Language of Language Arts) TCAs: 2(3F): Managing and Implementing Standards-Based ESL and Content Instruction 2(3G): Using Resources Effectively in ESL and Content Instruction 2(4J): Classroom-Based Assessment for ESL	Scenario cards	**TH**—This week will focus primarily on role-play in learning speaking skills for different situations and if formal or informal language is used in each given scenario. Students will be given cards with five different scenarios: talking to a cashier, talking to a parent, talking to a teacher, talking to a friend, and talking to a waitress. Students will be split into pairs and with each scenario they will switch roles. **DIV**—The teacher will ask students, "How do you speak to elders in your home country?" The students will then share their customs for speaking to older people. **L/ASSESS**—The teacher will walk around the room and assess the students' comprehension of the material and correct any incorrect sentences.
23	**Unit 1: Vocabulary of Operations and Algebraic Thinking— Coordinate Planes** Given a life-size coordinate plane and directions called out by the teacher, each student will locate at least two points or sections on the plane with 100% accuracy.	Standard 3 (Language of Mathematics) TCAs: 2(3F): Managing and Implementing Standards-Based ESL and Content Instruction 2(3G): Using Resources Effectively in ESL and Content Instruction	Life-size coordinate plane: http://www.pinterest.com/pin/408701734906236827/ Notebooks Pencils and erasers	**M**—The teacher will introduce the vocabulary of coordinate planes (x-axis, y-axis, etc.). She will draw and label each important section on the whiteboard, and students will draw and label in notebooks simultaneously. **ACT/P**—The students will divide into teams and take turns walking to the correct sections of a life-size coordinate plane (made out of painter's tape, masking tape, or sidewalk chalk) as the teacher calls them out.
24	**Unit 1: Vocabulary of Scientific Research and Method—Review Day** Given a study guide and review games, students will memorize the key Vocabulary words from Unit 1 with 100% accuracy.	Standard 4 (Language of Science) TCAs: 2(3F): Managing and Implementing Standards-Based ESL and Content Instruction 2(3G): Using Resources Effectively in ESL and Content Instruction	Study guide Around the World game Love, War, and Lightning PowerPoint game: http://www.teacherspayteachers.com/Product/Love-War-and-Lightning-Review-Game-Template-351559 Projector	**S**—The teacher will guide the students in filling in the answers on a study guide. The study guide will consist of vocabulary from the metric system, from time words, and from the students' self-selected vocabulary words in their binders. **ACT**—Then, the class will play Around the World and Love, War, and Lightning to review. **DIV**—During Around the World, different desks will be labeled with the students' home countries. When the students make it "around the world" and back to their home country, they will win.

DAY #	CONTENT/OBJECTIVE	STANDARDS	RESOURCES/MATERIALS	LEARNING ACTIVITIES/ASSESSMENTS
25	**Unit 1: United States Encounter, Colonization, and Devastation (1492–1763)** Students in Group 1 will define 9/10 words accurately. Students in Group 2 are missing less than two country names. Students in Group 3 will	Standard 5 (Language of Social Science) TCAs: 2(3F): Managing and Implementing Standards-Based ESL and Content Instruction 2(3G): Using Resources Effectively in ESL and Content Instruction 2(4J): Classroom-Based Assessment for ESL	Computers Headphones Web Quest: http://zunal.com/tasks.php?w=231516	The students will go to the computer lab and participate in a Web Quest about Christopher Columbus. First, students will go to the computer lab and split into three different groups. The groups will work together to complete the different assigned tasks. **SS/ASSESS**—Group 1 will find the definitions of vocabulary words related to Christopher Columbus. Group 2 will find the names of all the countries that Christopher Columbus traveled to, as well as the country where he was born and the country that he thought he was travelling to. Group 3 will find key dates in Christopher Columbus' life and present them in sentences using the correct past tense. **D/P**—Each group will present the information they found to the class. They will also choreograph a "discovery dance" to celebrate their findings during the WebQuest. **DIV**—Kinesthetic learners will learn through choreographing the dance, auditory learners will be able to learn through listening to the song, visual learners will be able to learn through the information seen on the computer screen.
26	**Types of Food in Different Cultures** Given instruction on how to correctly use "different than" and "like" in sentences and given blank exit tickets, students will correctly write 2/2 sentences using these structures.	Standard 1 (Social & Instructional Language) TCAs: 2(2c): Nature and Role of Culture 2(2d): Cultural Group and Identity 2(3F): Managing and Implementing Standards-Based ESL and Content Instruction	A rug Pillows Blank exit tickets	Students will sit on the floor and discuss types of food in America and in their own countries. They will talk about what is different, what is the same, what they like, and what they do not like. **H**—They will also discuss what types of food are healthy and are not healthy. The teacher will instruct them to use the structures, "____ is different than ____ because ____" and "____ is like ____ because ____". **CT/COLL**—The students with different tastes will have a debate. In the mini-debate, students with similar tastes will get into groups and work together to come up with two reasons why they like or dislike the chosen food. They will then present these reasons to the class. **CE**—Respect: the teacher will explain to the students the importance of being respectful toward other cultures and their customs, even when they are different. She will teach students that it is okay to be different and to not think the same way or like the same things, but that it is not okay to be disrespectful. At the end of class, students will write on exit tickets one sentence using "different than" and one sentence using "like" correctly.

DAY #	CONTENT/OBJECTIVE	STANDARDS	RESOURCES/MATERIALS	LEARNING ACTIVITIES/ASSESSMENTS
27	**Unit 1: Communication: Speaking, Listening** Given the grading rubric and video recording equipment, students will successfully produce a short video with five or less speaking mistakes.	Standard 2 (The Language of Language Arts) TCAs: 2(3F): Managing and Implementing Standards-Based ESL and Content Instruction 2(3G): Using Resources Effectively in ESL and Content Instruction 2(4J): Classroom-Based Assessment for ESL	Video camera	**TH**—The teacher will announce the assessment for the speaking and listening unit. With the assistance of the teacher, students will be split into four groups to produce their own video in which each group member will have a speaking role. The groups will have three options for their movie: Who Is My Hero?, Why 5th Grade Is the Best, or What I Want to Be When I Grow Up. **ASSESS**—The students will begin working on their unit project. They will listen to the teacher's instructions carefully, then begin discussing options for their project with their group members. The teacher will also equip the students with a rubric so they will know how they are going to be graded.
28	**Unit 1: Vocabulary of Operations and Algebraic Thinking—Review Day** Given a study guide with 10 blanks, students will fill them in with 10/10 accuracy.	Standard 3 (Language of Mathematics) TCAs: 2(3F): Managing and Implementing Standards-Based ESL and Content Instruction 2(3G): Using Resources Effectively in ESL and Content Instruction	Flash cards: http://quizlet.com/16864532/flashcards http://quizlet.com/17725876/math-symbols-used-in-algebra-flash-cards/ http://quizlet.com/24420937/5th-grade-common-core-math-vocabulary-flash-cards/ http://quizlet.com/17087701/coordinate-plane-vocabulary-slope-equations-flash-cards/	**M**—The teacher will create three stations in the room: one focused on numbers, one focused on math symbols, one focused on coordinate planes. She will divide the students into three groups and give them each 10 minutes at each station before calling for them to rotate. At the station, students will quiz each other on the flash cards. They will sit in a circle and one student will hold up a flash card; the student to their left will say the answer. If they are correct, the card is put in a "discard" pile. If they are incorrect, the card is put at the bottom of the question pile. The person who attempted to answer the card will then hold the next card up for the person on their left, and so on until their 15 minutes are complete. At the end of their time doing the flash card stations, students will fill in 10 blanks on a study guide.

DAY #	CONTENT/OBJECTIVE	STANDARDS	RESOURCES/MATERIALS	LEARNING ACTIVITIES/ASSESSMENTS
29	**Unit 1: Vocabulary of Scientific Research and Method—Assessment Day** Given a test with 25 questions, students will match, write, and circle definitions of vocabulary words with 25/25 accuracy.	Standard 4 (Language of Science) TCAs: 2(3F): Managing and Implementing Standards-Based ESL and Content Instruction 2(4J): Classroom-Based Assessment for ESL	Test of 25 questions	**S/ASSESS**—Students will take a test with different types of questions (matching, circling, true-false, writing definitions) to assess whether they have accurately learned the vocabulary from Unit 1.
30	**Unit 1: United States Encounter, Colonization, and Devastation (1492—1763)** Given an exam over the vocabulary terms and concepts covered, students will answer 19/20 questions correctly.	Standard 5 (Language of Social Science) TCAs: 2(3F): Managing and Implementing Standards-Based ESL and Content Instruction 2(4J): Classroom-Based Assessment for ESL	Quiz	**SS/ASSESS**—Students will take a 20-question quiz on the vocabulary terms they have been learning. The quiz will include matching, multiple-choice, and five vocabulary words they must use in a sentence.
31	**Transportation** Given a map and two locations, students will tell a partner how to get to both locations from a starting point on the map.	Standard 1 (Social & Instructional Language) TCAs: 2(2c): Nature and Role of Culture 2(3F): Managing and Implementing Standards-Based ESL and Content Instruction	PowerPoint with pictures Maps Projector	The teacher will teach students the names of different types of transportation (e.g., bus, taxi, car, airplane, train, bicycle, etc.). **CT/DIV**—The teacher will ask the class, "Which transportation is most common in the United States?" and "Which transportation is most common in your home country?" The students will then talk about why certain types of transportation are more popular in different places. Students will then learn how to use a map to give and receive directions.

DAY #	CONTENT/OBJECTIVE	STANDARDS	RESOURCES/MATERIALS	LEARNING ACTIVITIES/ASSESSMENTS
32	**Unit 1: Communication: Speaking, Listening** Given the grading rubric and video recording equipment, students will successfully produce a short video with five or less speaking mistakes.	Standard 2 (The Language of Language Arts) TCAs: 2(3F): Managing and Implementing Standards-Based ESL and Content Instruction 2(3G): Using Resources Effectively in ESL and Content Instruction	Video camera Note cards Construction paper, markers, glitter, and crayons	**A**—Student will be given time to create props for their video using construction paper, markers, glitter, and crayons. They will also be given time to write out note cards to help them remember their lines during the presentation. **TH**—Students will begin acting and creating their video. The teacher will assist the students in filming.
33	**Unit 1: Vocabulary of Operations and Algebraic Thinking—Assessment Day** Given a test with 25 questions, students will match, write, and circle definitions of vocabulary words with 100% accuracy.	Standard 3 (Language of Mathematics) TCAs: 2(3F): Managing and Implementing Standards-Based ESL and Content Instruction	Test of 25 questions	**M/ASSESS**—The students will take a 25-question test over the information in Unit 1. **CE**—Before the test begins, the teacher will give a short explanation of honesty and integrity, explaining why they are important character principles and how they relate to test-taking. After all the students have taken the test, the teacher will go over the answers with them immediately, answering any questions.
34	**BEGINNING OF UNIT 2: Vocabulary of Sound and Light: Introduction** Given a worksheet with seven blanks, students will fill them in with 7/7 accuracy.	Standard 4 (Language of Science) TCAs: 2(3F): Managing and Implementing Standards-Based ESL and Content Instruction	Science binders Pencils and drawing tools Pocket translators Dictionaries	**S**—The teacher will start with a review of the vocabulary words from Unit 1. She will ask students to raise their hands and explain what each word means. Next, the teacher will introduce the new unit: sound and light. She will teach the students the definitions of the basic vocabulary they need to know for the unit (including waves, wavelengths, etc.). The students will follow along, filling in seven blanks on a worksheet. The teacher will check at the end of the lesson to make sure they have filled in the blanks accurately.

DAY #	CONTENT/OBJECTIVE	STANDARDS	RESOURCES/MATERIALS	LEARNING ACTIVITIES/ASSESSMENTS
35	**Unit 1: United States Encounter, Colonization, and Devastation (1492–1763)** Given five questions about vocabulary terms and concepts, students will answer 4/5 correctly.	Standard 5 (Language of Social Science) TCAs: 2(3F): Managing and Implementing Standards-Based ESL and Content Instruction 2(3G): Using Resources Effectively in ESL and Content Instruction 2(4J): Classroom-Based Assessment for ESL	Note cards Colored pencils SMART Board	**A**—The students will have the opportunity to continue to listen to the John Adams audiobook while writing the next set of vocabulary terms on note cards. The students will be given clear instruction to write the vocabulary term and picture on one side of the card and the definition on the other side of the card. **COLL**—After the students have written the terms on note cards, they will have the opportunity to split into pairs and quiz each other on the new vocabulary terms. The teacher will walk around the room to assess the students' comprehension of the new vocabulary terms and answer any possible questions. **SS/ASSESS**—Once the students have reviewed the terms, they will play Around the World. **DIV**—During Around the World, different desks will be labeled with the students' home countries. When the students make it "around the world" and back to their home country, they win.
36	**Going to the Movies & Ordering at a Restaurant** Given a blank exit ticket, students will write down three sentences they learned in class with zero errors.	Standard 1 (Social & Instructional Language) TCAs: 2(2c): Nature and Role of Culture 2(3F): Managing and Implementing Standards-Based ESL and Content Instruction 2(4J): Classroom-Based Assessment for ESL	Pictures of movie posters Pictures of restaurants Blank exit tickets	The teacher will teach the students some key words about going to see a movie and ordering at a restaurant. **TH/COLL**—Then, students will role-play a restaurant and movie theatre, switching off roles. **ASSESS**—When they are done role-playing, they will write down three sentences they learned on an exit ticket for the teacher.

DAY #	CONTENT/OBJECTIVE	STANDARDS	RESOURCES/MATERIALS	LEARNING ACTIVITIES/ASSESSMENTS
37	**Unit 1: Communication: Speaking, Listening** Given the grading rubric and video recording equipment, students will successfully produce a short video with five or less speaking mistakes.	Standard 2 (The Language of Language Arts) TCAs: 2(3F): Managing and Implementing Standards-Based ESL and Content Instruction 2(3G): Using Resources Effectively in ESL and Content Instruction	Video camera Note cards Props	**T**—The students will finish recording and editing their videos. The groups will be given the opportunity to watch their video and decide if they would like to make any changes before presenting the video to the class the following week.
38	**BEGINNING OF UNIT 2: Vocabulary of Big Numbers and the Decimal System: Introduction and Numbers in the Thousands** Given a blank exit ticket, students will accurately write 3/3 numbers that the teacher reads to them.	Standard 3 (Language of Mathematics) TCAs: 2(3F): Managing and Implementing Standards-Based ESL and Content Instruction 2(4J): Classroom-Based Assessment for ESL	Buckets and bean bags for The Bucket Game Blank exit tickets	**M**—After reviewing the information from the last class, the teacher will introduce the concept of decimals. She will explain that in America, "big numbers" (such as thousands, millions, and billions) are separated with commas, not decimal points. She will then teach students how to say numbers in the thousands. **ACT/P**—Students will review numbers in the thousands playing The Bucket Game. **ASSESS**—Before students leave, the teacher will read three big numbers to the students and ask them to write them down on an exit ticket. **DIV**—Students with ADHD will have the opportunity to stand during the activities.
39	**Unit 2: Vocabulary of Sound and Light: Sound and Light Waves Introduction Song**	Standard 4 (Language of Science) TCAs: 2(3F): Managing and Implementing Standards-Based ESL and Content Instruction 2(3G): Using Resources Effectively in ESL and Content Instruction	Love, War, and Lightning PowerPoint game: http://www.teacherspayteachers.com/Product/Love-War-and-Lightning-Review-Game-Template-351559 "Sound & Light Waves" video: http://www.youtube.com/watch?v=YNE6zeLqEyU Projector	**S**—After working through any new words in the students' science journals, students will play the Love, War, and Lightning PowerPoint game to review the vocabulary that they learned on the introduction day of the unit. **CT/CE**—The teacher will ask students "Why is it important to know how light and sound work?" The students will share their answer with a partner. Then, the teacher will teach students that wisdom means "knowledge applied" and will introduce to them the character principles of loving to learn and of wisdom. **ACT/T/MUS/D/P**—The teacher will introduce the "Sound & Light Waves" video, giving the students the lyrics to look at. She will divide them into groups to start learning the dance moves step-by-step.

DAY #	CONTENT/OBJECTIVE	STANDARDS	RESOURCES/MATERIALS	LEARNING ACTIVITIES/ASSESSMENTS
40	**Unit 1: United States Encounter, Colonization, and Devastation (1492–1763)**	Standard 5 (Language of Social Science) TCAs: 2(3F): Managing and Implementing Standards-Based ESL and Content Instruction 2(3G): Using Resources Effectively in ESL and Content Instruction	Quizlet: (http://quizlet.com/5484012/us-history-vocab-flash-cards/) SMART Board Who Wants to Be a Millionaire game	**T**—Today, the students will go to the computer lab. At the computer lab, the students will review the new vocabulary terms through playing games on Quizlet. **T**—After the students have reviewed the terms on Quizlet, they will have the opportunity to participate in a SMART Board game of Who Wants to Be a Millionaire? The students will also be reminded to study for their vocabulary test the following week.
41	**Proper Field Trip Behavior** Given five expected behaviors, the students will accurately role-play 5/5 behaviors.	Standard 1 (Social & Instructional Language) TCAs: 2(2c): Nature and Role of Culture 2(3F): Managing and Implementing Standards-Based ESL and Content Instruction		The teacher will explain to students what behavior is expected of them when they go on a field trip the following week. **CT/COLL/CE**—The teacher will ask the class, "Why do you think good behavior is important?" and "How does behavior affect safety?" Each student will get together with a partner to discuss behavior. The teacher will remind them after their discussion of the character principle of obedience and how it relates to safety. **ACT/TH**—The students will role-play proper field trip behavior.
42	**Unit 1: Communication: Speaking, Listening** Given the grading rubric and materials needed for creating the video, students will create a video meeting 5/5 requirements listed on the rubric.	Standard 2 (The Language of Language Arts) TCAs: 2(3F): Managing and Implementing Standards-Based ESL and Content Instruction 2(4J): Classroom-Based Assessment for ESL	Test	**T**—The students will have the opportunity to watch the videos that each group created. The teacher will bring in snacks for the class to share as a celebration of their huge accomplishment. **L/ASSESS**—The teacher will use the grading rubric given to the students to assess each group's video.

DAY #	CONTENT/OBJECTIVE	STANDARDS	RESOURCES/MATERIALS	LEARNING ACTIVITIES/ASSESSMENTS
43	**Unit 2: Vocabulary of Big Numbers and the Decimal System: Numbers in the Millions** Given a blank exit ticket, students will accurately write 3/3 "millions" numbers.	Standard 3 (Language of Mathematics) TCAs: 2(3F): Managing and Implementing Standards-Based ESL and Content Instruction	Deck of UNO cards Dice Blank exit tickets	**M**—After reviewing numbers in the thousands, the teacher will introduce numbers in the millions, teaching students how to say them. Students will review the numbers by playing a game where they roll two dice and then flip over UNO cards next to each other until they have the number of cards laid out that they rolled on the dice. Then, they pretend that the cards next to each other are one big number and pronounce the name of the number. Last, the teacher will read off three numbers in the millions, asking students to accurately write them on an exit ticket.
44	**Unit 2: Vocabulary of Sound and Light: Visible Light** Given science binders, drawing supplies, and the names of the colors in the visible light spectrum, students will draw rainbows and accurately label 7/7 colors.	Standard 4 (Language of Science) TCAs: 2(3F): Managing and Implementing Standards-Based ESL and Content Instruction	Science binders Drawing supplies Paper "Sound & Light Waves" video	**S**—The teacher will introduce the visible light spectrum and the names of its colors to the students. She will use the acronym "ROY G. BIV" to help the students remember the orders of the colors. **A**—The students will then color rainbows in their science binders and label the colors with their English names. **T/MUS/D**—The teacher will again play the "Sound & Light Waves" video and students will practice singing along and doing the dance moves again.
45	**Unit 1: United States Encounter, Colonization, and Devastation (1492–1763)** Given an exam over the vocabulary terms and concepts covered, students will answer 19/20 questions correctly.	Standard 5 (Language of Social Science) TCAs: 2(3F): Managing and Implementing Standards-Based ESL and Content Instruction 2(4J): Classroom-Based Assessment for ESL	Quiz	**SS/ASSESS**—Students will take a 20-question test on the vocabulary terms they have been learning. The test will include matching, multiple-choice, and five vocabulary words they must use in a sentence.

DAY #	CONTENT/OBJECTIVE	STANDARDS	RESOURCES/MATERIALS	LEARNING ACTIVITIES/ASSESSMENTS
46	**Field Trip: Lunch and a Movie** Given a list of 20 vocabulary words, students will look and listen to see and hear at least 10 of the 20 while they are on their field trip.	Standard 1 (Social & Instructional Language) TCAs: 2(2c): Nature and Role of Culture 2(3F): Managing and Implementing Standards-Based ESL and Content Instruction	Transportation for a field trip to the movies and a restaurant Chaperones	In order to give students real-life practice ordering in a restaurant and buying tickets at the movies, the class will go to lunch and to see a movie. **COLL**—The teacher will ask parents and members of her Sunday School class to accompany her as chaperones. **CT/CE**: The teacher will remind students to be polite to their waiter or waitress. She will then ask students "Why is it important to be polite?" "Why is it important to appreciate others?" and "How do you feel when you are appreciated?" The students will then have the opportunity to share their answer with the teacher. Students will be given a checklist with 20 key vocabulary words and will have to look and listen for them while they are out. **DIV**—Advanced students will have the opportunity to receive more challenging words for their vocabulary terms.
47	**BEGINNING OF UNIT 2: Reading Comprehension** Given the pre-assessment, students will answer 75% of the questions correctly.	Standard 2 (The Language of Language Arts) TCAs: 2(3F): Managing and Implementing Standards-Based ESL and Content Instruction 2(3G): Using Resources Effectively in ESL and Content Instruction 2(4J): Classroom-Based Assessment for ESL	Pre-Assessment	**L/ASSESS**—The students will be given an end of the year, 4th grade reading comprehension exam. The teacher will use this exam to assess the students' current reading comprehension and target areas students may be struggling in.
48	**Unit 2: Vocabulary of Big Numbers and the Decimal System: Numbers in the Billions** Given blank exit tickets, students will accurately write 3/3 "billions" numbers that the teacher reads.	Standard 3 (Language of Mathematics) TCAs: 2(3F): Managing and Implementing Standards-Based ESL and Content Instruction	"Billions" worksheets Deck of UNO cards Dice Blank exit tickets	**M**—The teacher will explain numbers in the billions, and students will fill out a worksheet inserting commas where they belong in the billions. They will also play the UNO review game. At the end of class, students will write three numbers that the teacher reads on exit tickets.

DAY #	CONTENT/OBJECTIVE	STANDARDS	RESOURCES/MATERIALS	LEARNING ACTIVITIES/ASSESSMENTS
49	**Unit 2: Vocabulary of Sound and Light: Opacity** Given a definition of the terms related to opacity, a classroom full of objects, and a Bingo chart, students will accurately find and label the opacity of 12/12 objects.	Standard 4 (Language of Science) TCAs: 2(3F): Managing and Implementing Standards-Based ESL and Content Instruction 2(3G): Using Resources Effectively in ESL and Content Instruction	Opacity cards: http://www.doe.virginia.gov/testing/sol/standards_docs/science/2010/lesson_plans/grade5/force_motion_energy/sess_5.3c.pdf "Sound & Light Waves" video	**S**—After reviewing the names of the colors with the students and defining any words the students have written in their notebooks, the teacher will teach the difference between the terms opaque, translucent, and transparent. Students will glue the definitions from the Opacity Cards link in the resources section into their science notebooks. **ACT**—Then, they will use the Bingo-type chart at the link to have a scavenger hunt within the classroom to find four objects of each type within the classroom (a total of 12 objects). **T/MUS/D/P**—The teacher will again play the "Sound & Light Waves" video and students will practice singing along and doing the dance moves again.
50	**BEGINNING OF UNIT 2: United States Independence (1763–1791)**	Standard 5 (Language of Social Science) TCAs: 2(3F): Managing and Implementing Standards-Based ESL and Content Instruction 2(3G): Using Resources Effectively in ESL and Content Instruction	PowerPoint Music video: http://youtu.be/uZFRaWAtBVg Projector	**COLL**—The teacher will collaborate with the mainstream 5th grade history teacher to see what vocabulary terms and ideas will be used in the class for the particular unit and assess particular concepts that may be difficult for ESL students. **M**—To spark the students' interest in independence, the teacher will play the music video "Too Late to Apologize: A Declaration": http://youtu.be/uZFRaWAtBVg **SS**—Students will be asked what they think "independence" means and what independence meant for the United States. They will then have the opportunity of sharing their thoughts about what independence means with a partner. The teacher will walk around the room and evaluate the students' understanding of the concept. **T**—After the students have discussed the meaning of independence, the teacher will use a PowerPoint to portray the new vocabulary and concepts for this history unit.
51	**Going to the Mall** Given the opportunity to go to the mall, students will participate in 100% of the activities.	Standard 1 (Social & Instructional Language) TCAs: 2(2c): Nature and Role of Culture 2(3F): Managing and Implementing Standards-Based ESL and Content Instruction	Bus/transportation $5	**ACT**—Students will take a field trip to the mall. The teacher will demonstrate and teach appropriate casual conversation to use with friends while spending time at the mall. **M/CE**—Students will also have the opportunity to buy something small from the mall. Students will choose the correct amount of money to give the cashier and also count their change. The teacher will explain to the students the character principle of honesty in how it relates to returning extra money if the clerk overpays you.

DAY #	CONTENT/OBJECTIVE	STANDARDS	RESOURCES/MATERIALS	LEARNING ACTIVITIES/ASSESSMENTS
52	**Unit 2: Reading Comprehension**	Standard 2 (The Language of Language Arts) TCAs: 2(3F): Managing and Implementing Standards-Based ESL and Content Instruction	Homework	The teacher will use a PowerPoint to teach the students various helpful reading strategies. **L**—The students will work on their reading comprehension by bringing their reading homework from other classes and practicing reading strategies while doing their homework. The teacher will walk around the room to assist students and ask comprehension questions as they read.
53	**Unit 2: Vocabulary of Big Numbers and the Decimal System: Decimals to the Hundredth** Given individual whiteboards and markers, students will accurately write 5/5 numbers with decimals to the hundredth place as the teacher calls them out.	Standard 3 (Language of Mathematics) TCAs: 2(3F): Managing and Implementing Standards-Based ESL and Content Instruction	Individual whiteboards and markers	**M**—The teacher will teach students decimals to the hundredth place. To review, the teacher will call out numbers and students will hold up the written form on their whiteboards. Then, they will play Around the World as the teacher shows students written numbers and asks them to say the name of the number. **DIV**—During around the world, different desks will be labeled with the students' home countries. When the students make it "around the world" and back to their home country, they will win.
54	**Unit 2: Vocabulary of Sound and Light: Review Day** Given a fill-in-the-blank worksheet with key vocabulary missing from the "Sound & Light Waves" lyrics, the students will fill in the missing vocabulary words with 20/20 being correct.	Standard 4 (Language of Science) TCAs: 2(3F): Managing and Implementing Standards-Based ESL and Content Instruction	"Love, War, and Lightning" PowerPoint "Sound & Light Waves" video Fill-in-the-blank worksheet of the lyrics to the "Sound & Light Waves" song	**S**—Students will review their key vocabulary through playing the Love, War, and Lightning game. **T/MUS/D/P**—The teacher will again play the "Sound & Light Waves" video. Students will practice singing and dancing in their groups and then fill in a fill-in-the-blank worksheet of the lyrics to the song.

DAY #	CONTENT/OBJECTIVE	STANDARDS	RESOURCES/MATERIALS	LEARNING ACTIVITIES/ASSESSMENTS
55	Unit 2: United States Independence (1763–1791)	Standard 5 (Language of Social Science) TCAs: 2(3F): Managing and Implementing Standards-Based ESL and Content Instruction 2(3G): Using Resources Effectively in ESL and Content Instruction	Quizlet: (http://quizlet.com/5484012/us-history-vocab-flash-cards/) SMART Board Bingo game	CT—The teacher will ask students to remember the meaning of independence. She will ask them "Why is independence important?" Then she will give the class an opportunity to write a thank-you note to a veteran thanking them for keeping our nation free. T—The students will go to the computer lab. At the computer lab, the students will review the new vocabulary terms through playing games on Quizlet. T—After the students have reviewed the terms on Quizlet, they will have the opportunity to participate in a SMART Board game of Bingo. Students will split into two teams to compete in the game. The students will also be reminded to study for their vocabulary quiz the following week.
56	Favorite Sports Given a worksheet with 20 sporting vocabulary items, students will match 19/20 items correctly.	Standard 1 (Social & Instructional Language) TCAs: 2(2c): Nature and Role of Culture 2(3F): Managing and Implementing Standards-Based ESL and Content Instruction 2(4J): Classroom-Based Assessment for ESL	Soccer ball Basketball Kickball	H/CE—The teacher will instruct students on different vocabulary terms used for sporting events. She will point out the importance of being active through things like sports in order to maintain a healthy lifestyle. She will also teach them the character principle of good sportsmanship. COLL—The students will also have an opportunity to discuss their favorite sport with a partner. ASSESS—After the students have learned the vocabulary terms associated with sporting events, they will match 20 sporting vocabulary terms. ACT—After students have completed their matching worksheet, they will have the opportunity to go outside and play soccer, basketball, or kickball.
57	Unit 2: Reading Comprehension	Standard 2 (The Language of Language Arts) TCAs: 2(3F): Managing and Implementing Standards-Based ESL and Content Instruction 2(3G): Using Resources Effectively in ESL and Content Instruction	Computers Headphones: http://www.funenglishgames.com/readinggames.html http://www.jumpstart.com/parents/games/reading-games http://mrnussbaum.com/readingpassageindex/	T—The students will have an opportunity to go to the computer lab to work on their reading comprehension. Students will be able to choose to visit one of the following websites to play reading comprehension games: http://www.funenglishgames.com/readinggames.html http://www.jumpstart.com/parents/games/reading-games http://mrnussbaum.com/readingpassageindex/

DAY #	CONTENT/OBJECTIVE	STANDARDS	RESOURCES/MATERIALS	LEARNING ACTIVITIES/ASSESSMENTS
58	**Unit 2: Vocabulary of Big Numbers and the Decimal System: Decimals to the Hundredth** Given individual whiteboards and markers, students will accurately write 5/5 numbers with decimals to the thousandth place as the teacher calls them out.	Standard 3 (Language of Mathematics) TCAs: 2(3F): Managing and Implementing Standards-Based ESL and Content Instruction	Individual whiteboards and markers	M—The teacher will teach students decimals to the thousandth place. To review, the teacher will call out numbers and students will hold up the written form on their whiteboards. Then, they will play Around the World as the teacher shows students written numbers and asks them to say the name of the number. DIV—During Around the World, different desks will be labeled with the students' home countries. When the students make it "around the world" and back to their home country, they will win.
59	**Unit 2: Vocabulary of Sound and Light: Assessment Day** Given 20 key vocabulary terms, students will define 20/20 correctly.	Standard 4 (Language of Science) TCAs: 2(3F): Managing and Implementing Standards-Based ESL and Content Instruction	Test with a list of 20 key vocabulary terms	ASSESS—Students will take a test in which they must define 20 key vocabulary terms. DIV—They may write the English definition of the word, write the word's translation in their native language, or draw a picture that accurately shows the meaning of the word. ACT—The students will perform the "Sound & Light Waves" song together.
60	**Unit 2: United States Independence (1763–1791)** Given a quiz over the vocabulary terms and concepts covered, students will answer 19/20 questions correctly.	Standard 5 (Language of Social Science) TCAs: 2(3F): Managing and Implementing Standards-Based ESL and Content Instruction 2(4J): Classroom-Based Assessment for ESL	Quiz	SS/ASSESS—Students will take a 20-question test on the vocabulary terms they have been learning. The test will include matching, multiple-choice, and five vocabulary words they must use in a sentence.

DAY #	CONTENT/OBJECTIVE	STANDARDS	RESOURCES/MATERIALS	LEARNING ACTIVITIES/ASSESSMENTS
61	**Chores** Given five chores in the Let's Get Clean game, the students will participate and help in finishing all five chores.	Standard 1 (Social & Instructional Language) 2(3F): Managing and Implementing Standards-Based ESL and Content Instruction	Vacuum cleaner Window cleaner Paper towels Dish detergent Multipurpose cleaner	**T**—Using a PowerPoint, the teacher will review common chores. **COLL/DIV**—The teacher will divide students into five groups for conversation. After the students have been placed in groups, they will share the chores they are responsible for in their home. They will also share the names for different chores in their native language. **ACT**—The students will learn about household chores during this lesson. At the end of the lesson, they will participate in the Let's Get Clean game in which each group will be assigned a chore. The team who finishes their chore most thoroughly will win! **CE/CT**—The teacher will ask students "Why is helping others important?" and "How can you help with chores?" The students will learn about helping others through helping their parents with household chores.
62	**Unit 2: Reading Comprehension** Given 10 review questions regarding fiction and non-fiction on the Wheel of Fortune game, students will be able to answer 9/10 questions correctly.	Standard 2 (The Language of Language Arts) TCAs: 2(3F): Managing and Implementing Standards-Based ESL and Content Instruction 2(3G): Using Resources Effectively in ESL and Content Instruction	SMART Board PowerPoint Review questions	**LA**—Students will learn to distinguish the differences between fiction and non-fiction literature. The teacher will give a PowerPoint presentation about the differences between fiction and non-fiction. **ASSESS**—The students will be split into two teams to play a SMART Board Wheel of Fortune game to review the differences between fiction and non-fiction. Once the students have finished playing the game, they will fill out a chart marking the differences between fiction and non-fiction. Students will be instructed to study the chart for a quiz the following week.
63	**Unit 2: Vocabulary of Big Numbers and the Decimal System: Review Day** Given a study guide with blanks, students will fill in the blanks with 20/20 accuracy.	Standard 3 (Language of Mathematics) TCAs: 2(3F): Managing and Implementing Standards-Based ESL and Content Instruction	Buckets and bean bags Study guide	**M**—The teacher will review the key facts that students need to know for their test the following week. She will give them a study guide with 20 blank terms and the class will fill in the blanks together. **ACT**—Students will play The Bucket Game to review as well.

DAY #	CONTENT/OBJECTIVE	STANDARDS	RESOURCES/MATERIALS	LEARNING ACTIVITIES/ASSESSMENTS
64	**BEGINNING OF UNIT 3: Vocabulary of Matter: Introduction—Definition of Mass & The Phases** Given a set of objects, students will accurately identify whether they are solid, liquid, or gas with 5/5 accuracy.	Standard 4 (Language of Science) TCAs: 2(3F): Managing and Implementing Standards-Based ESL and Content Instruction 2(3G): Using Resources Effectively in ESL and Content Instruction	Science binders "States of Matter" video: http://www.brainpop.com/science/matterandchemistry/statesofmatter/ Projector	**S/T**—The teacher will introduce the states of matter by playing the "States of Matter" video (in the resources section). Over the entirety of Unit 3, she will break down the content of the video, focusing on a different section each day. For the first day, she will use examples of different types of substances in the room (e.g., water, a book, a balloon filled with gas, etc.) to help the students recognize the differences between the three states of matter. The students then will have to identify the objects on their own.
65	**Unit 2: United States Independence (1763–1791)** Given the resources about locations to visit in Philadelphia, students will be able to write five sentences about their favorite location with five or less writing errors.	Standard 5 (Language of Social Science) TCAs: 2(3F): Managing and Implementing Standards-Based ESL and Content Instruction 2(3G): Using Resources Effectively in ESL and Content Instruction	Computers Educational websites: http://www.visitphilly.com/ http://www.visitphilly.com/history/philadelphia/independence-hall/ http://www.visitphilly.com/museums-attractions/philadelphia/national-constitution-center/ http://www.visitphilly.com/history/philadelphia/valley-forge-national-historical-park/ http://www.ushistory.org/libertybell/	**T/SS**—Students will go to the computer lab to prepare for their field trip next week. They will be preparing for a trip to Philadelphia with the rest of their history class to observe important locations and documents relevant to independence in the United States. The class will be researching important facts about the places they will be visiting. They will be able to research using the following websites: http://www.visitphilly.com/ http://www.visitphilly.com/history/philadelphia/independence-hall/ http://www.visitphilly.com/museums-attractions/philadelphia/national-constitution-center/ http://www.visitphilly.com/history/philadelphia/valley-forge-national-historical-park/ http://www.ushistory.org/libertybell/ **LA**—Students will also write down five factual sentences about their favorite historical sight. **M**—To spark the students' interest in independence, the teacher will play the music video "Too Late to Apologize: A Declaration" again: http://youtu.be/uZFRaWAtBVg

DAY #	CONTENT/OBJECTIVE	STANDARDS	RESOURCES/MATERIALS	LEARNING ACTIVITIES/ASSESSMENTS
66	**Making a Phone Call** Given 12 sentences, each containing one error in phone etiquette or grammar, the students will correct the mistakes with 12/12 accuracy.	Standard 1 (Social & Instructional Language) TCAs: 2(2c): Nature and Role of Culture 2(3F): Managing and Implementing Standards-Based ESL and Content Instruction	*All Clear Listening and Speaking 1* Textbook and audio CD	The students will listen to the audio CD recording of the dialogue from page 20 of *All Clear Listening and Speaking 1*. Then, the teacher will ask the class the questions listed on page 20. **COLL**—As directed by the textbook on page 21, the students will divide into pairs and practice saying the dialogue to each other. The teacher will explain, using pages 21–23, what things are polite and impolite to say on the telephone. **CT/CE**—The teacher will ask students "Why is it important to be polite?" and "How do you feel when someone is rude to you?""Why is it important to be polite?" Finally, the students will complete the error correction exercise on page 29.
67	**Unit 2: Reading Comprehension** Given a 20-question quiz, students will be able to answer 19/20 questions correctly.	Standard 2 (The Language of Language Arts) TCAs: 2(3F): Managing and Implementing Standards-Based ESL and Content Instruction 2(3G): Using Resources Effectively in ESL and Content Instruction 2(4J): Classroom-Based Assessment for ESL	Quiz Article: https://www.superteacherworksheets.com/reading-comp/5th-skydiving.pdf	**ASSESS**—The students will be given a 20-question quiz about the differences between fiction and non-fiction. The students will be expected to answer multiple-choice, true-false, and fill-in-the-blank questions. Students will be given instructions to read a non-fiction article about skydiving as their homework. They will be instructed to highlight any vocabulary words they don't currently know.
68	**Unit 2: Vocabulary of Big Numbers and the Decimal System: Assessment Day** Given a test with 20 terms, students will correctly match or define 20/20.	Standard 3 (Language of Mathematics) TCAs: 2(3F): Managing and Implementing Standards-Based ESL and Content Instruction	Test of 20 terms	**M/ASSESS**—Students will take a test that consists of 20 matching and short answer questions. **DIV**—Students may answer the short answer questions either by writing a definition in English, by writing the word in their native language, or by drawing a picture or example that accurately illustrates the word's meaning.

DAY #	CONTENT/OBJECTIVE	STANDARDS	RESOURCES/MATERIALS	LEARNING ACTIVITIES/ASSESSMENTS
69	**Unit 3: Vocabulary of Matter: Temperature and Phases** Given cutouts of water in its solid, liquid, and gas forms, students will glue them into their science binders and draw arrows, labeled with temperatures, to show the change temperature makes on the state of matter with 3/3 accuracy.	Standard 4 (Language of Science) TCAs: 2(3F): Managing and Implementing Standards-Based ESL and Content Instruction 2(3G): Using Resources Effectively in ESL and Content Instruction	Science Binders "States of Matter" video: http://www.brainpop.com/science/matterandchemistry/statesofmatter/ Projector Solids and Liquids game: http://www.bbc.co.uk/schools/scienceclips/ages/8_9/solid_liquids.shtml	**S/T**—The teacher will replay the section of the "States of Matter" video that deals with the effect of temperature on states of matter. Students will then play the online "Solids and Liquids" game to review. Next, they will take cutouts of water in its solid, liquid, and gas states and draw arrows and labels that show how heating and cooling affects the states of matter.
70	**Unit 2: United States Independence (1763–1791)** Given the field trip and activity sheets, students will participate 100% of the time and fill out their activity sheets with 100% accuracy.	Standard 5 (Language of Social Science) TCAs: 2(3F): Managing and Implementing Standards-Based ESL and Content Instruction 2(3G): Using Resources Effectively in ESL and Content Instruction	Transportation Chaperones Lunch money Activity sheets	**ACT/SS**—Students will go on a field trip to Philadelphia. During their field trip, they will visit the Liberty Bell, visit Independence Hall, and see the Declaration of Independence. **COLL**—Parents and other teachers from the school will accompany the class as chaperones. **A**—Students will also be given turns taking pictures of different sights with the teacher's camera. These photos will be used for an activity later in the unit. Students will also be given activity sheets to accompany each sight they see. They will be expected to study their activity sheets to prepare for next week's quiz.
71	**Christmas** Given a numbered outline and five strips of paper containing key parts of the Christmas story, students will paste the parts of the story onto the paper in the proper order with 5/5 accuracy.	Standard 1 (Social & Instructional Language) TCAs: 2(1A): Describing Language	A children's bible containing the story of Christ's birth Blank, numbered outlines Strips of paper containing key parts of the Christmas story in both written and picture form Glue	**B**—To practice listening comprehension, the teacher will read the Christmas story to the children aloud. She will then ask the class to answer questions to ensure they understood what happened in the story. To practice speaking comprehension, she will ask them to turn to a partner and retell the story. **ASSESS**—Finally, the students will paste strips of paper containing key parts of the Christmas story in the correct order onto an outline. **DIV**—The fact that the parts of the Christmas story will be in both written and picture form will cater to the needs of students at different levels.

DAY #	CONTENT/OBJECTIVE	STANDARDS	RESOURCES/MATERIALS	LEARNING ACTIVITIES/ASSESSMENTS
72	**Unit 2: Reading Comprehension** Students will be able to define all of the words they didn't know with 100% accuracy. Each group will come up with three elements of non-fiction in *Rosa Parks: My Story* by Rosa Parks with 3/3 correct reasons.	Standard 2 (The Language of Language Arts) TCAs: 2(3F): Managing and Implementing Standards-Based ESL and Content Instruction 2(3G): Using Resources Effectively in ESL and Content Instruction	Article: https://www.superteacherworksheets.com/reading-comp/5th-skydiving.pdf Flash cards YouTube clip	**T**—The teacher will show a short YouTube clip about skydiving to spark the students' interest in the topic. **CE**—After the clip, the teacher will ask the students to talk about the character principle of bravery and if they think skydiving is a brave thing to do or not. **LA**—Students will discuss the chapters that they read in the article about skydiving. They will bring the list of vocabulary words they didn't know to class, write the word definitions, and make flash cards for the words they didn't know. The teacher will break students into five groups and the groups will each come up with three reasons why the article is non-fiction. The groups will also discuss their favorite and least favorite part of the article. The students will be instructed to read the fiction story *The Hidden Treasure* for the next class period and answer the comprehension questions that accompany the story.
73	**BEGINNING OF UNIT 3: Vocabulary of Fractions, Introduction** Given a list of 10 key terms, students will draw a number or symbol that is represented by the term with 10/10 accuracy.	Standard 3 (Language of Mathematics) TCAs: 2(3F): Managing and Implementing Standards-Based ESL and Content Instruction 2(3G): Using Resources Effectively in ESL and Content Instruction	PowerPoint Construction paper Blank wall Painter's tape Markers "Fraction Wall": http://www.pinterest.com/pin/408701734906178653/	**M/T**—The teacher will remind students of key vocabulary related to adding, subtracting, multiplying, and dividing. She will also introduce the words "fraction," "numerator," "denominator," and "mixed number." Students will practice saying the words aloud as the teacher puts them up on the board. Then, they will complete a worksheet to see if they can match each word with a symbol or set of numbers that represents it. **ACT**—Students will each write down the name of a fraction from one half to one tenth. Then, the students will tape their pieces of paper together to make a visual fraction representation, as demonstrated in the link in the resources section.

DAY #	CONTENT/OBJECTIVE	STANDARDS	RESOURCES/MATERIALS	LEARNING ACTIVITIES/ASSESSMENTS
74	**Unit 3: Vocabulary of Matter: Atoms, Molecules, Elements, Compounds** Given a matching worksheet, students will correctly match terms with a picture that describes them with 6/6 accuracy.	Standard 4 (Language of Science) TCAs: 2(3F): Managing and Implementing Standards-Based ESL and Content Instruction 2(3G): Using Resources Effectively in ESL and Content Instruction	Science binders "States of Matter" video: http://www.brainpop.com/science/matterandchemistry/statesofmatter/ Projector "5th Grade Physical Science Vocabulary": http://www.ocde.us/Science/Documents/5thgrade_physicalsci_voc.PDF?Mobile=1&Source=%2FScience%2F_layouts%2Fmobile%2Fview.aspx%3FList%3D611f1cff-8c32-4316-a97c-588cde53df20%26View%3D57199a25-7495-4150-8829-842557993dda%26CurrentPage%3D1	**S/T**—The teacher will replay the section of the "States of Matter" video that deals with what atoms and molecules are. Next, the teacher will introduce elements and compounds using the definitions in the "5th Grade Science Vocabulary" link. The students will complete a worksheet to match the terms they learn with their correct definitions. **ACT**—If time allows, the students will review everything they have learned so far in Unit 3 by playing Science Around the World. **DIV**—During Around the World, different desks will be labeled with the students' home countries. When the students make it "around the world" and back to their home country, they will win.
75	**Unit 2: United States Independence (1763–1791)** Given a 20-question quiz, students will be able to answer 19/20 questions correctly.	Standard 5 (Language of Social Science) TCAs: 2(3F): Managing and Implementing Standards-Based ESL and Content Instruction 2(3G): Using Resources Effectively in ESL and Content Instruction 2(4J): Classroom-Based Assessment for ESL	Quiz Pictures Scrapbook paper Stickers Glue Markers	**SS/ASSESS**—Students will be given a 20-question quiz covering the factual information they learned during their field trip based on the activity sheets they completed during the field trip. **A**—Students will use the pictures from their field trip last week to create a "class memory book." The teacher will print out the photos and each student will be given a piece of scrapbook paper to decorate using their favorite pictures, stickers, and short descriptions of their favorite part of the trip.

DAY #	CONTENT/OBJECTIVE	STANDARDS	RESOURCES/MATERIALS	LEARNING ACTIVITIES/ASSESSMENTS
76	**Injury and Illness** Given six sentences, each containing one error, students will correct the errors with 6/6 accuracy.	Standard 1 (Social & Instructional Language) 2(3F): Managing and Implementing Standards-Based ESL and Content Instruction	*All Clear Listening and Speaking 1* Textbook and audio CD	The class will start off, as directed on page 99 of *All Clear Listening and Speaking 1*, with a comparison of the sounds used to express pain in their native language. Next, the students will listen to the audio recording of the dialogue on page 100. As a class, they will discuss the answers to the questions following the dialogue. **COLL**—Next, they will divide into pairs, as directed by page 101, and practice saying the dialogue to each other. The teacher will explain the nine common English phrases related to illness and injury on pages 101–109. The students will complete the error correction exercise on page 111.
77	**Unit 2: Reading Comprehension** Given five comprehension questions, students will be able to answer 5/5 correctly.	Standard 2 (The Language of Language Arts) TCAs: 2(3F): Managing and Implementing Standards-Based ESL and Content Instruction 2(3G): Using Resources Effectively in ESL and Content Instruction 2(4): Classroom-Based Assessment for ESL	The Hidden Treasure: https://www.superteacherworksheets.com/reading-comp/5th-hiddentreasure.pdf A bible	**ASSESS**—The teacher will review the students' answers from the article "The Hidden Treasure." The students will be expected to answer all questions fully and accurately. The students will write down the vocabulary words that weren't familiar and find definitions for them. **CE/B**—The teacher will read the students the parable of the hidden treasure and explain the character principles of sacrificing something good for something better and of seeking heavenly treasure instead of earthly treasure. **ACT**—After writing down the definitions, the students will go outside for a scavenger hunt for "hidden treasures." Before they are allowed to open their treasure, students will be required to tell the teacher one of the aspects of fiction or non-fiction.

DAY #	CONTENT/OBJECTIVE	STANDARDS	RESOURCES/MATERIALS	LEARNING ACTIVITIES/ASSESSMENTS
78	**Unit 3: Vocabulary of Fractions: Basic Vocabulary** Given a set of cards, some containing terms, some containing definitions, and some containing examples, students will correctly put together four sets of three.	Standard 3 (Language of Mathematics) TCAs: 2(3F): Managing and Implementing Standards-Based ESL and Content Instruction	"Adding and Subtracting Fractions" video: http://www.brainpop.com/games/dropzone/ Projector	**M**—The teacher will teach the students the words "common denominator," "lowest common denominator (LCD)," "mixed number," and "equivalent fractions." **T**—The teacher will then have the students watch the "Adding and Subtracting Fractions" video for reinforcement. Next, they will match terms with their definitions and with examples. The teacher will ask the students to bring any word problems from their class for ESL class next week.
79	**Unit 3: Vocabulary of Matter: Solutions** Given a worksheet with pictures demonstrating the terms "solute," "solvent," and "solution," the students label the pictures with 3/3 accuracy.	Standard 4 (Language of Science) TCAs: 2(3F): Managing and Implementing Standards-Based ESL and Content Instruction	Science binders	**S**—Students will learn the definitions of the terms solute, solvent, and solution. **ACT**—The students will make their own solutions by dissolving various substances in water. They will experiment with different things (salt, oil, etc.) to see what will and will not dissolve in water. Last, the students will complete a worksheet in which they label "solute," "solvent," and "solution" correctly.
80	**Unit 2: United States Independence (1763–1791)** Given the questions "Why do people want to be free?" and "How can we be heard by our government?" students will be able to write three answers to each question with five or less writing errors.	Standard 5 (Language of Social Science) TCAs: 2(3F): Managing and Implementing Standards-Based ESL and Content Instruction 2(3G): Using Resources Effectively in ESL and Content Instruction	Paper Pencil	**CT/SS**—In order to process the information they have learned so far in their ESL and history class, students will contemplate the following questions: Why do people want to be free? How can we be heard by our government? **DIV**—The teacher will ask students, "What is the government like in your country?" and "How is the government in your country different from the government in the United States?" **LA**—Once the teacher has given the students the questions, students will be split into five groups to talk about these questions. After sharing their ideas with their group, each group member will write down three reasons why people want to be free and three ways we can be heard by the government.

DAY #	CONTENT/OBJECTIVE	STANDARDS	RESOURCES/MATERIALS	LEARNING ACTIVITIES/ASSESSMENTS
81	**Weather** Given a lesson about vocabulary words used in describing weather, students will tell the class about the weather in their country with five or less speaking errors.	Standard 1 (Social & Instructional Language) 2(3F): Managing and Implementing Standards-Based ESL and Content Instruction	PowerPoint Computers	**T**—The students will go to the computer lab to look up the weather. Once they arrive at the computer lab, they will go to weather.com and look up the weather for the day. The teacher will then give a lesson about different types of weather and the vocabulary used to describe the types of weather. **DIV**—After the students look up the weather for their current setting, they will look up the weather for their home country. **COLL**—After the lesson, they will each use the vocabulary words to tell a group of three other students about the weather in their home country.
82	**Unit 2: Reading Comprehension**	Standard 2 (The Language of Language Arts) TCAs: 2(3F): Managing and Implementing Standards-Based ESL and Content Instruction 2(3G): Using Resources Effectively in ESL and Content Instruction	Word Detective game: http://www.smarttutor.com/free-resources/free-reading-lessons/fifth-grade-reading/ Wheel of Fortune game Review questions	**T**—The students will go to the computer lab to play Word Detective. This is a game where the students learn to pay close attention to clues within a story in order to answer the comprehension questions. The teacher will also hold a review session for the upcoming test. The students will play a review game of The Wheel of Fortune. The review game will include questions about fiction, nonfiction, and reading comprehension strategies.
83	**Unit 3: Vocabulary of Fractions: Word Problems** Given a word problem containing three unnecessary pieces of information, the students will identify and cross out the unnecessary information with 3/3 accuracy.	Standard 3 (Language of Mathematics) TCAs: 2(3F): Managing and Implementing Standards-Based ESL and Content Instruction	Word problems from students' main math class Elmo/overhead projector	**M**—The teacher will explain to the students that some of the things in word problems are very necessary and some are distracting. She will project the math problems that the students brought in and show examples of how to narrow out information that is not important. **CE**—The teacher will relate distractions in word problems to distractions in life. She will explain how, just like we need to get rid of distractions in word problems, we must get rid of distractions in life. **ASSESS**—The class will then narrow out words of one problem together, and finally, they will do a word problem of the teacher's creation by themselves.

DAY #	CONTENT/OBJECTIVE	STANDARDS	RESOURCES/MATERIALS	LEARNING ACTIVITIES/ASSESSMENTS
84	**Unit 3: Vocabulary of Matter: Review Day** Given a study guide, students will fill in the blanks with 20/20 accuracy.	Standard 4 (Language of Science) TCAs: 2(3F): Managing and Implementing Standards-Based ESL and Content Instruction 2(3G): Using Resources Effectively in ESL and Content Instruction	Science binders ZAP! review game: http://mathtastrophe.wordpress.com/2012/07/23/made-4-math-monday-4/	**ACT**—The students will play the ZAP! review game to learn the terms from a study guide. The students will then individually fill in the blanks on a study guide with information from Units 1, 2, and 3 in preparation for the midterms in both ESL class and in their regular science class. Students will be informed that their ESL midterm (due the following week) will be a binder check. The teacher will ensure that they have been keeping up with their vocabulary words from science class all along and have pasted into the binders all of the resources that she gave them in ESL class.
85	**Unit 2: United States Independence (1763–1791)** **REVIEW DAY**	Standard 5 (Language of Social Science) TCAs: 2(3F): Managing and Implementing Standards-Based ESL and Content Instruction 2(3G): Using Resources Effectively in ESL and Content Instruction	SMART Board Who Wants to Be a Millionaire game	**T**—The teacher will help the students review for the upcoming unit test through a SMART Board review game of Who Wants to Be a Millionaire. **ACT**—Students will be split into two groups and the groups will answer questions from the unit. The winner of the game will receive two bonus points on their test. After the game, the students will be given time to fill out a study guide for next week's test. At the end of the class period, the teacher will go over the correct answers with the class so that they can prepare for the test.
86	**Parts of the Body** Given a worksheet with 11 pictures and names of body parts, students will accurately match 11/11 pictures with their proper names.	Standard 1 (Social & Instructional Language) TCAs: 2(3F): Managing and Implementing Standards-Based ESL and Content Instruction 2(3G): Using Resources Effectively in ESL and Content Instruction	"Doctor! Doctor!" song: http://genkienglish.net/doctorsong.htm Projector Body Parts worksheet: http://www.anglomaniacy.pl/bodyPT1.pdf	**CT/CE/COLL/H**—The teacher will ask students "Why is it important to take care of our bodies?" and "What can happen if we don't take care of our bodies?" Each student will talk about the question with a partner while the teacher walks around to listen. The teacher will lead the discussion toward the conclusion that it is very important to take care of our bodies since they are God's temple. The teacher will teach the students the names of different parts of the body. They will review by learning and singing the "Doctor! Doctor!" song. **DIV**—The teacher will ask students, "How is going to the doctor in your home country different than going to the doctor in the United States?" and "How is going to the doctor in your home country similar to going to the doctor in the United States?" **TH**—The students will act out going to the doctor. They will act out the symptom they are given on a card and practice proper doctor's office etiquette. **T**—Finally, they will use the body parts worksheet to correctly match pictures to names of body parts.

DAY #	CONTENT/OBJECTIVE	STANDARDS	RESOURCES/MATERIALS	LEARNING ACTIVITIES/ASSESSMENTS
87	**Unit 2: Reading Comprehension**	Standard 2 (The Language of Language Arts) TCAs: 2(3F): Managing and Implementing Standards-Based ESL and Content Instruction 2(4J): Classroom-Based Assessment for ESL	Test	**ASSESS**—Students will be given a 30-question multiple-choice, short answer, and matching test about reading comprehension. The test will assess the students' comprehension of the material covered in the last unit as well as their reading comprehension.
88	**Unit 3: Vocabulary of Fractions: Word Problems** Given a word problem, students will correctly identify and circle three necessary pieces of information.	Standard 3 (Language of Mathematics) TCAs: 2(3F): Managing and Implementing Standards-Based ESL and Content Instruction	Word problems from students' main math class Elmo/overhead projector	**M**—The teacher will explain to the students that some of the things in word problems are very necessary and some are distracting. Using the word problems that the students brought in from their math class, the teacher will project them for the whole class to see and demonstrate how to find words and pieces of information that are especially important. She will then give the students a word problem of their own to identify the important pieces of information.
89	**Unit 3: Vocabulary of Matter: Assessment Day ("MIDTERM")** Having been given science binders, weekly vocabulary words, and handouts, students will have correctly included all required information from Units 1, 2, and 3.	Standard 4 (Language of Science) TCAs: 2(3F): Managing and Implementing Standards-Based ESL and Content Instruction	Science binders	**S/ASSESS**—The teacher will ensure that they have been keeping up with their vocabulary words from science class all along and have pasted into the binders all of the resources that she gave them in ESL class.
90	**Unit 2: United States Independence (1763–1791)** **UNIT TEST** Given the 30-question unit test, students will be able to answer 25/30 questions correctly.	Standard 5 (Language of Social Science) TCAs: 2(3F): Managing and Implementing Standards-Based ESL and Content Instruction 2(4J): Classroom-Based Assessment for ESL	Test	**SS/ASSESS**—Students will be given the 30-question unit test covering the vocabulary and information they covered while studying United States independence. The test will contain 15 multiple-choice, 5 fill-in-the-blank, 5 true-false, and 5 short answer.

DAY #	CONTENT/OBJECTIVE	STANDARDS	RESOURCES/MATERIALS	LEARNING ACTIVITIES/ASSESSMENTS
91	**Holidays** Given a piece of paper and craft supplies, students will be able to draw a picture of their favorite holiday tradition from their home country and the United States with 100% accuracy.	Standard 1 (Social & Instructional Language) TCAs: 2(3F): Managing and Implementing Standards-Based ESL and Content Instruction	PowerPoint Paper Markers Crayons	**T**—The teacher will give the students a lesson about the major holidays in the United States using a PowerPoint presentation. **ACT**—After the teacher tells the class about the major holidays in the United States, she will break the students into five groups to discuss holidays. The students will discuss the differences between traditions in their home country and the United States. **DIV**—Students will compare and contrast holidays in the United States with holidays from their home country. **A**—After discussing the differences in traditions in their home country and the United States, students will create a craft. They will choose their favorite holiday, then create a comparison chart. On one side of the paper, they will draw pictures representing their favorite holiday tradition from their home country and on the other side of the chart they will draw a picture of a tradition from the United States.
92	**BEGINNING OF UNIT 3: Writing** Given the pre-assessment, students will answer all questions with 10 or less writing errors.	Standard 2 (The Language of Language Arts) TCAs: 2(3F): Managing and Implementing Standards-Based ESL and Content Instruction 2(4J): Classroom-Based Assessment for ESL	Pre-Assessment	**ASSESS**—Students will be given a pre-assessment to assess their writing abilities. The pre-assessment will be given in written and verbal form. The students will be asked to write different types of sentences, write a topic sentence, and write three full paragraphs about a topic of their choice.
93	**Unit 3: Vocabulary of Fractions: Measuring Area** Given four key vocabulary words, students will compose a song or poem that includes all four words.	Standard 3 (Language of Mathematics) TCAs: 2(3F): Managing and Implementing Standards-Based ESL and Content Instruction		**M**—Students will learn the vocabulary "area," "side," "length," and "rectangle." The teacher will show them that the side of a rectangle can be measured in a fraction so that they might have to calculate the area by multiplying fractions. **ACT/COLL**—Students will get into groups and compose a song or write a poem that helps them remember their four vocabulary words.

DAY #	CONTENT/OBJECTIVE	STANDARDS	RESOURCES/MATERIALS	LEARNING ACTIVITIES/ASSESSMENTS
94	**BEGINNING OF UNIT 4: Living Systems— Introduction, Organisms, and Cells**	Standard 4 (Language of Science) TCAs: 2(3F): Managing and Implementing Standards-Based ESL and Content Instruction 2(3G): Using Resources Effectively in ESL and Content Instruction	Science binders Projector "Cells" video: http://www.brainpop.com/science/cellularlifeandgenetics/cells/	**S/T**—The teacher will use the "Cells" Video (see link in resources section) to introduce the topic of how cells are the building blocks of organisms. For the first day, the students will watch only the first bit of the video. **ACT**—The teacher will then allow the students to build things out of Legos, asking them to call the Legos "cells" and the thing they build an "organism."
95	**BEGINNING OF UNIT 3: United States: Founding the Nation (1776–1791)** Given a poster board, students will list the values they want to incorporate in their country with five or less writing errors.	Standard 5 (Language of Social Science) TCAs: 2(3F): Managing and Implementing Standards-Based ESL and Content Instruction 2(3G): Using Resources Effectively in ESL and Content Instruction	Poster board Markers Video clip: http://www.history.com/topics/american-revolution/american-revolution-history/videos/the-founding-fathers-unite	**COLL**—The teacher will collaborate with the mainstream 5th grade history teacher to see what vocabulary terms and ideas will be used in the class for the particular unit and assess particular concepts that may be difficult for ESL students. **M**—To spark the students' interest in the new unit, the teacher will play a video clip from the History channel: http://www.history.com/topics/american-revolution/american-revolution-history/videos/the-founding-fathers-unite **SS/CT/CE**—Students will be asked the question, "What are our values and principles?" After this question is asked, students will break into groups to discuss the values and principles that would be important when founding a country. **A**—Each group will be given a poster to decorate showing the values and principles they would incorporate if they were founding a country. The group may also create a flag and name for the country. **DIV**—Kinesthetic learners will learn through creating the craft. Visual learners will learn through watching the video. Auditory learners will learn through listening to the video.

DAY #	CONTENT/OBJECTIVE	STANDARDS	RESOURCES/MATERIALS	LEARNING ACTIVITIES/ASSESSMENTS
96	**Going to the Doctor** Given a set of instructions on taking medicine, students will accurately answer 5/5 questions.	Standard 1 (Social & Instructional Language) TCAs: 2(3F): Managing and Implementing Standards-Based ESL and Content Instruction	*The Berenstain Bears Go to the Doctor* book Written instructions on taking a medicine	**H**—First, the teacher will ask the students when they have been to the doctor or might have to go. Then, the teacher will read *The Berenstain Bears Go to the Doctor* to the class. Then, she will introduce some key vocabulary words to the students about going to the doctor. **COLL/ACT**—Next, the students will role-play. They will divide into pairs and the "patient" will practice telling the "doctor" what hurts. The "doctor" will then assign a treatment. Finally, they will look at a set of "instructions" on taking medicine and answer questions about the instructions.
97	**Unit 3: Writing** Given the lecture from the teacher, the students will be able to write four sentences using verbs, nouns, adjectives, and adverbs with five or less writing errors.	Standard 2 (The Language of Language Arts) TCAs: 2(3F): Managing and Implementing Standards-Based ESL and Content Instruction 2(3G): Using Resources Effectively in ESL and Content Instruction 2(4J): Classroom-Based Assessment for ESL	Mad Lib: https://www.teachervision.com/reading-and-language-arts/printable/31845.html "Parts of Speech" song: https://www.teachervision.com/reading-and-language-arts/printable/31845.html Paper Pencil	To begin the lesson and spark students' interest in writing, the class will begin with a "Mad Lib." This will help students begin to understand the parts of speech and how to incorporate them into their writing. **T**—The teacher will then play the "Parts of Speech" song to spark the students' interest in different parts of speech. This week, the teacher will review the meaning and place of verbs, nouns, adjectives, and adverbs. She will demonstrate their use in sentences and students will write down their definitions on flash cards. **CE/B**—The teacher will connect the concept of parts of speech to the idea of all Christians being part of the Body of Christ. She will point out the character principle of fulfilling our duties and callings, saying that it is important that each member of the body fulfill their purpose. **ASSESS**—To assess the students' understanding of these four parts of speech, the teacher will ask the students to write four sentences using the four parts of speech.
98	**Unit 3: Vocabulary of Fractions—REVIEW DAY** Given a study guide with blanks, students will fill in the blanks with 30/30 accuracy.	Standard 3 (Language of Mathematics) TCAs: 2(3F): Managing and Implementing Standards-Based ESL and Content Instruction	Study guide with 30 blanks	**M**—To review the concepts from throughout the semester, students will go through a study guide together, filling in the blanks. Next, they will play Around the World to review. **DIV**—During Around the World, different desks will be labeled with the students' home countries. When the students make it "around the world" and back to their home country, they will win.

DAY #	CONTENT/OBJECTIVE	STANDARDS	RESOURCES/MATERIALS	LEARNING ACTIVITIES/ASSESSMENTS
99	**Unit 4: Living Systems—Cells & Their Functions** Given a quiz over cells, students will answer the questions with 9/10 accuracy.	Standard 4 (Language of Science) TCAs: 2(3F): Managing and Implementing Standards-Based ESL and Content Instruction 2(3G): Using Resources Effectively in ESL and Content Instruction	Science binders "Cells" video: http://www.brainpop.com/science/cellularlifeandgenetics/cells/ Projector Cells activity: http://www.brainpop.com//science/cellularlifeandgenetics/cells/activity/ Cells quiz: http://www.brainpop.com/science/cellularlifeandgenetics/cells/quiz/	**S/T**—The class will finish watching the "cells" video. Then, they will complete the cells activity (see the link in the resources section) together as a class. The students will take the review quiz afterward.
100	**United States: Founding the Nation (1776–1791)**	Standard 5 (Language of Social Science) TCAs: 2(3F): Managing and Implementing Standards-Based ESL and Content Instruction 2(3G): Using Resources Effectively in ESL and Content Instruction	PowerPoint Vocabulary words	**T**—The teacher will use a PowerPoint to portray the new vocabulary and concepts for this history unit. After the PowerPoint, the students will play a game of Around the World to review the meaning of the new terms.
101	**Outdoor Chores** Students will participate in 100% of the activities. Given 10 matching questions, students will answer 9/10 correctly.	Standard 1 (Social & Instructional Language) TCAs: 2(3F): Managing and Implementing Standards-Based ESL and Content Instruction	Rakes Snow shovels Warm clothing	**T/CE**—The teacher will give a brief introduction to different chores that occur outside using a PowerPoint. She will again highlight the character principles of obedience and hard work, talking about the importance of doing chores. **COLL**—She will ask one of the facilities staff members to tell the students about mowing the lawn, trimming hedges, shoveling snow, etc. **ACT**—Depending on the weather, students will either go out and shovel snow or rake leaves. After they do the chore, they will be able to jump in the leaves or play in the snow. **ASSESS**—The students will be given a 10-question worksheet in which they will match the season of the year with the outdoor chores that accompany it.

DAY #	CONTENT/OBJECTIVE	STANDARDS	RESOURCES/MATERIALS	LEARNING ACTIVITIES/ASSESSMENTS
102	**Unit 3: Writing** Given the lecture from the teacher, the students will be able to write four sentences using pronouns, prepositions, conjunctions, and interjections with five or less writing errors.	Standard 2 (The Language of Language Arts) TCAs: 2(3F): Managing and Implementing Standards-Based ESL and Content Instruction 2(3G): Using Resources Effectively in ESL and Content Instruction 2(4J): Classroom-Based Assessment for ESL	Mad Lib: https://www.teachervision.com/reading-and-language-arts/printable/31845.html Paper Pencil	To begin the lesson and spark students' interest in writing, the class will begin with a "Mad Lib." This will help students begin to understand the parts of speech and how to incorporate them into their writing. This week, the teacher will review the meaning and place of pronouns, prepositions, conjunctions, and interjections. She will demonstrate their use in sentences and students will write down their definitions on flash cards. **ASSESS**—To assess the students' understanding of these four parts of speech, the teacher will ask the students to write four sentences using the four parts of speech.
103	**Unit 3: Vocabulary of Fractions—ASSESSMENT DAY (MIDTERM)** Given a test with 30 terms, students will match them to an example equation or definition with 28/30 accuracy.	Standard 3 (Language of Mathematics) TCAs: 2(3F): Managing and Implementing Standards-Based ESL and Content Instruction 2(4J): Classroom-Based Assessment for ESL	A test with 30 terms	**M**—Students will take a test in which they must match the math terms to an example equation or definition.
104	**Unit 4: Living Systems—Classification** Given a worksheet with definitions and terms, students will match 10/10 correctly.	Standard 4 (Language of Science) TCAs: 2(3F): Managing and Implementing Standards-Based ESL and Content Instruction 2(3G): Using Resources Effectively in ESL and Content Instruction	Science binders "Classification of Living Things": http://www.softschools.com/science/biology/classification_of_living_things/ Animal Classification Jeopardy: http://www.tangischools.org/Page/8208 Projector	**CT**—The teacher will ask students "Why are living things classified?" and "How are living things classified?" **S**—Using the information from "Classification of Living Things" (see link in resources section), the teacher will introduce the students to how animals are classified. **ACT/T**—The students will play Animal Classification Jeopardy to review. Last, students will be given a chart where they match terms to their correct definitions.

DAY #	CONTENT/OBJECTIVE	STANDARDS	RESOURCES/MATERIALS	LEARNING ACTIVITIES/ASSESSMENTS
105	**United States: Founding the Nation (1776–1791)** Given 20 flash cards, students will define 19/20 vocabulary words and concepts correctly.	Standard 5 (Language of Social Science) TCAs: 2(3F): Managing and Implementing Standards-Based ESL and Content Instruction 2(3G): Using Resources Effectively in ESL and Content Instruction	Computers Flash cards Markers	**T**—Today, the students will go to the computer lab. At the computer lab, the students will review the new vocabulary terms through playing games on Quizlet. **A**—Students will also be given the opportunity to create and decorate 20 flash cards to use at home. These will be used as a study guide for next week's quiz.
106	**Going to the Dentist** Given three questions about going to the dentist, students will answer 3/3 correctly.	Standard 1 (Social & Instructional Language) TCAs: 2(3F): Managing and Implementing Standards-Based ESL and Content Instruction 2(3G): Using Resources Effectively in ESL and Content Instruction	Berenstain Bears "Visit the Dentist" video: http://www.youtube.com/watch?v=2qhELwf-Ggg Projector Dental Care Vocabulary and Practice: http://www.esl-lab.com/vocab/v-dental-care.htm	The students will first watch the "Visit the Dentist" video. The teacher will ask questions after they watch the video and explain anything the students did not understand. **CE**—The teacher will highlight the character principle of bravery, explaining how the bear in the story was brave to behave at the dentist even when she was afraid. Next, the teacher will give the students a list of words they need to know when going to the dentist, given at the link in the resources section. Finally, take the three-question practice quiz to test their understanding.
107	**Unit 3: Writing** Given a 20-question quiz about the parts of speech, students will answer 19/20 correctly.	Standard 2 (The Language of Language Arts) TCAs: 2(3F): Managing and Implementing Standards-Based ESL and Content Instruction 2(4J): Classroom-Based Assessment for ESL	Quiz	**ASSESS**—Students will be given a 20-question matching and multiple-choice quiz about the eight parts of speech they have learned the past 2 weeks.

DAY #	CONTENT/OBJECTIVE	STANDARDS	RESOURCES/MATERIALS	LEARNING ACTIVITIES/ASSESSMENTS
108	**BEGINNING OF UNIT 4: Vocabulary of Measurements, Introduction** Given eight objects to measure, students will write eight complete sentences recording their measurements.	Standard 3 (Language of Mathematics) TCAs: 2(3F): Managing and Implementing Standards-Based ESL and Content Instruction	Rulers, yardsticks, tape measures, measuring cups and spoons, and a scale Paper and writing utensils Grapes, water, and nut-free trail mix	**M**—The teacher will introduce the term "measurement" to the students. She will also introduce the terms "unit,""unit cube,""convert,""length," "width,""height," and "base." **ACT**—The students will be given rulers, tape measures, yardsticks, and measuring cups and spoons, and a scale. They will then be given a worksheet and divided into groups to move between various stations in the classroom. At one station, they will measure the length of a textbook, a desk, and a bookshelf. At the next, they will weigh various classrooms objects (e.g., an apple, an eraser). At the third, they will measure out ½ cup of grapes, 1 cup of water, and 2 tablespoons of nut-free trail mix to have as a snack at the end of class. They will record their findings on a piece of paper using complete sentences (e.g., The book is 6 inches long. The apple weighs 10 ounces.)
109	**Unit 4: Living Systems—Survival** Given 10 definitions, students will choose the correct term with 10/10 accuracy.	Standard 4 (Language of Science) TCAs: 2(3F): Managing and Implementing Standards-Based ESL and Content Instruction 2(3G): Using Resources Effectively in ESL and Content Instruction	Science binders Animal survival flash cards: http://quizlet.com/36590313/animal-survival-jpj-flash-cards/ Individual whiteboards and markers	**S/ACT**—Students will replay Animal Classification Jeopardy to review the concepts they have learned so far in Unit 4. The teacher will introduce the vocabulary words relevant to survival or organisms. Then, the class will go through the flash cards together. The students will play Around the World to review. **DIV**—During Around the World, different desks will be labeled with the students' home countries. When the students make it "around the world" and back to their home country, they will win. **CT/COLL**—The teacher will ask the class "What things do we, as human beings, need to survive?" The students will discuss the answer in groups of three. **ASSESS**—Last, the teacher will call out a definition and the students will write the term on their whiteboards and hold it up for the teacher to see if they know it.
110	**United States: Founding the Nation (1776–1791)** Given a 20-question quiz, students will be able to answer 19/20 questions correctly.	Standard 5 (Language of Social Science) TCAs: 2(3F): Managing and Implementing Standards-Based ESL and Content Instruction 2(4J): Classroom-Based Assessment for ESL	Quiz	**SS/ASSESS**—Students will take a 20-question test on the vocabulary terms they have been learning. The test will include matching, multiple-choice, and five vocabulary words they must use in a sentence.

DAY #	CONTENT/OBJECTIVE	STANDARDS	RESOURCES/MATERIALS	LEARNING ACTIVITIES/ASSESSMENTS
111	**Jobs** Students will write a five-sentence paragraph describing what they want to be when they grow up with five or less writing errors.	Standard 1 (Social & Instructional Language) TCAs: 2(3F): Managing and Implementing Standards-Based ESL and Content Instruction	PowerPoint presentation YouTube dance video: http://www.tlc.com/tv-shows/dance-kids-atl/dance-kids-atl-videos/lets-go-to-work.htm Doctor Pencils Paper	**CT**—The teacher will ask the class, "What do you want to be when you grow up?" and "Why do you want to be a _____ when you grow up?" "Will you have to work hard to become a _____?" **T/P/D/CE**—The teacher will give a short presentation about different types of jobs using a PowerPoint. The class will also watch the dance video "Let's Go to Work." The students will have the opportunity to dance along with the video. The teacher will highlight the importance of hard work and diligence when it comes to achieving our dream jobs. **COLL**—The teacher will ask a doctor to come to the class and share about his profession. The students will be given the opportunity to ask questions about his profession. **ACT**—Students will be split up into five groups to discuss their parents' jobs as well as what they want to be when they grow up. **ASSESS**—Students will write a five-sentence paragraph describing what they want to be when they grow up and why.
112	**Unit 3: Writing** The Writing Process Student will be able to identify and list the five parts of the writing process with 4/5 accuracy.	Standard 2 (The Language of Language Arts) TCAs: 2(3F): Managing and Implementing Standards-Based ESL and Content Instruction 2(3G): Using Resources Effectively in ESL and Content Instruction 2(4J): Classroom-Based Assessment for ESL	Writing process video: http://www.teachertube.com/viewVideo.php?video_id=214689	**T/LA**—The teacher will give a short PowerPoint presentation about the five stages of the writing process which is prewriting, writing, revising, editing, and publishing. After giving the short presentation, she will play a short clip about the writing process from Teacher Tube. **ASSESS**—The students will be given a five-part worksheet about the writing process. They will need to list the parts of the writing process in the correct order.

DAY #	CONTENT/OBJECTIVE	STANDARDS	RESOURCES/MATERIALS	LEARNING ACTIVITIES/ASSESSMENTS
113	**Unit 4: Vocabulary of Measurements: Metric Units** Given a list of metric unit terms, students will write a paragraph-long story that includes at least five of the terms correctly.	Standard 3 (Language of Mathematics) TCAs: 2(3F): Managing and Implementing Standards-Based ESL and Content Instruction 2(3G): Using Resources Effectively in ESL and Content Instruction	"Measuring Metrically with Maggie": http://www.mathsisfun.com/measure/metric-system-introduction.html	**M/T**—The teacher will teach the students the vocabulary of the metric system (e.g., centimeter, meter, liter, etc.). She will project the story about an alien named Maggie on the screen and read it to the class. At the end, students will be asked to write their own story using at least five terms of measurement.
114	**Unit 4: Living Systems—Review Day** Given a list of options for their unit assessment, students will choose one option and begin to work on it.	Standard 4 (Language of Science) TCAs: 2(3F): Managing and Implementing Standards-Based ESL and Content Instruction	Science binders	**S**—The teacher will explain that for the assessment for Unit 4, students will be required to give a short presentation on something they learned in class. They may do one of the following: 1. Use household items to make a larger-than-life "cell," and label at least seven key parts. 2. Create a flowchart showing the different ways that animals are classified and use it to classify at least five animals. 3. Research two animals and list at least three survival tactics of each in either a paper or an oral presentation to the teacher. **DIV**—The variety of options for assessment meets the needs of students with different learning styles and levels of English.
115	**United States: Founding the Nation (1776–1791)** Given computers and websites as resources, each group will be able to come up with 10/10 accurate facts and accomplishments of their assigned founding father.	Standard 5 (Language of Social Science) TCAs: 2(3F): Managing and Implementing Standards-Based ESL and Content Instruction 2(3G): Using Resources Effectively in ESL and Content Instruction	Computers Websites for research: http://www.archives.gov/exhibits/charters/constitution_founding_fathers.html http://constitutioncenter.org/learn/educational-resources/founding-fathers/ http://americanhistory.about.com/od/revolutionarywar/tp/foundingfathers.htm	**T**—In order to supplement the material they are learning in their history class and solidify the concepts and prominent characters involved in the founding of the United States, students will begin working on a video recording project. **CT**—The teacher will ask the class, "Why are the founding fathers important?" and "How did the founding fathers impact present-day?" **SS**—Students will be split into seven groups and each group will be assigned one of the following characters: John Adams Thomas Jefferson Benjamin Franklin James Madison Alexander Hamilton George Washington John Jay During this class period, the students will go to the computer lab and begin researching their character. They will find interesting facts, pictures, and accomplishments. Each group will collectively find 10 interesting facts/accomplishments and 5 pictures.

DAY #	CONTENT/OBJECTIVE	STANDARDS	RESOURCES/MATERIALS	LEARNING ACTIVITIES/ASSESSMENTS
116	**Going to the Grocery Store** Given a scavenger hunt worksheet with a list of five items, students will accurately retrieve 5/5.	Standard 1 (Social & Instructional Language) TCAs: 2(2c): Nature and Role of Culture 2(3F): Managing and Implementing Standards-Based ESL and Content Instruction Standard 1 (Social & Instructional Language)	Grocery store List of vocabulary terms Scavenger hunt worksheet Nonperishable foods	**ACT**—The class will take a field trip to the grocery store. The teacher will first explain key vocabulary of common grocery store terms and the names of popular foods. **COLL**—After the instruction time, the students will divide into pairs and complete a scavenger hunt, finding five nonperishable items in the grocery store and bringing the items to share with the group. (The teacher will save these items for a cooking lesson next week.)
117	**Unit 3: Writing** Prewriting Given the instruction about brainstorming, students will be able to write down five ideas with less than five writing errors.	Standard 2 (The Language of Language Arts) TCAs: 2(3F): Managing and Implementing Standards-Based ESL and Content Instruction 2(3G): Using Resources Effectively in ESL and Content Instruction	YouTube clip: https://www.youtube.com/watch?v=tgpSG2mbhPs	**LA**—The students will begin to write a story using the strategies they have been learning about writing. This week the teacher will focus on helping the students with prewriting. **CE**—The teacher will tell the students that they must include a hero who shows some kind of good character principle. It can be honesty, integrity, diligence, obedience, politeness, or any similar character trait. **T**—The teacher will show a quick YouTube clip about brainstorming. **ACT**—Students will choose a brainstorming strategy and be given time in the class to brainstorm. Once they are given 15 minutes to brainstorm, they will share their ideas with a partner. The teacher will walk around the room and assist students in brainstorming. The students will be informed that they may continue brainstorming through the week, but will need to have a topic chosen by the following week.
118	**Unit 4: Vocabulary of Measurements: Line Plots** Given a description of what line plots are, students will define a line plot accurately and will draw an example of one.	Standard 3 (Language of Mathematics) TCAs: 2(3F): Managing and Implementing Standards-Based ESL and Content Instruction 2(3G): Using Resources Effectively in ESL and Content Instruction	"Hands On (and Feet On and Breath On!) Line Plots": http://www.theteacherstudio.com/2013/05/hands-on-and-feet-and-breath-on-line.html?spref=fb Pom-poms and straws Masking tape Paper and writing utensils Stickers and pre-drawn line plot	**M**—The teacher will define a line plot. Then, using the activities from the website link in the resources section, the class will transition between three stations, where they will measure the distance of their own jumps and of how far they can blow a pom-pom. They will then put stickers on a line plot recording their data. Rather than doing the third station listed on the website, the third station the ESL students go to will require them to write down the definition of a line plot and draw a picture of one.

DAY #	CONTENT/OBJECTIVE	STANDARDS	RESOURCES/MATERIALS	LEARNING ACTIVITIES/ASSESSMENTS
119	**Unit 4: Living Systems—Assessment Day** Given an assignment description from day 114 above, students will: 1. Accurately label seven parts of a larger-than-life "cell" of their design 2. Accurately classify five animals using a flowchart of their design or 3. List at least three survival techniques each of two different animals	Standard 4 (Language of Science) TCAs: 2(3F): Managing and Implementing Standards-Based ESL and Content Instruction 2(4J): Classroom-Based Assessment for ESL	Science binders	**S/ASSESS**—The students will present their projects to the teacher. They will have done one of the following: 1. Use household items to make a larger-than-life "cell," and label at least seven key parts. 2. Create a flowchart showing the different ways that animals are classified, and use it to classify at least five animals. 3. Research two animals and list at least three survival tactics of each in either a paper or an oral presentation to the teacher. **DIV**—The variety of options for assessment meets the needs of students with different learning styles and levels of English.
120	**United States: Founding the Nation (1776–1791)** PRACTICE DAY	Standard 5 (Language of Social Science) TCAs: 2(3F): Managing and Implementing Standards-Based ESL and Content Instruction 2(3G): Using Resources Effectively in ESL and Content Instruction	Old clothes	**SS/LA/TH**—Given the information students found while researching their assigned founding father last week, they will practice dressing up as the character and rehearsing the facts they wrote last week. The teacher will walk around the classroom and help each group with their pronunciation, grammar, and fluency. **A**—Students will be given the opportunity to design their own costumes using old clothes that have been donated by the teacher and parents. They will be given the opportunity to conduct a "dress rehearsal" prior to videotaping next week.

DAY #	CONTENT/OBJECTIVE	STANDARDS	RESOURCES/MATERIALS	LEARNING ACTIVITIES/ASSESSMENTS
121	**Cooking** Given matching items with names and pictures of common kitchen items, students will accurately match 10/10.	Standard 1 (Social & Instructional Language) TCAs: 2(2c): Nature and Role of Culture 2(3F): Managing and Implementing Standards-Based ESL and Content Instruction	Groceries School's kitchen (including utensils, etc.) Kitchen items worksheet	Students will learn the names of common kitchen items as well as some kitchen safety tips. **CT/COLL**—The teacher will ask the class, "Why is it important to know how to cook?" and "Who does the cooking in your home?" The students will answer the questions in groups of three. **DIV/COLL**—Students will also discuss in groups of three what the grocery stores are like in their home country in comparison to the grocery stores in the United States. **ACT**—Using the items purchased at the grocery store the week before, students will cook together under the teacher's supervision. Students will complete a worksheet, matching the name of a kitchen item to its picture.
122	**Unit 3: Writing** Drafting Given instruction regarding drafting, students will begin writing their draft with 100% class participation.	Standard 2 (The Language of Language Arts) TCAs: 2(3F): Managing and Implementing Standards-Based ESL and Content Instruction 2(3G): Using Resources Effectively in ESL and Content Instruction	PowerPoint Projector Paper Pencils	**LA/CE**—The students will continue to write a story about their hero with good character, using the strategies they have been learning about writing. This week the teacher will focus on helping the students with drafting. **T**—Using a PowerPoint presentation, the teacher will instruct students regarding how to write a draft and tips for writing. This week, the students will be given class time to begin writing their rough draft. The teacher will walk around the room to assist students. The teacher will also unveil the surprise that students will actually be able to publish their own book. This will be used to motivate students to put forth their best effort since they will be published authors.
123	**Unit 4: Vocabulary of Measurements: Volume** Given a cloze style exit ticket, students will fill in 3/3 blanks with the proper English comparative and superlative forms of the word "big."	Standard 3 (Language of Mathematics) TCAs: 2(1A): Describing Language 2(2B): Language Acquisition and Development	Chex cereal Measuring cups Napkins Cloze exit ticket Writing utensils	**M/ACT**—The teacher will ask the students to use the measuring cups and spoons from last week's cooking activity to measure out Chex cereal for each member of the class. The teacher will explain the idea of volume and then tell her students that each measuring cup will hold a certain volume of cereal. The students will practice English comparatives and superlatives as they talk about volume. For example, "This cup is big. This cup is bigger. This cup is the biggest. Juan has a tablespoon of cereal. Lily has more cereal. Ali has the most cereal." **ASSESS**—The students will write the correct forms of "big, bigger, and biggest" in a cloze style exit ticket.

DAY #	CONTENT/OBJECTIVE	STANDARDS	RESOURCES/MATERIALS	LEARNING ACTIVITIES/ASSESSMENTS
124	**Unit 5: The Ocean: Introduction** Given an exit ticket with a list of three places, students will accurately identify each of them as either "close," "closer," or "closest," to the ocean with 3/3 accuracy.	Standard 4 (Language of Science) TCAs: 2(1A): Describing Language 2(2B): Language Acquisition and Development 2(2C): Nature and Role of Culture 2(2D): Cultural Groups and Identity 2(3E): Planning for Standards-Based ESL and Content Instruction 2(3F): Managing and Implementing Standards-Based ESL Content Instruction	Maps, such as the following: http://www.mapsofworld.com/africa/ http://www.50states.com/us.htm#.U1WTWfldVWw http://www.mapsofworld.com/usa/states/north-carolina/ Computer and projector Exit ticket	**S**—The class practices speaking by discussing whether or not they have ever seen the ocean and whether or not their homes (both in their native country and in the United States) are close to the ocean. They will learn the names of all the different oceans (Pacific, Indian, etc.). **T**—The class will continue their study of comparatives and superlatives by discussing as a class how close countries are to the ocean, using maps that the teacher will project. (Raleigh is close to the ocean, Greenville is closer, Wilmington is closest, etc.) Finally, students will be given an exit ticket with a list of three places they have looked at as a class and will correctly identify them as "close," "closer," or "closest" to the ocean.
125	**United States: Founding the Nation (1776–1791)** Recording Day Given the opportunity to record their video about a founding father, students will record with 100% effort and participation.	Standard 5 (Language of Social Science) TCAs: 2(3F): Managing and Implementing Standards-Based ESL and Content Instruction 2(3G): Using Resources Effectively in ESL and Content Instruction	Video camera Props Notes Computers Quizlet: http://quizlet.com/32886237/founding-of-a-nation-flash-cards/	**T**—Students will take turns recording their presentation. Students must be prepared with any props they plan on using as well as notes to help them remember their lines. The teacher will assist students in operating the video camera. Students who are not presently recording will review themes and vocabulary terms from the unit using Quizlet.

DAY #	CONTENT/OBJECTIVE	STANDARDS	RESOURCES/MATERIALS	LEARNING ACTIVITIES/ASSESSMENTS
126	**Valentine's Day** Given the name of a teacher in the school, students will write a note to that teacher telling them that they are appreciated with fewer than five spelling and grammar errors.	Standard 1 (Social & Instructional Language) TCAs: 2(1A): Describing Language 2(2B): Language Acquisition and Development 2(2C): Nature and Role of Culture 2(2D): Cultural Groups and Identity	A bible Paper Writing utensils	First, the teacher will explain that Valentine's Day is coming up the next week. The class will sit in a circle and discuss whether or not their culture celebrates Valentine's Day. If they do celebrate the holiday, they will tell the class their family's related. If they do not celebrate Valentine's Day, they will tell the class about any similar holidays (e.g., International Women's Day) in their home culture. **CE/CT**—She will ask students what they think love is. Then she will ask them to tell stories of how people have showed them love and to brainstorm together how they can show love to others. **B**—Next, the teacher will read them Romans 5:6–11, explaining how God loved us enough to send His Son to die for us while we were still sinners. Finally, to show teachers in the school that they are loved and appreciated, the students will write notes to different teachers in the school.
127	**Unit 3: Writing** Revising Given the video about revision, students will make at least 10 revisions to their story and 10 revisions to their partner's story.	Standard 2 (The Language of Language Arts) TCAs: 2(3F): Managing and Implementing Standards-Based ESL and Content Instruction 2(3G): Using Resources Effectively in ESL and Content Instruction	Video: https://www.youtube.com/watch?v=RBKqgOvmJ8w	**LA/CE**—The students will continue to write a story about a hero with good character, using the strategies they have been learning about writing. This week the teacher will focus on helping the students with revising. **T**—The teacher will show students a short, fun video about revising in order to spark their interest and teach them the basics of revision. **COLL**—After spending 20 minutes making revisions on their story, students will trade papers with a partner. The partner will check for any mistakes and write any ideas on a separate piece of paper. **ASSESS**—After the students have made revisions, the teacher will collect all of the stories. The teacher will check the stories and mark mistakes so the students can fix them next class period.

DAY #	CONTENT/OBJECTIVE	STANDARDS	RESOURCES/MATERIALS	LEARNING ACTIVITIES/ASSESSMENTS
128	**Unit 4: Vocabulary of Measurements: Conversions** Given an exit ticket, students will write a definition of the word "convert" with fewer than three grammar errors.	Standard 3 (Language of Mathematics) TCAs: 2(1A): Describing Language 2(2B): Language Acquisition and Development	Bible Paper Drawing utensils Exit ticket	**M**—The teacher will explain the idea of converting one unit to another. The class will review the metric unit terms. **B**—The teacher will explain, from Ephesians 4:22–24, how as Christians we are converted from our old nature to a new nature when Christ saves us. **ACT**—To further understand the idea of "converting" something, the students will play a game in which they must convert a squiggle drawn by another student into a drawing of something recognizable. **ASSESS**—Finally, the students will write an exit ticket in which they must write a definition of the word convert in their own words, with fewer than three grammar errors.
129	**Unit 5: The Ocean: Geology** Given definitions of one vocabulary term from their classmates, each student will accurately guess their one term based on their classmates' definitions.	Standard 4 (Language of Science) TCAs: 2(1A): Describing Language 2(2B): Language Acquisition and Development	Geology of the ocean terms: https://docs.google.com/viewer?a=v&pid=sites&srcid=c29sdGVhY2hlci5jb218bzx0ZWFjaGVyLWNvbXxne Do0MjA5Ym0ZDYzNTNmMjlm Bingo chart maker: http://edubakery.com/Super-Bingo-Cards-Maker/Editor Vocabulary review games: https://www.google.com/url?sa=t&rct=j&q=&esrc=s&source=web&cd=2&cad=rja&uact=8&ved=0C C0QFjAB&url=http%3A%2F%2Fmershonwvis.cusie.cmswiki.wikispaces.net%2Ffile%2Fview%2FVOCABULARY_REVIEW_ACTIVITIES%255B1%255D.docx%2FVOCABULARY_REVIEW_ACTIVITIES%255B1%255D.docx%2F228854802%2FVOCABULARY_REVIEW_ACTIVITIES%255B1%255 D.docx&ei=9phVU67slsiT8QG104 HIDA&usg=AFQjCNFuQRaYPB7O tjCebAFsGTIJbVP7hg&bvm=bv.65058239,d.b2U	**S**—Using the eight terms at the link in the resources section, the teacher will define eight key terms related to the geology of the ocean. **ACT**—To review the terms together (guided practice), students will be divided into groups of four, and each group will be given a teacher-made bingo chart with terms from the teacher. The teacher will then call out definitions, and students will decide as a group which term matches that definition. They will color in the square they think matches and then hold their Bingo chart up for the teacher to check. The first team to get a row of correct terms (a Bingo) will win. Finally, the class will play Vocabulary Review Games link in the resources section, to review the terms. Each student will have a vocabulary term on their back and will have to accurately guess their term based on the definitions their classmates give.

DAY #	CONTENT/OBJECTIVE	STANDARDS	RESOURCES/MATERIALS	LEARNING ACTIVITIES/ASSESSMENTS
130	**United States: Founding the Nation (1776–1791)** Movie Day After watching each group's movie about the founding fathers, students will be able to write two new facts about each founding father with 2/2 accuracy.	Standard 5 (Language of Social Science) TCAs: 2(3F): Managing and Implementing Standards-Based ESL and Content Instruction 2(3G): Using Resources Effectively in ESL and Content Instruction	Popcorn Projector Paper Pencils	**T**—Students will celebrate the completion of their project by having a movie day during class. **ASSESS**—Students will watch each group's movie and write down at least two new things they learned about each founding father.
131	**Joining a Club** Given the presentations about different club activities, students will write two paragraphs about the activities they tried and which club they would like to join with less than five writing errors.	Standard 1 (Social & Instructional Language) TCAs: 2(3F): Managing and Implementing Standards-Based ESL and Content Instruction 2(3G): Using Resources Effectively in ESL and Content Instruction	Club representatives Club activities Writing utensils Paper	**COLL**—The teacher will collaborate with the middle school teachers to have representatives of different middle school clubs join the class. Each club representative will give a short presentation about their club to spark students' interest in the new opportunities that will be available in middle school. **ACT**—After the short presentation is given, each club representative will lead a group activity for the students to try. The students may choose to try three different activities. **ASSESS**—After the students have tried three club activities, they will write two paragraphs about the activities they tried and which club they would like to join when they enter middle school.
132	**Unit 3: Writing** Editing	Standard 2 (The Language of Language Arts) TCAs: 2(3F): Managing and Implementing Standards-Based ESL and Content Instruction 2(3G): Using Resources Effectively in ESL and Content Instruction	Paper Writing utensils Classical music Music player	**LA/CE**—The students will continue to write a story about a hero with good character, using the strategies they have been learning about writing. This week the teacher will focus on helping the students with editing. The teacher will give students their papers from last week. During the class period, students will be responsible for making changes to their book in order to get it ready for publishing. **MUS**—The teacher will play classical music while the students are editing. **CT**—The teacher will ask students, "Why is editing important?" and "Are there things other than writing that we edit or fix?"

DAY #	CONTENT/OBJECTIVE	STANDARDS	RESOURCES/MATERIALS	LEARNING ACTIVITIES/ASSESSMENTS
133	**Unit 4: Vocabulary of Measurements: Review Day** Given a list of 20 key vocabulary words, students will write definitions in English with 20/20 defined accurately.	Standard 3 (Language of Mathematics) TCAs: 2(3F): Managing and Implementing Standards-Based ESL and Content Instruction	Study guide consisting of a list of 20 words Envelopes Printed terms and definitions	**M/COLL**—The teacher will ask the ESL students' math teacher for a copy of the exams they will be taking in math class in the future over the Measurements unit. She will take 20 of the students' key vocabulary words that will be on the test and will create a list of them with room for the students to write definitions. **ACT**—The students will play a matching game in which the teacher divides the class into two teams and gives them envelopes containing printed definitions of each term as well as each key term. They will then practice matching the words with their definitions. The first team will correctly match all the terms and definitions. Finally, students will collaborate with a partner to fill in their study guides with the proper definitions.
134	**Unit 5: The Ocean: Physical Characteristics** Given eight definitions and a list of eight terms, students will correctly match 7/8 terms and definitions.	Standard 4 (Language of Science) TCAs: 2(1A): Describing Language 2(2B): Language Acquisition and Development	*The Magic School Bus on the Ocean Floor* by Joanna Cole ELMO projector Ocean vocabulary: http://www.lcps.k12.va.us/education/components/scrapbook/default.php?sectiondetailid=24508 Vocabulary Review Games link (see day 129) Numbered papers with definitions of each of the key eight vocabulary terms Paper Handouts (one for each student) with each of the eight terms	**S/DIV**—The teacher will start the class off with listening and reading practice by reading *The Magic School Bus on the Ocean Floor* by Joanna Cole, projecting the book on the ELMO projector as she reads so that the class can follow along. This will help both auditory and visual learners benefit from the book. Next, the teacher will define eight words from the Ocean Vocabulary list on the link in the resources section (from "salinity" to "pressure"). **ACT**—According to the description of the "Definition Search Game" (see the Vocabulary Review Game link in day 129), students will walk around to different numbered papers around the room, each paper having the definition of one of the key terms of the day. Students will then match number of the definition with the correct term on their paper.

DAY #	CONTENT/OBJECTIVE	STANDARDS	RESOURCES/MATERIALS	LEARNING ACTIVITIES/ASSESSMENTS
135	**United States: Founding the Nation (1776–1791)** Review Day Given the review game, students will answer 90% of the questions correctly.	Standard 5 (Language of Social Science) TCAs: 2(3F): Managing and Implementing Standards-Based ESL and Content Instruction	Review questions Who Wants to be a Millionaire game Study guide	**SS/T**—Students will have the opportunity to review the information they learned in the unit "Founding the Nation." During the first part of the class, the teacher will split the students into two groups. The two teams will play Who Wants to Be a Millionaire using questions from the unit. After playing the review game, students will be given time to fill in the study guide for next week's test.
136	**Signs** Given a matching worksheet with 20 signs and their meanings, they will answer 19/20 correctly.	Standard 1 (Social & Instructional Language) TCAs: 2(3F): Managing and Implementing Standards-Based ESL and Content Instruction	PowerPoint	**T/CE**—The teacher will give a lesson about common signs using a PowerPoint. The lesson will include traffic signs, pedestrian signs, safety signs, bathroom signs, etc. The teacher will remind the students that signs are for our safety and health, reiterating the character principle of obedience. **ACT**—After learning the different signs, the students will participate in a game to review the different signs. The teacher will put a picture of the sign on the PowerPoint and students will learn a hand motion to represent what the sign means. For instance, the students will stretch forth their hand when the stop sign appears. **DIV/COLL**—The students will get into groups of four and compare and contrast different signs from the United States with signs in their home country. **ASSESS**—Students will do a matching worksheet with 20 signs and their meanings.
137	**Unit 3: Writing** Bookmaking Day Given access to a computer, students will type out their story with less than three grammatical errors.	Standard 2 (The Language of Language Arts) TCAs: 2(3F): Managing and Implementing Standards-Based ESL and Content Instruction 2(3G): Using Resources Effectively in ESL and Content Instruction	Bookmaking kit: http://www.studenttreasures.com/programs/elementary Crayons, markers, colored pencils	**CT**—The teacher will ask the class, "What makes a great author?" and "How can you become a great author?" **LA**—Today, students will be given a free book kit. The kit will include pages that will be sent to the publisher and later published. During the class period, students will type out their story and print it out to paste it on the book pages. **A**—On the other side of the page, students will have the opportunity to draw pictures that correspond to their story. The teacher will give students the opportunity to continue working on their book until next week's class.

DAY #	CONTENT/OBJECTIVE	STANDARDS	RESOURCES/MATERIALS	LEARNING ACTIVITIES/ASSESSMENTS
138	**Unit 4: Vocabulary of Measurements: Assessment Day** Given a test of 20 questions, students will answer 20/20 correctly.	Standard 3 (Language of Mathematics) TCAs: 2(4A): Issues of Assessment for ESL	Math vocabulary test consisting of 20 questions	M—Students will take a test in which they must answer six multiple-choice questions, six matching questions, and eight short answer questions correctly.
139	**Unit 5: The Ocean: Ecology** Given an exit ticket, students will write down two of the key vocabulary terms from the day and define them with 2/2 accuracy.	Standard 4 (Language of Science) TCAs: 2(1A): Describing Language 2(2B): Language Acquisition and Development	Ocean vocabulary: http://www.lcps.k12.va.us/education/components/scrapbook/default.php?sectiondetailid=24508 "I have, Who has?" cards: http://mscraftynyla.blogspot.com/2012/12/what-are-i-have-who-has-games.html Exit tickets	S—The teacher will define the last 13 vocabulary words on the list at the Ocean Vocabulary link in the resources section. ACT—Each member of the class will be given a card with a definition on one side and an unrelated term on the other. They will play "I have, who has?" (A version of this game for math is explained at the link in the resources section.) The first person will look at the definition on their card and say, "Who has ____?" (e.g., Who has "an ebb and flow of the ocean caused by the moon's gravity"?) The person who has the term that matches that definition will say, "I have ____!" (e.g., I have "tide"!). Then they will look at the definition on the other side of their card and say, "Who has ____?" And so it will continue until the entire class has matched a term and definition. ASSESS—The teacher will ask the students to write on an exit ticket at least two terms and their definitions that they remember from class that day.
140	**United States: Founding the Nation (1776–1791)** Given the test covering the unit, students will be able to answer 30/35 questions correctly.	Standard 5 (Language of Social Science) TCAs: 2(3F): Managing and Implementing Standards-Based ESL and Content Instruction	Test	SS/ASSESS—Students will be given a 35-question test made up of multiple-choice, true-false, and fill-in-the-blank questions.

DAY #	CONTENT/OBJECTIVE	STANDARDS	RESOURCES/MATERIALS	LEARNING ACTIVITIES/ASSESSMENTS
141	**National Parks** Given information about different national parks in Virginia, students will write three sentences about which park they would like to visit with three or less writing errors.	Standard 1 (Social & Instructional Language) TCAs: 2(3F): Managing and Implementing Standards-Based ESL and Content Instruction 2(3G): Using Resources Effectively in ESL and Content Instruction	Handout Paper Writing utensil Transportation Packed lunch	Students will learn about the different national parks located within the United States and specifically Virginia. ACT—In order to gain an appreciation for state and national parks, students will take a field trip to the Jamestown National Park. During this trip, students will learn different vocabulary words about national parks and Jamestown. After the field trip, students will be given a list of different national parks in Virginia. They will write three sentences about which park they would like to visit next and why.
142	**Unit 3: Writing** Publishing/Review Day Given the task of reading their story aloud, students will read their story with five or less grammar and pronunciation errors.	Standard 2 (The Language of Language Arts) TCAs: 2(3F): Managing and Implementing Standards-Based ESL and Content Instruction 2(3G): Using Resources Effectively in ESL and Content Instruction	Bookmaking kit: http://www.studentreasures.com/programs/elementary Envelope Postage	LA/COLL—Student will split into groups to share their completed story. Each student will take a turn reading their story in front of their group. The teacher will walk around the room to assess reading fluency as well as pronunciation. After students have shared their stories with their classmates, they will put the book pages into the provided envelope. The envelope will then be sent to publishing. T—After the students have shared their story, they will play Around the World to review the information for their test on the writing unit next week. DIV—During Around the World, different desks will be labeled with the students' home countries. When the students make it "around the world" and back to their home country, they will win.
143	**Unit 5: Geometry: Review of Coordinate Planes** Given a life-size coordinate plane and directions called out by the teacher, each student will locate at least two points or sections on the plane with 100% accuracy.	Standard 3 (Language of Mathematics) TCAs: 2(3F): Managing and Implementing Standards-Based ESL and Content Instruction	Life-size coordinate plane: http://www.pinterest.com/pin/408701734906236827/ YouTube video (Teaching Geography through Dance): https://www.youtube.com/watch?v=41NQwGXRkP8 Notebooks	M—The teacher will ask students to turn to the section of their notebooks from Unit 1 (day 23) when they learned about coordinate planes. They will review together all of the terms related to coordinate planes. ACT/P—The students will repeat the activity from day 23. They will divide into teams and take turns walking to the correct sections of a life-size coordinate plane (made out of painter's tape, masking tape, or sidewalk chalk) as the teacher calls them out. D/P/T—The students will have the opportunity to watch "Teaching Geography through Dance." Students will learn the moves and geography terms accompanying each dance move.

DAY #	CONTENT/OBJECTIVE	STANDARDS	RESOURCES/MATERIALS	LEARNING ACTIVITIES/ASSESSMENTS
144	**Unit 5: The Ocean—Review Day** Given a study guide consisting of a set of 23 definitions, students will provide the correct term for at least 20/23 terms.	Standard 4 (Language of Science) TCAs: 2(3F): Managing and Implementing Standards-Based ESL and Content Instruction	Virginia SOL test review questions: http://www.virginiasol.com/test/waves.htm Ocean flash cards: http://quizlet.com/831636/5th-grade-unit-5-science-geology-all-shook-up-flash-cards/ Study guide containing 23 definitions	**S/COLL/DIV**—First, the teacher will print out sets of the 23 ocean vocabulary flash cards from Quizlet. Students will pair together to take turns quizzing each other on the flash cards. A higher-level learner and a lower-level learner will work together. Next, the students will be given a study guide consisting of a set of the 23 definitions from the Quizlet flash cards. As a class, they will fill in the 23 terms that match each definition. **ACT**—Finally, students will use the 15 questions of the SOL Test Review to play Around the World as they review for their science test the next week.
145	**BEGINNING OF UNIT 4: US—Legacy for Us Today** Given the critical thinking question "What are our rights and responsibilities?" students will be able to write down two rights and two responsibilities with less than two grammatical errors.	Standard 5 (Language of Social Science) TCAs: 2(3F): Managing and Implementing Standards-Based ESL and Content Instruction	Bulletin board supplies Markers	**COLL**—The teacher will collaborate with the mainstream 5th grade history teacher to see what vocabulary terms and ideas will be used in the class for the particular unit and assess particular concepts that may be difficult for ESL students. **SS/CT**—Students will be asked the question, "What are our rights and responsibilities?" After this question is asked, students will break into groups to discuss the question and share their opinion. **CE**—The teacher will discuss the meaning of responsibility. **A**—Students will be given the opportunity to help the teacher decorate a new bulletin board. On the new bulletin board, one side will be devoted to rights and one side will be devoted to responsibilities. Students will be allowed to write down two rights and two responsibilities they have as a citizen of the United States.
146	**Easter** Given between one and five lines of text, students will read their lines with 100% accuracy.	Standard 1 (Social & Instructional Language) TCAs: 2(1A): Describing Language 2(2B): Language Acquisition and Development	Children's bible containing the story of Christ's death, burial, and resurrection	**B**—The teacher will read the students the story of Christ's death, burial, and resurrection. **TH/ACT/P**—The students will then act out the story of Christ's death, burial, and resurrection. The teacher will assign roles to the students (apostles, soldiers, Christ, the women, Joseph of Arimathea, etc.). She will give each student between one and five lines of text to read that corresponds with their character. More advanced students will have more lines. After they have acted out the story, she will ask the students how many of them have heard the story before. She will ask if any of them have asked Christ to be the Lord of their life and will explain how to be saved, asking if any of the students would like to pray to receive Christ.

DAY #	CONTENT/OBJECTIVE	STANDARDS	RESOURCES/MATERIALS	LEARNING ACTIVITIES/ASSESSMENTS
147	**Unit 3: Writing Assessment** Given the test, students will answer 25/30 questions correctly.	Standard 2 (The Language of Language Arts) TCAs: 2(3F): Managing and Implementing Standards-Based ESL and Content Instruction	Test	**LA/ASSESS**—Students will take a test covering the writing unit. The test will be made up of multiple-choice, true-false, and short answer questions.
148	**Unit 5: Geometry: Two-Dimensional Figures on Coordinate Planes** Given Geoboards, students will accurately make three separate two-dimensional shapes located at the points the teacher calls out with 3/3 accuracy.	Standard 3 (Language of Mathematics) TCAs: 2(1A): Describing Language 2(2B): Language Acquisition and Development	Geoboards (either material ones or online ones such as the one at this website): http://www.mathplayground.com/geoboard.html)	**M**—The teacher will explain what two-dimensional figures are and the difference between one-, two-, and three-dimensional figures. She will then explain how two-dimensional figures can be drawn on coordinate planes. **ACT**—The class will practice making two-dimensional shapes on a coordinate plane using Geoboards. **COLL/DIV/ASSESS**—In pairs (one high-level English speaker with one lower-level English speaker), students will make shapes located at the proper point as the teacher calls out instructions. They will then hold up their creation for the teacher to check.
149	**Unit 5: The Ocean—Assessment Day** Given a test with eight matching questions, eight multiple-choice questions, and four short answer questions, students will answer the questions with at least 18/20 accuracy.	Standard 4 (Language of Science) TCAs: 2(4A): Issues of Assessment for ESL	A test of 20 questions (eight matching, eight multiple-choice, and four short answer)	**S/ASSESS**—The students will take a 20-question test, in which they will answer eight matching questions, eight multiple-choice questions, and four short answer questions.
150	**Unit 4: US–Legacy for Us Today**	Standard 5 (Language of Social Science) TCAs: 2(3F): Managing and Implementing Standards-Based ESL and Content Instruction	PowerPoint Projector Review game Post-it notes Marker	**T**—The teacher will use a PowerPoint to portray the new vocabulary and concepts for this history unit. After the PowerPoint, the students will play a game of Post-it Practice to review the terms. http://k6educators.about.com/od/lessonplanheadquarters/a/5-Successful-Review-Activities-For-Elementary-Students.htm After students have played the review game, they will be given time to make flash cards for next week's vocabulary quiz.

DAY #	CONTENT/OBJECTIVE	STANDARDS	RESOURCES/MATERIALS	LEARNING ACTIVITIES/ASSESSMENTS
151	**Spring Vocabulary** Given the matching sheet with 10 springtime vocabulary words, students will answer 9/10 questions correctly.	Standard 1 (Social & Instructional Language) TCAs: 2(3F): Managing and Implementing Standards-Based ESL and Content Instruction 2(3G): Using Resources Effectively in ESL and Content Instruction	Springtime vocabulary words: http://www.enchantedlearning.com/wordlist/spring.shtml Coat hanger Cotton balls Construction paper Glue A bible	**LA**—Students will memorize vocabulary words associated with springtime. **CT/COLL**—Students will be asked, "Why does new life occur in the spring?" and "What is the weather like in the spring?" They will get together in groups of three to discuss the questions. Then, each group will agree on a short answer to share with the entire class. **CE/B**—The teacher will then read the Ephesians 4:22–24 to the students, about how they have a new self. She will teach them the character principle of taking off the old self and putting on the new self. http://www.enchantedlearning.com/wordlist/spring.shtml **A**—After students have memorized the springtime vocabulary, they will make an "April Showers" craft. http://spoonful.com/crafts/april-showers-mobile **ASSESS**—When students have completed the craft, they will be given a matching worksheet containing 10 of the springtime vocabulary words.
152	**BEGINNING OF UNIT 4: Unique Grammar: Idioms** Given the video, review games, and lesson about idioms, students will be able to complete the matching sheet with 18/20 questions answered correctly.	Standard 2 (The Language of Language Arts) TCAs: 2(3F): Managing and Implementing Standards-Based ESL and Content Instruction	YouTube video: https://www.youtube.com/watch?v=WVHlVblgUH0 Idiom games: http://www.aasd.k12.wi.us/staff/boldtkatherine/readingfun3-6/readingfun_idioms.htm	**LA/T**—Students will begin to learn idioms in the English language. To begin this unit, students will watch a 15-minute video about idioms on YouTube: https://www.youtube.com/watch?v=WVHlVblgUH0 **DIV**—The teacher will discuss the most common idioms found in the English language, then she will give students the opportunity to share idioms in their native language and the English translation. **ASSESS**—After students have watched the YouTube video, they will go to the computer lab to play review games about popular English idioms: http://www.aasd.k12.wi.us/staff/boldtkatherine/readingfun3-6/readingfun_idioms.htm Once students have completed the review games, they will be given a 20-question matching worksheet.

DAY #	CONTENT/OBJECTIVE	STANDARDS	RESOURCES/MATERIALS	LEARNING ACTIVITIES/ASSESSMENTS
153	**Unit 5: Geometry: Categories and Properties** Given an exit ticket, students will accurately define 3/3 terms they studied in class that day.	Standard 3 (Language of Mathematics) TCAs: 2(1A): Describing Language 2(2B): Language Acquisition and Development	Exit tickets	**M**—The teacher will explain the definitions of the words "properties" and "categories" as they relate to geometry. She will explain that students can determine what category a two-dimensional shape belongs in based on its properties. They will then review some common terms that students will need to know about properties of shapes (e.g., angle, side, equilateral, etc.). **ACT**—To review the terms they have learned in the class period, the class will play Around the World. **DIV**—During Around the World, different desks will be labeled with the students' home countries. When the students make it "around the world" and back to their home country, they will win. **ASSESS**—Before class ends, the students will write on an exit ticket three terms and definitions they remember.
154	**Unit 6: The Surface of the Earth: Introduction, Rocks, and Rock Cycle** Given eight definitions called out by the teacher, the students will accurately write the correct term no less than 7/8 times.	Standard 4 (Language of Science) TCAs: 2(1A): Describing Language 2(2B): Language Acquisition and Development	Rock cycle link: http://pmt-5th-grade-science.wikispaces.com/Rock+Cycle Computer and projector Individual whiteboards and whiteboard markers	**S**—Using the 15 vocabulary words included in the steps from diagram in the Rock Cycle link in the resources section, the teacher will provide definitions of key terms for students. **ACT/T/DIV**—Students will be divided into pairs (one higher-level English speaker with one lower-level English speaker). They will then play the game Four Corners to review the vocabulary. Each corner will be labeled "A," "B," "C," or "D." Then, the teacher will put a definition up on the screen with multiple-choice options of terms ("a" through "d") underneath. Students will walk with their partner to the corner of the room that they decide corresponds with the correct term. The teacher will then show them the correct answer. Pairs will get points for the number of answers they get correct. The team with the most points will win in the end. **ASSESS**—Finally, students will return to their seats. The teacher will call out eight definitions, one by one. After she calls out each term, students will write the term that matches each definition on their whiteboards and hold them up for the teacher to check.

DAY #	CONTENT/OBJECTIVE	STANDARDS	RESOURCES/MATERIALS	LEARNING ACTIVITIES/ASSESSMENTS
155	**Unit 4: US–Legacy for Us Today** Given a 20-question quiz, students will be able to answer 19/20 questions correctly.	Standard 5 (Language of Social Science) TCAs: 2(3F): Managing and Implementing Standards-Based ESL and Content Instruction 2(4J): Classroom-Based Assessment for ESL	Quiz	**SS/ASSESS**—Students will take a 20-question test on the vocabulary terms they have been learning. The test will include matching, multiple-choice, and five vocabulary words they must use in a sentence.
156	**Healthy Eating** Given an empty brainstorming chart, students will write down five ways they can eat more healthily.	Standard 1 (Social & Instructional Language) TCAs: 2(1A): Describing Language 2(2B): Language Acquisition and Development	"Berenstain Bears—Too Much Junk Food" video: http://www.youtube.com/watch?v=h61O9D_5pSw Empty brainstorming chart Writing utensils	**T/H**—The students will watch the 11½- minute video about eating healthily. **CT**—The teacher will ask the students to discuss whether healthy eating is something that is important in their culture or not. She will then ask the students to have a discussion about whether or not they eat healthily. Finally, they will brainstorm five things they can do to eat more healthily.
157	**Unit 4: Unique Grammar: Idioms** Students will be able to write five sentences using idioms correctly with three or less writing errors.	Standard 2 (The Language of Language Arts) TCAs: 2(3F): Managing and Implementing Standards-Based ESL and Content Instruction	*There's a Frog in My Throat* by Loreen Leedy	**LA**—To begin the class, the teacher will read *There's a Frog in My Throat* by Loreen Leedy. While the teacher is reading the book, students will raise their hand each time they hear an idiom. The first student to raise their hand will tell the class the meaning of the idiom. **ASSESS**—After the teacher has finished reading the book, she will give the class an assignment to write five sentences using idioms. After the students have written five sentences using idioms, they will fill out the study guide for next week's quiz.
158	**Unit 5: Geometry: Properties Hierarchies** Given a poster board, markers, and magazines, each student will either paste one picture of food in its correct location or will write the name of a property correctly on the poster board to make a food properties hierarchy.	Standard 3 (Language of Mathematics) TCAs: 2(1A): Describing Language 2(2B): Language Acquisition and Development 2(2C): Nature and Role of Culture 2(2D): Cultural Groups and Identity	Poster board Markers Magazines with pictures of foods	**M**—The teacher will teach the students the concept of hierarchies and connect them back to the classification keys they learned about in Unit 1 of Science. To prepare them for making and understanding properties hierarchies in their other classes, the teacher will ask them to make a hierarchy of different properties of foods. **COLL/CT**—As a class, they will brainstorm different properties of food (e.g., breakfast food, lunch food, dinner food; sweet, salty, cold, hot, etc.). **ACT**—They will then draw a hierarchy onto a poster board, cutting out pictures of different types of foods from magazines and gluing them into the proper categories where they belong.

DAY #	CONTENT/OBJECTIVE	STANDARDS	RESOURCES/MATERIALS	LEARNING ACTIVITIES/ASSESSMENTS
159	**Unit 6: The Surface of the Earth: History of the Earth** Given an exit ticket with three questions, students will answer 3/3 with complete sentences.	Standard 4 (Language of Science) TCAs: 2(1A): Describing Language 2(2B): Language Acquisition and Development	Computers YouVersion online bible: https://www.bible.com/bible/1/gen.1.kjv Jesus film: http://jesusfilmmedia.org/video/1_529-jf-0-0/english/jesus Projector Exit ticket	**S/B/CT/CE/COLL**—The students will practice their speaking by having a discussion time. The teacher will ask them whether they believe in Evolution or in Creation and why. They will divide into groups of three to discuss the question, then each group will nominate a speaker to summarize what they said to the whole class. **DIV**—The students will go to the YouVersion website (see link in the resources section) and pull up a copy of the bible in their native language if it is available (If it is not, they will read it in English). They will read and/or listen to Genesis 1 in their native language (meeting the needs of students with diverse backgrounds and learning styles). When they have finished, the teacher will read Genesis chapter 1 aloud in English. She will ask the students if there was anything they did not understand and if they have any questions. **T**—Finally, the students will go to the Jesus Film website (see the link in the resources section) and watch the first 2½ minutes of the film in their native language. Then the teacher will project and play that section of the film in English for the students. On an exit ticket, students will be asked to use complete sentences to answer three questions. 1. Do they think the world was formed through Evolution or Creation? 2. Why do they think what they do? 3. Has their opinion changed since the beginning of class? (If the students do not believe that God created the world, she will follow up with them in person, sharing the Gospel and the evidence for a Creator and against Evolution.)
160	**Unit 4: US—Legacy for Us Today** Given the writing assignment, students will write at least one full-page essay including an introduction, body, and conclusion with five or less writing errors.	Standard 5 (Language of Social Science) TCAs: 2(3F): Managing and Implementing Standards-Based ESL and Content Instruction	Paper	**SS/LA/CT**—Students will be given a critical thinking writing assignment. Their writing prompt will be "What is my legacy?" In this short essay, students will recall the impact of the founding fathers and discuss how they wish to make an impact in the world and their country. Students will write at least one page of text and the essay must include an introduction, body, and conclusion.

DAY #	CONTENT/OBJECTIVE	STANDARDS	RESOURCES/MATERIALS	LEARNING ACTIVITIES/ASSESSMENTS
161	**Going to the City Pool** Given the 10-question quiz covering pool vocabulary, students will answer 9/10 questions correctly.	Standard 1 (Social & Instructional Language) TCAs: 2(3F): Managing and Implementing Standards-Based ESL and Content Instruction 2(3G): Using Resources Effectively in ESL and Content Instruction	Pool vocabulary: http://www.english-test.net/esl/learn/english/grammar/ii805/esl-test.php	**LA/T**—Students will learn vocabulary words about going to the pool and play online review games to help memorize the vocabulary: http://www.english-test.net/esl/learn/english/grammar/ii805/esl-test.php **MUS/T**—After memorizing the vocabulary relating to swimming and going to the pool, the teacher will play the Swimming Song: http://www.watchknowlearn.org/Video.aspx?VideoID=43642&CategoryID=7100 **ACT/COLL/P/CE**—The students will take an afternoon trip to the city pool; this will also be counted as PE class, and the PE instructor will accompany the class and help teach them about swimming. The teacher will mention the character principle of wisdom and carefulness when it comes to pool safety. **ASSESS**—After students return from the pool, they will be given a 10-question matching worksheet covering the pool vocabulary they have learned. **DIV**—Kinesthetic learners will be able to learn through the activity of swimming. Auditory learners will be able to learn through listening to the song. Visual learners will be able to learn using the online review games.
162	**Unit 4: Unique Grammar: Idioms** Given the 20-question quiz covering idioms, students will answer 18/20 questions correctly.	Standard 2 (The Language of Language Arts) TCAs: 2(3F): Managing and Implementing Standards-Based ESL and Content Instruction	Quiz	**LA/ASSESS**—Students will take a 20-question quiz covering the idioms they learned last week. The quiz will include matching, multiple-choice, and two idioms they will need to use in a sentence.

DAY #	CONTENT/OBJECTIVE	STANDARDS	RESOURCES/MATERIALS	LEARNING ACTIVITIES/ASSESSMENTS
163	**Unit 5—Geometry: Geometry Review Day** Given a checklist of five math review games, students will complete 5/5.	Standard 3 (Language of Mathematics) TCAs: 2(3F): Managing and Implementing Standards-Based ESL and Content Instruction	Computers (one for each student) A checklist with the links to each of the following games— 2D Shapes game: http://www.math-play.com/shapes-jeopardy/shapes-jeopardy.html Polygon Vocabulary Review: http://www.ixl.com/math/geometry/polygon-vocabulary Coordinate Plane Review: http://www.ixl.com/math/geometry/coordinate-plane-review Triangle Classification Review: http://www.ixl.com/math/geometry/classify-triangles Quadrilateral Classification Review: http://www.ixl.com/math/geometry/classify-quadrilaterals	**M/T**—The students will go to the computer lab and play math computer games to review the vocabulary that they have learned related to geometry.

DAY #	CONTENT/OBJECTIVE	STANDARDS	RESOURCES/MATERIALS	LEARNING ACTIVITIES/ASSESSMENTS
164	**Unit 6: The Surface of the Earth: The Interior of the Earth & Plate Tectonics** Given three Oreo cookies and the definitions of different types of plate boundaries, students will work individually to correctly break and form their cookies to demonstrate 3/3 types of plate boundaries. Given five Styrofoam cups labeled with each of the layers of the earth, students will work in groups of four to stack them in the proper order, with 5/5 accuracy.	Standard 4 (Language of Science) TCAs: 2(1A): Describing Language 2(2B): Language Acquisition and Development	Oreo Plate Tectonics: http://homeschooljournal-bergblog.blogspot.com/2012/05/oreo-plate-tectonics.html Oreo cookies Styrofoam cups for the cup game (see the link below for concept idea): http://www.pinterest.com/pin/408701734906497291/ List of the layers of the earth: http://volcano.oregonstate.edu/vwdocs/vwlessons/lessons/Earths_layers/Earths_layers2.html	**S/ACT**—Using the process and techniques described in the process at the Oreo Plate Tectonics link in the resources section, the teacher will explain the various types of plate boundaries to students. Then, the students will be given three Oreo cookies each and asked to demonstrate each of the types of plate boundaries using the cookies. (Then they can eat them, of course!) Next, for the interior of the earth, the teacher will introduce the names of the layers of the earth. She will then divide students into groups of four and give them a stack of Styrofoam cups with the name of each layer written on the top edge of the cup. Students will be given "ready, set, go!" and then they will work together to stack the cups in the proper order (with the innermost layer on the bottom and the outermost layer on top).
165	**5th Grade Social Science Review Day/ SOL Preparation**	Standard 5 (Language of Social Science) TCAs: 2(3F): Managing and Implementing Standards-Based ESL and Content Instruction	Pre-assessment (similar to SOL test)	**SS/ASSESS**—The teacher will present students with a 50-question practice test that will mimic the Social Science SOL. Based on the results from the test, the teacher will determine the areas that need more clarification and emphasis before the students take the Social Science SOL assessment. After students are finished with the assessment, they will be rewarded with going outside for a 15-minute recess.
166	**SOL Test Prep** Given an oral assessment of five questions, students will answer with 5/5 accuracy.	Standard 1 (Social & Instructional Language) TCAs: 2(4A): Issues of Assessment for ESL	An old copy of an SOL test	The teacher will explain to the students the format of the SOL tests they are required to take. Using an old copy of an SOL test as an example, she will explain what types of questions will be on the tests, how long it will take, and what the students may and may not do. **ASSESS**—The teacher will ask the students five questions out loud to make sure they have understood the information she has presented.

DAY #	CONTENT/OBJECTIVE	STANDARDS	RESOURCES/MATERIALS	LEARNING ACTIVITIES/ASSESSMENTS
167	**5th Grade Language Arts Review Day/SOL Preparation**	Standard 2 (The Language of Language Arts) TCAs: 2(3F): Managing and Implementing Standards-Based ESL and Content Instruction	Pre-assessment (similar to SOL test) Movie	**LA/ASSESS**—The teacher will present students with a 50-question practice test that will mimic the Language Arts SOL. Based on the results from the test, the teacher will determine the areas that need more clarification and emphasis before the students take the Language Arts SOL assessment. After students are finished with the pre-assessment, they will have the opportunity to watch a short movie for the remainder of the class period.
168	**Unit 5: Yearlong Review Day** Given a blank exit ticket, students will accurately write the definitions to three vocabulary words of their choice.	Standard 3 (Language of Mathematics) TCAs: 2(3F): Managing and Implementing Standards-Based ESL and Content Instruction	"Mathematics Vocabulary Cards": http://www.doe.virginia.gov/instruction/mathematics/resources/vocab_cards/math_vocab_cards_5.pdf Blank exit tickets Writing utensils	**M/COLL**—The class will review together all of the contents of the Mathematics Vocabulary Flash Cards. The students will get into groups of four and take turns reading one flash card each. **ACT**—After reviewing the material in the flash cards, students will play math Around the World for further review. **DIV**—During Around the World, different desks will be labeled with the students' home countries. When the students make it "around the world" and back to their home country, they will win. **ASSESS**—On an exit ticket, students will write three definitions of vocabulary words they will need to know for next week's geometry test.
169	**Unit 6: The Surface of the Earth: Erosion & Pollution** Given eight scenarios, students will label them with 8/8 accuracy.	Standard 4 (Language of Science) TCAs: 2(1A): Describing Language 2(2B): Language Acquisition and Development	"Weather, Erosion, and Deposition Sorting Activity": http://www.teacherspayteachers.com/Product/FREE-Weathering-Erosion-and-Deposition-Sorting-Activity-354192	**S/CT/CE**—The teacher will define key terms the students need to know (such as deposition, weathering, pollution, erosion, watershed, etc.). The students will then practice speaking by having a discussion on what humans' role should be in taking care of the earth. The teacher will ask them to share anything they know of that the bible has to say about taking care of the earth. She will ask them to think of some examples of human-caused "wear & tear" on the earth and "wear & tear" from other causes. Finally, students will be given the eight examples from the link in the resources section and will label them with the correct term (weathering, deposition, or erosion).

DAY #	CONTENT/OBJECTIVE	STANDARDS	RESOURCES/MATERIALS	LEARNING ACTIVITIES/ASSESSMENTS
170	**5th Grade Social Science Review Day/ SOL Preparation**	Standard 5 (Language of Social Science) TCAs: 2(3F): Managing and Implementing Standards-Based ESL and Content Instruction	Computers Social Science games: http://www.collierschools.com/weblessons/students_online/5Social.htm PowerPoint presentation Study guide	**SS/T**—Students will have the opportunity to go to the computer lab to play review games in preparation for the SOL assessment: http://www.collierschools.com/weblessons/students_online/5Social.htm After students have played a few review games individually, the teacher will give a review lesson of the materials they have covered throughout the year. Once they have received the review lesson, students will be given class time to fill out a study guide regarding information that will be covered in the Social Science SOL assessment.
171	**Review Day** Given the review game and PowerPoint presentation, students will be able to fill out the complete study guide with 100% accuracy.	Standard 1 (Social & Instructional Language) TCAs: 2(3F): Managing and Implementing Standards-Based ESL and Content Instruction 2(3G): Using Resources Effectively in ESL and Content Instruction	Sink or Swim game: http://k6educators.about.com/od/lessonplanheadquarters/a/5-Successful-Review-Activities-For-Elementary-Students.htm Review questions Study guide	**T/CE**—The teacher will give a short PowerPoint presentation reviewing the 40 vocabulary terms students will need to know for the test. These vocabulary terms will be pulled from the lessons and activities covered in the Social and Instructional Language class period. The teacher will also remind the students of the character principles of wisdom and carefulness in relation to pool safety. After the teacher has reviewed the terms with the class, they will play a review game called "Sink or Swim." After the class has played the review game, they will be given time to fill out the study guide.
172	**5th Grade Language Arts Review Day/SOL Preparation**	Standard 2 (The Language of Language Arts) TCAs: 2(3F): Managing and Implementing Standards-Based ESL and Content Instruction	Computers Language Arts games: http://www.gameclassroom.com/language-arts-games/5th-grade PowerPoint presentation Study guide	**T**—Students will have the opportunity to go to the computer lab to play review games in preparation for the SOL assessment: http://www.gameclassroom.com/language-arts-games/5th-grade After students have played a few review games individually, the teacher will give a review lesson of the materials they have covered throughout the year. Once they have received the review lesson, students will be given class time to fill out a study guide regarding information that will be covered in the Language Arts SOL assessment.

DAY #	CONTENT/OBJECTIVE	STANDARDS	RESOURCES/MATERIALS	LEARNING ACTIVITIES/ASSESSMENTS
173	**Final Assessment Day— Mathematics SOL Test** Given the mathematics section of the Virginia SOL test, students will complete it.	Standard 3 (Language of Mathematics) TCAs: 2(4A): Issues of Assessment for ESL	Mathematics SOL test	**M/ASSESS**—The students will take the mathematics section of the state SOL test.
174	**Unit 6: Yearlong Review Day** Given seven terms from their year of science vocabulary, students will accurately define 7/7.	Standard 4 (Language of Science) TCAs: 2(3F): Managing and Implementing Standards-Based ESL and Content Instruction	Paper Writing utensils "Vocabulary Snowball Fight" instructions (see the link in day 129's resources section) Study guide with key terms for the SOL test	**S**—Each student will be given seven terms each written by itself on its own sheet of paper. Students will then need to define each term, each definition being written on a new set of paper. **ASSESS**—They will raise their hands when they have finished so the teacher can make sure they have defined the terms accurately. **COLL/ACT**—Finally, students will crumple all of their papers and toss them to each other and all over the room. They will team up with a partner and race to un-crumple papers and match terms and definitions. The first student to match seven terms and definitions accurately will win, but all of the students must ultimately find seven matching terms and definitions. Finally, the teacher will send the students home a study guide consisting of a list of key terms and definitions to study in preparation for next week's SOL test.
175	**ASSESSMENT DAY** Social Science SOL Assessment Students will take the SOL assessment with 100% participation and a good attitude.	Standard 5 (Language of Social Science) TCAs: 2(4A): Issues of Assessment for ESL	Social Science SOL test	**SS/ASSESS/COLL**—The ESL teacher will collaborate with the students' social studies teacher to have the students take the Social Science portion of the state SOL in the ESL classroom. If needed, the ESL teacher will provide students with modifications such as a bilingual dictionary and reading the test aloud to the student.

DAY #	CONTENT/OBJECTIVE	STANDARDS	RESOURCES/MATERIALS	LEARNING ACTIVITIES/ASSESSMENTS
176	**ASSESSMENT DAY** Given the 40-question vocabulary test, students will answer 35/40 questions correctly.	Standard 1 (Social & Instructional Language) TCAs: 2(3F): Managing and Implementing Standards-Based ESL and Content Instruction 2(4A): Issues of Assessment for ESL	Test	**ASSESS**—Students will take a comprehensive 40-question test made up of multiple-choice, fill-in-the-blank, and true-false questions.
177	**ASSESSMENT DAY** Language Art SOL Assessment Students will take the SOL assessment with 100% participation and a good attitude.	Standard 2 (The Language of Language Arts) TCAs: 2(4A): Issues of Assessment for ESL	Language Arts SOL test	**LA/ASSESS**—The students will take the Language Arts portion of the state SOL. If needed, the ESL teacher will provide students with modifications such as a bilingual dictionary and reading the test aloud to the student.
178	**Tutoring Day** Given assignments from content area teachers, each student will ask the ESL teacher at least two questions.	Standard 2 (The Language of Language Arts) Standard 3 (Language of Mathematics) Standard 4 (Language of Science) Standard 5 (Language of Social Science) TCAs: 2(5M): Professional Development and Collaboration	Assignments from content area teachers	**COLL**—The ESL teacher will ask the students' content area teachers to give them any assignments or test preparation materials that the students need to work on. Students will spend class period working on the materials and asking the teacher about anything they do not understand.

DAY #	CONTENT/OBJECTIVE	STANDARDS	RESOURCES/MATERIALS	LEARNING ACTIVITIES/ASSESSMENTS
179	**Unit 6: The Surface of the Earth—Assessment Day: Science SOL Tests** Students will take the SOL assessment with 100% participation and a good attitude.	Standard 4 (Language of Science) TCAs: 2(4A): Issues of Assessment for ESL	Science SOL Test	**S/ASSESS**—The students will take the science section of the state SOL test.
180	**LAST DAY OF SCHOOL** Given instructions to bring food items and participate in games, students will be attentive and give 100% class participation.		Food items Paper plates, cups, napkins, decorations Balloons Games Movie	**CT/CE**—Students will talk about their favorite part of 5th grade. They will be asked, "How have you grown in the past year?" The teacher will remind them of the importance of hard work as a student and praise their efforts from the past school year. **DIV**—The students will then talk about the differences between their culture and culture in the United States. They will recall the different things they learned about the United States the past school year. **ACT**—Play games Watch movie Eat food

SAMPLE #2 WITH TESL COURSE INTEGRATION CURRICULUM PROJECT

TEACHER CANDIDATE'S NAME:
CONTENT SUBJECT AREA: *ESL*
GRADE LEVEL: *8th Grade, Level 3*
TEXTBOOK NAME WITH PUBLICATION INFORMATION:

Allen, J., Applebee, A. N., Burke, J., Carnine, D., Jackson, Y., & Jago, C. (2012). *Literature: Grade 8.* Orlando, FL: Houghton Mifflin Harcourt Publishing Company.

Azar, B. S. (2002). *Understanding and using English grammar* (3rd ed.). White Plains, NY: Pearson Education.

Beck, R. B., Black, L., Krieger, L. S., Naylor, P. C., & Shabaka, D. I. (2009). *Ancient world history: Patterns of interaction.* Evanston, IL: McDougal Littell.

Bennet, J. M., Burger, E. B., Chard, D. B., Hall, E. J., Kennedy, P. A., & Renfro, F. L. (2010). *Mathematics: Course 3.* Austin, TX: Holt McDougal.

Daise, D., Falk, R., Norloff, C., & Zante, J. V. (2005). *Grammar links 3* (2nd ed.). Boston, MA: Houghton Mifflin Company.

Frank, D. V., Jones, T. G., Little, J. G., Miaoulis, B., Miller, S., & Pasachoff, J. M. (2009). *Physical science.* Upper Saddle River, NJ: Pearson Education Inc.

Mikulecky, B. S., & Jeffries, L. (2007). *Advanced reading power: Extensive reading, vocabulary building, comprehension skills, reading faster.* White Plains, NY: Pearson Education, Inc.

Mission Statement:
The ESL department of Cornerstone Middle School strives to provide all levels of language learners with a multicultural learning environment that promotes and encourages long-term academic, social, and professional excellence by supplying students with opportunities to further develop their knowledge of the English language through differentiated methods of application and collaboration, and supplemental lessons from other disciplines of academia.

DAY #	CONTENT/OBJECTIVE	STANDARDS	RESOURCES/MATERIALS	LEARNING ACTIVITIES/ASSESSMENTS
	• Skills • Knowledge • Dispositions • Concepts • Themes • Values	• VA SOLs • National Standards • TCAs	*Include (1) resources to assist the teacher in planning and implementing lessons and (2) materials students need to participate.* • Books • Technology • Supplies • Community organizations • Guest speakers • Websites	*After each code below, list the day #'s in which the element is present. Codes are not required in every day's lesson but should be distributed appropriately throughout. You may create other codes if necessary to reflect special considerations not listed here.* *Simply listing the code is not sufficient. A brief explanation is needed to describe what the legend is referring to. For example, instead of just listing "CE," describe what character trait is being taught and how it relates to the lesson. Instead of just listing "ACT," describe how the students will be engaged in active learning.*

DAY #	CONTENT/OBJECTIVE	STANDARDS	RESOURCES/MATERIALS	LEARNING ACTIVITIES/ASSESSMENTS
	Key: Green—Science day Red—Math day Brown—LA day Blue—History day Yellow—Social Studies day Purple—ACCESS testing or review GM—Weekly grammar connection			**ACTIVITY LEGEND** (*All of the Activity Codes are* **required** *to be integrated at least once each week. It's important to show a variety of the legends distributed throughout the project.*): ACT = Active Learning—Day #: 1, 7, 10, 12, 18, 19, 21, 22, 27, 28, 33, 37, 40, 46, 47, 49, 50, 56, 62, 63, 65, 66, 73, 76, 80, 85, 86, 90, 91, 96, 102, 106, 108, 109, 111, 115, 122, 127, 132, 135, 137, 139, 142, 150, 152, 153, 155, 160, 165, 168, 169, 175, 177, 180 ASSESS = Assessment Activity—Day #: 2, 3, 4, 6, 8, 12, 13, 16, 22, 23, 24, 25, 29, 31, 36, 42, 43, 48, 51, 53, 59, 60, 61, 63, 65, 69, 72, 74, 77, 80, 81, 83, 84, 88, 89, 90, 91, 92, 94, 95, 97, 99, 100, 101, 102, 103, 109, 112, 114, 116, 119, 120, 123, 125, 126, 128, 129, 130, 131, 134, 136, 137, 139, 142, 145, 146, 147, 148, 149, 150, 154, 155, 157, 159, 163, 170, 176, 178 COLL = There are different types of collaboration: (1) teacher with community members/organizations or other educators and (2) students with other students or community members—Day #: 1, 5, 8, 10, 12, 16, 19, 20, 24, 25, 26, 28, 30, 33, 35, 36, 37, 41, 43, 44, 46, 50, 52, 58, 60, 61, 63, 64, 65, 66, 68, 71, 73, 78, 82, 83, 85, 86, 91, 92, 94, 95, 99, 100, 103, 104, 105, 107, 110, 111, 112, 117, 118, 123, 126, 127, 132, 134, 135, 138, 139, 140, 141, 143, 144, 147, 151, 152, 153, 156, 161, 162, 164, 165, 171, 172, 175, 180 CE = Character Education—Day #: 1, 6, 14, 19, 24, 27, 34, 39, 40, 47, 48, 50, 57, 62, 64, 65, 70, 75, 78, 80, 85, 88, 92, 96, 98, 107, 113, 119, 123, 124, 125, 126, 127, 128, 129, 130, 131, 132, 136, 148, 157, 162, 164, 167, 169, 173, 178 CT = Critical Thinking Activity—Day #: 2, 3, 5, 6, 8, 11, 15, 17, 21, 26, 29, 30, 35, 37, 42, 47, 48, 52, 53, 58, 60, 61, 63, 65, 66, 73, 77, 83, 84, 85, 88, 89, 91, 92, 93, 94, 95, 105, 109, 113, 115, 118, 126, 128, 129, 130, 131, 133, 139, 141, 144, 146, 152, 154, 156, 158, 159, 160, 162, 166, 167, 172, 176, 179 DIV = Diversity Consideration—Day #: 1, 7, 13, 14, 19, 23, 24, 28, 33, 36, 41, 43, 44, 45, 49, 50, 56, 57, 61, 64, 67, 70, 78, 79, 83, 85, 88, 89, 94, 99, 107, 108, 109, 114, 115, 117, 122, 123, 126, 132, 133, 134, 135, 142, 145, 147, 152, 153, 158, 165, 167, 172, 173, 180 T = Technology—Day #: 1, 4, 5, 6, 12, 13, 14, 17, 19, 21, 22, 24, 25, 27, 29, 32, 35, 38, 40, 43, 44, 45, 47, 51, 52, 53, 54, 57, 58, 60, 63, 64, 65, 68, 70, 71, 80, 82, 85, 86, 88, 89, 92, 93, 95, 96, 98, 103, 104, 105, 108, 112, 114, 115, 117, 118, 119, 121, 122, 123, 125, 129, 131, 135, 136, 137, 138, 140, 142, 143, 148, 150, 153, 154, 155, 156, 157, 159, 160, 161, 162, 164, 166, 167, 170, 173, 175, 177, 179, 180

DAY #	CONTENT/OBJECTIVE	STANDARDS	RESOURCES/MATERIALS	LEARNING ACTIVITIES/ASSESSMENTS
				***INTEGRATION LEGEND** (A variety of interdisciplinary integrations should be included at least once per 9 weeks. **Not all are necessary**, only those that can reasonably be integrated into your subject area. If a code is not used at all, enter N/A after "Day #'s" for that code.):*
				A = Art—Day #: 15, 30, 35, 42, 57, 86, 110, 143, 153
				B = Biblical principles—Day #: 40, 48, 65, 132, 148
				D = Dance—Day #: 12, 78, 90, 115, 122, 157
				H = Health—Day #: 44, 45, 84, 155
				L = Language arts—Day #: 4, 5, 8, 12, 14, 22, 25, 26, 27, 32, 44, 45, 46, 48, 51, 55, 56, 57, 58, 59, 60, 63, 66, 82, 84, 87, 93, 98, 101, 103, 107, 113, 118, 133, 135, 137, 140, 145, 150, 151, 152, 154, 155, 157, 160, 170, 175, 176, 178
				M = Math—Day #: 7, 11, 16, 21, 26, 31, 36, 41, 46, 51, 54, 59, 65, 81, 86, 91, 94, 105, 114, 119, 136, 141, 146, 151, 156, 161, 166, 171, 177, 178
				MUS = Music—Day #: 29, 37, 81, 90, 115, 122, 157, 179, 180
				P = Physical education/movement—Day #: 12, 46, 47, 49, 50, 62, 70, 76, 85, 90, 102, 115, 155, 157, 158, 165, 168, 169
				S = Science—Day #: 6, 9, 11, 15, 20, 25, 30, 35, 40, 42, 45, 50, 53, 58, 62, 68, 69, 80, 85, 90, 96, 102, 107, 116, 121, 134, 139, 144, 149, 154, 159, 164, 165, 169, 175, 176
				SS = Social Science—Day #: 7, 13, 23, 24, 25, 28, 33, 38, 39, 43, 48, 49, 50, 52, 61, 64, 67, 83, 88, 89, 92, 95, 109, 115, 133, 138, 143, 148, 153, 158, 163, 164, 168, 177, 178
				TH = Theatre—Day #: 46, 47, 49, 117, 142
1	**Social (Class Greetings and Introductions)** Given a world map, students will introduce themselves, where they are from, and what their native language is in complete sentences and with less than five speaking errors.	WIDA Standard 1 Grade 8 Level 3 VSOL: ENGL 8.2 TCA 2(2c)	PPT—introduction, CE principle, and world map Syllabus	**T/CE**—Teacher introduction and personal character principle with PowerPoint Pass out class syllabus to students. Go over class expectations/ guidelines/content and schedule with students. **T/DIV/COLL/ACT**—PPT displays a world map. Students use it to introduce themselves, they go to the screen, point out where they are from, and state what their native language is.

DAY #	CONTENT/OBJECTIVE	STANDARDS	RESOURCES/MATERIALS	LEARNING ACTIVITIES/ASSESSMENTS
2	**Pre-Assess Reading/Writing** Given 25 practice questions from the reading/writing parts of an old copy of the ACCESS test, students will complete as much as they can to the best of their abilities in the time frame of one class period.	WIDA Standard 2 Grade 8 Level 3 VSOL: ENGL 8.4–8 TCA: 2(4h)	ACCESS practice test or old version of test Pencil Paper	**ASSESS/CT**—Students need to be seated at every other desk. Teacher distributes practice ACCESS test for reading and writing. Oral directions for the test are given to the students. Students complete the test as best as they can.
3	**Pre-Assess Speaking/ Listening** Given 25 practice questions from the listening/speaking parts of an old copy of the ACCESS test, students will complete as many questions as they can to the best of their abilities in the time frame of one class period.	WIDA Standard 1 and 2 Grade 8 Level 3 VSOL: ENGL 8.2a, b, h TCA: 2(4h)	ACCESS practice test or old version of test Pencil Paper	Students need to be seated at every other desk. **ASSESS/CT**—Teacher distributes practice ACCESS test for speaking and listening. Oral directions for the test are given to the students. Students complete the test as best as they can.
4	**Review Reading/ Writing** Given a short story, students will answer 8 out of 10 questions based on reading comprehension and vocabulary correctly. Given the same short story, students will answer in writing two out of three discussion questions using complete sentences.	WIDA Standard 2 Grade 8 Level 3 VSOL: ENGL 8.4b, 5, 6 TCA: 2(1a, b) 2(2e, f) 2(4i, j)	PPT on parts of speech, sentence structure, and paragraphs Book (ESL reading language): *Advanced reading power: Extensive reading, vocabulary building, comprehension skills, reading faster* Comprehension & vocabulary worksheet	**L/T**—Teacher uses PPT to review parts of speech, structure of a basic sentence in the English language, and parts of a paragraph. Teacher reads an example short story and works with students to answer comprehension/vocabulary questions. **ASSESS**—Students are given a copy of their own short story with 10 comprehension and vocabulary questions to answer. Students are allowed to finish for HW.

DAY #	CONTENT/OBJECTIVE	STANDARDS	RESOURCES/MATERIALS	LEARNING ACTIVITIES/ASSESSMENTS
5	**Review Speaking/ Listening** After hearing an audio clip of a short passage being read, students will answer three out of five questions related to the audio clip correctly. Given the same audio clip, students will discuss their thoughts about the subject of the clip with a partner in complete sentences and using no more than five grammatical speaking errors.	WIDA Standard 1 Grade 8 Level 3 VSOL: ENGL 8.2d, e, f, h TCA: 2(1a, b) 2(3e, f) 2(4h, j)	PPT on listening and speaking skills Audio files of short story Worksheets	**L**—Teacher uses PPT to review listening and speaking skills. Teacher focuses on tone, pitch, social cues, vocabulary, and keeping attention. **T**—Teacher plays an audio clip. Then, teacher asks students questions related to the material they just heard. Teacher leads students in conversation about the audio clip. **COLL/CT**—Teacher distributes a worksheet with questions for students to answer based on another audio clip they will hear for their individual practice. Students listen to an audio clip of a short passage from a story. They answer the questions. Then students are to partner up and discuss their personal thoughts about audio clip. They are not to share answers from the worksheet.
6	**Intro to Science** Given information about dry ice and water, students will compose in a complete sentence and with less than four grammatical errors a hypothesis about what happens when the two mix.	WIDA Standard 4 Grade 8 Level 3 VSOL: PS.1, PS.5a/b TCA: 2(1a, b) 2(3e, f, g) 2(4h, j)	PPT on physical science and scientific method Video clip of Coke and Mentos: http://www.youtube.com/watch?v=Vn5sV8aQG_k Worksheet	**CE**—Teacher opens with mini-lesson on starting day and week with moments of silence. **T/S**—Teacher uses PPT to review definition and concepts of physical science and scientific inquiry (scientific method). Give copies of PPT to LD students. **T**—Teacher uses video clip of Coke and Mentos reaction to walk students through steps of scientific inquiry. Teacher will guide students in how to write each step. **ASSESS/CT**—Students are given facts sheet about dry ice and water and will have to write their own hypothesis about what they expect to happen when the two mix.

DAY #	CONTENT/OBJECTIVE	STANDARDS	RESOURCES/MATERIALS	LEARNING ACTIVITIES/ASSESSMENTS
7	**Intro to Math** Given the order of operations, students will create their own acronym using each term in its correct order and using a country name for each letter.	WIDA Standard 3 Grade 8 Level 3 VSOL: MATH 8.1a TCA: 2(1a, b) 2(3e, f) 2(4j)	Textbook—*Mathematics: Course 3*	**M** –Teacher and students look at the math textbook together. Teacher explains that the chapters have specific vocabulary and reading/comprehension hints in each section. For practice, teacher has students identify vocabulary of a chapter, give their own definition, and then read the correct definition. Teacher then calls on students to read several of the reading and comprehension hints. **SS/DIV/ACT**—Teacher explains the order of operations PEMDAS as the foundational concepts of higher level math and reviews the operations. Teacher has students stand up and form each letter with their hands as they are repeated out loud. Then has students create their own acronym with PEMDAS using a country from the world for each letter. A list of country names will be given to each student.
8	**Intro to LA** Given five descriptions of books and a list of genres, students will label each description with the appropriate genre, labeling four out of five correctly.	WIDA Standard 2 Grade 8 Level 3 VASOL: ENGL 8.5b TCA: 2(1a) 2(2c) 2(3e) 2(4j)	PPT discussing genre; incl. list of example book descriptions	**L**—Teacher asks students, "What is literature? Why do we read literature?" Teacher will discuss with students the role literature plays in defining and describing culture and why it is important to read literature. Teacher then describes *genre* and gives a brief explanation of many different kinds of genre (i.e., short stories, poems, fiction, non-fiction, historical fiction, sci-fi, fantasy, mystery, etc.). **Activity** **CT**—Teacher gives students the titles of a couple example books and a brief description of each book. Based on the description, students must identify what genre each book fits into. **COLL**—Students pick the genre they are most interested in. They then write their own two- to three-sentence description of a book they would like to read in that genre. Students will exchange papers and identify the genre of their friends' descriptions. Provide extra guidance to LD students during this activity. **ASSESS**—Teacher gives students a worksheet with five additional titles and descriptions. Students match each description with the correct title.

DAY #	CONTENT/OBJECTIVE	STANDARDS	RESOURCES/MATERIALS	LEARNING ACTIVITIES/ASSESSMENTS
9	**Intro to History (Graphic Organizers)** Given an example of how to complete a graphic organizer and a section from their world history textbook, students will properly outline the five characteristics of civilization by providing at least two supporting details for each chosen characteristic.	WIDA Standard 5 Grade 8 Level 3 VASOL: WHI.3 TCA: 2(1a) 2(3f) 2(4j)	History textbook—*Ancient World History: Patterns of Interaction*—reference pages 19–21 Main idea graphic organizer template	**SS**—Teacher will teach students how to identify the main idea of a section in their history book. Students will also be instructed on how to use graphic organizers to help them in organizing new information read in their textbook. Teacher will give students tips on how to read a chapter in their history book. They will explain the importance of titles, subtitles, headings, and bold-faced or highlighted words and how taking note of them may assist students in understanding the main idea. Give LD students a copy with summarized information. Explain to students what the *main idea* is and how to identify it in a passage. Teacher will briefly explain different kinds of graphic organizers which may help students outline a chapter (Ex. Venn diagram, for comparing & contrasting; main idea bubble map, large bubble for main idea and small bubbles for supporting details; cause & effect organizer). Teacher will demonstrate the use of a main idea bubble map with the students by outlining a specific section in class. Teacher will then have students identify other main and supporting points from the text. Students will then outline a new section of the text.
10 GM1	**Science Chapter 1** Given a listening quiz on 10 vocabulary words from Chapter 1, students will provide the correct definition for each word, with 80% accuracy.	WIDA Standard 4 Grade 8 Level 3 VASOL: PS.2a, b, c, d, e, f TCA: 2(1a) 2(3f) 2(4i)	Paper, scissors Notebook paper	**COLL/ACT**—Students will work together to compile a list of 10 vocabulary words they do not know from Chapter 1. Allow students to move around and work anywhere they want in the classroom. **ACT/SS**—Students will create and utilize a graphic organizer to help each other study the vocabulary words. [Students will take a piece of paper and fold it in half, hot dog-style. They will then cut 9 slits on the front half of the paper, making tabs to write the 10 words. The students will then write their own definition for each of the words on the side of the paper that is covered by the tabs. **COLL**—Students will quiz each other on the definitions for practice. Have students complete listening quiz, recording their answers on a sheet of notebook paper.

DAY #	CONTENT/OBJECTIVE	STANDARDS	RESOURCES/MATERIALS	LEARNING ACTIVITIES/ASSESSMENTS
11	**Math Chapter 1** Given the four mathematical operations, students will give two additional words or phrases that can be used to express each mathematical operation, answering 90% correctly.	WIDA Standard 3 Grade 8 Level 3 VSOL: MATH 8.2, 8.3a, 8.4 TCA: 2(1a) 2(3f) 2(4j)	Textbook—*Mathematics: Course 3*, Chapter 1 Section 2	**M**—Focus on section 2. Teach the students the word phrases and expressions listed. Work through each example in the book with the students (including the word problems), asking them reinforcement questions along the way. Students will complete similar problems independently. **CT**—Have students complete "Think and Discuss" on bottom of page 11 as their exit ticket. 1. Give two words or phrases that can be used to express each operation: addition, subtraction, multiplication, and division. 2. Express 5 + 7n in two different ways.
12	**LA Story/Plot/Main Idea** After instruction, students will identify and describe the types of conflict and the different stages of the plot of a story with 100% accuracy.	WIDA Standard 2 Grade 8 Level 3 VSOL: ENGL 8.5c/h TCA: 1(1e, f, g, h, i) 1(2b, c, d, e) 1(3a, b, e) 1(5a, e) 1(6d) 2(1a, b) 2(2d) 2(3e, f, g) 2(5k)	Duck Tape PPT on story/plot/main idea	Teacher rearranges the room and leaves a big open space in the middle. Teacher uses tape to form an outline of a mountain on the floor. Teacher places five "X's" on the outline for the different stages of the plot of a story. **L/D/P/ACT/COLL/T**—Students come to class and sit on the floor at the bottom of the mountain. Teacher uses PPT review conflict in a story. Teacher plays short polar bear clip of mountain climbing. Teacher puts image up from page 30 in text on screen. Students stand up and move to the bottom left of the outlined mountain. Students must do the mountain climbing dance movement to all reach the first "X." Teacher explains what the first "X" is in relation to the stages of a plot in a story. Students and teacher repeat this process for every "X" on the mountain. Students sit back on floor. Teacher guides students on how to develop the stages of a plot based on a short story prompt. **ASSESS**—For review, teacher asks students collectively what conflict is and the different stages of the plot of a story. Teacher does not call on LD students.

DAY #	CONTENT/OBJECTIVE	STANDARDS	RESOURCES/MATERIALS	LEARNING ACTIVITIES/ASSESSMENTS
13	**History (Maps)** Given a blank world map, students will label the five oceans and the seven continents, getting at least 10 out of 12 correct.	WIDA Standard 5 Grade 8 Level 3 VASOL: WHI.1b, c TCA: 2(1b) 2(2d) 2(2j)	World map Continents and oceans online games: http://www.sheppardsoftware.com/World_Continents.htm	**SS**—Display an ancient world map for students (to 1500 A.D.). Discuss the areas where the ancient civilizations lived and major geographic features of the time. Display a modern world map. Discuss with students how the maps have changed over time. Review the seven continents and five oceans with them. **DIV**—Have students identify which continent they are from. Review concepts of country, state, and city. Have students identify what continent, state, and city they are currently in. **T**—Play online review games of continents. **ASSESS**—Students will complete a quiz on the continents and oceans.
14	**Social** Given a thesaurus and instruction on adjective clauses, students will write a five-sentence paragraph demonstrating proper use of adjective clauses, with three out of three clauses written correctly.	WIDA Standard 1 Grade 8 Level 3 VASOL: ENGL 8.8b TCA: 2(1a, b) 2(3f) 2(i)	Thesaurus PPT presentation on adjectives, personality, and grammar point Text: *Grammar Links 3*	**DIV**—Ask students about their families, particularly how many brothers and sisters they have. Ask them if they think there's a difference in people's personalities based on when they were born (i.e., firstborn, middle child, baby). **T**—Use PPT to review adjectives that could describe someone's personality with students (i.e., friendly, kind, open-minded, creative, insecure, rude, practical, realistic, etc.). Stress the importance of displaying the POSITIVE character traits. Have students take the birth-order personality quiz. Have students discuss their results and whether or not the results were accurate. **L**—Tell students that adjectives are a good way to describe somebody's characteristics or personality, but they can use adjective clauses, as well (as demonstrated in the quiz). Teach adjective clauses. **CE**—Ask students to think about which character traits they would most like to have in a best friend. Have students write a five-sentence paragraph describing their ideal best friend. *If needed, students will finish for homework.

DAY #	CONTENT/OBJECTIVE	STANDARDS	RESOURCES/MATERIALS	LEARNING ACTIVITIES/ASSESSMENTS
15 GM2	**Science Chapter 2** Given Section 3 of Chapter 2 in the textbook, students will identify the different changes which matter can undergo, accurately describing four specific examples.	WIDA Standard 4 Grade 8 Level 3 PS.5a, b TCA: 2(1a) 2(3f) 2(4j)	Four-square graphic organizer	Students will answer review questions about Chapter 2. They will identify and describe the main idea of the chapter. **S/A/CT**—Students will create a vocabulary four-square for matter. They will provide the word, the definition, an example sentence using the word, and they will draw a picture representing *matter*. Students will take home a Venn diagram worksheet where they will compare and contrast physical and chemical changes. They must provide at least two specific examples of both.
16	**Math Chapter 1** Given an oral/listening quiz on this chapter's vocabulary, students will recall and say the proper definition for each word, with 80% accuracy.	WIDA Standard 3 Grade 8 Level 3 VASOL: MATH 8.1a TCA: 2(1a) 2(3e, g) 2(4i, j)	Textbook—*Mathematics: Course 3*, Chapter 1	Students will review their Venn diagrams and their examples of different kinds of physical and chemical changes. **M**—Students will take the vocabulary from Sections 1, 3, and 4 of Chapter 1 and categorize them into groups of nouns, adjectives, or verbs. Students will use their textbooks to find the definition of each word. They will then rewrite the definitions in their own words. **COLL/ASSESS**—Students will exchange papers in order to peer-check each other's definitions. They may study together for a few minutes with a partner. Listening quiz/oral activity: Each partner will quiz the other partner on the vocabulary words on their list. Students will say the answer out loud.
17	**LA** Given information on how to use context clues to identify the meaning of an unknown word, students will create their own context to describe a vocabulary word that has multiple meanings, correctly describing one of them with zero errors.	WIDA Standard 2 Grade 8 Level 3 VSOL: ENGL 8.4b TCA: 2(1a, b) 2(2d) 2(3e) 2(4i)	Zip, zap, zop worksheet	**T**—Ask students what they do when they come to a new word in a text. Explain the different ways students could find the definition of a word they don't know. Explain the best option is for them to GUESS the meaning of a word, and why. Use PPT to explain what *context* and *context clues* are and how examining the two can help a student identify the meaning of a new word. **L**—Give students a couple examples of words they do not know within a context. Have students identify the *context clues* that will help them find the words' meaning. Students will then guess the meaning of the example words. Next, give students a couple examples of words that have a different meaning based on different context. Show them how to use context clues to identify the meaning in each context. Indep. Pract: Students complete the *zip, zap, zop* worksheet. Each worksheet has three paragraphs. Each paragraph has a specific vocabulary word that has been replaced by a fun made-up word (such as zip, zap, or zop). The student will use the context clues to figure out what the missing word is. [At least one of the paragraphs should be a word that has multiple meanings] **CT**—Students create their own zops. Have class identify each student's zop.

DAY #	CONTENT/OBJECTIVE	STANDARDS	RESOURCES/MATERIALS	LEARNING ACTIVITIES/ASSESSMENTS
18	**History Chapter 1** Given a quiz on five chapter vocabulary words, students will provide the correct definition for each of the five words, with 100% accuracy.	WIDA Standard 5 Grade 8 Level 3 VASOL: WHI.1, 2 TCA: 2(1a) 2(3f) 2(4j)	Index cards History textbook—*Ancient World History: Patterns of Interaction*	**COLL/ACT**—Have students split into groups of two. They will work together to identify five new vocabulary words that they do not know. Students will then get index cards and write the new words on the front of the cards. They will research the definitions using an online dictionary or their textbook, and they will write the definition in their own words on a separate index card (20 min.) Then, one student from each group will meet with a member from a different group. Partner LD students with advanced students. Each student will have a few minutes to teach their vocabulary words to their friend (5 min. = SPEED TEACHING! 30 seconds per each word). When the students are finished teaching each other, the teacher will gather all the index cards (both with the vocab word and the definition) and they will lay them out facing down. Students will then play a matching game with the cards. The goal is to match each vocab word with its correct definition (15–20 min.). As the students are playing the game, the teacher will choose five vocab words from the words the students studied and will record the students' definition. The teacher will then prepare a brief oral test that will ask students to identify the correct definition of each word. Students will number a sheet of paper from 1–5. The teacher will say the five vocab words, one at a time. The student must listen to what the teacher is saying and then write down the correct definition for each word after it is said.
19	**Social** After conducting an interview with a local professional, students will outline an informative essay about the professional's job, properly utilizing in-text quotes and citations with 100% accuracy.	WIDA Standard 1 Grade 8 Level 3 VASOL: ENGL 8.1a, b, c, d TCA: 2(1b) 2(2c) 2(4i)	List of possible interview questions Members of the community that have agreed to be interviewed by students	Ask students if they've ever done an interview before. **DIV/T/CE**—Use PPT to instruct students on what an interview is and typical questions prospective employers may ask. Explain that interviews could also be for scholarships, college interviews, or in order to learn new information from a new source. Give tips on how to conduct oneself in an interview, both as the interviewer and the interviewee. Teach students that they need to be professional and then teach them how to be professional. **ACT/COLL/TH**—Have students mock interview each other. Students will use the list of practice interview questions. **COLL**—Have a list of professionals from the community which have agreed to be interviewed by students. Students will each pick somebody from the list to interview. They should interview someone with a job they would like to have one day. Community members will come in at a later date in the semester so students may interview them. After completing their interview, students will outline an essay they will write later about the job they learned, including quotes from the person they interviewed.

DAY #	CONTENT/OBJECTIVE	STANDARDS	RESOURCES/MATERIALS	LEARNING ACTIVITIES/ASSESSMENTS
20 GM3	**Science Chapter 3 (Reading)** Given a selection of elements, students will have to classify them in their state of matter, determine their shape, and describe their volume with 80% accuracy.	WIDA Standard 4 Grade 8 Level 3 VSOL: PS.2c/d/f TCA: 2(1a, b) 2(e, f) 2(4i, j)	Whiteboard, markers Textbook: *Physical Science* Paper Pencil	**S**—Teacher makes a flowchart for the entire chapter to show how the concepts in each section are related. Teacher skims each section of the chapter with students and lists key terms and concepts on the flowchart. Teacher focuses on titles, section headings, highlighted/underlined passages, and side notes/figures. Teacher explains key concepts while students define key terms. Once complete, the flowchart should identify what the states of matter are, how matter changes states, how gases behave, and what graphs of behavior show. Students copy the flowchart piece by piece during teacher instruction. **COLL**—Students then partner up and classify elements by their state, shape, and volume.
21	**Math Chapter 2 Listening/Writing** Given three mathematical equations, students will produce statements for each that lists 100% of the steps to solve them.	WIDA Standard 3 Grade 8 Level 3 VSOL: MATH 8.2 TCA: 2(1a, b) 2(3e, f) 2(4h, i, j)	Textbook—*Mathematics: Course 3* PPT game Paper Pencil	**M**—Teacher lists vocabulary on board from the first three sections. Vocabulary is reviewed with students. **T/ACT**—Teacher leads students in a PowerPoint vocabulary matching game. Students have to come to the board to answer problems. Teacher explains how the specific vocabulary of each section is used to help understand the example problems in the chapter. Teacher identifies the vocabulary usage in example problems from each section, then explains how to read these problems and write out the problems in English sentences. Students are given an example problem to identify vocabulary in and rewrite in an English sentence. **CT**—Students are given three mathematical equations to translate into English sentences for HW.

DAY #	CONTENT/OBJECTIVE	STANDARDS	RESOURCES/MATERIALS	LEARNING ACTIVITIES/ASSESSMENTS
22	**LA (Science quiz 20 min)** Given an authentic text, students will identify the examples of figurative language and explain their use in the text, correctly identifying and explaining four out of five examples.	WIDA Standard 2 Grade 8 Level 3 VSOL: ENGL 8.5a TCA: 2(1a, b) 2(3e, f) 2(4i)	Cartoon example of alliteration Clip of "Sarah Cynthia Sylvia Stout" poem MP3	L—Explain to students what a *literary device* is. Describe *alliteration*—show cartoon example. T—Describe *hyperbole*—show video clip from *Despicable Me* "It's so fluffy I'm gonna die!" Explain why authors use alliteration and hyperbole. ACT—Listening Act: Give class handout of Shel Silverstein's "Sarah Cynthia Sylvia Stout" poem. Play audio recording. Have students circle examples of alliteration and underline examples of hyperbole. Students write why these devices are used in the poem. They will share their answers with the class. ASSESS—Students will use the last 20 minutes of class to take the science quiz.
23	**History Chapter 2** Given a quiz on the four ancient civilizations addressed in this chapter, students will identify the important aspects of each culture, answering 80% of the questions correctly.	WIDA Standard 5 Grade 8 Level 3 WHI.2 b, c, d, e TCA: 2(1a) 2(3f) 2(4j)	Four-square graphic organizer History textbook—*Ancient World History: Patterns of Interaction*	DIV/SS—Students will use a four-square graphic organizer to identify and characterize the four major ancient cultures discussed in this chapter (Mesopotamian, Egyptian, Indian, and Chinese). After identifying each of these and placing the name of the culture at the top of each square on the graphic organizer, students will then identify the major advances and characteristics of each society that differentiated it from the rest. After students are given time to complete their graphic organizer, the teacher will review the organizer with the students to ensure that students correctly filled out their organizer. Each student will be called upon to share at least one answer with the class. ASSESS—After the review, the teacher will hand each student a brief quiz on the main ideas of the chapter. The quiz will ask questions concerning the four ancient cultures and the most important and noteworthy aspects of their civilization.

DAY #	CONTENT/OBJECTIVE	STANDARDS	RESOURCES/MATERIALS	LEARNING ACTIVITIES/ASSESSMENT
24	**Social (Fall Season) Present perfect and present perfect progressive** Given pictures of fall scenarios, students will use the present perfect or present perfect progressive to form and tell five sentences describing these scenarios to a partner with no more than one incorrect verb usage.	WIDA Standard 1 Grade 8 Level 3 VSOL: ENGL 8.2a/c/h TCA: 2(1a, b) 2(2c, d) 2(3f, g) 2(4h, i, j)	Technology (PPT, video clip) Whiteboard, markers	**CE**—Teacher opens with lesson about beauty. Relates beauty with the seasons (fall). **SS/DIV**—Teacher asks students what their favorite season is and when that season occurs in their native country. Teacher explains the Fall season and shows students short video clip of the Fall season. Teacher tells students that they will converse with a partner about the Fall, but must first learn new verb forms. Teacher explains the present perfect and present perfect progressive tense to students. Students copy definitions, concepts, and examples for a review lesson the following week. Partner LD students with Gifted students. **ASSESS/COLL/T**—Teacher gives students several examples and then has students create several examples using Fall vocabulary. Teacher then uses a PowerPoint to show pictures of Fall activities, weather, events, etc. Students partner up and describe to one another what is happening in the picture while using one of the newly learned tenses. Teacher evaluates, monitors, and guides learning during this time.
25 GM4	**Science Chapter 4 (Writing)** Given the key terms for the first two sections of Chapter 4, students will describe the purpose of the periodic table and how it is organized by composing a paragraph with less than five grammatical errors.	WIDA Standard 4 Grade 8 Level 3 VSOL: PS.4a/b/c TCA: 2(1a, b) 2(3f) 2(4j)	Textbook: *Physical Science* Technology (video clip) Paper Pencil	**SS/L**—Teacher reviews grammar lesson from previous week with students. **S/COLL/T**—Students are split into groups of two. Groups take 25 minutes to define vocabulary from Section 1 and 2 of Chapter 4. Teacher shows short video clip to review the periodic table with students. **ASSESS**—Individually, students use their vocabulary definitions to write a paragraph that describes what the periodic table organizes and how it is organized.

DAY #	CONTENT/OBJECTIVE	STANDARDS	RESOURCES/MATERIALS	LEARNING ACTIVITIES/ASSESSMENTS
26	**Math Chapter 2** After learning about rational numbers and reciprocals, students will construct their own division problem using rational numbers and then explain how to answer it with 100% accurate description of each step.	WIDA Standard 3 Grade 8 Level 3 VSOL: MATH 8.2, 8.3a TCA: 2(1a, b) 2(3e, f) 2(4j)	Textbook—*Mathematics: Course 3* Whiteboard, markers Paper Pencil	**M/COLL**—Have students partner up to define vocabulary from the last three sections of Chapter 2 (should not be much). Partner boys with girls as is possible. Teacher asks students for examples of reciprocals. Teacher explains when and why reciprocals are used. Call on students to explain each part of the fraction, the relationship between a fraction and its reciprocal, and when reciprocals are used. **L**—Go through example 4 on page 86 with students to show how to read and answer math problems. **CT**—Explain to students that they will write their own division problem using rational numbers. Also explain that they will need to give a step-by-step description of how to answer it. Give students a Math Test Study Guide for their upcoming Math Language Test.
27	**LA Synonyms/ Antonyms** After hearing 10 unknown SAT words, students will use a thesaurus to look up synonyms and antonyms for each word with 80% accuracy.	WIDA Standard 2 Grade 8 Level 3 VSOL: ENGL 8.2h, 8.4c TCA: 2(1a, b) 2(2d) 2(3e, f, g) 2(4h, i, j)	Whiteboard, markers Technology (PPT) Thesaurus Paper Pencil	**CE**—Teacher writes proverb about integrity on the board. Teacher asks students what it means, and then for words that mean the same thing. Teacher asks for words that mean the opposite. **T/L**—Teacher uses this character principle to introduce synonyms and antonyms. Teacher uses PPT to define and explain synonyms/ antonyms and their usage. Teacher reads students sentences and asks for synonyms of basic English vocabulary in the sentences. Teacher also asks for antonyms. **L/ACT**—Teacher distributes thesauruses to students. Teacher reads 10 SAT words to students. Students look up words for synonyms and antonyms and then record their findings on blank sheet of notebook paper.

DAY #	CONTENT/OBJECTIVE	STANDARDS	RESOURCES/MATERIALS	LEARNING ACTIVITIES/ASSESSMENTS
28	**History Chapter 3** Given the vocabulary from Chapter 3, students will construct a graphic organizer that divides the terms into people, places, events/things and will give the definition for each term with 90% accuracy.	WIDA Standard 5 Grade 8 Level 3 VSOL: WHI 1a, 3e TCA: 2(1a, b) 2(2c, d) 2(3f, g) 2(4j) 2(5k)	Whiteboard, markers Indo-European Language Chart History textbook—*Ancient World History: Patterns of Interaction* Paper Pencil	**SS**—Teacher asks students what they know about the time period from 2000 B.C–50 B.C. **ACT/DIV/COLL**—Teacher writes every student's native language on the board. Students come up to the board and write their initials under their native language. Students then gather in groups based on their native language. Teacher asks students what similarities their language has with other languages. Teacher then explains to students the importance of the history of the Indo-Europeans. Teacher shows Indo-European language chart to students. Students see the similarities and differences in language based on Indo-European history. **COLL**—Students stay in the groups that they are in to define vocabulary of Chapter 3. Students create a graphic organizer that splits the vocabulary into three groups: people, places, and events/things. Students categorize each vocabulary word and then define it. This assignment is to be turned in at the end of class.
29	**Social** Given eight incomplete model sentences, students will orally compose with a partner eight completed sentences using a combination of the past perfect and past progressive tenses with less than four speaking and grammatical errors.	WIDA Standard 1 Grade 8 Level 3 VSOL: ENGL 8.2c/f TCA: 2(1a, b) 2(3e, f, g) 2(4h, i, j) 2(5k)	Text: *Understanding and Using English Grammar*, Ex. 16 on page 47 Audio clip of Verb Tense Song Technology (PPT) Worksheet	**T/MUS**—Teacher uses PPT and song to introduce and explain the past perfect and past progressive tenses to students. Teacher gives students incomplete example sentences for students to read aloud to the teacher and fill-in-the-blank with the correct tense of the verb missing. Teacher gives students a worksheet to complete. The worksheet has 10 sentences that use verbs in the simple past tense. Students are to rewrite half of the sentences with the past perfect and the other half with past perfect progressive. **ASSESS/CT**—Students then partner up and orally complete eight prewritten sentences using a combination of the two verb tenses discussed in this lesson. Allow LD students to have no more than three grammatical errors more than everyone else.

DAY #	CONTENT/OBJECTIVE	STANDARDS	RESOURCES/MATERIALS	LEARNING ACTIVITIES/ASSESSMENTS
30 GM5	**Science Chapter 4 (Focus on Last Three Sections)** Given a worksheet of the periodic table, scissors, and glue, students will work together to brainstorm how to organize their own new version of the periodic table, sensibly and systematically categorizing and placing *each* element in a new spot with zero errors.	WIDA Standard 4 Grade 8 Level 3 VASOL: PS.4a, b TCA: 2(1a) 2(2d) 2(3e, f, g)	Periodic table worksheets Scissors, glue, paint, other craft supplies	**S**—Review the concept of elements with the class. Look at the Periodic Table. Examine the keys with the students. Quickly review how the elements are organized. Have students point out where the symbol, atomic number, and atomic mass are on each element square. Review the definition of each. **A**—Students will each pick an element. They will use construction paper, paint, glue, glitter, pom-poms, etc., to create and decorate their element as it appears on the periodic table. Ask students: Why is the periodic table organized the way it is? (i.e., by atomic mass; elements are grouped together by similar properties; zigzag line separates metals from nonmetals, etc.). Class discussion: If you were Mendelev, how would you have organized the periodic table? Would you have grouped or placed the elements differently? **COLL/CT**—Give students a printable of the periodic table. As a class, students will decide how they are going to organize their own version of the periodic table. They may cut up the elements into whatever sections they choose in order to create the new table. As a group, students will work together to put together a short paragraph explaining why they organized their new periodic table the way they did. The paragraph will be collected as an exit ticket.
31	**Math Chapters 1–2 (Test)** Given a test on the first two chapters, students will use their knowledge of the vocabulary and concepts to match vocabulary words, translate mathematical equations into discourse statements, and write mathematical equations based on given discourse statements with 75% accuracy.	WIDA Standard 3 Grade 8 Level 3 VSOL: MATH 8.1a, 8.2, 8.3a TCA: 2(4h, i, j)	Math test	**ASSESS/M**—Teacher distributes test and testing folders. Students put up testing folders and take test. Students turn test in to teacher. After test, students take rest of time to read.

DAY #	CONTENT/OBJECTIVE	STANDARDS	RESOURCES/MATERIALS	LEARNING ACTIVITIES/ASSESSMENTS
32	**LA** Given a clip of a radio interview, students will choose at least three quotes from the interview and will write a sentence with a lead-in for each one, demonstrating proper grammar and mechanics with 100% accuracy.	WIDA Standard 2 Grade 8 Level 3 VASOL: ENGL 8.7f, 8.8b TCA: 2(1b) 2(3e, g) 2(4j)	Radio interview clips	(*Ties into community interview project) Lesson on quotations! **L**—Instruct students on how to create and include quotes in a paper. Discuss: how to choose an effective quote, how to properly cite each quote, mechanics of in-text quotes. **T**—Listening activity: Have students listen to clips of radio interviews. Students will then choose three quotes from the interview. They will write a lead-in for each quote, demonstrating proper mechanics for each quote. If there is extra time, students may receive help on material from other classes.
33	**History Chapter 4** Given a section in the chapter, students will work in groups to define key vocabulary words in the section, defining them with 100% accuracy.	WIDA Standard 5 Grade 8 Level 3 VASOL: WHI.3a, b, c, e TCA: 2(1a) 2(3f) 2(4j)	History textbook—*Ancient World History: Patterns of Interaction,* Sections 1–4 of Chapter 4	**DIV/SS**—Divide students into groups of four based on language proficiency. Assign each student one of the following empires discussed in the chapter: Egyptian, Nubian, Assyrian, Persian, China (Qin Dynasty). **COLL/ACT**—The members of each group will work together to identify the most important and interesting aspects of each empire. They must record when and how each power came into being, when and how each fell, their greatest accomplishments, and their legacy. Students will also compile a list of the vocabulary associated with each empire. Once they have provided their own definition for each word, teacher will regroup students so that one member from each original group is in the new group. Students will share the information about their empire, and the vocabulary words they thought were important from the section.
34	**Social** After conducting an interview with a local professional, students will write an informative essay about the professional's job, properly utilizing in-text quotes and citations with 100% accuracy.	WIDA Standard 1 Grade 8 Level 3 VASOL: ENGL 8.1a, b, c, d TCA: 2(1b) 2(2d) 2(3e)	Online interview survey Local professionals	*Continuation of day 19 **CE**—Review with students what it means to be professional and how to speak and act professionally. Local professionals come in so that students may conduct their interview. Refreshments follow. Students are to begin writing their essay. It is due the following Friday. Extend the due date for LD students until the following Monday on case by case basis. After the interview has been submitted, students will take a brief online survey as homework. The survey will ask students' opinions on the effectiveness of interviewing to find information.

DAY #	CONTENT/OBJECTIVE	STANDARDS	RESOURCES/MATERIALS	LEARNING ACTIVITIES/ASSESSMENTS
35 GM6	**Science Chapter 5** Given an example of a common metal object, students will write a brief paragraph describing the metal and two of its properties, with zero mistakes in subject-verb agreement. GRAMMAR CONNECTION	WIDA Standard 4 Grade 8 Level 3 VASOL: PS. 2d, e TCA : 2(1a) 2(3f) 2(4j)	Paper, colored pencils, index cards	**T**—Use a PPT to teach students about proper subject-verb agreement. Use sentences discussing chapter concepts as examples. **S**—Review with students the concepts and definitions of metals, alloys, metallic bonding, metallic properties, conductivity, and luster. Have students make flash cards with the definitions for each. **A/CT**—Students will create a product label. Have them choose a familiar metal object for which they are going to make the label. The label must describe at least two of the metal's properties. Then explain why it has those properties, and how they enhance the properties and make the product beneficial to the consumer. Students may include drawings on their label. **COLL**—Students work with teachers to ensure they are using proper subject-verb agreement.
36	**Math Chapter 3** Given a two-variable equation, students will describe in a paragraph with less than four grammatical errors how to find the solution.	WIDA Standard 3 Grade 8 Level 3 VSOL: MATH 8.4 TCA 2(1a) 2(2c, d)	Textbook—*Mathematics: Course 3* Notebook paper Writing utensil	**M/DIV**—Teacher reviews vocabulary for chapter with students. The math term "origin" is introduced in this chapter. Teacher connects this word with the meaning "beginning." Students are asked to verbally share their personal origin with the class. Students discuss their cultural heritage. **COLL**—As students are sharing, other students are to write one question they would like to ask their classmates about their heritage. After discussion, teacher explains to students how to read and solve math equations that have two variables. Teacher explains this skill by walking students through example 3a of Section 1. Students then are to read and solve example 3b on their own. Provide a worksheet explanation of lesson to LD students. Allow them to take this worksheet home to study. **ASSESS**—Teacher assigns HW for students to solve a problem with two variables. Students are to write a paragraph that describes step-by-step how to solve the equation.

DAY #	CONTENT/OBJECTIVE	STANDARDS	RESOURCES/MATERIALS	LEARNING ACTIVITIES/ASSESSMENTS
37	**LA—Media Literacy Lesson** After conducting an interview with a local professional, students will write an informative paragraph about the professional's job, properly utilizing in-text quotes and citations with 100% accuracy.	WIDA Standard 2 Grade 8 Level 3 VASOL: ENGL 8.1a, b, c TCA: 2(1b) 2(2d) 2(3e)	Brainstorming graphic organizer List of example interview questions	**MUS**—Students will brainstorm topics they want to talk to their interviewee about. Give students 5 minutes while playing relaxing classical music. **CT**—Students will choose and prepare interview questions for their interview project. **ACT/COLL**—Students will collaborate with teacher and classmates to determine the best questions to ask their chosen professional. Students will ask professional questions, take responses, and formulate a paragraph that summarizes the professional's job.
38	**History Chapter 5 (WebQuest)** Given the vocabulary from Chapter 5, students will identify and rewrite (in their own words) the definitions for each vocabulary word, defining them with 100% accuracy.	WIDA Standard 5 Grade 8 Level 3 VASOL: WHI.5 TCA: 2(1a) 2(3f) 2(4j)	Zunal webquest: http://zunal.com/webquest.php?w=211372 Fishbone chart	**SS/T**—Students will be divided into five groups. Divide LD students proportionally. Each group will be assigned one section of the chapter. Students will locate the bold-faced vocabulary words in their section. They will look up the definitions for each word using the dictionary resource website attached to the WebQuest. They will copy and paste the definitions into a Word document. Below each definition they will write a new definition in their own words in complete sentences. Each group must produce one copy with each group member's work. This will be collected at the end of the week.
39	**Social—History WebQuest** Given a blank fishbone chart, students will describe, compare, and contrast the four governments of ancient Greece, filling in (completing) each blank with 100% accuracy.	WIDA Standard 1 Grade 8 Level 3 VASOL: WHI.5a, c TCA: 2(1a) 2(2c) 2(3e) 2(4j)	Zunal webquest: http://zunal.com/webquest.php?w=211372 Fishbone chart	**CE**—Teach students a mini-lesson on politics. Teach them that they should always vote for the candidate who has the best interest of the people in mind in relation to a high moral standard. **SS**—Students will use their books to research the four different forms of political structures in ancient Greece. As a group, they will complete the fishbone chart by filling in the lines with the following pertinent information: what each form of government is, what its effects were on ancient Greece, and any similarities between the different systems. Each student will collaborate with the others in their group, discuss their research, and work together to complete the chart. Each group will turn in a single copy of the chart at the end of the day. *Interview projects are due today! Remind students about online survey. Outcome of the surveys will be discussed next Friday.

DAY #	CONTENT/OBJECTIVE	STANDARDS	RESOURCES/MATERIALS	LEARNING ACTIVITIES/ASSESSMENTS
40 GM7	**Science Chapter 6** Given a video on chemical reactions, students will actively listen and watch the video to identify and record no less than 20 scientific vocabulary words.	WIDA Standard 4 Grade 8 Level 3 VSOL: PS 5.a, b TCA: 2(2d) 2(3f, g) 2(4j)	Open space Science textbook: *Physical Science* Video about chemical reactions Notebook paper Writing utensil	**CE/B**—Open class with mini-lesson about how to handle change. Use proverb from bible but do not cite passage reference. **S/COLL**—Teacher has students stand up and make one big group in the middle of the classroom. Teacher reviews concepts of chemical change. Students pretend to be a chemical. Teacher describes phases/types of chemical change. **ACT**—Students act out the phases by physically changing the form of their group in response to teacher instruction. Students sit back down in their seats and teacher reviews vocabulary of the chapter by calling on students to read the definitions. Teacher is selective to make sure LD students are not singled out. Teacher answers questions about definitions as they arise. **T**—Teacher plays video about chemical reactions. Students listen for scientific vocabulary in the video. Students record every scientific word they hear.
41	**Math Chapter 3** Given a collective but divided summary of the heritage questions students had for their classmates, students will construct both a table and a graph that displays 100% of the data collected.	WIDA Standard 3 Grade 8 Level 3 VSOL: MATH 8.13a TCA: 2(a, b) 2(2d) 2(3f) 2(4h, j)	Textbook—*Mathematics: Course 3* Whiteboard Markers Notebook paper Writing utensil Heritage question worksheet	**M**—Students define the vocabulary listed in Section 4 with a partner. Teacher reviews vocabulary with students. Students read definitions out loud. Teacher does this by calling on students. Teacher has students open books to Section 5. Students popcorn-read to read through the opening paragraph and the different uses of graphs and tables. Teacher guides students through one of the examples and teaches them how to construct tables and graphs based on given information. **COLL/DIV**—Teacher then explains to students that they will use the questions they created for their classmates to construct their own table and graph. Teacher distributes a sheet that lists the topics of the questions the students had for their classmates in the last math lesson. If time permits, teacher calls on several students to answer some of the questions their classmates had. Students use the information given to produce a table and a graph that explains the relationship between the questions.

DAY #	CONTENT/OBJECTIVE	STANDARDS	RESOURCES/MATERIALS	LEARNING ACTIVITIES/ASSESSMENTS
42	**LA (Science quiz 20 min)** Given a list of idioms, students will construct three complete sentences using at least one idiom correctly in each.	WIDA Standard 2 Grade 8 Level 3 VSOL: ENGL 8.5a/8.8 TCA: 2(3e, f)	Science quiz Text—*Monkey Business* PPT Notebook paper Writing utensil Youtube clip: http://www.youtube.com/watch?v=E9DxGe94uoc	**S/ASSESS**—Teacher distributes science quiz to students. Students take no more than 15 minutes to complete. **L**—Teacher reads a passage from *Monkey Business*. Students record any idioms they hear. Teacher uses PPT to give instruction on idioms. Teacher explains how to find literal and metaphorical meanings of idioms. **T**—Show students a video clip from YouTube about idioms. Teacher guides students to determine meanings of idioms. Teacher then shows students how to create their own sentences with idioms. Students construct their own sentences. Teacher monitors this process. **A/ASSESS/CT**—Students are given a sheet of idioms. Students choose three idioms and create their own sentences. Students then flip the sheet over and draw the literal representation of their idiom.
43	**History Chapter 5 (WebQuest)** Given research about the cause and effects of the ancient Greek wars and the conquest of Alexander the Great, students will identify and orally present a list of these wars and at least three of the causes of these wars and effects with less than four grammatical errors.	WIDA Standard 5 Grade 8 Level 3 VSOL: WHI 5d,g ENGL: 8.2a/b/f/g/h TCA: 2(1b) 2(4j)	Laptop History textbook—*Ancient World History: Patterns of Interaction* Notebook paper Writing utensil WebQuest link: http://zunal.com/webquest.php?w=211372	**SS/COLL/DIV/T**—Students divide into the groups they have been working in for the entirety of the WebQuest assignment. Teacher assigns each group two of the four wars ancient Greece was involved with. Students use textbook and resources found in WebQuest to identify causes and effects of the wars. In groups, students record their research. **CT**—After students have completed this part of the assignment, they are to connect with another group and share research orally. Complete sentences and English are to be used. Students record all the information they learn from their collaborating group. **ASSESS**—Students turn in one copy of notes to the teacher. During the WebQuest activity, teacher monitors, guides, observes, and assesses learning achievement.

DAY #	CONTENT/OBJECTIVE	STANDARDS	RESOURCES/MATERIALS	LEARNING ACTIVITIES/ASSESSMENTS
44	**Social (First 9 Wks)** Given a list of phrasal verbs and verb-preposition combinations, students will write 10 sentences that incorporate examples from the list with 90% accuracy.	WIDA Standard 1 Grade 8 Level 3 VSOL: ENGL 8.7g ENGL 8.8b, k TCA: 2(2b) 2(f)	Whiteboard Markers PPT about food Worksheet	**DIV/COLL/H**—Teacher opens with student-based discussion about food. Teacher guides students to talk about their favorite native food. Students actively listen to their fellow classmates and participate in discussion. **L**—Teacher continues the conversation about food, but introduces the grammar of phrasal verbs and verb preposition combinations. Teacher instructs students on these two aspects of grammar. **T**—Then teacher uses PPT to teach and show students examples of how to use these phrases. Students fill in blanks of sentences on PPT. PPT is all about shopping for food and ordering food in restaurants. Students are given a worksheet that lists phrasal verbs and verb preposition combinations and are asked to use at least 10 of them to create their own sentences. Make sure worksheet has illustrations for LD students. *Review outcome of surveys today!
45 GM8	**Science Chapter 7** Given instruction on acids and bases, students will research, identify, classify, and state in compete sentences five household objects or foods that are either acidic or basic.	WIDA Standard 4 Grade 8 Level 3 VSOL: PS 2.b TCA: 2(2d) 2(4h)	Science textbook: *Physical Science* Laptops Whiteboard, markers Notebook paper Writing utensil	**L/S**—Students popcorn-read Section 3. Teacher reviews vocabulary with students as they appear in text. **DIV/H**—Teacher explains that acids and bases are commonly used in everyday life. Teacher gives examples of foods and household items that fall into one of the two categories. **T**—Teacher takes students to computer lab or passes out portable laptops to students. Teacher explains to students that they are to research common everyday items that are either acidic or basic. Students identify and classify their research. Then students create five sentences that explain the categorization of the items they found.

DAY #	CONTENT/OBJECTIVE	STANDARDS	RESOURCES/MATERIALS	LEARNING ACTIVITIES/ASSESSMENTS
46	**Math Chapter 4** Given five numbers, students will either explain in complete sentences how to write at least four out of five numbers in scientific notation or standard notation. Students will then write four out of five numbers in the correct notation.	WIDA Standard 3 Grade 8 Level 3 VSOL: Math 8.1b, 8.2 ENGL 8.6k, l TCA: 2(1b) 2(3g)	Textbook—*Mathematics: Course 3* Vocabulary handout Open space Whiteboard Markers Notebook paper Writing utensil	**M**—Teacher reviews vocabulary with students from previous chapter. Teacher uses text page 159 to ask students questions. **L**—Teacher writes vocabulary list from chapter preview on board. Teacher and students go through each section and read the definition of each vocabulary word together. Teacher makes vocabulary relatable to students by connecting terms with personal experiences. Teacher also gives students a handout of all vocabulary. **TH/P/ACT/COLL**—Teacher has students turn to Section 4 in their text. Teacher instructs students how to write numbers in scientific notation. Teacher also explains how to write numbers in standard notation if they are already in scientific notation. Teacher has students act out these two processes. Students line up and are assigned different parts for each notation. Teacher writes a number on the board and students move positions depending on the type of notation. The purpose of the movement in this activity is to show students the different steps they must take when writing numbers in these two types of notation. **ASSESS**—Students are then given five numbers. Some are in scientific notation. Some are in standard notation. Students are to write in complete sentences how to write the given number in its opposite notation. Then students are to write the number in its other notation.
47	**Social—Halloween** Given a diversity of candy, students will write a paragraph with less than four grammatical errors about the candy they received during the trick-or-treating skit and about the candy they hope to receive when they actually go trick-or-treating.	WIDA Standard 1 Grade 8 Level 3 VSOL: ENGL 8.7d,/g, 8.8b/e/g. TCA: 2(2c, d) 2(5k)	Candy PPT on Halloween Short storybook about Halloween Open space Notebook paper Writing utensil	**CE**—Teacher reads a short story about Halloween to students. Teach students about the importance of giving. **T**—Teacher uses PPT to teach the history of Halloween in America. Teacher asks students if they celebrate this holiday in their native culture. Teacher gives examples of other cultures' celebration of Halloween. **ACT/TH/P**—Teacher explains the process of trick-or-treating. Students then move and spread out their desks around the classroom. Each student is given five pieces of candy to give away in a skit about trick-or-treating. Half of the students go trick-or-treating while the other half hands out candy. Students switch roles once all the candy has been passed out. **CT**—Students write a paragraph with no more than four grammatical errors about the candy they received and the candy they hope to receive when they actually go trick-or-treating.

DAY #	CONTENT/OBJECTIVE	STANDARDS	RESOURCES/MATERIALS	LEARNING ACTIVITIES/ASSESSMENTS
48	**LA/History Chapter 6 (Writing)** Given information about Christianity and Judaism, students will construct a Venn diagram that compares and contrasts the two religions with four facts, written in complete sentences, in each column.	WIDA Standard 2 and 5 Grade 8 Level 3 VSOL: WHI 6.h, i TCA: 2(3f) 2(4j)	History textbook—*Ancient World History: Patterns of Interaction* Maps of the apostles' journeys Judaism facts sheet Notebook paper Writing utensil	**CE/B**—Write a proverb from the bible on the board to introduce topic. **SS/DIV**—Teacher opens class with discussion on world religions. Students are asked to list and describe the religions they know. **L**—Teacher and students read Section 3 of Chapter 6 together. Discuss the role of Christianity during this time period and in this context with students. **SS**—Teacher distributes several maps of the apostles' missionary journeys to students. Students interpret the path of the apostles' trips and then orally describe them to teacher and fellow students. **CT/ASSESS**—Teacher gives Judaism facts sheet to students, and has students create a Venn diagram that compares and contrasts Judaism with Christianity.
49	**Social—Voting** Given a reading passage about voting in America, students will answer five out of six reading comprehension questions correctly.	WIDA Standard 1 Grade 8 Level 3 VSOL: ENGL 8.5m TCA: 2(2c, d)	Open space YouTube clip on voting: http://www.youtube.com/watch?v=ar7r5aG_B0Y A ballot from the previous presidential election Voting reading passage Reading comprehension worksheet	Teacher has classroom set up before students arrive. **SS**—Teacher shows students a short video clip on voting. **DIV**—Teacher explains what voting is, why it occurs, when it happens, and who the voting process is for. Teacher also explains the qualifications and processes internationals have to take in order to vote in America. **ACT/TH/P**—Students participate in mock voting experience. A ballot from the previous presidential election is used. As students are voting, teacher hands out a reading passage. Students have to answer reading comprehension questions derived from the passage.

DAY #	CONTENT/OBJECTIVE	STANDARDS	RESOURCES/MATERIALS	LEARNING ACTIVITIES/ASSESSMENTS
50 GM9	**Science Chapter 8** Given a vocabulary quiz on the words from Chapter 8, students will correctly define each vocabulary word, with 80% accuracy.	WIDA Standard 4 Grade 8 Level 3 PS.2b, d, f TCA: 2(1a, b) 2(2c) 2(e, f) 2(i, j)	Ball, basket	**S**—Review main ideas of the chapter. Ask students if they have any questions regarding their assigned readings for the class. **L**—Have students share new English they have learned from this chapter. Each student will make a list of new words they do not know from the chapter. They will find the definitions in the back of the book. Students should rewrite them and put them in their own words. Collect students' vocabulary lists. **COLL/ACT/P/DIV/CE**—Split students into two teams based on gender. Each team will stand in a single-file line facing the front of the classroom. Stand at the front of the classroom with a ball in your hand. Place a basket on top of a desk at the front of the room, as well. Teacher will say the definition of a vocabulary word from the chapter. Whoever says the correct vocabulary word first has the chance to make a basket. Only the member from each team who is at the front of the line may attempt to answer the question, receiving no help from their teammates. Give students a mini-lesson on cheating. Talk about why it is wrong and the consequences. Students receive 1 point for providing the correct vocabulary word and 2 points for making a basket. The team who wins gets candy! Students should study and prepare for a vocabulary exam the next day.
51	**Math/LA Chapter 4** Given a list of math vocabulary, students will break words apart by their affixes and then record their definitions with 80% accuracy.	WIDA Standard 2 and 3 Grade 8 Level 3 VASOL: ENGL 8.4c TCA: 2(1a) 2(3f) 2(4j)	Science vocabulary quiz PPT on affixes	**ASSESS**—Science vocabulary quiz. **L/M/T**—Use a PPT to teach suffixes, prefixes, and other word parts (use "irrational" as an example). Guide students on how to break up math vocabulary and then define it. For independent practice, assign a few words and math problems similar to the guided practice. Have students also define these words. Collect independent practice for assessment of understanding.

DAY #	CONTENT/OBJECTIVE	STANDARDS	RESOURCES/MATERIALS	LEARNING ACTIVITIES/ASSESSMENTS
52	**History Chapter 6** Given a vocabulary quiz on Chapter 6, students will identify the correct definition for each word, completing it with 80% accuracy.	WIDA Standard 5 Grade 8 Level 3 VASOL: WHI.6 TCA: 2(1b) 2(2d) 2(3g) 2(4j)	Computer access History textbook—*Ancient World History: Patterns of Interaction*	**COLL/SS/T/CT**—Students will split into four groups. Each group will be assigned one section of Chapter 6. Students will identify the vocabulary words from their section and identify which words are nouns and which are proper nouns. After categorizing the vocabulary words, the students will define each of the words. They will then create a PPT with one word on each slide. Each slide must contain the word, its definition, and a picture that represents the word. PPTs will be uploaded online by the end of class. Students will study PPT as homework. Vocabulary test the following day.
53 GM10	**Science Chapter 9** Given a verbal question asked by a teacher, students will respond with a sentence using the correct modal verb with 100% accuracy.	WIDA Standard 4 Grade 8 Level 3 VASOL: ENGL 8.8d TCA: 2(1a) 2(3f) 2(4j)	History vocabulary quiz PPT on modals Activity sheet with acceleration word problems	**ASSESS**—Students will take History vocabulary quiz. **T/L**—Start with Grammar Connection. Use PPT to teach students about modals (i.e., must, could, would, etc.). **CT/S**—Provide students with an activity sheet with acceleration word problems on it. Each word problem will also have questions asking the student to make a prediction about a certain event that is dependent upon time and speed. Without solving the problems, have students guess which modal phrase corresponds to each situation. (Ex. If the train accelerates at this rate, what are the chances Rob will make it to Pittsburgh on time? Possible answer: He *might* make it to Pittsburgh on time.) **ASSESS**—Students will orally demonstrate their ability to use modal verbs as an exit ticket.
54	**Math Chapter 5** Given time to study the vocabulary and definitions of this chapter, students will choose three vocabulary words and write sentences using each one appropriately with 100% accuracy.	WIDA Standard 3 Grade 8 Level 3 VASOL: MATH 8.3a TCA: 2(1b) 2(2d) 2(3e) 2(4i)	Access to game websites	Have students split up into groups and review vocabulary on page 270 together. **T/COLL/M**—Students will split into groups and design a game using the website provided. Each group will make a game for five vocabulary words, including the proper definition for each one. When they are finished, each group will be able to try the other groups' games. (Play lightning rounds! 4–5 min/game.) As an exit slip, students will write three sentences correctly using three of the new vocabulary words.

DAY #	CONTENT/OBJECTIVE	STANDARDS	RESOURCES/MATERIALS	LEARNING ACTIVITIES/ASSESSMENTS
55	**LA** Given a prompt, students will work together to write an essay about a sample topic and read it aloud to the class, with fewer than four grammatical errors.	WIDA Standard 2 Grade 8 Level 3 VASOL: ENGL 8.7a, b, d, e, g, h 8.8b, d, g TCA: 2(1a) 2(3f) 2(4h, i)	PPT on how to write a three-paragraph essay. Paper, pencil	**L**—Use a PPT to instruct students on how to write a basic three-paragraph informative essay. **COLL**—Students will then each work in groups of three to write a short, cohesive essay about one of the sample topics. (Each student can write one paragraph.) After working with teacher to ensure there are no grammatical errors in the essay, students will read their essays to the class.
56	**History Chapter 7** Given the opportunity to research a particular historical topic, students will create a three-paragraph informative essay about their topic, with fewer than five grammatical errors.	WIDA Standard 5 Grade 8 Level 3 VASOL: ENGL 8.7d, g TCA: 2(1a) 2(3f) 2(4j) 2(5k)	Access to Internet/computers	**DIV**—Each student will choose whether they would like to learn more about ancient China or ancient India. Then, they will pick one of the following topics to research concerning the country they chose: major religions, major historical works of art, major works of literature, or famous historical places. Students will write an essay discussing one major religion, work, or place. **ACT/L**—After the first draft of their paper has been written, students will peer-evaluate each other's paper for grammatical errors. Allow students to get up and move to switch partners. After revising, students will submit papers to the teacher. Articles will be due the following Monday.
57	**Social** Given instruction on American slang, students will create their own slang dictionary including five terms and an example sentence for each, demonstrating proper use of 5 out of 5 slang terms.	WIDA Standard 1 Grade 8 Level 3 VASOL: ENGL 8.1e ENGL 8.5a TCA: 2(1a) 2(2c) 2(4j)	Cardstock paper, notebook paper *Lilo & Stitch* movie	Slang day! **L**—Use PPT to instruct students about common American slang. Use examples that are applicable to students. Guided practice: Have students use each new slang term in a sentence, making sure they demonstrate a proper understanding of each phrase. **DIV**—Explain that slang terms vary from area to area. Even in the US, different states and areas of the country will have different popular slang terms. Example: Hawaii **CE**—Explain to students what slang words are appropriate and acceptable in this region. **T**—Play clips from *Lilo & Stitch*. Have students listen for new slang words and phrases. **A**—Students will create their own dictionary for slang terms. Today, they must include five slang terms, providing an example sentence for each word, and at least three illustrations. Students may add pages for additional slang terms they will learn at school. In order to help LD students, give all students a slang term review handout to use and take home.

DAY #	CONTENT/OBJECTIVE	STANDARDS	RESOURCES/MATERIALS	LEARNING ACTIVITIES/ASSESSMENTS
58 GM11	**Science Chapter 10** Given one of Newton's laws of motion, students will divide into groups and will orally present facts and related concepts about the law assigned to them with less than three speaking errors.	WIDA Standard 4 Grade 8 Level 3 VSOL: PS 10a.b.c TCA: 2(1a) 2(2i)	Science textbook: *Physical Science* Student Edition Audio CD Laptops Notebook paper Writing utensil	Collect students' history articles. **S**—Teacher begins by asking if there are any vocabulary words in the chapter the students are not familiar with. Teacher reviews these words with students. **L/COLL**—Teacher breaks students into groups by language level proficiency. Teacher plays Student Edition Audio CD of Section 2 and 3 of Chapter 10 for students to actively listen to. These sections focus on Newton's Laws of Motion. **CT/T**—Teacher gives instructions to students to form a short oral presentation on these laws. Each group receives a law to research information about and then present on. Each group also receives a laptop. Teacher explains that each presentation needs to include the definition of the law, an explanation of how the law works, and an example of the Law of Motion in motion. Teacher explains to students the resources they are allowed to use, and that the presentations will be on the following day.
59	**Math Chapter 5** Given math instruction on indirect measurement, students will write in complete sentences and with less than two grammatical errors a problem that uses indirect measurement to measure an object at home or school.	WIDA Standard 3 Grade 8 Level 3 VSOL: MATH 8.7a/b TCA: 2(2c, d) 2(4j)	Textbook—*Mathematics: Course 3* Whiteboard Markers Notebook paper Writing utensil	**ASSESS**—Teacher takes the first 15 minutes of class to listen to the students' oral report on Newton's Laws of Motion. **M**—Teacher begins instruction with a lesson on the tense of math problems. Teacher explains to students what tense math problems are generally written in. Students read through the exercises of Section 7 and record on a sheet of paper every verb they find in the present tense. **L**—Teacher then reviews with students the vocabulary and concepts of Section 7. Teacher instructs students how to write problems that use indirect measurements. **ASSESS**—As an exit slip, students write at least one math problem with indirect measurement to measure an object at home or school. Remind students of science quiz.

DAY #	CONTENT/OBJECTIVE	STANDARDS	RESOURCES/MATERIALS	LEARNING ACTIVITIES/ASSESSMENTS
60	**LA—Science Quiz** Given instruction and a list of sentences that can be combined by an adjective clause, in pairs, students will dialogue through the list and combine the sentences with an adjective clause with 90% accuracy.	WIDA Standard 2 and 4 Grade 8 Level 3 VSOL: ENGL 8.3c, 8.8 TCA: 2(1a) 2(3e)	Science quiz PPT Text—*Understanding And Using English Grammar* Laptop Worksheet	**ASSESS**—Teacher passes out science quiz. Students take no more than 12 minutes to complete it. **L**—Teacher instructs students on adjective clauses. Specific instruction will include pronouns that act as the subject, pronouns that act as the object of the verb, pronouns that act as the object of a preposition, and the usual patterns of adjective clauses. Teacher uses example sentences to guide students on how and when to use adjective clauses. Teacher then models for students how to choose which adjective clause pronoun to use. Students complete example sentences with teacher aid if needed. **ASSESS/COLL/CT/T**—Students split into pairs and are given worksheet (page 273 from *Understanding And Using English Grammar*). Each pair then receives a mobile laptop. Students follow directions on worksheet and record themselves speaking with the microphone. One student asks the question on the worksheet, and the other student replies with an adjective clause. Students switch roles halfway through the assignment. Give students a study guide for history test. Explain that history test is the following day.
61	**History Chapter 8 (Test)** Given a test on Chapters 5–7, students will answer questions with 90% accuracy.	WIDA Standard 5 Grade 8 Level 3 VSOL: WHI5,6, 7 TCA: 2(1a) 2(2d) 3(3f) 2(4j)	History test History textbook—*Ancient World History: Patterns of Interaction*	**ASSESS/SS**—Give students a history test that consists of 20 questions about the language discussed in Chapters 5–7. Give students 25 minutes to complete this. Collect tests after 25 minutes. **COLL/DIV/CT**—Write the vocabulary word "migration" on board. Talk to students about common causes and effects listed in Chapter 8 Section 2 of text. Have students split into groups. Split LD students up proportionally. Have students tell their family history of migration and discuss the causes and effects of their family's migration as well as how it has affected their use of their native language. Take the last 15 minutes of class for this activity. Monitor students and listen for correct usage of English grammar and terms.

DAY #	CONTENT/OBJECTIVE	STANDARDS	RESOURCES/MATERIALS	LEARNING ACTIVITIES/ASSESSMENTS
62 GM12	**Science Chapter 11** Given a lesson on density, students will use scientific and comparative vocabulary to compare and contrast the densities of hot and cold air in complete sentences with less than two grammatical errors.	WIDA Standard 4 Grade 8 Level 3 VSOL: PS1.j, 2.d ENGL 8.8e TCA: 2(1a) 2(3e, f) 2(4h, i)	Iceberg picture Science textbook: *Physical Science* Whiteboard Markers Notebook paper Pencil	**CE/ACT/P**—Show students a picture of an iceberg. Talk about how an iceberg is 90% underwater. Have students act out this relationship of what is seen and what is not seen. Have 10% of students stand in front of a row of desks. Then have the rest of the class hide behind the row of desks. Relate this to our character and relationship with others. Use this principle to introduce the term of density. **S**—Have students define the vocabulary from Section 2 on their own. Once students are close to finishing, have students popcorn-read each sentence of the density section. In order to help LD students, teacher records all vocabulary on one file and sends to all students by e-mail. Verbally and visually explain to students what density is and how to compare the density of substances. Give students several substances to compare. Guide them through the process of comparing. **CT**—Have students write down their comparisons. Give them a problem to do on their own. Review it with them. Then ask students to compare the densities of hot and cool air by imagining a hot air balloon. Have students write their answer in complete sentences. Remind students about the grammar test next class.
63	**Thanksgiving** Given a test over the language of grammar studied, students will answer all questions with 80% accuracy.	WIDA Standard 1 Grade 8 Level 3 VSOL: ENGL 8.6 TCA: 2(3g) 2(4h, j)	PPT game Grammar test Pencil	**COLL/ACT/T**—Divide students into groups of 4. Play short review game using PPT animation. Students will come to board to interact with the game. **ASSESS/CT**—Distribute grammar test to students. Students take the test and read a book on their own after they are finished.

DAY #	CONTENT/OBJECTIVE	STANDARDS	RESOURCES/MATERIALS	LEARNING ACTIVITIES/ASSESSMENTS
64	**Thanksgiving** While watching a Thanksgiving video, students will fill in the blank scripted dialogue that correlates with the video with 75% accuracy.	WIDA Standard 1 Grade 8 Level 3 VSOL: 8.2h TCA: 2(1b) 2(2c, d) 2(3f) 2(4i)	Worksheet Pencil Thanksgiving history video: http://websidestories.pagesperso-orange.fr/thanks/Untitled-2.htm	**CE**—Teach students about the value of family, friends, and community. Use this to introduce the lesson. **DIV**—Ask students what they usually do to celebrate the Thanksgiving holiday. **SS**—Explain to students that they are going to watch a video that describes the American tradition of Thanksgiving. Also explain that they will fill out the blanks of a scripted dialogue that correlates with the video. Therefore, they must actively listen the whole time. Pass out scripted dialogue worksheet. Add illustrations to worksheet for LD students. **COLL/T**—Tell students they will watch the video three times. Have students pair up to watch the video and fill out the worksheet for the first showing. Then have students split away from their partners for the last two showings of the video clip. During the last showing of the video, pause the video at indicated spots on the worksheet and ask students open-ended questions about Thanksgiving. **ASSESS**—After the third viewing, have students turn in their worksheet and grade it for listening comprehension.

DAY #	CONTENT/OBJECTIVE	STANDARDS	RESOURCES/MATERIALS	LEARNING ACTIVITIES/ASSESSMENTS
65	**Math Chapter 6** Given five word problems from this chapter, students will work together to identify and list all of the different parts of the problems and then solve the problems with 100% accuracy.	WIDA Standard 3 Grade 8 Level 3 VSOL: MATH 8.2 ENGL 8.6a, b, k TCA: 2(1a, b) 2(3f) 2(4h, j)	PPT Candy Whiteboard Markers Worksheet Pencil	**CE/B**—Use PPT for the entire lesson. Introduce lesson by describing a sports team. Indicate that every team in any context has members that play different parts. Even religious groups show the different roles people play. Show summary passage of Romans 12:3–4. Connect the different roles of a team to percent. Everyone acts as a percentage to the whole of the team. **ACT**—Then pass out packaged candy to students. Have them make different percentages with their candy to review terms of Chapter 6. For LD students, give all students a list of percentages. **T/M**—On the PPT bring up word problems from Chapter 6. Ask students if they know how to read them and answer them. If students respond positively, have them display their solutions on the board. Then have them explain how they broke apart the word problem to derive their answer. If students don't respond, teach them how to read these word problems. Break the word problems apart and look for the components needed to make a mathematical expression. Teach students about the word "of" in word problems. Do this with one word problem and then solve it for the students. Then display two word problems for students and guide them through the process of identifying/listing all the different parts and then finding a solution. **COLL/CT/ASSESS**—Split students into pairs and give them five word problems from the chapter. Have them identify and list the different parts of the word problem, write a mathematical expression, and then solve it to find the solution to the word problem. Have students turn in for completion grade, but allow them to take the assignment home for HW if not completed. Collect it the following class period.

DAY #	CONTENT/OBJECTIVE	STANDARDS	RESOURCES/MATERIALS	LEARNING ACTIVITIES/ASSESSMENTS
66 GM12	**LA** Given instruction on gerunds and infinitives, students will create five sentences which use a gerund or an infinitive with 100% accuracy, get them approved by the teacher, and then teach their constructed sentences with a partner with no more than one speaking error.	WIDA Standard 2 Grade 8 Level 3 VSOL: ENGL 8.2b, c, e, 8.8 TCA: 2(1a, b) 2(3f) 2(4h, i)	Whiteboard Markers Gerunds and infinitives handout Notebook paper Pencil	**L**—List sentences which contain gerunds and infinitives on the board. Ask students what they know about these two aspects of English grammar. Have them try to determine what sentences have gerunds and which have infinitives. **CT**—Give students a handout that reviews these two aspects of grammar in terms of what they, how they are formed, and what function they serve. Verbally teach students as they actively listen and follow along on their handout. After lesson, have students decide what sentences on the board contain gerunds and which ones contain infinitives. Then have students identify the newly learned terms in the sentences. Ask them how they came to their conclusion. **COLL/ACT**—Guide students to write two sentences on their own. One must contain a gerund. The other one must contain an infinitive. Then have students create five sentences using a combination of the two new aspects of grammar they just learned. Approve all of the students' work and then have them teach a partner their sentences. Explain that they must identify to their partner the gerunds and infinitives in their sentences.
67	**History Chapter 9** Given vocabulary from this chapter, students will write a sentence about the significance of each with no more than one grammatical error.	WIDA Standard 5 Grade 8 Level 3 VSOL: ENGL8.7e, g TCA: 2(1b) 2(2d) 2(3g)	History textbook—*Ancient World History: Patterns of Interaction* Whiteboard Markers Notebook paper Pencil	**SS/DIV**—Have students open text. Look at the titles of each section in the chapter with students. Then identify with the students the different people groups discussed in each section. Have students apply what they learned in the last history lesson about migration to describe the migration paths of the people groups in this chapter. List all the vocabulary from chapter on the board. Have students read about each term. Teach students to read the context around the term for clarity in meaning. In order to help LD students, teacher records all vocabulary on one file and sends to all students by e-mail. With the class, identify vocabulary in Section 1. Read the context in which each term is found. Then, guide students to construct a sentence for each term that describes its significance. Have students read through the next two sections on their own and write sentences for each term.

DAY #	CONTENT/OBJECTIVE	STANDARDS	RESOURCES/MATERIALS	LEARNING ACTIVITIES/ASSESSMENTS
68	**Science Review** Given a review over the language of science from the chapters discussed so far, students will answer review questions with 90% accuracy.	WIDA Standard 4 Grade 8 Level 3 VSOL: PS1.j,2.b.d.f, 10.a.b.c TCA: 2(1a) 2(3f, g)	PPT game	**S/T/COLL**—Split students into teams. Review the important concepts and terms from each chapter. Play Connect the Stars PPT game with students to review the language of science.
69	**Social Science Test** Given a test that addresses questions about the language of science learned from the beginning of the year, students will answer all questions with 80% accuracy.	WIDA Standard 1 and 4 Grade 8 Level 3 VSOL: PS1.j,2.b.d.f, 10.a.b.c TCA: 2(4j)	Science test Pencil	Arrange classroom before students arrive for test-taking environment. **S/ASSESS**—Give students a science language test. Allow students to read after test is complete.

DAY #	CONTENT/OBJECTIVE	STANDARDS	RESOURCES/MATERIALS	LEARNING ACTIVITIES/ASSESSMENTS
70	**LA—Haiku** Given time to brainstorm and write their own Haiku, students will explain the use of symbolism in their own poem, given a detailed and accurate two-sentence answer with no more than two grammatical errors.	WIDA Standard 2 Grade 8 Level 3 VASOL: ENGL 8.5a, 8.8 TCA: 2(1a) 2(2c, d)	PPT presentation on Japanese Haiku poetry Computer access (for teacher only); projector National Geographic resource on Basho: http://ngm.nationalgeographic.com/2008/02/bashos-trail/bashos-trail-interactive Paper and pencil	**DIV/T**—Begin with PPT presentation on Japanese Haiku poetry. Explain the typical 5-7-5 poetry pattern, and give many examples of Haikus. Use poems by famous Japanese poets such as Basho, Murakami, etc. Explain *why* the poets wrote these poems. Discuss the freedom writing in Haikus brings to an individual and how they are able to express feelings and newfound truths in a succinct and artful way. Also discuss the theme of nature and self-discovery present in many Japanese haikus. Demonstrate how Basho's poetry is an example of this. **T**—Use the links from *National Geographic* to show students how Basho went on a journey of self-discovery. He wrote many of his Haikus on this journey. **P**—Take students on a walk outside around the campus. Have students take note of things they see in the nature around them (i.e., Is it a rainy day? Is the sun shining brightly? Is there a chill in the air? Have the leaves begun to change color? etc.). As the students record what is going on in the nature around them, have them think about how it relates to what is going on in their own life. (If it's sunny outside, does it match the joy they are feeling inside? If the leaves are changing colors, does it resemble change that is going on in their own lives?) Once inside, give students time to write their own Haiku about the things they saw and considered in their walk. Students must include at least one example of symbolism in their Haiku. They will then write a couple sentences explaining the symbolism in their poem and its meaning in their lives. **CE**—As an exit slip, students will write a character trait they would like to exhibit this week. They will also write how they will demonstrate it.

DAY #	CONTENT/OBJECTIVE	STANDARDS	RESOURCES/MATERIALS	LEARNING ACTIVITIES/ASSESSMENTS
71	**Math Finish Chapter 6 and Review** After being given time to study vocabulary for their upcoming math exam, students will write one sentence telling how they feel about their upcoming test with zero grammatical errors.	WIDA Standard 3 Grade 8 Level 3 VASOL: MATH 8.3a ENGL 8.8 TCA: 2(1a, b) 2(3e) 2(4i, j) 2(5l)	PPT presentation on Chapter 6 Student computer access Vocabulary review flash cards on Quizlet.com	**T**—Use PPT presentation to review vocabulary from the rest of Chapter 6. Give students the chance to offer their own definition for each word before giving them the answer. **COLL**—Ask students what concepts and language they have struggled with in Chapter 6. If only a few students need help, use this time to provide individualized help in a small group. **T**—Students that do not need help may use the computers to review vocabulary flash cards on Quizlet to ensure that they fully understand the language they will be tested on the next day. After the review group has finished, they may do this, as well. As an exit slip, students will write one grammatically correct sentence saying how they feel about tomorrow's test.
72	**Math Test** Given a test on the language of Chapters 1–6 in the textbook, students will provide the correct answer for each question with 80% accuracy.	WIDA Standard 3 Grade 8 Level 3 VASOL: MATH 8.1a, b MATH 8.2 MATH 8.3a MAT 8.4	Math exam over Chapters 1–6 Students should bring books to read	**ASSESS**—Before class begins, organize the desks so that there is a copy of the math test at every other seat. Students may read a book of their choice when they are finished with the test.
73	**History Review** Given review questions for the test over Chapters 1–9, students will answer questions correctly with 80% accuracy.	WIDA Standard 5 Grade 8 Level 3 VASOL: WHI.1, 2, 3, 4, 5, 6, 7 TCA: 2(1b) 2(2f) 2(5l)	Letter to parents about Christmas party Resources for centers: Historical figure matching game Sample essay/critical thinking questions worksheet Packet of sample test questions	**COLL**—Send letter about Christmas party out today. Encourage parental involvement. **ACT**—Students will go to four different centers to study for their history exam. Center #1: Students will play a matching game. They will match the name of a historical figure with a quote that describes them. Center #2: **COLL**—Students will verbally quiz each other on vocabulary. The student that defines the most vocabulary words correctly will earn a bonus point for their exam. Center #3: **CT**—Students will look at sample essay/critical thinking questions for their exam. They will choose one and brainstorm how they would answer the question. Center #4: **COLL**—Students will quiz each other on sample test questions.

DAY #	CONTENT/OBJECTIVE	STANDARDS	RESOURCES/MATERIALS	LEARNING ACTIVITIES/ASSESSMENTS
74	**History Test** Given a text on the language and main ideas of Chapters 1–9, students will provide the correct answer for each question with 80% accuracy.	WIDA Standard 5 Grade 8 Level 3 VASOL: WHI.1, 2, 3, 4, 5, 6, 7 TCA: 2(4h, i, j)	History test over Chapters 1–9 Students should bring their own books to read	**ASSESS**—Arrange classroom before students arrive. Organize the desks so that there is a copy of the history test at every other seat. When students finish their exam, they may quietly read at their seat.
75	**All Subject Help** Given time to study or receive assistance in all subject areas, students will spend 50 minutes studying for their upcoming exams.		Students should bring textbooks to class, along with any assignments they would like help with	Students will bring to class any assignments or projects from other classes that they need help with. Students may also quiz each other and play review games. Teacher will especially work with students who are struggling at this time. **CE**—As an exit slip, students will write one positive character trait they saw a classmate display today. They will write the student's name on the slip, as well. Teacher will display these notes on the bulletin board.
76	**LA Review** Given review questions from the previous semester, students will answer questions correctly with 80% accuracy.	WIDA Standard 2 Grade 8 Level 3 VASOL: ENGL. 8.1a, b, c 8.2b, c, e, h 8.4b, c 8.5a, b, c, h 8.7a, b, d, e, f, g, h 8.8 TCA: 2(2f, h, i)	Review test questions	**P/ACT**—Students will play the Around the World review game answering questions from the previous semester's lessons and assignments. One student will begin their journey "around the world" to start. They will go to their friend's desk. Both students will stand up. The teacher will ask a question. Once the teacher finishes the question, the first student to answer the question *correctly* will advance to the next student's desk. The game will continue on as such. The game is finished when a student makes it back to their original desk.

DAY #	CONTENT/OBJECTIVE	STANDARDS	RESOURCES/MATERIALS	LEARNING ACTIVITIES/ASSESSMENTS
77	**LA Test** Given a listening and reading comprehension test on LA information covered thus far, students will provide the correct answer for each question with 80% accuracy.	WIDA Standard 2 Grade 8 Level 3 VASOL: ENGL 8.1a, b, c 8.2b, c, e, h 8.4b, c 8.5a, b, c, h 8.7a, b, d, e, g, h, f 8.8 TCA: 2(2f, h, i)	LA test on information learned to this point in the semester	**CT/ASSESS**—Rearrange room before students arrive. Arrange desks so tests are placed at every other desk. Students take test. Students may read silently once they have finished their exam.
78 Carlie	**Christmas Holidays** Given the opportunity to share about their own holiday traditions, students will give a brief oral presentation with no more than two grammatical errors.	WIDA Standard 1 Grade 8 Level 3 VASOL: ENGL 8.2a, b, c, d, g, h TCA: 2(2d) 2(4i, j) 2(5l)	Typical Christmas decorations (i.e., manger scene, miniature Christmas tree, poinsettia, star, wrapped Christmas gift, etc.). Students should bring in a prop that represents their own holiday traditions	**CE**—Share the Christmas story with students. Explain that this is the original reason for the season. Also explain how today, we use it as a time to show love and generosity to the people around us. (We show love because Christ showed us love. We give gifts because God gave us the biggest and best gift, Jesus.) Explain the character trait of generosity and how it applies to the Christmas season. Use props to explain examples of typical Christmas traditions in America. **DIV/COLL/D**—Give each student the opportunity to come up and explain Christmas traditions in their country/family. Send a letter out to parents a week before to gain support and parental involvement. Encourage the use of props, costumes, pictures, songs, dance, etc. Invite parents and family members to class this day.
79	**Christmas Party (Winter Break)** Given a vocabulary sheet on words dealing with Christmas, students will write a short story using five of the words correctly, with less than three grammatical errors.	WIDA Standard 1 Grade 8 Level 3 VASOL: ENGL 8.8 TCA: 2(2d) 2(5l, m)	Sugar cookies, sprinkles, recipe and ingredients for icing Movie: *A Charlie Brown Christmas* Christmas vocabulary activity sheet	**COLL**—Make sugar cookies in Christmas shapes before class. Collaborate with the Home Economics teacher. At the beginning of class, students will meet at the Home Ec. room. Home ec. teacher will provide students with a butter cream icing recipe and will instruct students how to make homemade icing. Students will work in groups to make icing, and will then ice and decorate their sugar cookies. **T/DIV**—Students will enjoy cookies, spiced cider, and eggnog as they watch *A Charlie Brown Christmas*. Students will be given a fun Christmas vocabulary sheet to work on during the movie.

DAY #	CONTENT/OBJECTIVE	STANDARDS	RESOURCES/MATERIALS	LEARNING ACTIVITIES/ASSESSMENTS
80	**Review Science (start of third 9 wks)** Given a review over the language of science, students will take a pre-assessment for science with 100% of the questions answered.	WIDA Standard 4 Grade 8 Level 3 VSOL: PS1 TCA: 2(4h, i) 2(5k)	*Hitch* movie clip Pre-assessment test Pencil	**CE/T**—Begin every day as if it were on purpose. Relate this to the start of a new 9 weeks and the second half of the year. Show students a clip from the movie *Hitch*. **S**—Verbally review with students the scientific language learned before Christmas break. Teacher plays the questioner role. **ASSESS**—Give students a pre-assessment on the scientific language they will learn about for the rest of the year.
81	**Review Math** Given a pre-assessment for the language of math, students will complete 100% of the questions asked.	WIDA Standard 3 Grade 8 Level 3 VSOL: MATH 8 TCA: 2(3e, f) 2(4i) 2(5k)	Order of operations rap video: http://www.youtube.com/watch?v=d0xutl2sUt0 Whiteboard Markers Pre-assessment test Pencil	**MUS**—Play a song for the students which will review the order of operations. **ACT**—List several math word problems on the board. Have students come up to the board and write the math equation that correlates with each. Encourage LD students to come to the board. **M/ASSESS**—Give students a pre-assessment over the language of math they will study for the rest of the year.
82	**Review LA** Given a pre-assessment writing exercise over the grammar of the English language, students write in complete sentences and with less than four grammatical errors whether or not they know and understand the grammar topics that will be taught for the remainder of the year.	WIDA Standard 2 Grade 8 Level 3 VSOL: ENGL 8.4, 8.5, 8.6, 8.7, 8.8 TCA: 2(1a) 2(3f) 2(4i) 2(5k)	PPT Grammar topics list Pencil Notebook paper	**T/COLL/L**—Use a PPT to display sentences with fill-in-the-blanks. Call on students and have them fill in the blank with the correct word or phrase. Each of these sentences will review the grammar students learned from before winter break. **ASSESS**—Then give students a list of the grammar topics that will be discussed throughout the rest of the year. Have students write in complete sentences and state whether or not they know these topics and understand how to use these forms of grammar.

DAY #	CONTENT/OBJECTIVE	STANDARDS	RESOURCES/MATERIALS	LEARNING ACTIVITIES/ASSESSMENTS
83	**Review History** Given a pre-assessment over the language of history, students will answer 100% of the questions asked.	WIDA Standard 5 Grade 8 Level 3 VSOL: WHI 7, 8, 9, 10, 11, 12, 13 TCA: 2(1b) 2(2c, d) 2(4h, i) 2(5k)	Pre-assessment test Pencil	**COLL/DIV/CT**—Split students into groups. Divide students first by cultural background. Then, take students from each culture to form a diverse cultural group. Once in these multicultural groups, have students discuss the history of their native country. Give students about 10 minutes to do this. **ASSESS/SS**—Have students return to their desk. Pass out pre-assessment and encourage students to answer all the questions on world religions and language. Allow students to read after pretest is completed.
84	**Extra Review** Given a list of topics to discuss about their winter break, students will give an oral speech no more than 3 minutes long about what they did over winter break with no more than three speaking errors.	WIDA Standard 1 Grade 8 Level 3 VSOL: 8.2a.b.c.d.h TCA: 2(1b) 2(3e, f) 2(4h, i, j) 2(5k)	PPT Whiteboard Markers Notebook paper Pencil	Review with students how to form a speech. Reteach the different parts of a speech. On the board, list the topics Food, Activities, Travel, Presents, and Weather. **H/CT**—Have students choose one or two of these topics, use a blank sheet of paper to write down ideas about these topics, and then form a speech that includes at least one or two of these topics. Give the students 15 minutes to do this. **ASSESS/L**—Take the last 20 minutes for students to give oral speeches.
85 GM13	**Science Chapter 12** Given a lesson on asking questions in English as well as the scientific concept of work, in groups, students will write six questions about the section of work assigned to them with less than three grammatical errors.	WIDA Standard 4 Grade 8 Level 3 VSOL: PS10.a.c.d TCA: 2(1a, b) 2(2d) 2(3e, f) 2(4h)	2 granite building blocks PPT Science textbook: *Physical Science* Notebook paper Pencil	**ACT/P**—Bring in two granite building blocks. Have students attempt to pick up the blocks. Have students sit back down and use this activity to introduce the scientific concept of work. **CE/T/S/CT/DIV**—Explain to students that when they learn new concepts and terms, they should always ask questions. Use a PPT to explain the general types of questions asked in English: who, what, when, where, why, and how. Then have students open text to Chapter 12. Read the first few paragraphs of Section 1 with students and guide them through the process of asking questions about work. Make it personal. Have students answer questions with personal responses about work. **COLL**—Split students into groups. Assign each group a portion of the first two sections to read and write six questions about using the English question model. Then assign each group a portion of Section 3 to write six questions about. Have students present one of their questions orally to the class as a review at the end of the lesson.

DAY #	CONTENT/OBJECTIVE	STANDARDS	RESOURCES/MATERIALS	LEARNING ACTIVITIES/ASSESSMENTS
86	**Math Chapter 7** Given the definitions for all the vocabulary in Chapter 7, students will match all the terms with 100% accuracy.	WIDA Standard 3 Grade 8 Level 3 VSOL: MATH 8.9b, 8.10a TCA: 2(3g)	Abbott & Costello clip: http://www.youtube.com/watch?v=XnlCFjDn97o Textbook—*Mathematics: Course 3* Colored note cards Pencil	**T**—Show students YouTube clip from Abbott and Costello math problems. Explain to students that they need to have a good foundation of math terms and concepts before they can begin a new field of study. Relate this to the foundations of geometry. **M/A**—Have students work with a partner to define the new vocabulary words in Chapter 7. Explain again the importance of the terms/concepts. To define these words, have students make flash cards. On one side of the cards, have students list the term or concept. On the other side of the card, have students write the definition and draw a picture that relates to the word. **COLL/ACT**—When students are finished defining all the words, have students play a memory matching game with the flash cards. Teach students how to play the game and then let them play with their partners.
87	**LA** Given instruction on verb+ gerund and infinitive relationships, students will identify 8 out of 10 verb+ gerund and infinitive relationships and will label them in correct order with 100% accuracy.	WIDA Standard 2 Grade 8 Level 3 VSOL: ENGL 8.5a, b TCA: 2(1a, b) 2(3f)	Grammar Textbook—*Grammar Links 3* Worksheet Review worksheet Pencil	**L**—Review gerunds and infinitives with students. Answer any questions students may have about these aspects of grammar. Pass out *Grammar Links 3* textbook to everyone in the class. Have students turn to Chapter 13. Give students 15 minutes to read through the red section of the Grammar Briefing 1 section. Teach the students for approximately 15 minutes about verbs+ gerunds and infinitives. Explain to them the different forms and functions. Go through each of the red sections with students. Ask students example questions from the book. For LD students, give all students an explanation worksheet to review the lesson. Make sure the worksheet has illustrations. Give students a reading passage and have them identify all the verb+ gerund and infinitive relationships in the passage. Have them label which word comes first and which word comes second.

DAY #	CONTENT/OBJECTIVE	STANDARDS	RESOURCES/MATERIALS	LEARNING ACTIVITIES/ASSESSMENTS
88	**History Chapter 10** Given the geographical map found on page 264 of text and instruction about trade in ancient Arabia, students will write a paragraph of at least five sentences with less than three grammatical errors about the reasons why trade and the spread of Islam flourished in this ancient civilization.	WIDA Standard 5 Grade 8 Level 3 VSOL: WHI 8a, b ENGL 8.7d, g, 8.8 TCA: 2(1b) 2(2c, d) 2(3e, f, g) 2(4j)	Qur'an Whiteboard Markers Video on ancient Arab culture: http://www.youtube.com/watch?v=fWw2QZ7zbeQ History textbook—*Ancient World History: Patterns of Interaction* Notebook paper Pencil	**CE/DIV**—Write a moral code from the Qur'an, but do not indicate to students that it is from the holy book of Islam. Ask students what they think about the code. Ask students if they have heard moral codes like the one listed from their faith or upbringing. Ask students if they are unfamiliar with any vocabulary from this chapter. Review verbally with students any terms not already learned. In order to help LD students, teacher records all vocabulary on one file and sends to all students by e-mail. **T**—Show students a video about ancient Arabian culture that focuses on trade and religion. Motivate students to actively watch and listen to the video by promising a reward at the end of the day. **CT/SS**—Show students the map of ancient Arabia on page 249 in text. Have students interpret map and critically think about why trade and religion would flourish in this location. Then guide students to locate the passages of each section that focus on trade and religion. Explain to students that they will write a paragraph about the reasons why trade and the spread of Islam flourished during this time period. Help students identify one reason. Have them record this. **ASSESS**—Then have students identify and record other reasons. If students finish this in class, have them start writing the paragraph. If time does not permit, have student write paragraph for HW. Tell students that they will have a quiz over the reading passages from this chapter that deals with trade and religion at the beginning of the next class. Give students candy as they leave for actively watching and listening to the video.

DAY #	CONTENT/OBJECTIVE	STANDARDS	RESOURCES/MATERIALS	LEARNING ACTIVITIES/ASSESSMENTS
89	**Social (MLK Lesson)** Given a reading passage about MLK's life, students will provide the correct answer for each question, answering 12 out of 12 reading comprehension questions correctly.	WIDA Standard 1 Grade 8 Level 3 WIDA Standard 5 Grade 8 Level 3 VSOL: 8.6b, I TCA: 2(2d) 2(3f, g) 2(4j)	I Have a Dream video: http://www.youtube.com/watch?v=HRlF4_WzU1w MLK reading passage Worksheet Pencil	**ASSESS/SS**—Give students a reading comprehension quiz over Chapter 10 in the History text. **DIV**—Ask students to list and describe important figures from their native country/heritage. Have students recall what they know about MLK. **CT**—Have students record on paper why they think MLK is so important to American History. Then call on students by name to read their answers. **T**—Play video of MLK's "I Have A Dream" speech. Students are to actively listen. Then give students a revised reading passage on the biography of MLK's life. Allow students enough time to read through passage once in class and to ask questions if they arise. Have students answer reading comprehension questions.
90 GM14	**Science Chapter 13 (Jan. 22)** Given a reading comprehension worksheet, students will provide the correct answer for each question, answering 10 out of 10 questions correctly.	WIDA Standard 4 Grade 8 Level 3 VSOL: PS6a.b TCA: 2(1b) 2(3g) 2(4j)	"I Want To Dance With Somebody" song Science textbook: *Physical Science* Whiteboard Markers Worksheet Review worksheet	**MUS/D/ACT/P**—Have an '80s energetic dance song playing when students come into the classroom. Have students set their things down and lead them in a short and fun energetic dance. **S**—Allow students to sit anywhere they want to in the room. Have them open their science text to Chapter 13. Explain to them that they are going to be reviewing the language of the chapter which focuses on energy and its different forms. Have students popcorn-read each paragraph from Section 1 and 2. Stop and explain the scientific formulas with students. Show on the board how to write them out and explain them. Also, review verbally with the students the different concepts and terms they read as they come across them. Give all students a review worksheet of the terms. **ASSESS**—With the last 15 minutes of class, give students a reading comprehension worksheet to complete.

DAY #	CONTENT/OBJECTIVE	STANDARDS	RESOURCES/MATERIALS	LEARNING ACTIVITIES/ASSESSMENTS
91	**Math Chapter 7** Given the vocabulary from Chapter 7, students will create their own definitions and record them in a journal that they also will begin for the remainder of the year to review what they learn in and still struggle with after each ESL math class with no more than three grammatical errors.	WIDA Standard 3 Grade 8 Level 3 VSOL: ENGL 8.7d, g, 8.8 TCA: 2(1a, b) 2(4h, i)	Math flash cards Math journal Pencil	**ACT/M/COLL**—Have students pull out their Chapter 7 flash cards. Let them play one memory game with their partner, and then have students switch partners. Inform students that they do not have to stay in their seats. Review with students how to write their own definitions for math terms. Construct several new definitions with students. Have students construct one or two definitions on their own. **CT/ASSESS**—Introduce the math journal project to students. Explain to students that for the remainder of the year, they will be journaling about their math experience in relation to English after every math content day in ESL class. Let students know that in their journal entries they will need to rewrite any new vocabulary they learn, an overview of what they learned in each lesson, and anything they are still struggling with. Show students the preview guide from Chapter 7 (page 329 in TE) for an example of what this looks like. Have students start this journal in class so that they can ask questions if they arise. Then explain that this project will be due at the end of the year, but will be turned in frequently for checks.
92	**History/LA (Chapter 11)** Given instruction on how to write a personal opinion essay and on the church division under the Byzantine Empire, students write an essay that compares and contrasts the Roman Catholic Church and the Eastern Orthodox Church and answers personal opinion questions about this subject with 100% correct usage of personal pronouns.	WIDA Standard 2 Grade 8 Level 3 VSOL: WHI7d ENGL 8.7b, c, d, e, g, h, 8.8 TCA: 2(1a, b) 2(3f, g) 2(4i)	Whiteboard Markers History textbook—*Ancient World History: Patterns of Interaction* PPT Notebook paper	**CE**—Explain the concept of division and why it occurs. Discuss the pros and cons. Use this to introduce lesson. **SS**—Have students look at the diagram on page 305 that deals with church division. Verbally have students identify two or three comparisons and contrasts between the two church systems. **COLL**—Split students into pairs and give them two personal questions to discuss with their partner: "What do you think was the most important issue dividing the two churches?" and "Do you think the conflict between the two churches will ever be healed? Why or why not?" Give students 10 minutes to discuss these questions. **T**—Have students go back to desks. Use PPT to review the parts of an essay. Then teach students how to write a personal opinionated essay. Teach students what pronouns to use and when to use them. Show students example passages that have been extracted from personal opinion essays to further explain this new concept. **CT**—Tell students that they will be writing an essay over the next week outside of class that compares and contrasts the divisions of the church and also expands on the personal opinion questions they answered with their partners. Guide students on how to form the essay and divide each section. **ASSESS**—Have students turn in on next history day. Extend the date for LD students on a case by case basis.

DAY #	CONTENT/OBJECTIVE	STANDARDS	RESOURCES/MATERIALS	LEARNING ACTIVITIES/ASSESSMENTS
GM15 93	**LA** Given a list of modals, students will match 10 out of 10 commonly used modals with their specific function and then will correctly use each modal in a sentence with no grammatical errors.	WIDA Standard 2 Grade 8 Level 3 VSOL: ENGL 8.5a, 8.8 TCA: 2(1a, b) 2(3e, f) 2(4i, j)	Whiteboard Markers *The Little Engine That Could* PPT Modal handout Worksheet Pencil	Answer any questions students may have about history essay. L—Write 10 commonly used modals on the board. Read a short passage that contains an excess of modals. Have students stand up every time they hear a modal used. T/CT—After reading, instruct students on what modals are. Use a PPT to explain the different forms and functions of modals. On the PPT, make sure to include at least one example sentence for each modal and its negative. Give students a fill-in-the-blank handout to complete as they actively listen to the lesson. Every few modals, have students create a sentence on their own using the example modal. Ask students if they have any questions about the different forms of modals and their functions. Pick modals at random and have students create sentences with them. Then show example sentences and have students identify the modals. Review with students the different functions of the modals listed on the board. Distribute a matching worksheet to students. Have them match all the commonly used modals they have learned with their appropriate function. Then have them create a sentence for each function on the same worksheet.
94	**Math Chapter 8** Given an overview of Chapter 8, in a group, students will orally present the vocabulary and language about perimeter, area, and volume of geometric shapes and figures with less than four grammatical speaking errors.	WIDA Standard 3 Grade 8 Level 3 VSOL: MATH 8.11 ENGL: 8.2a, b, c, g, h TCA: 2(1a, b) 2(3f) 2(4h, i)	Textbook—*Mathematics: Course 3* Notebook paper Pencil Math journal	M—Read through the opening paragraphs of Sections 1–5 with students. Have students popcorn-read these sections. Stop and review the vocabulary with students when they are addressed. After reading each section, look at the first two or three examples of each section. Guide students on how to read these example problems and explain them. COLL/DIV/ASSESS—Split students into five groups based on language levels. Group struggling students with advanced students. Assign each group a section to form an oral presentation on. Have each group orally define each vocabulary word and then orally describe how to read and solve the first two example problems in the HW section of each chapter. Grade groups based on speaking skills and mastery of content they are presenting. Have groups actively listen to each other's presentations. CT—Have students journal in their math journal for HW about the lesson.

DAY #	CONTENT/OBJECTIVE	STANDARDS	RESOURCES/MATERIALS	LEARNING ACTIVITIES/ASSESSMENTS
95	**History Chapter 12** Given instruction on Buddhism, in groups, students will orally summarize what Buddhism is, its origin, and what role it played in China, Japan, Korea, or SE Asia with no more than two speaking errors.	WIDA Standard 5 Grade 8 Level 3 VSOL: WHI 4d ENGL: 8.2a, b, c, g, h, 8.9a, c, TCA: 2(3f, g) 2(4h, i, j)	Computers Resource list Notebook paper Pencil Study guide	**ASSESS**—Students turn in personal opinion essay on church division in the Byzantine Empire. **T/COLL/SS**—Take students to the computer lab to do research. Split students into four groups. Explain to students that they need to research what Buddhism is, its origin, and what role it has played in the nation(s) assigned to their group. **CT**—Give students a list of resources they can use or go to do research. Have students research at least two facts about each subtopic. Then have students work together to form an oral presentation on their research. Limit presentations to 5 minutes per group. Indicate that each student must speak an equal amount. Remind students to only use English. Inform students that they will present on Friday, which means they have 2 days to prepare in or out of class. Help students understand unfamiliar vocabulary while they are researching. Give students a study guide for a history language test next history class.
96	**Science Chapter 14** Given five vocabulary words from the chapter, in groups, students will orally describe the term/concept in their own words and will include an example to match the term with no more than two speaking errors.	WIDA Standard 4 Grade 8 Level 3 VSOL: ENGL: 8.2a, b, c, g, h PS7.d TCA: 2(1a, b) 2(3f) 2(4i)	Science textbook: *Physical Science* Notebook paper Pencil Mobile devices, tablets, iPads, etc. Study guide	**CE**—Ask students if they have ever heard of the phrase, "The argument was heated." Explain to students what the use of the word "heated" means in this context. Then explain to students that they should avoid conversations and situations of that nature. **S**—Have students open text and popcorn-read all the bold-faced vocabulary words from the chapter. After each term is introduced, review with students orally. Also, for every couple of terms ask for a real-life example. Guide them and help them come up with an example. In order to help LD students, teacher records all vocabulary on one file and sends to all students by e-mail. **ACT/T**—After all vocabulary words have been addressed, split students into groups. Give each group five vocabulary words from the chapter. Have them rewrite the definition in their own words and come up with an example of each. Allow students to use their mobile devices and tablets for this part of the assignment and sit anywhere they want to in the room or hallway right outside the class. With the remaining time, have each group present their words. Make sure everyone speaks. Give students a study guide for a science language test next science day.

DAY #	CONTENT/OBJECTIVE	STANDARDS	RESOURCES/MATERIALS	LEARNING ACTIVITIES/ASSESSMENTS
97	**Social** Given instruction on how to answer ACCESS test questions, as a class, students will answer three ACCESS test questions correctly.	WIDA Standard 1 Grade 8 Level 3 VSOL: ENGL 8.5, 8.6 TCA: 2(4h, i, j) 2(5k)	ACCESS Practice Test Pencil SMART Board	**ASSESS**—Take the first 25 minutes of class to listen to the students' oral presentations on Buddhism. Have students record what they learn from other groups. Give them an outline to take notes on and then turn in. Use the second half of class to begin preparing students to take the ACCESS test. Reiterate that all the activities the students have done throughout the year have served the purpose to prepare students to take the ACCESS test. Use the SMART Board to bring up the ACCESS practice test and start teaching students how to read and answer the various types of questions. Guide students through two problems. Then allow them to work together as a class to answer three problems.
98 GM16	**Social/LA** Given a lesson on present and past unreal conditionals, students will construct an outline for their personal unreal or impossible story and write the first paragraph of the story with less than two grammatical errors.	WIDA Standard 2 Grade 8 Level 3 VSOL: ENGL 8.7b, d, e, g, 8.8 TCA: 2(1a, b) 2(3e, f) 2(4h, i)	Grammar Textbook—*Grammar Links 3* Whiteboard Markers Notebook paper Pencil	**CE**—Talk to students about accomplishing everything they want to do, so they don't have to be wishful or hopeful for something unnecessary. Give a personal example. Then use this to introduce the lesson. **L**—Show students pictures on page 360 of the *Grammar Links 3* textbook. Guide students through process of identifying the present and past unreal conditionals. Ask students if they have ever heard these phrases heard. If they respond positively ask when. Proceed to make up generic examples of when they could be used. Teach students the "if" and "result" clauses. Relate this to what students already know about cause-effect relationships. Explain that these conditionals are used to talk about unreal or impossible situations. Then teach the students the difference between present and past conditionals with the unreal. Give students a few examples to work through. **CT**—Have students create their own unreal or impossible story. Have them make an outline for the entire story, but also require them to write the first paragraph of the story with less than two grammatical mistakes. Provide help if necessary.

DAY #	CONTENT/OBJECTIVE	STANDARDS	RESOURCES/MATERIALS	LEARNING ACTIVITIES/ASSESSMENTS
99	**LA** Given a worksheet on the error analysis of coordinating conjunctions, students will identify the improper use of conjunctions in each sentence, correctly providing the correct answer for each with 80% accuracy.	WIDA Standard 2 Grade 8 Level 3 VASOL: ENGL 8.8 TCA: 2(3e, f)	Textbook: *Understanding and Using English Grammar* *Conjunction Junction* video http://youtu.be/RPoBE-E8VOc Activity sheet on coordinating conjunctions	Use PPT presentation to instruct students on Coordinating Conjunctions. Include explanation and examples of parallel structure and paired conjunctions. **T**—Show video of *Schoolhouse Rock's Conjunction Junction.* After instruction, give students a few examples that they can work out with a partner for guided practice. Teacher will continue to interact with students at this time. Students will complete a written activity sheet including error analysis.
100	**Math Chapter 8 (last 5 sections)** Given chapter review math problems, students will write sentences describing how to properly solve each problem with less than two grammatical errors.	WIDA Standard 3 Grade 8 Level 3 VASOL: MATH 8.7a TCA: 2(2b) 2(4i, j)	Rubric for students to assess each other's speaking Math journal	**COLL/ASSESS/DIV**—Students will be divided into pairs. Each pair will be assigned a review section on page 448 from Sections 8-6 through 8-10. Individuals in each pair will take turns orally describing how to solve each problem. For the student that is not speaking at the moment, they will listen actively and assess the other student's use of language using the provided rubric. Students will correct each other. As a group, students will then record their answers in writing for each problem. These papers will be collected at the end of class. **CT**—Have students journal in their math journal for HW about the lesson.
101	**History Test Chapters 10–12 Language** Given an oral exam over Chapters 10–12 of their history textbooks, students will answer all questions with 80% accuracy.	WIDA Standard 5 Grade 8 Level 3 VSOL: WHI 4d, 7d, 8a, b TCA: 2(3e, f) 2(4i, j)	History test Science study guide Pencil	**ASSESS**—Students will take history exam. Teacher will present student with different questions or topics. Students must provide the correct answer and show that they are able to fully describe and explain answers using proper terminology and English grammar. Have students turn in history test when they are finished. Hand them a study guide for the science test. Motivate students to start studying for the test. Give students directions for poster board project for history Chapters 10–12. Indicate that they will need to prepare a poster board presentation on the three religions they learned. Let students know they will give a 4–5-minute presentation on their project.

DAY #	CONTENT/OBJECTIVE	STANDARDS	RESOURCES/MATERIALS	LEARNING ACTIVITIES/ASSESSMENTS
102	**Social** After taking a learning style quiz, students will write a paragraph describing whether or not they accurately described them with no more than two spelling or conventional errors.	WIDA Standard 1 Grade 8 Level 3 VASOL: ENGL 8.8b, g TCA: 2(3e) 2(4h)	Copies of learning styles quiz Paper and pencil ACCESS practice test	**ASSESS**—Have students complete learning style quiz. **ACT/P**—In order to see what students have each learning style, call each learning style one at a time. If a student scored strongly in that particular learning style, have students move to a designated area of the room. **LA**—Have students write a short paragraph describing whether or not they thought the test was accurate. Encourage them to focus on using proper spelling and writing conventions in this paragraph. Collect from the students. **ASSESS**—Last 25 minutes use for ACCESS test practice.
103 GM17	**Science Test** Given a test on the language of science discussed in Chapters 12–14 of the text, students will answer 30 out of 30 questions correct.	WIDA Standard 4 Grade 8 Level 3 PS1, 7.d, 10.a.b.c TCA: 2(4j)	Science test Pencil	Pre-arrange classroom for test. **ASSESS/S**—Give students test as they come in. Have them read the directions and begin immediately. Have students flip their test over when they are finished. Allow students to read when they are finished.

DAY #	CONTENT/OBJECTIVE	STANDARDS	RESOURCES/MATERIALS	LEARNING ACTIVITIES/ASSESSMENTS
104	**LA** Given a list of sources and interview questions for potential news stories, students will evaluate the validity of the sources and the effectiveness of the interview questions, providing a detailed explanation as to why each is or is not appropriate.	WIDA Standard 2 Grade 8 Level 3 VASOL: ENGL 8.3a, b, d TCA: 2(1a)	Grammar quiz Pencil Literature textbook—*Literature: Grade 8* PPT on sources, quotations, and sound-bites "Deep Impact" newscast—from textbook's "Media Smart" DVD "A Grand Slam" magazine article from the textbook's supplemental resources CD-ROM	**ASSESS**—Give students 15 minutes to take a grammar quiz on Chapters 14, 15, 16 (seven questions). Direct students to page 910 of their literature books. Call on three different students and have each one read one of the paragraphs out loud. **T**—Use PPT presentation to instruct students on the definitions of source, quotations, and sound-bites. Include examples of types of sources (i.e., witnesses and officials, experts, visual sources, sources as counterpoints). Explain to students that we can't always believe everything we hear, even if it's on the news. Explain that it is important to evaluate the sources from which they are receiving information. Give students 5 minutes to brainstorm how to evaluate sources. Facilitate discussion on evaluating sources. Fill in the gaps of what students do not mention with information in prepared PPT. **T**—Have students watch newscast on "Deep Impact"—included on textbook's "Media Smart" DVD. Assess for understanding. **COLL**—Have students pair up with a partner to evaluate the sources used in the news segment. Ask them whether or not the sources were valid and the sound-bites used were used properly. Each group will then share their opinions with the class. Students will then read the magazine article titled "A Grand Slam." Students will answer the questions on page 912 of their textbook on their own. **COLL**—Students will work together in small groups to brainstorm possible news stories that could be covered in their own school or neighborhood. They must include a list of possible sources for each news story and questions they would ask each source in order to receive solid information. Questions must be open-ended to encourage strong sound-bites that could be used in the students' media piece. Students will then exchange their sources and interview questions with students in other groups. Each group must then evaluate each other's sources and the effectiveness of the interview questions.

DAY #	CONTENT/OBJECTIVE	STANDARDS	RESOURCES/MATERIALS	LEARNING ACTIVITIES/ASSESSMENTS
105	**Math Chapter 9** Given a word problem, students will verbally explain how to solve the problem and write down the explanation with fewer than two grammatical errors.	WIDA Standard 3 Grade 8 Level 3 VASOL: MATH 8.13a, b TCA: 2(1a, b)	Student computer access Access to http://quizlet.com/ Math journal	**COLL/T**—Divide students into five groups. Split students by language proficiency. Put advanced students with struggling students. Assign each group one of the following sections of the chapter: Sections 9.1–9.5, found on pages 462–486. Students will work in groups to define the vocabulary from their chapter. Students will use computers to create a set of Quizlet vocabulary flash cards for each section. Encourage students to use these flash card sets to study for their next test and their regular math class. Also, have each group choose one word problem from their section. Have them work together to orally explain how to solve the problem. As an exit slip, have each group write down their oral explanation.
106	**History Chapter 13** Given multiple activities to complete in centers, students will choose their favorite center and write a paragraph explaining why they enjoyed it so much and what they learned from it with no more than two grammatical errors.	WIDA Standard 5 Grade 8 Level 3 VASOL: WHI.9a, b, c TCA: 2(1b) 2(3e, f, g) 2(4i, j)	History textbook—*Ancient World History: Patterns of Interaction* Paper and pencil Student computer access Activity sheet on homonyms from the chapter	**ACT**—Students will participate in centers concerning Chapter 13 in their History books. Divide students into five groups. Each group will participate in one of the five centers at a time. The centers activity will span two days (continued day 108). Students will be given a checklist outlining the activities that will be completed at each center. This checklist, along with student work, will be collected at the end of the second day of centers. Center 1: Students will read about Charlemagne on pages 356–357 of their textbook. They will then create a list describing Charlemagne's empire. Center 2: **COLL**—After reading the section on Feudalism on page 360 and examining the illustration on 361, students will each be assigned a role from the feudal system. Each must define their role and explain it to the other students in their group. They will have 1 minute to describe their role to the others. Center 3: **CT**—Students will read section titled "The Vikings Invade from the North" on pages 358–359. They must then answer the following Critical Thinking question: How did geography play a role in ending Viking attacks in Europe? Center 4: **T/COLL**—Students will use computers and the Internet to research *chivalry* in the Middle Ages. They may also use their textbooks. Students will work together to create their own modern-day code of chivalry that they think would be applicable to the classroom. Center 5: **L**—Students will be given an activity sheet. The sheet will provide students with the definition of homonyms, and three chapter vocabulary words: *knight, serf,* and *manor*. Students will provide a definition for each word. They will then identify a homonym for each vocabulary word along with its definition.

DAY #	CONTENT/OBJECTIVE	STANDARDS	RESOURCES/MATERIALS	LEARNING ACTIVITIES/ASSESSMENTS
107	**Science Chapter 15** Given a vocabulary word from the chapter, students will design a science experiment relating to the word, writing out each step with less than three errors in the use of scientific language.	WIDA Standard 4 Grade 8 Level 3 VASOL: PS.8a, b, c TCA: 2(1a, b) 2(3f) 2(4i, j)	Science textbook: *Physical Science* Pencil and paper	**S/L**—Assign each student one of the following vocabulary words from the text: wavelength, frequency, speed, rarefaction, compression, resonance. Have students create a hypothetical science experiment to show proof of each concept. Students will write out directions for conducting the science experiment using proper scientific terms and following the outline of the scientific method. They will also include a hypothesis to accompany their experiment.
108 GM18	**Social (Valentine's Day)** Given the story of St. Valentine, students will write a short essay on why they think Valentine was or was not brave, with no more than three errors in spelling or grammar.	WIDA Standard 1 Grade 8 Level 3 VASOL: ENGL 8.8g TCA: 2(1b) 2(2d) 2(5l)	Valentine's Day packet found at: http://www.abcteach.com/free/r/rc_valentine_legend.pdf Movie—*A Charlie Brown Valentine*	**COLL**—A week before Valentine's Day, send out a letter to parents. Explain that there will be a Valentine's Day party in ESL class the following Friday. Invite parents to participate in the celebration by volunteering to send in cookies or candy to help celebrate. Encourage students to bring in valentines for other students in the class. **CE**—Discuss the courage that St. Valentine exemplified in his interactions with the Emperor. Explain why courage is a valuable character trait to have. Have the classroom decorated with hearts and red and white decorations. Begin class by explaining Valentine's Day. Describe typical traditions, symbols associated with the holiday, the meaning behind it, etc. **DIV**—Ask students to share about similar holidays in their countries. Give them a chance to share their customs and traditions. Give students Valentine's Day handouts. Read "The Story of St. Valentine." **COLL/ACT**—Students may then exchange valentines and get cookies. Encourage them to work on the rest of the Valentine's Day packet as they watch *A Charlie Brown Valentine*. They should at least finish the essay section by the end of class. Collect packet as an exit slip.

DAY #	CONTENT/OBJECTIVE	STANDARDS	RESOURCES/MATERIALS	LEARNING ACTIVITIES/ASSESSMENTS
109	**History Chapters 10–12** Given time to prepare outside of class, students will present a poster board project about the three religions they studied in Chapters 10–12 with no more than three speaking errors.	WIDA Standard 2 Grade 8 Level 3 VASOL: ENGL 8.2a, b, c, h; ENGL 8.8 TCA: 2(2d) 2(4i, j)	Poster board projects	**DIV/SS/ACT/CT**—Use class time for students to present their poster board projects about the three major religions they recently took a test on. Grade students on content and speaking skills. Have other students listen to each other's presentations and record one fact about each presentation. Have students turn their facts sheet in before they leave and include this in the final score of this project.
110	**Math Chapters 7–9 Test** Given a test over the language and application of the mathematical skills in Chapters 7, 8, & 9, students will correctly answer each question with 80% accuracy.	WIDA Standard 3 Grade 8 Level 3 VASOL: MATH 8.6, 8.8 TCA: 2(4h, j)	Math test—Chapters 7–9	Students will have 5 minutes to ask questions and review for the test. **ASSESS**—Students will sit at every other desk during the test. When students have finished the test, they may read quietly at their seats.
111	**History Chapter 14** Given a section of Chapter 14, students will work together to outline their section and identify the main idea of each sub-section with 100% accuracy.	WIDA Standard 5 Grade 8 Level 3 VASOL: WHI.12a, b, c TCA: 2(1b) 2(2d) 2(3e, f) 2(4j)	History textbook—*Ancient World History: Patterns of Interaction* Pencils and paper Material for creating interactive bulletin board including construction paper, staples, bulletin board borders, etc.	**COLL**—Students will be divided into four groups. Each group will be responsible for outlining one section of the chapter. Split students up based on language proficiency. Put advanced students with struggling students. Among each group, students may choose to divide up their chapter into smaller sections for individuals to outline, that way they will be able to finish their chapter in time. Students will be sure to identify the main idea of each paragraph in their section and put it on their outline. **COLL/A/ACT**—Once the groups have each finished their outline, students will work with the teacher in order to create a condensed outline of the entire chapter. Students will then design a bulletin board showing the outline of the chapter. The bulletin board must be interactive. *Synthesis*

DAY #	CONTENT/OBJECTIVE	STANDARDS	RESOURCES/MATERIALS	LEARNING ACTIVITIES/ASSESSMENTS
112	**Science Chapter 16** Given a list of new vocabulary words, students will write a sentence correctly using each new word, with no more than two grammatical errors.	WIDA Standard 4 Grade 8 Level 3 VASOL: PS.8a, d; WHI.12a, b, c TCA: 2(1a) 2(4i, j)	Science textbook: *Physical Science* Paper and pencil Material for creating interactive bulletin board including construction paper, staples, bulletin board borders, etc.	**T**—Students will identify unknown vocabulary words from Chapter 16. After using the computers to identify the meaning of each word, they will write a sentence for each, using each vocabulary word properly. **COLL**—Students will use the last 25 minutes to work on their bulletin board project.
113 GM19	**LA/History Centers!** Given multiple activities to complete in centers, students will choose their favorite center and write a paragraph explaining why they enjoyed it so much and what they learned from it with no more than two grammatical errors.	WIDA Standard 5 Grade 8 Level 3 VASOL: WHI.9a, b, c TCA: 2(1b) 2(3e, f, g) 2(4i, j)	History textbook—*Ancient World History: Patterns of Interaction* Paper and pencil Student computer access Activity sheet on homonyms from the chapter	**CE**—Ask each student to share with a neighbor one way they have seen them display a positive character trait this week. **ACT/COLL/CT/L**—Continue history centers from day 106.

DAY #	CONTENT/OBJECTIVE	STANDARDS	RESOURCES/MATERIALS	LEARNING ACTIVITIES/ASSESSMENTS
114	**Math Chapter 10** Experimental and Theoretical Probability Given instruction on the language of experimental and theoretical probability, students will write 4 out of 4 mathematical equations correctly after reading four word problems that discuss probability.	WIDA Standard 3 Grade 8 Level 3 VSOL: MATH 8.12, 8.13a ENGL 8.6a, 8.7d, g, 8.8 TCA: 2(1a, b) 2(2d) 2(3f) 2(4j)	Textbook—*Mathematics: Course 3* PPT Worksheet Pencil Math journal	**DIV**—Review the term "probability" with students. Verbally ask students probability questions about real-life situations such as sports events, school lunch options, etc. **M**—Then verbally review the vocabulary from the first four sections of Chapter 10 that deal with experimental and theoretical probability. Frequently ask students if they understand and if any further explanation needs to be given. DO not single out LD students. Have students record on a sheet of paper a short description of each vocabulary term reviewed. **T**—Then use a PPT to display word problems from each of the first four sections. Describe to students how to read each word problem, review what they learned about splitting the word problems into parts, and then teach them how to write mathematical equations from the information given in each problem according to the language introduced in this chapter. **ASSESS**—Guide students through the process of writing mathematical equations from word problems for this specific chapter. Then give students a worksheet with four multiple-choice word problems. Verbally give students directions and have them read along on their worksheet. Have students read each word problem, break up its parts, write a mathematical equation for the word problem, and then choose the correct equation for each problem. Students are not to solve the problem.
115	**History Chapter 15** Given a review over three ancient empires of West Africa, students will create a chart that divides each empire and lists at least three facts about each that are written with a 100% correct subject-verb agreement.	WIDA Standard 5 Grade 8 Level 3 VSOL: WHI 10d ENGL 8.8d TCA: 2(1b) 2(3g) 2(4j)	Personally recorded video "Gati Bongo" song Notebook paper Pencil History textbook—*Ancient World* *History: Patterns of Interaction*	**T/ACT/MUS/D/P/DIV/CT**—Show students a video of West Africans dancing to tribal music. Play a West African tribal song for students. Have students get out of their seats and dance like the people they saw in the video. Have video playing so students can model dance. Do this with the students. After a brief period of dancing, have students sit back down and write a sentence or two about what they think the song is trying to communicate on a blank sheet of notebook paper. Collect these papers. **SS**—Have students turn in their books to Chapter 15 Section 2. Review with students the terms and concepts introduced in the passages about the empires of Ghana, Mali, and Songhai. Have students create a chart for the three empires that divides them and gives three facts about each. Tell students they must write in complete sentences.

DAY #	CONTENT/OBJECTIVE	STANDARDS	RESOURCES/MATERIALS	LEARNING ACTIVITIES/ASSESSMENTS
116	**Science Quiz Chapters 15–16 HW Help Day** Given a quiz on the language of science from Chapters 15–16, students will answer 20 out of 20 questions correct.	WIDA Standard 4 Grade 8 Level 3 VSOL: PS.8a, b, c, d TCA: 2(4j)	Notebook paper Pencil	**ASSESS/S**—Give students a science language quiz. Allow them 30 minutes to complete the quiz. Students may read a book until the 30 minutes has passed if they finish early. Collect quizzes from students. Have students work on HW from other subjects. Monitor and help students if they need it.
117	**Social** Given instruction on how to answer ACCESS questions, students will answer 4 out of 4 ACCESS practice test questions correctly.	WIDA Standard 1 Grade 8 Level 3 VSOL: 8.2a, c, g, h, 8.5, 8.6, 8.7, 8.8 TCA: 2(1a, b) 2(d) 2(3f, g) 2(4h, i) 2(5k)	Life without manners clip: http://www.youtube.com/watch?v=xPmtssXaSQ8 PPT ACCESS practice test Pencil	**T**—Show students a YouTube clip about life without manners. Use this to introduce lesson. **DIV**—Ask students if they have any polite customs in their native country/culture. Then teach students a variety of mannerisms in America. Make sure to include instruction on conversation with peers, the opposite sex, teachers, adults, coworkers, meals, public and private settings. **T/COLL/TH**—Use PPT to list common mannerisms. Have students partner up and then role-play and use different mannerisms with each other. Use last 25 minutes for ACCESS test practice. Bring up questions from all subjects on the ACCESS. Teach students how to read questions. Then give students a worksheet with four questions to answer. Have them complete as much as possible in class and then complete the rest for HW.
118 GM20	**LA** Given an introduction to noun clauses, with a partner, students will identify 5 of 5 noun clauses in prewritten sentences and will then create five new sentences using the same noun clauses with no grammatical errors.	WIDA Standard 2 Grade 8 Level 3 VSOL: ENGL 8.4b, 8.7g, 8.8 TCA: 2(1a, b) 2(3e, f) 2(4i, j)	PPT Reading passage from *The Cat In The Hat* Grammar Textbook—*Grammar Links 3* Cut out sheets of example sentences Notebook paper Pencil	**T/CT**—Put a short reading passage on the screen with all the noun clauses of the passage deleted. Use *The Cat In The Hat* for reading passage. Ask students what is missing from the passage. Ask them why they think something is missing. **L**—Explain that all the sentences are missing noun clauses. Give students a summarized description of noun phrases and their functions from the *Grammar Links 3* textbook. Teach students what noun clauses are, their placement in sentences, uses, and function. Guide students through recognizing noun clauses in sentences. Give students a list of several noun clauses and have them create sentences with the different clauses **COLL**—Pair students up and give each pair a list of five sentences. Have students identify the noun clause in each sentence. Then have them create five new sentences with the noun clauses they just identified. *Continue Chapter 20 in the following week.

DAY #	CONTENT/OBJECTIVE	STANDARDS	RESOURCES/MATERIALS	LEARNING ACTIVITIES/ASSESSMENTS
119	**Math Chapter 10 Probability and Counting** Given instruction on how to read math equations from the last half of Chapter 10, students will write two of their own equations that deal with probability, predictions, counting, or permutations with full inclusion of each part of a math equation and with no more than one grammatical error.	WIDA Standard 3 Grade 8 Level 3 VSOL: MATH 8.12, 8.13a ENGL 8.7d, g, 8.8 TCA: 2(1a, b) 2(3e, g) 2(4j)	Textbook - *Mathematics: Course 3* PPT on making decisions: http://www.youtube.com/watch?v=vuyW1BWVOrw PPT and handout Math textbook Notebook paper Pencil Math journal	When students first come into the classroom, ask them if they are struggling with any of the terms, concepts, and language of the second half of Chapter 10. Help students as needed. **CE/T**—Explain to students that we have to be wise when we make decisions. As we make decisions, we should always weigh the consequences of the decisions. One way we can do this is by making predictions. Show students a short video about bad decision-making. **M**—Review with students the major terms of each section by using a PPT to show students examples of probability and counting numbers. For LD students, give all students a copy of the PPT to follow along. Guide students through the process of reading math equation examples from Sections 5–8. Have students use prior knowledge to identify the different parts of the problems. **ASSESS**—Assign students the task of writing two math equations that either deal with predictions, probability, counting, or permutations. Explain that they must write solvable math problems with no more than one grammatical error and with 100% accurate content material. Have students turn in assignment on the following day.
120	**History Test Chapters 13–15** Given a listening test on the language learned from Chapters 13–15 in the history textbook, students will respond in writing to 14 of 20 questions correctly.	WIDA Standard 5 Grade 8 Level 3 VSOL: WHI 10d ENGL 8.2h TCA: 2(4j)	Notebook paper Pencil Teacher copy of test	Have classroom arranged where students cannot cheat on the test. Tell students to get out a blank sheet of notebook paper. **ASSESS**—Deliver the history test orally. Read each question three times and have students actively listen and answer each question. At the end of the test, ask students if they need any questions repeated. Repeat any question only once. Repeat up to five questions. Collect the tests from the students. Allow students to read or work on other assignments if time permits.

DAY #	CONTENT/OBJECTIVE	STANDARDS	RESOURCES/MATERIALS	LEARNING ACTIVITIES/ASSESSMENTS
121	**Science Chapter 17** Given an example outline of a science chapter, students will work in groups to outline the topics, subtopics, key concepts, and key terms in Chapter 17 with 100% accuracy.	WIDA Standard 4 Grade 8 Level 3 VSOL: PS9.a.b ENGL 8.6a, g, k TCA: 2(1a, b) 2(3f) 2(4j)	PPT Paper Pencil	Ask LD students what their favorite food to cook in the microwave is. Explain to students that a microwave uses microwaves to cook their food. Use this icebreaker to lead into lesson over the language of Chapter 17. **T**—Use PPT to review with students how to outline a chapter. Show students an example of another outlined chapter. Guide students through the process of identifying and understanding each point in the example outline. **S**—Split students into groups and have them outline Chapter 17. Have them divide their outline by title, topic, subtopic, key concept(s), and key term(s) for each section. Explain to them that they must include every part of a standard outline and must use proper English writing techniques/skills. Collect group outlines at the end of class.
122	**Social** Given instruction on how to complete the ACCESS test, students will orally respond to one question with no speaking or grammatical errors.	WIDA Standard 1 Grade 8 Level 3 VSOL: ENGL 8.2b, c, e, 8.6k TCA: 2(2d) 2(3f) 2(4i, j) 2(5k)	Audio clip of "Take Me Out To The Ball Game" "Sports Bloopers" video from YouTube: http://www.youtube.com/watch?v=f9PRw90UNNM Practice ACCESS test Microphone system	**ACT/MUS/D/T**—Have students walk into the song "Take Me Out To The Ball Game." Have them stand at their seats until the song is over. Encourage them to dance. Then show students a short clip of sports bloopers. **DIV**—Ask students to list all the different sports they know. Then ask the students to divide the list into fall, winter, spring, and summer sports. Introduce and explain to students sports they don't already know. Have students write a short paragraph to be turned in for class participation about their favorite sport. Use the last 30 minutes of class for ACCESS test practice. Use the Internet to pull up an oral practice question. Teach the students how to answer this type of problem. Have them make an outline of how to form their oral discussion. Then give students a practice topic and have them outline their response. Use the microphone system in the classroom to record each student's oral discussion. Individually help LD students.

DAY #	CONTENT/OBJECTIVE	STANDARDS	RESOURCES/MATERIALS	LEARNING ACTIVITIES/ASSESSMENTS
123	**LA** **ACCESS Review** Given commonly missed questions from previous ACCESS reading and listening tests, in groups, students will answer 15 out of 15 questions correctly.	WIDA Standard 2 Grade 8 Level 3 VSOL: ENGL 8.2c, h, 8.5, 8.6 TCA: 2(1a) 2(2d) 2(3e, f) 2(4h) 2(5k)	ACCESS practice test PPT ACCESS worksheet ACCESS audio recordings Pencil	**CE**—Have students close their eyes and spend 2 minutes focusing on something that makes them happy. Remind them to spend time every day and in stressful situations to stop and relax. Connect this skill to their ACCESS test they are about to take. **DIV/COLL/T**—Break students into groups based on culture groups. Use a PPT to display commonly missed questions on the ACCESS reading and listening tests. Have students identify the right answer and explain the wrong answer. Allow students to speak in their native language to better understand the review. Indicate that they can only give their answers in English though. **ASSESS**—Distribute a worksheet with practice ACCESS listening and reading comprehension questions to the groups. Have students answer the questions in their groups. Play the recordings for the listening questions twice, and then let students work together to answer the rest of the questions.
124	**MATH** **ACCESS Review** Given eight new vocabulary words, students will define and rewrite their own definitions of these words with 100% accuracy.	WIDA Standard 3 Grade 8 Level 3 VSOL: ENGL 8.7, 8.8, 8.9 TCA: 2(1a) 2(3e, g) 2(4h) 2(5k)	ACCESS practice test Dictionaries Pencil Paper Math journal	**CE**—Have students close their eyes and spend 2 minutes focusing on something that makes them happy. Remind them to spend time every day and in stressful situations to stop and relax. Connect this skill to their ACCESS test they are about to take. Show students vocabulary questions from previous ACCESS tests. Explain to students how they need to answer these types of questions. Ask students to solve two problems. Distribute a list of eight common ACCESS vocabulary words and a dictionary to each student. Have students define the words and then rewrite their own definitions. Give LD students extra encouragement. Have students write a journal entry for HW.

DAY #	CONTENT/OBJECTIVE	STANDARDS	RESOURCES/MATERIALS	LEARNING ACTIVITIES/ASSESSMENTS
125	**History** **ACCESS Review** Given a prewritten essay that answers a writing prompt from an old ACCESS test, students will identify 100% of the different parts of the essay that are necessary to receive a passing score on the ACCESS test.	WIDA Standard 5 Grade 8 Level 3 VSOL: ENGL 8.7, 8.8 TCA: 2(1a) 2(3e, g) 2(4h, i) 2(5k)	ACCESS practice test PPT Pencil Paper	**CE**—Have students close their eyes and spend 2 minutes focusing on something that makes them happy. Remind them to spend time every day and in stressful situations to stop and relax. Connect this skill to the ACCESS test they are about to take. **T**—Use a PPT to review the different parts of an essay. Display an essay prompt from an old ACCESS test. Guide students through the process they would take in order to write an essay based on the given prompt. Then show students an example essay that answers the given prompt. Have students identify the different parts that make up an essay and address any new parts that the ACCESS test may look for. **ASSESS**—Give students an old essay prompt and a copy of a response essay to that prompt. Have them individually identify the different parts that make up that essay. Collect work at the end of class.
126	**Science** **ACCESS Review** Given an oral prompt question from a practice ACCESS test, students will deliver an oral speech to their partner with no speaking errors.	WIDA Standard 4 Grade 8 Level 3 VSOL: ENGL 8.2b, c, e TCA: 2(1a) 2(3e, g) 2(4h, i) 2(5k)	ACCESS practice test ACCESS audio recordings Pencil Paper	**CE**—Have students close their eyes and spend 2 minutes focusing on something that makes them happy. Remind them to spend time every day and in stressful situations to stop and relax. Connect this skill to the ACCESStTest they are about to take. **T**—Give students a list of oral response questions from old ACCESS tests. Review with students how to read these prompts and review with them how to form responses to these types of questions. Have students listen to recordings of example responses to these questions. Address the types of responses that are required by the ACCESS Test. Have students actively listen for speaking errors and the quality of English. **ASSESS/DIV/COLL/CT**—Partner students up by gender. Give each pair an example oral prompt. Have students form personal responses and then deliver an oral speech to their partner. Have students listen for speaking errors in their partner's speech. Address speaking errors as a class.

DAY #	CONTENT/OBJECTIVE	STANDARDS	RESOURCES/MATERIALS	LEARNING ACTIVITIES/ASSESSMENTS
127	**Social** **ACCESS Review** Given a review over the ACCESS test, in teams, students will answer 100% of the review questions correctly.	WIDA Standard 1 Grade 8 Level 3 VSOL: ENGL 8.2g, h TCA: 2(1a) 2(3e, g) 2(4h, i) 2(5k, m)	ACCESS practice test ACCESS test schedule PPT Whiteboard Markers Study guide	**CE**—Have students close their eyes and spend 2 minutes focusing on something that makes them happy. Remind them to spend time every day and in stressful situations to stop and relax. Connect this skill to the ACCESS test they are about to take. Ask students if they have any questions about the test. Address questions as they arise. Explain to students the schedule for the ACCESS test for the following week. **COLL/ACT**—Split students into teams. Play PPT review game with students. Have students come up to the board to play-answer questions and record points. **COLL**—Give students a study/review handout to look over during their weekend of rest. Coordinate with other teachers to make sure ESL students do not have other HW. Express the importance of this test to other content area teachers.
128	**ACCESS Test** Given the reading portion of the ACCESS test, students will answer all the questions with 100% accuracy.	WIDA Standard 2 Grade 8 Level 3 VSOL: ENGL 8.4, 8.5, 8.6 TCA: 2(1a) 2(3e) 2(4h)	ACCESS test Paper Pencil	**CE**—Have students close their eyes and spend 2 minutes focusing on something that makes them happy. Remind them to spend time every day and in stressful situations to stop and relax. Connect this skill to the ACCESS test they are about to take. **ACCESS/CT**—Administer the reading portion of the ACCESS test to students. Give them as much time as they need. Allow them to read when they are finished.
129	**ACCESS Test** Given the writing portion of the ACCESS test, students will write an essay with no grammatical or content description mistakes.	WIDA Standard 2 Grade 8 Level 3 VSOL: ENGL 8.7, 8.8 TCA: 2(1a) 2(3e) 2(4h)	ACCESS test Paper Pencil	**CE**—Have students close their eyes and spend 2 minutes focusing on something that makes them happy. Remind them to spend time every day and in stressful situations to stop and relax. Connect this skill to the ACCESS test they are about to take. **ACCESS/CT**—Administer the writing portion of the ACCESS test to students. Give them as much time as they need. Allow them to read when they are finished.

DAY #	CONTENT/OBJECTIVE	STANDARDS	RESOURCES/MATERIALS	LEARNING ACTIVITIES/ASSESSMENTS
130	**ACCESS Test** Given the listening portion of the ACCESS test, students will respond to all the questions with 100% accuracy.	WIDA Standard 2 Grade 8 Level 3 VSOL: ENGL 8.2h TCA: 2(1a) 2(3e) 2(4h)	ACCESS test ACCESS audio recordings Paper Pencil	**CE**—Have students close their eyes and spend 2 minutes focusing on something that makes them happy. Remind them to spend time every day and in stressful situations to stop and relax. Connect this skill to the ACCESS test they are about to take. **ACCESS/CT**—Administer the listening portion of the ACCESS test to students. Give them as much time as they need. Allow them to read when they are finished.
131	**ACCESS Test** Given the oral portion of the ACCESS test, students will prepare and deliver an oral presentation with no speaking or content description errors.	WIDA Standard 2 Grade 8 Level 3 TCA: 2(1a) 2(3e) 2(4h) VSOL: ENGL 8.2a, b, c, e	ACCESS test Voice recording system Paper Pencil	**CE**—Have students close their eyes and spend 2 minutes focusing on something that makes them happy. Remind them to spend time every day and in stressful situations to stop and relax. Connect this skill to the ACCESS test they are about to take. **ACCESS/T/CT**—Administer the oral portion of the ACCESS test. Give students as much time as they need to prepare what they are going to say. Have them record themselves when they are ready to complete the test. Allow them to read when they are finished.
GM21 132	**Social** Given time to verbally discuss what they thought about the ACCESS test, students will write a one- to two-paragraph reflection about the test and on how they think they did with no more than two grammatical errors.	WIDA Standard 1 Grade 8 Level 3 VSOL: ENGL 8.2b, c, e, h, 8.7d, e, g, 8.8b, c, d, e, g TCA: 2(1a, b) 2(2d) 2(3e, f, g) 2(4h, i)	Whiteboard Markers Pencil Paper	**CE/B/ACT**—Display several quotes about the importance of rest to students. Have one of the quotes be from Scripture. Explain to students that they need to take the weekend to rest and regenerate from a week-long of testing. Have students lay their heads on the desk. Let them close their eyes for 30 minutes. Then ask students if that felt good? Relate to CE. **COLL/DIV**—Split students up into groups of three or four based on nationality. Have groups be diverse. Have students orally discuss their thoughts about the ACCESS with one another. Then lead a discussion with the class about their reflection of test. Have all students write one to two paragraphs on their reflection of the ACCESS and about how they think they did.

DAY #	CONTENT/OBJECTIVE	STANDARDS	RESOURCES/MATERIALS	LEARNING ACTIVITIES/ASSESSMENTS
133	**History Chapter 16 (First Half)** Given instruction on how to skim-read sections of a book, students will skim-read Chapter 16 in order to identify the important dates listed and will create a timeline of events that uses complete sentences with no grammatical errors.	WIDA Standard 5 Grade 8 Level 3 VSOL: WHI 11 ENGL: 8.6, 8.7, 8.8 TCA: 2(1a, b) 2(3f) 2(4j)	Example college rubric History textbook—*Ancient World History: Patterns of Interaction* Pencil Paper	**DIV**—Ask students if they know the history of the Americas. Take a few minutes to introduce the Native Americans of both North and South America and their importance. **CT**—Give students example HW assignments from upper level language arts classes and college classes. Explain to students that they will have an excess of reading to do in their later education. Therefore, they need to know how to skim-read and when to skim-read. **SS**—Teach students the skills of skim-reading and then teach them when it is appropriate to skim-read. Give students a sample passage from Chapter 16 Section 1 and guide them through the process of skim-reading. **L**—Assign students the timeline assignment in which they will skim-read the entire chapter and make a timeline of important dates and events. Indicate to students that they need to write the facts about the events in complete sentences. Allow students to work with a partner. Provide extra instruction to LD students as needed.
134	**Science Chapter 18** Given in-class reading time, students, in groups, will correctly respond to 10 out of 10 reading comprehension questions over Chapter 18 in the science text.	WIDA Standard 4 Grade 8 Level 3 VSOL: PS.9a, b, c, d, e ENGL 8.6 TCA: 2(1a, b) 2(3f) 2(4j)	Lights Science textbook: *Physical Science* Reading comprehension worksheet Pencil	Have one small light on when students come into the classroom. Tell them to be very quiet. Have them sit down at their desk. Turn all lights off. Turn two small lights on then turn one off. Then turn three lights on. Then turn all the lights off. Finally turn all the lights back on. Explain to students that they will be learning about the language of science concerning light during this class period. Ask students what concepts/terms they think may be related to light. **DIV/COLL/S**—Split students into five groups based on reading level and assign each group a section to read from Chapter 18 in their text. Have students popcorn-read the section by switching off every paragraph. Monitor students as they read. Answer any questions the students may have. Verbally review with the students the concepts and terms of each chapter. **ASSESS**—Give each group a reading comprehension worksheet to complete. Have them turn the worksheet in before they leave.

DAY #	CONTENT/OBJECTIVE	STANDARDS	RESOURCES/MATERIALS	LEARNING ACTIVITIES/ASSESSMENTS
135	**LA** Given a short clip of the movie *Shrek*, students will record four examples of quoted/reported speech they hear and will create two example sentences of quoted/reported speech with no more than one grammatical error.	WIDA Standard 2 Grade 8 Level 3 VSOL: ENGL 8.2h, 8.7, 8.8 TCA: 2(1a, b) 2(3f, g) 2(4h, j)	PPT and handout Quoted/reported speech worksheet Pencil *Shrek* movie Paper	**ACT/COLL/DIV**—Have students sit boy-girl-boy-girl in a circle on the floor in the classroom. Teach them the game Telephone. Have students play the game. Compare the last response with the initial quote. Use this to introduce the grammar lesson on quoted speech. **T/L**—Use a PPT to teach students the function of both quoted and reported speech, their differences, the verb tenses they use, and the modals they use. For LD students, give all students a corresponding handout with illustrations. For each new concept, give students example sentences. Have them read the sentences out loud. Give students a quoted/reported speech worksheet. Guide students through each question. **T**—Play a short clip from the movie *Shrek*. Have all students record, in complete sentences, the quoted and reported speech they hear as well as create quoted and reported speech based off what they hear.
136	**Math Chapter 11** Given instruction on how to read equations with variables on both sides, students will describe in complete sentences how to solve equations with variables on both sides with no grammatical errors.	WIDA Standard 3 Grade 8 Level 3 VSOL: MATH 8.15a, c ENGL 8.7, 8.8 TCA: 2(1a, b) 2(3f) 2(4j)	Whiteboard Markers Textbook—*Mathematics: Course 3* Paper Pencil Math journal	**CE**—Teach a mini-lesson on dealing with arguments. Explain that there are two sides to every argument. Relate this to equations and how there are some equations with two sides. **T/M**—Guide students through the vocabulary of the chapter. Ask students if they have any questions. Use a PPT to review with students how to read two-sided equations. Then show students how to answer these types of equations in writing. Guide students through two problems. Have students pair up and answer two questions in writing. **ASSESS**—Then have students answer three questions individually by writing out the answers to equations with variables on both sides. Have students write a journal entry for HW.

DAY #	CONTENT/OBJECTIVE	STANDARDS	RESOURCES/MATERIALS	LEARNING ACTIVITIES/ASSESSMENTS
137	**Social** Given instruction on basic English vocabulary concerning foods and colors, students will complete a matching worksheet with 100% accuracy.	WIDA Standard 1 Grade 8 Level 3 VSOL: ENGL 8.6b TCA: 2(1a, b) 2(2d) 2(3f) 2(4j)	Color-distorting sunglasses Colored poster boards Whiteboard Markers Matching worksheet Pencil	**ACT**—As students come into the classroom give them color-distorting sunglasses. Have them wear these sunglasses for 10 minutes. Ask students if they know the acronym ROYGBIV. Explain what this is and then review with students the seven basic colors of the color spectrum and how to pronounce them in English. Show students seven different poster boards. Ask students what color they see as you hold up each board. Take a poll. Each poster board needs to be one of the colors of ROYGBIV. Then have students take off glasses. Hold up each board again, ask the students what color it is, and then show them the poll. Have students, as a class, verbally repeat the different colors in English. **L/T**—Ask students if they have ever learned the English vocabulary for different foods. Have students list the foods they know in English. Make a list on the whiteboard. Then make a chart on the whiteboard that provides a section for each of the seven colors. Ask students what color each of the foods they listed is. Place the food in the correct section of the chart. Then use a PPT to teach students new foods. As each new food item is introduced, ask students what color it is. Add their responses to the chart. **ASSESS**—Give students a matching worksheet to complete. Explain that they need to match the correct color with each food item. Have students complete for HW if they do not finish in class.
138 GM22	**History Chapter 16 (Last Half)** Given information on the Aztecs and Incas, students will write an informational essay comparing and contrasting the two cultures, with no more than two spelling mistakes and no more than two grammar mistakes.	WIDA Standard 5 Grade 8 Level 3 VASOL: WHI.11a, b ENGL 8.7a, b, d, e ENGL 8.8g TCA: 2(3f) 2(4i, j)	PPT presentation on the Aztecs and Incas Compare and contrast graphic organizer Paper and pencil	**T**—Use a PPT presentation to review the major points of Section 3 (about the Aztecs) and Section 4 (about the Incas). Students should take notes during instruction. Students will complete a graphic organizer comparing and contrasting the two civilizations. **COLL**—Students will pair up and review their organizers together. Teacher will go around to the groups at this time to ensure that students understand the information and that they have completed their graphic organizers correctly. Students will use the rest of the class time to write a short three-paragraph compare and contrast essay on the two civilizations.

DAY #	CONTENT/OBJECTIVE	STANDARDS	RESOURCES/MATERIALS	LEARNING ACTIVITIES/ASSESSMENTS
139	**Science Quiz on Chapter 18** **Teach Chapter 19** Given a set of magnets and small metal objects, students will display and explain different concepts of the chapter on magnets, describing at least five concepts correctly.	WIDA Standard 4 Grade 8 Level 3 VASOL: PS.9a, b, c, d, e PS11b ENGL 8.8 TCA: 2(1b) 2(3f) 2(4h, j) 2(5l)	Quiz on Chapter 18 Worksheet—list of vocabulary Magnets, compass, paper clips, coins, other small metal objects (**COLL** with science teacher to get this) Science textbook: *Physical Science*	**ASSESS**—Students will be given a listening quiz on Chapter 18. Given a definition for a vocabulary word, students will be expected to provide the proper term, or else provide the proper definition for a vocabulary term. Students will also listen to sentences from the textbook that have been adjusted to have grammatical errors. Students will then need to adjust the sentences on their quiz paper. **COLL**—Divide students into groups of three or four based on language proficiency. Each group will identify words or concepts from the chapter that were new to them or perhaps that they still do not understand. Students will have a discussion about the meaning and importance of each word or concept. **ACT/CT**—Each group will then be given a collection of magnets and different kinds of metals. Students will use the magnets to demonstrate different concepts from the chapter. Each student must use the following words in their explanation to the group: magnet, magnetic pole, magnetic force, magnetic field, temporary magnet, permanent magnet, and compass. Informally assess students as you walk around the room.
140	**LA** Given the opportunity to listen to the reading of *Mama, I'll Give You the World*, students will properly identify at least five examples of figurative language with 100% accuracy. Given instruction on literary devices, students will write a short story correctly utilizing three kinds of literary devices.	WIDA Standard 2 Grade 8 Level 3 VASOL: ENGL 8.5a TCA: 2(1b) 2(4i; j) 2(5k)	PPT on figurative language/literary devices Schotter, Roni, & Gallagher S. Saelig. (2006). *Mama, I'll give you the world.* New York, NY: Schwarts & Wade Books Worksheet with list of literary devices Paper and pencil	**T**—Use PPT presentation to instruct students on different kinds of figurative language/literary devices, including alliteration, simile, metaphor, imagery, symbolism, etc. (A few of these have been taught earlier in the year, so just review them quickly.) Provide a couple examples for each. **CT—Listening Activity:** Read the book *Mama, I'll Give You the World* out loud to students. Encourage students to practice their critical listening skills. Students will be given a worksheet with each kind of literary device listed. Each student will record at least one example under each. Students will then choose three kinds of literary devices. They must then write a short story using each of the literary devices correctly. **COLL**—At the end of class, students will switch stories with a partner so they may go home and read their story for fun. Each student must return the story the next day with at least one positive comment, and one correction or suggestion for improvement. Remind students that their story will be graded on their use of literary devices. If needed, students will correct their paper for homework. It will be collected on this week's social day.

DAY #	CONTENT/OBJECTIVE	STANDARDS	RESOURCES/MATERIALS	LEARNING ACTIVITIES/ASSESSMENTS
141	**Math Chapter 12/Study Guide for Test Next Week** Given sections 1 and 2 of Chapter 12, students will verbally explain how to graph linear equations and identify the slope of a line with 100% accuracy. Given three linear equations, students will write each equation using point-slope form and verbally explain one of the equations to their partner with 100% accuracy.	WIDA Standard 3 Grade 8 Level 3 VASOL: MATH 8.15a TCA: 2(1b) 2(3e, f)	Textbook—*Mathematics: Course 3* Study guide for next week's math test over Chapters 10, 11, and 12 Math journals	**COLL**—Give students 12–15 minutes to identify any vocabulary they do not understand from the chapter. They may ask other students for the definitions of each word to clarify their understanding. **COLL**—Assign each student a partner. Looking at Section 1 of Chapter 12, students will each take turns verbally explaining how to graph linear equations. Looking at Section 2, students will verbally explain to each other how to identify the slope of a line. From Section 4, assign students three equations where they need to write the point-slope form of the equation. After they have done so, each student will choose one equation that they will verbally explain to each other. Teacher will go around the room observing students and informally assessing their answers. Teacher will give assistance when needed. Review: Provide study guide for the math test next week. Students may begin reviewing the vocabulary therein and working on the sample test questions if there is time left at the end of class. **CT**—Students will write an entry in their math journals for HW. They should record the vocabulary words they learned in class today, assess the progress in their understanding of English mathematical vocabulary, and write a brief overview of what they learned today. They should also write down any questions they have pertaining to the information discussed in class today, and anything they are still struggling with.

DAY #	CONTENT/OBJECTIVE	STANDARDS	RESOURCES/MATERIALS	LEARNING ACTIVITIES/ASSESSMENTS
142	**Social** Given instruction on good American manners, students will use their previous knowledge of accepted manners in their culture to write a compare & contrast paragraph, correctly comparing manners in the two cultures with 100% accuracy and no more than two grammatical errors.	WIDA Standard 1 Grade 8 Level 3 VASOL: ENGL 8.7a, b, d, e, g ENGL 8.8b, d, g TCA: 2(1a) 2(2d) 2(4h)	Teacher: PPT—Intro to American Manners Table settings, plastic ware, and snack foods Hypothetical practice situations written on slips of paper Students: Paper and pencil	**T**—Use PPT presentation to introduce students to good American manners. Explain what manners are appropriate in different situations, and why it is important to know what manners are acceptable in the culture you are living in. **DIV**—Ask students to share examples of good manners in their own culture. **TH**—Create a hypothetical situation where students are going to a friend's house for a birthday dinner. There, the students will meet their friend's family members for the first time, and they will be expected to appropriately greet and carry on conversation with each family member (grandmother, crazy uncle, older sister, little brother, mom and dad, etc.). They will also be expected to use proper table manners during the meal. Instruct students through each hypothetical conversation, and instruct them through proper American table manners. **ACT/TH**—Students will role-play conversations for different common social situations (i.e., meeting a new person, formal introductions, asking someone out on a date, fancy dinner party, meeting someone's family members, etc.). Divide students into groups of two. Write down different situations on small slips of paper and put them in a hat. Each group will pick two to three hypothetical situations to practice. **ASSESS**—For homework, students will write a paragraph about one of their assigned situations. Allow LD students to write less than a paragraph. They will compare and contrast the actions of the manners of their own culture to the actions of the manners expected in America. The paragraphs will be graded on accuracy, spelling, and grammar.

DAY #	CONTENT/OBJECTIVE	STANDARDS	RESOURCES/MATERIALS	LEARNING ACTIVITIES/ASSESSMENTS
143 GM22	**History Chapter 17 (First Half)** Given time to research a famous work of art from the Renaissance, students will present information about their piece to class, accurately conveying at least five major facts about the work of art.	WIDA Standard 5 Grade 8 Level 3 VASOL: WHI.13a, c, d TCA: 2(3f) 2(4i, j)	History textbook—*Ancient World History: Patterns of Interaction* List of five artists	Ask students to review questions that cover Sections 1 and 2 of the chapter. Questions will cover what they already should have learned in their history class. They will cover details such as where did the Renaissance start, what ideals and morals did the Renaissance value, who were some major historical figures of the time and why they were significant (Shakespeare, etc.). **A/T/COLL**—Students will each be assigned one of five famous works of art from the Renaissance time period. They will use the Internet to print a picture of the piece and research information about it. Students will then be split into groups of five (each student in the group will have a different work of art). Students then will each have 2 to 4 minutes to share their piece of art with their group. ***For tomorrow:** Divide students into groups of five. Place more advanced students with students that have lower language ability. Each student in each group will be assigned to a different section of Chapter 20 in their science books. They must come to class tomorrow prepared to "teach" the main ideas of their section to their other group members. Students should identify the main ideas of the section, explain major vocabulary and concepts, as well as provide a real-life application to the information. Students should focus on being able to convey the ideas of the chapter to others *orally*. They will have 5–6 minutes to teach their section.
144	**Science Chapter 20** Given a section from the chapter, students will identify the main points of the lesson and teach it to a small group of students, accurately conveying at least three major points of information.	WIDA Standard 4 Grade 8 Level 3 VASOL: PS.11a, b TCA: 2(1a, b) 2(2d) 2(3e, f, g) 2(4i) 2(5k)	Science textbook: *Physical Science* Section outline Other homework Study guide	**CT/COLL**—Students will have the first 10–15 minutes to finish preparing to teach their section of the chapter in their small groups. While each student is teaching their section, the other students in the group are to write down new facts or ideas or vocabulary they are learning. By the end of the group presentations, each student should have at least four facts written down. This will be collected as an exit slip. Students must also hand in an outline of their mini-lesson. If there is additional time at the end of class, students may ask teacher for help with homework from other classes, or they may study the vocabulary from Chapter 20. Give students a study guide for next week's science language test.

DAY #	CONTENT/OBJECTIVE	STANDARDS	RESOURCES/MATERIALS	LEARNING ACTIVITIES/ASSESSMENTS
145	**LA** Given the short story "Babe the Blue Ox" and a short worksheet, students will answer each reading comprehension question correctly with 90% accuracy.	WIDA Standard 2 Grade 8 Level 3 VASOL: ENGL 8.5b, c TCA: 2(2d) 2(3e, f)	Folktales: "The Birth of Paul Bunyan": http://americanfolklore.net/folklore/2010/07/the_birth_of_paul_bunyan.html "Babe the Blue Ox": http://americanfolklore.net/folklore/2010/07/babe_the_blue_ox.html Reading and listening comprehension quizzes	**ASSESS/DIV**—Ask students if they know what a folktale is. Ask students if they think folktales exist in every culture. Have them share brief examples of folktales in different cultures. Ask students if they know of any American folktale stories. Read students the story "The Birth of Paul Bunyan," explaining that this is one of America's most famous folktales. Ask students listening comprehension questions after the story is finished. Review answers together as a class. Explain to students that they will read another famous American folktale, this time on their own. Give students a copy of "Babe the Blue Ox." Have them read it to themselves and complete a worksheet of reading comprehension questions afterward. Collect students' reading and listening comprehension quizzes. Have students think of a folktale from their culture that they could share with the rest of the class. Students will use the next social day (day 147) to prepare their folktale presentation. Exit slip: Have students write down a folktale they could possibly share with the class.
146	**Math Test Chapters 10–12** Given a math exam over Chapters 10–12, students will provide the correct answer for each question with 85% accuracy.	WIDA Standard 3 Grade 8 Level 3 VASOL: MATH 8.12, 8.13a, 8.15a TCA: 2(1a) 2(4h, i, j)	Math test over Chapters 10–12 Math journals	**ASSESS**—Students will take the exam over Chapters 10–12. The first part of the exam will be listening. Students must listen carefully to the questions and write down the answers on their paper. The second part will be multiple-choice. It will cover topics such as the math skills addressed in the chapters, grammar, and mathematical language. For the third part, students will be given two problems they will need to verbally explain how to solve: (1) students will verbally explain how to graph a linear equation; (2) students will explain how to put a linear equation into point-slope form **CT**—For HW, students will write a journal entry about how they felt they did on their math test. They will also discuss the progress they have made concerning their math language skills since their last math exam.

DAY #	CONTENT/OBJECTIVE	STANDARDS	RESOURCES/MATERIALS	LEARNING ACTIVITIES/ASSESSMENTS
147	**Social** Given instruction on folktales, students will choose a folktale from their own culture and orally present it to the class with less than three grammatical errors.	WIDA Standard 1 Grade 8 Level 3 ENGL: 8.2a, b, c, g TCA: 2(1a) 2(4h) 2(5l)	Note for parents Props, etc., for folktale presentation	**DIV**—Students will have chosen a folktale from their own culture to share with the class. Students will use today to begin working on their presentation. Students must orally present their folktale, but they may present it in a variety of ways. For example, students could collaborate with other students to present their story as a drama. Students could present their folktale through poetry or also include song and dance. Each presentation will be graded based on creativity as well as the student's oral skills. Students must also include a visual. The visual could be a poster, costume, dance, prop, or work of art. **COLL**—Include parental involvement. Send a note home informing parents of the folktale presentation. Tell parents that their input and assistance is welcome, and invite them to the presentation day. Students will present their folktale on LA day 160.
148	**History Chapter 17 (Last Half)** Given a review over how to outline a chapter of a textbook, students will construct an outline for the last two sections of Chapter 17 with 100% accuracy.	WIDA Standard 5 Grade 8 Level 3 VSOL: WHI.13 ENGL 8.6k TCA: 2(1a) 2(3f) 2(4j)	Whiteboard Markers PPT History textbook—*Ancient World History: Patterns of Interaction*	**B/CE**—Write Ephesians 2:8–9 on the board. Explain to students that the main idea of these verses is what led to the Reformation of the Church in the 16th century. **T/SS**—Review with students the Reformation. Then use a PPT to review with students how to outline a chapter. Have students outline the last two sections of Chapter 17. Allow them to ask questions about any concepts or terms they are unsure of. **ASSESS**—Follow up with students orally by means of questions to rate their reading comprehension.
149	**Science—Listening Test Chapters 19–20** Given an auditory skills test over the language of science, students will answer 20 out of 20 questions.	WIDA Standard 4 Grade 8 Level 3 VSOL: ENGL 8.2h TCA: 2(1a) 2(3f) 2(4h)	Listening test Pencil Paper Sentence-type review handout	**S/ASSESS**—Deliver auditory skills test over the language of science to students. Read each question three times for students to listen, comprehend, and respond. Collect test from students and give them a handout that reviews the different forms a sentence can take in the English language. Explain that the next grammar lesson will cover this aspect of language.

DAY #	CONTENT/OBJECTIVE	STANDARDS	RESOURCES/MATERIALS	LEARNING ACTIVITIES/ASSESSMENTS
150	**LA—Review All Types of Sentences** Given a sentence-type worksheet, students will identify all of the different kinds of sentences and then construct an example sentence of their own for each sentence-type with 100% accuracy.	WIDA Standard 2 Grade 8 Level 3 VSOL: ENGL 8.8b TCA: 2(1a, b) 2(3h, f) 2(4j)	Whiteboard Markers PPT Sentence-type worksheet Pencil Paper	**L**—Review with students the different structures of sentences: SVO, SOV, VSO, VOS, OVS, and OSV. Then explain to students that there are multiple types of sentences. **T**—Use a PPT to show sentence types that the students already know. Then show students new sentence types they are most likely unfamiliar with. Use example sentences that connect the different sentence types with the different types of learners in the classroom. **ACT**—Write sentences on the board and then have students identify the type of sentence. Ask for three volunteers to create and write out one type of sentence on the board. Call on at least one LD and encourage them to come to the board. Ask students if they need any extra help. **ASSESS**—Give students a worksheet to complete and turn in before they leave.
151	**Math Chapter 13** Given a list of the vocabulary of Chapter 13, in groups, students will define the words and concepts and then construct mathematical sentences using these terms with no grammatical or content errors.	WIDA Standard 3 Grade 8 Level 3 VSOL: MATH 8.15c ENGL 8.87, 8.8 TCA: 2(1a) 2(3f) 2(4j)	Textbook—*Mathematics: Course 3* Paper Pencil Math journal	**L/M/COLL**—Ask students if they have any questions about the language or content of this chapter. Split students into groups and explain to them the importance of the terms in this chapter. Split students into groups based on language proficiency. Partner advanced students with LD students. Explain that the terms in this chapter will be applied to other disciplines of math they will learn in years to come. Have the groups take the vocabulary terms from the chapter and define them. Then have the groups create authentic sentences with these terms. Review all the terms verbally with students before they leave. Have students write a journal entry for HW.

DAY #	CONTENT/OBJECTIVE	STANDARDS	RESOURCES/MATERIALS	LEARNING ACTIVITIES/ASSESSMENTS
152	**Social** Given the task to orally describe their extracurricular activities, students will record in complete sentences and with no grammatical errors three things their partner does after school.	WIDA Standard 1 Grade 8 Level 3 VSOL: ENGL 8.2a, b, c, e, f, h TCA: 2(1a, b) 2(2d) 2(3e, f, g) 2(4h, j)	Objects from after-school activities: sports balls, books, mini TV, video games, markers, etc. Whiteboard Markers Pencil Paper	**ACT/L**—Rearrange the classroom to have six different stations. At each station, have an after-school activity (sports, books, TV/video games, art, etc.). Have students come into the classroom and sit on the floor. Explain to them the importance of being able to communicate in all aspects of their lives. Teach them the questions "What did you do yesterday?" and "What do you like to do for fun?" Then teach the students how to respond. Ask students verbally what types of activities they participate in after school. Teach the students the vocabulary for other types of activities. **COLL/CT/DIV**—Pair students up by gender and have them ask each other what they do after school. Have them record three things their partner does after school. Indicate that they need to write in complete sentences.
153	**History Chapter 20 (First Half)** Given class instruction on how to make charts, students will make an explorer/settler chart for Chapter 20 that lists the names of the early North and South American settlers, the years of their discoveries/settlement, and a complete sentence description of the explorers/settlers with no grammatical or content mistakes.	WIDA Standard 5 Grade 8 Level 3 VSOL: WHI 11 ENGL 8.7d, g, 8.8 TCA: 2(1a) 2(2c) 2(3f) 2(4j)	History textbook—*Ancient World History: Patterns of Interaction* Paper Pencil Ruler	Ask students if they have ever gone exploring. If so, ask them if they found anything. Was it important? Why or why not? **DIV/COLL/T/SS**—Review with students the first two sections of Chapter 20 by means of a PPT. Have students partner up based on language proficiency and then have them skim-read the first two sections. Indicate that they need to find the names of the explorers/settlers or groups of settlers, the year of their discovery/settlement, and a brief description about the explorers/settlers. Have students record all this on notebook paper. **ACT/A**—Teach students how to make charts on paper. Let students use rulers to make charts accurate. Have students make a chart for this chapter and then have them enter the information they recorded from their skim-reading activity. Every student must turn in a chart. Ask students if they have any questions about the language. Address these questions as they arise.

DAY #	CONTENT/OBJECTIVE	STANDARDS	RESOURCES/MATERIALS	LEARNING ACTIVITIES/ASSESSMENTS
154	**Science Chapter 21** Given a list of vocabulary from Chapter 21, students will create and deliver a PPT presentation, with no more than two speaking errors, over one of the words from the list.	WIDA Standard 4 Grade 8 Level 3 VSOL: PS.11a, b, c, d ENGL 8.2b, c, e TCA: 2(1a, b) 2(3f, g) 2(4h, j)	Science textbook: *Physical Science* PPT Laptop	**S/T/L/CT**—Have students identify all of the vocabulary words from their text. Assign each student one word to create and deliver a PPT presentation on. Distribute a laptop to each student. Have them open PPT. Indicate that they need to have three slides in their presentation. They need to have one slide for the definition of their word, one slide that gives the word used in a sentence, and then one slide which asks a review question about the word. Give students 15 minutes to do this. Have students send their PPT to the teacher. **ASSESS**—Use the last 25 minutes of class for student presentations. Pull up every PPT one by one. Have students come up to the board to present their PPT. Grade students on their communication abilities.
155	**LA—Prepositions** Given teacher instruction, students will complete 9/10 sentences by filling in the blank with a concise and accurate prepositional phrase and then determine whether the prepositional phrase functions adverbially or adjectivally.	WIDA Standard 2 Grade 8 Level 3 VSOL: ENGL 8.2h, 8.5a, 8.7e, f TCA: 2(1a, b) 2(3f) 2(4j)	Sandwich ingredients PPT and handout Preposition worksheet Pencil	**H/L/P/ACT**—Ask students what constitutes a noun phrase. And ask what a subject is and a predicate is. Transition into lesson by talking about adding detail to sentences. Use sandwich example to describe detailed sentences. Explain that sandwiches with more ingredients taste better, just like sentences with more detail look and sound better. Give students sandwich ingredients for them to make a sandwich. Explain that this will help them remember prepositions better. Prepositions can fit into the detail portion of sentences. **T**—Show students a PPT slide show of pictures that have arrows pointing to things that can be explained by using a preposition. For LD students, give all students a handout that corresponds to the PPT. Ask students to give the word that describes what the arrow is pointing at in the picture. Discuss what a preposition is. Explain that it is a word that signals that a noun phrase is coming. Explain that together a preposition and the following noun phrase form a prepositional phrase. Ask students to give examples of prepositions and then ask for examples of prepositional phrases. Show students examples of complete sentences with prepositional phrases and ask students to clarify what the phrase in the sentence is. A prepositional phrase can serve adjectivally or adverbially depending on what the object of the preposition modifies. Show students how to distinguish the two functions of prepositional phrases. Give examples of prepositional phrases functioning adjectivally and adverbially. **ASSESS**—Give students a worksheet with incomplete sentences and have them fill in the blanks with a prep. phrase. Next to each sentence, ask students to write whether the phrase functions adjectivally or adverbially. Have students complete for HW if they do not finish in class.

DAY #	CONTENT/OBJECTIVE	STANDARDS	RESOURCES/MATERIALS	LEARNING ACTIVITIES/ASSESSMENTS
156	**Math Chapter 13** Given instruction on how to solve a word problem from this chapter, in pairs, students will teach their partner how to solve a given problem by verbally guiding their partner through the equation with no more than two speaking errors.	WIDA Standard 3 Grade 8 Level 3 VSOL: MATH 8.15a, c, 8.17 ENGL 8.2a, b, c, e TCA: 2(1a) 2(3f) 2(3h, j)	PPT Paper Pencil Math journal	Collect HW. **T/M**—Pull up word problems from previous chapters on the PPT. Have students answer word problems by describing the different steps in solving these problems. Teach students how to solve word problems from Chapter 13. Guide students through three word problems then split students into pairs. **COLL/CT**—Give each pair two word problems. Have students teach their partner how to solve one of the word problems to their partner. Monitor the students and listen for speaking errors. Have students write a journal entry for HW.
157	**Social** Given instruction on how to communicate about summer activities, students will write a three-paragraph mini-essay that uses at least five prepositions to describe their plans for the summer.	WIDA Standard 1 Grade 8 Level 3 VSOL: ENGL 8.7, 8.8 TCA: 2(1a, b) 2(2d) 2(3e, g) 2(4h, i, j)	Beach items (chair, umbrella, sand tools) Hawaiian music "Rocket Power" video clip PPT Paper Pencil	**CE/MUS/L/T/P/D**—Rearrange the classroom for a beach setting. As students walk into the classroom give them a pair of sunglasses and a lei to put on. Also have Hawaiian music playing. Let students dance to music if they want to. Have students sit on the floor. Explain to students the importance of planning for the future. Transition to have them think about planning for the future. Verbally ask students if they know any English terms to describe summertime activities. Write these terms on the board. Show students a clip from the show "Rocket Power" and ask them to identify activities they could perform in the summertime. Teach students the new vocabulary for these activities. As each new term is introduced have students stand up if they think they would participate in the activity. **ASSESS**—Have students go back to their desks. Instruct them to write a three-paragraph mini-essay about their summertime plans. Explain to them that they need to divide their essay by the different months of summer. Have students write their hypothetical plans for each month. Tell the students that they need to use five prepositions that they recently learned in this writing activity. Have students complete for HW if they do not finish.

DAY #	CONTENT/OBJECTIVE	STANDARDS	RESOURCES/MATERIALS	LEARNING ACTIVITIES/ASSESSMENTS
158	**History Chapter 20 (Last Half)** **Review for test** Given two reading passages from Chapter 20, students will provide written answers to four different critical thinking questions with 100% accuracy. Given example review questions for the upcoming test, students will provide the correct answer for each question with 80% accuracy.	WIDA Standard 5 Grade 8 Level 3 VASOL: WHII.4a, c TCA: 2(3e, f) 2(4h)	History textbook—*Ancient World History: Patterns of Interaction* List of critical thinking questions Review questions for test—including take-home list of possible essay questions Study guide for upcoming history exam	**SS**—Students will outline the causes of African slavery that are listed in Section 3. They will then identify the effects of each cause. Have students share the identified causes and effect with the class. **CT/DIV**—After reading the section on page 566 entitled "The Causes of African Slavery," students will answer the following critical thinking questions on a sheet of paper: — How had Africans built up immunity to European disease? — Why were Spain and Portugal the early leaders in the slave trade? After reading the section on page 567 entitled "Slavery Spreads Throughout the Americas," students will answer the following critical thinking questions: — Why does the number of slaves transported by the British to the United States understate the scope of slavery there? — How was British involvement in the slave trade similar to that of the Spanish? **P—Review:** Play review game with students. Divide students into two teams. Ask questions to one team at a time. If a team provides the right answer they will receive one point and they may shoot a basket. If they make the basket, they will get one extra point. Make sure that LD students are getting involved in the game. Ask students questions to prepare them for their upcoming test over Chapters 16, 17, and 20. Questions will be similar to what will appear on the test. There will be three kinds of questions: (1) Listening comprehension questions that focus on main idea, vocabulary, and grammar. (2) Short answer questions. (3) Questions where students must orally describe the major components of certain given topics and apply proper historical vocabulary and language, as well as correct grammar. Give students a paper of essay questions that may potentially appear on the test. Also give students a study guide for the upcoming test.

DAY #	CONTENT/OBJECTIVE	STANDARDS	RESOURCES/MATERIALS	LEARNING ACTIVITIES/ASSESSMENTS
159	**Science Chapter 22** Given time to reflect on their school year, students will write a reflection paragraph about their improvement in science and language, demonstrating proper organization and no more than one grammatical error. Given a chapter vocabulary list, students will properly identify the meaning for each unknown word and provide a sentence correctly using each word with 90% accuracy.	WIDA Standard 4 Grade 8 Level 3 VASOL: PS.11d TCA: 2(1b) 2(3a, f, g)	Student computer access Science textbook: *Physical Science* Chapter vocabulary list Pencil and paper	**ASSESS/CT**—Each student will write a reflection today. Give students time to think about where they were at the beginning of the year, both with their knowledge of science and their language ability. Students will write a paragraph describing where they were at the beginning of the year, and where they are now. Ask them to describe different steps they took or different occurrences that led them to where they are now. Paragraph will be collected at the end of class. Provide extra help and encouragement for LD students. Class discussion: Ask students to share their experiences with the class, if they would like. **T/S**—Students will be given a vocabulary list from the chapter. Students will work independently to identify the correct meaning for the words they are unfamiliar with. Students may use dictionaries, their textbooks, and the Internet. They must provide a picture for each new word, and provide a sentence using each word correctly. If students do not have time to finish, they may turn it in as homework the next day.
160	**LA** Given instruction on folktales, students will choose a folktale from their own culture and orally present it to the class with less than three grammatical errors.	WIDA Standard 2 Grade 8 Level 3 VASOL: ENGL 8.5b, c, d TCA: 2(1a) 2(4h) 2(5l)	Students should bring any props or pictures, etc., they need to give their presentations Cookies and drinks for students and parents	PRESENTATION DAY!!! **L/ACT/ COLL/T**—Students will present their own traditional folktales to the class today. Provide refreshments for students and parents. *Continued from days 145 & 147.

DAY #	CONTENT/OBJECTIVE	STANDARDS	RESOURCES/MATERIALS	LEARNING ACTIVITIES/ASSESSMENTS
161	**Math Chapter 14** Given a mathematical skill dealing with polynomials, students will prepare a brief lesson on applying that skill for their peers, and present it with 100% accuracy.	WIDA Standard 3 Grade 8 Level 3 VASOL: MATH 8.15a TCA: 2(1a) 2(4h)	PPT presentation on polynomials Paper and pencil Math journals	**T**—Use PPT presentation to review concept of and examples of polynomials. **M/COLL**—(Math language activity) Divide students into groups of four. Each student in each group will be assigned to one section and one skill. They will need to teach this skill to their classmates. The four skills will be classifying polynomials, simplifying polynomials, adding polynomials, and subtracting polynomials. Each student must provide an example of their mathematical skill and three practice equations for their classmates to work through. At the end of each student's mini-teaching presentation to their group, the students will have time to solve the three practice equations for that specific skill. Collect students' solved example equations. **CT**—Once each group is finished, they may begin on their journal entry for this week. The entry should follow the typical pattern of their previous entries.
162	**Social** After researching different exhibits at the Metro Richmond Zoo, students will work together in groups to prepare a short 2–3-minute oral presentation on their chosen exhibit, with no more than two grammatical errors.	WIDA Standard 1 Grade 8 Level 3 VASOL: ENGL 8.2a, b, c ENGL 8.8 TCA: 2(1b) 2(5l, m)	Computer access	**CE**—Give students a mini-lesson about the value of life. Explain that animals have a life value as well. Inform students about the upcoming field trip on day 165. Go over rules and expectations for the day, and what students will need to bring with them. **T**—Use the Metro Richmond Zoo website to give students a sneak peak of the animals they might see at the zoo. **T/COLL/CT**—Students will use the computers to research different activities they can do at the zoo, or different exhibits or animals they can see. Students will then work together in groups of three or four. Each group will choose one activity, exhibit, or animal they would like to see at the zoo. Each group will explain what their exhibit is and why they would like to go there. Each group will give a brief 2–3-minute oral presentation on their exhibit. Inform students that their presentations will be graded on grammatical correctness and that they should aim to have no grammatical errors. Also, each group member should participate in speaking during the presentation. Write the exhibits down and try to get to as many of them as possible on the day of the field trip.

DAY #	CONTENT/OBJECTIVE	STANDARDS	RESOURCES/MATERIALS	LEARNING ACTIVITIES/ASSESSMENTS
163	**History Test Chapters 16, 17, 20** Given a history exam over Chapters 16, 17, & 20, students will answer listening comprehension, short answer & essay, and oral questions correctly with 85% accuracy.	WIDA Standard 5 Grade 8 Level 3 VASOL: WHI.11a, b WHI.13a, c, d TCA: 2 (4i, j)	History exam	**ASSESS/SS**—Students will be given a history exam over Chapters 16, 17, & 20. The first part of the exam will be listening comprehension. Each question will be read aloud to the class three times. These questions will focus on main ideas and vocabulary from the book, as well as grammar. The second part of the exam will consist of short answer and essay questions. Students will be graded on correctness, content, and grammar. The final part of the exam is an oral test. Students will be given two to three topics. They must describe the major components/important facts of each topic, properly applying historical vocabulary and language and correct grammar.
164	**Science—In-Class Group Project** Given time to create a new computer or cell phone app, students will give a group presentation on the app, accurately conveying its usefulness and its required inputs and outputs with 100% accuracy.	WIDA Standard 4 Grade 8 Level 3 VASOL: PS.11c TCA: 2(1b) 2(4i, j)	PPT presentation on electronics, input and output, and other concepts from Chapters 21 & 22 Computer access	**CE**—Briefly discuss the importance of technology in our world. How would the world look without computers and smartphones? Teach students how to be appreciative of the small things in life (2–3 min.). **T/S**—Use short PPT presentation to quickly review concepts of electronics, input and output, and a couple of other important chapter vocabulary words if necessary (5–7 min.). **COLL**—Divide students into small groups based on language proficiency. Have groups think about different computer and cell phone apps. They will then brainstorm ideas for a new app they want to create. **CT**—Each group will then write a proposal for their new app, describing its usefulness (why people would need it), its required inputs and outputs, and how they would market it. They should describe different ways the app could be used in multiple situations. Students will present their idea for the new app to the class, focusing on using proper grammar and sentence structure.

DAY #	CONTENT/OBJECTIVE	STANDARDS	RESOURCES/MATERIALS	LEARNING ACTIVITIES/ASSESSMENTS
165	**Field Trip!!!** After going to the Metro Richmond Zoo, students will orally describe their favorite part of the day and why, with no grammatical errors.	WIDA Standard 1 Grade 8 Level 3 VASOL: ENGL 8.2e, 8.8 TCA: 2(1b) 2(l, m)	Bus Directions to zoo Zoo map List of what exhibits students want to visit	**ACT/P/COLL/S**—Today, we will go to the Metro Richmond Zoo! The bus will leave early in the morning before school starts and return soon after the school day ends. **DIV**—Students will be divided into groups. Each group will be assigned a chaperone. Each group will be given a checklist of exhibits to go to. They should try and visit as many exhibits as possible. On the bus ride home, the teacher will ask each student to share his or her favorite part of the day. Students will be encouraged to use proper grammar and vocabulary. Teacher may correct grammar if needed.
166	**Math Chapter 14** Given example problems from Sections 5 and 6 of the chapter, students will provide a written explanation of how to solve each problem, with 100% accuracy and no more than one to two grammatical errors.	WIDA Standard 3 Grade 8 Level 3 VASOL: MATH 8.15a ENGL 8.8 TCA: 2(3f)	Textbook—*Mathematics: Course 3* Math journals	**M**—Briefly review simplifying, adding, and subtracting polynomials on the board with students. Walk them through explaining an example problem of each to refresh students of the language. **T**—Refresh students about the FOIL method. If students do not know the FOIL method, they may use the classroom iPads to find what it is. Have students examine Sections 5 and 6 of Chapter 14. Students will write out how to solve thre different example problems for each section (Section 5—Multiplying Polynomials by Monomials; Section 6—Multiplying Binomials). Explain to students that their explanations will be graded on accuracy and grammar. **CT**—If more class time remains, students may begin their math journal entry for the week. The entry should follow the general outline of their past journal entries, including what they learned in class today and how their English ability in the subject area of math has improved.

DAY #	CONTENT/OBJECTIVE	STANDARDS	RESOURCES/MATERIALS	LEARNING ACTIVITIES/ASSESSMENTS
167	**Social** Given a review on positive character traits, students will identify five character traits they would like to display and write a sentence describing how they could display each one, with no more than two grammatical or spelling errors.	WIDA Standard 1 Grade 8 Level 3 VASOL: ENGL 8.8g TCA: 2(1f)	PPT on character traits	**CE/DIV**—Ask students for examples of positive character traits. Ask students why it is important to display positive character traits. Ask if certain cultures view traits differently. **T**—Use PPT presentation to review examples of positive character traits with students. Have students create a list of five character traits they would like to have or improve on. They must write a sentence or two describing why they would like to display each one. **CT**—Students will then think of ways they can display each characteristic. They will write a sentence giving an example of how they could display each one. Students should focus on proper spelling and grammar in these sentences. If there is extra class time, students may read a book of their choice or get help with their other classes.
168	**History Review for Final Test** Given review questions from history ESL class this year, students will provide the correct answer for each question with 90% accuracy.	WIDA Standard 5 Grade 8 Level 3 VASOL: WHI&WHII TCA: 2(4i, j)	History review questions	**SS/ACT/P**—Students will play Around-the-World in order to review for the history final exam, answering review questions from the semester's lessons and assignments. One student will begin their journey "around the world" to start. They will go to their friend's desk. Both students will stand up. The teacher will ask a question. Once the teacher finishes the question, the first student to answer the question *correctly* will advance to the next student's desk. The game will continue on as such. The game is finished when a student makes it back to their original desk. Students will answer questions concerning main ideas from each chapter, vocabulary, other language they have learned in history class, and grammar. Students will be given examples of possible essay questions to take home in order to prepare for the final exam.

DAY #	CONTENT/OBJECTIVE	STANDARDS	RESOURCES/MATERIALS	LEARNING ACTIVITIES/ASSESSMENTS
169	**Science (Nature Walk Day, Relate to Biology for 9th Grade Prep)** Given a question about what they are most excited to learn next year, students will answer orally, with fewer than three grammatical errors.	WIDA Standard 4 Grade 8 Level 3 WIDA Standard 1 Grade 8 Level 3 VASOL: ENGL 8.8 TCA: 2(1a, b) 2(3g)	Study guide	**ACT/P**—Students will go on a nature walk today, either near the school or to a local park (if it's within walking distance). **S**—During the walk, tell students they will be taking biology in 9th grade. Ask students if they know what biology is. Encourage students to share their previous knowledge about biology, discussing certain biological concepts they already know. Explain to students that there are many types of biology, including animal, plant, and human biology. Ask students to share which one interests them the most and why. **CE**—Ask students to observe their surroundings. Have them cite different examples of biology around them. Take time to stop and look at the small things. Remind them about the value of life humans and animals have. Extend the lesson about value of life to plants and all biological creatures. Continue a constant discussion about biology and biological concepts. Ask students what they are most excited to learn about in biology next year. Students will respond with near perfect grammar. Give students a study guide over the language of science they will be tested on for the final exam.
170	**LA** Given instruction on modifying adverbial phrases, students will write three example sentences correctly modifying adverbial phrases, with no more than one spelling error.	WIDA Standard 2 Grade 8 Level 3 VASOL: ENGL 8.8g TCA: 2(1a, b)	Chapter 18: *Understanding and Using English Grammar* PPT presentation on modifying adverbial phrases PPT handout Pencils and paper	**L/ASSESS**—Grammar Connection: **T**—Teacher will use a PPT presentation to instruct students about changing time clauses to modify adverbial phrases. For LD students, give all students a corresponding handout with illustrations. After learning the material and working through a few examples with the teacher as a class, students will complete an activity sheet where they will change the adverb clauses to modifying adverbial phrases. Students will then write three example sentences properly utilizing modifying adverbial phrases. Students should be sure to use correct spelling. Teacher will collect checklist and student work at the end of class as an exit slip.

DAY #	CONTENT/OBJECTIVE	STANDARDS	RESOURCES/MATERIALS	LEARNING ACTIVITIES/ASSESSMENTS
171	**Math Review for Final Test** Given review questions from math ESL class this year, students will provide the correct answer to each question with 90% accuracy.	WIDA Standard 3 Grade 8 Level 3 VASOL: ENGL 8.2h MATH 8.2–8.17 TCA: 2(4h, i, j)	Math journals Study guide for math test	**COLL**—Divide students into groups based on language proficiency. Have students verbally share an entry from their journal with their group members. Then have the group members switch journals with another group member. Have all students edit their group members' work. Have students return the edited journals to their owners. Have students turn in Math Journal! Review: Ask students if they have any particular skills or mathematical vocabulary/language they would like to practice. Review these together as a class. Provide students with a worksheet of potential grammar questions that could appear on the test. Give them time to work on it independently. **COLL**—Once students have finished reviewing the grammar questions, give them a packet of potential test questions reviewing the main ideas and mathematical language students have learned this year. Give all students a study guide for the final language of math exam.
172	**Social (Lesson for Memorial Day)** Given the opportunity to read the poem "In Flanders Fields", students will identify the poem's main idea and the meaning of its symbols, with 100% accuracy.	WIDA Standard 1 Grade 8 Level 3 VASOL: ENGL 8.4a, 8.5a,h TCA: 2(5m)	Thank you gift for guest speaker American flag and red white and blue decorations "In Flanders Fields" poem and activity packet: http://www.theholidayzone.com/veterans/In_Flanders_Fields_BW.pdf	**COLL**—Bring in a member of the community that used to serve in the US Armed Forces. Have them introduce the students to Memorial Day, explaining what it's about, the history behind it, and how Americans generally observe the day. Have them share their story about serving in the US military and what makes Memorial Day special to them. Encourage students to ask questions at the end of the presentation. **DIV**—Ask students to share about similar holidays in their own culture. **CT**—Provide students a handout of the poem "In Flanders Fields." Analyze the poem together as a class. Work together with the students to identify the main idea of the poem. Ask students to identify what they think the crosses represent. Ask students to identify possible meanings that the poppies symbolize. Give students time to independently answer the questions on the "In Flanders Field" worksheet. Collect the worksheet as an exit ticket.

DAY #	CONTENT/OBJECTIVE	STANDARDS	RESOURCES/MATERIALS	LEARNING ACTIVITIES/ASSESSMENTS
173	**Movie** Given an episode from the TV series "Captain Planet," students will record at least 20 vocabulary words they are unfamiliar with.	WIDA Standard 2 Grade 8 Level 3 VSOL: ENGL 8.2h TCA: 2(1a, b) 2(2d) 2(4j)	"Captain Planet" video clip Paper Pencil	**T/DIV/CE**—Play one episode from the TV Series "Captain Planet." Relate video to the character principle of taking care of the Earth. Have students actively watch and listen to the video. Have students record at least 20 vocabulary words they are unfamiliar with. Allow LD students to list less than 20.
174	**Movie** Given an episode from the TV series "Captain Planet," students will identify/ list in correct sentences with no grammatical errors five usages of modals and the context in which they are heard.	WIDA Standard 2 Grade 8 Level 3 VSOL: 8.2h TCA: 2(1a, b) 2(2d) 2(4j)	"Captain Planet" video clip Paper Pencil	**T/DIV/CE**—Play one episode from the TV Series "Captain Planet." Relate video to the character principle of taking care of the Earth. Have students actively watch and listen to the video. Have students identify and record five examples they hear of modals being used. Allow LD students to only list three modals. Indicate to students that they must write in complete sentences.
175	**Science and LA Review** Given a PPT review game, students will work together to successfully answer all questions with no help from the teacher.	WIDA Standard 2 Grade 8 Level 3 WIDA Standard 4 Grade 8 Level 3 VSOL: ENGL 8.2g PS 6–12 TCA: 2(1a) 2(3f) 2(4j)	PPT Science/LA study guide	**COLL/ACT/T/L/S**—Divide students into groups. Allow the groups to sit anywhere in the classroom, but indicate that they need to be able to see the screen. Verbally review with students the different concepts they learned concerning the languages of science and language arts. Use a PPT game to review the two types of languages. If groups are not able to answer a question themselves, have them collaborate with other groups to discover the correct answer. At the end of class, pass out another study guide for students to review in order to prepare for the test.

DAY #	CONTENT/OBJECTIVE	STANDARDS	RESOURCES/MATERIALS	LEARNING ACTIVITIES/ASSESSMENTS
176	**Science/LA Language Test** Given a summative assessment over the language of science and language arts, students will answer all questions with 100% accuracy.	WIDA Standard 4 Grade 8 Level 3 WIDA Standard 2 Grade 8 Level 3 VSOL: ENGL 8.4, 8.6 PS6–12 TCA: 2(1a) 2(3f) 2(4h, i, j)	Science/LA test Pencil	**L/S/CT/ASSESS**—Pass tests out to students. Give them the whole class period to work on it. Monitor students as they take the test. Answer questions if they arise. Have students read if they finish early.
177	**Math and History Review** Given a classroom adventure game, students will work together to successfully answer all questions with no help from the teacher.	WIDA Standard 3 Grade 8 Level 3 WIDA Standard 5 Grade 8 Level 3 VSOL: ENGL 8.2g WHI&WHII MATH 8.2–8.17 TCA: 2(1a) 2(3f) 2(4j)	Duck Tape PPT Candy Study guide	**ACT/T/CT/M/SS**—Move all the desks to one side of the classroom. Use Duck Tape to make a game board on the floor. Use the layout of Chutes and Ladders to make the game board. Have students come in and sit on the floor. Verbally review with them the concepts they have learned concerning the languages of math and history. Then divide students into groups. Use a PPT to display questions to the students. Have groups answer the questions and move from one space to the next based on their answer. If students are unsure as to how to answer a question, have them collaborate with other groups to answer the question. If students collaborate between groups, allow both teams to advance on the game board. Pass out candy to students at the end of the game. Then pass out another study guide for students to review in preparation for their test.
178	**Math/History Language Test** Given a summative assessment over the language of history and math that the students have studied, students will answer all questions with 100% accuracy.	WIDA Standard 3 Grade 8 Level 3 WIDA Standard 5 Grade 8 Level 3 VSOL: ENGL 8.4, 8.6 WHI & WHII MATH 8.2–8.17 TCA: 2(1a) 2(3f) 2(4h, i, j)	Math/history test Pencil	**ASSESS/M/SS**—Pass tests out to students. Give them the whole class period to work on it. Monitor students as they take the test. Answer questions if they arise. Have students read if they finish early.

DAY #	CONTENT/OBJECTIVE	STANDARDS	RESOURCES/MATERIALS	LEARNING ACTIVITIES/ASSESSMENTS
179	**Reflection Day** Given time to reflect, students will write in complete sentences and with no grammatical errors their overall personal reflection of the school year with specific reference to this class.	WIDA Standard 1 Grade 8 Level 3 WIDA Standard 2 Grade 8 Level 3 VSOL: ENGL 8.7, 8.8 TCA: 2(1a, b) 2(3e, f) 2(4h, i)	Paper Pencil "It's Closing Time" song List of food items	**CE/MUS/L/CT/T**—As students come into the classroom, have them sit down at their desk and take out a sheet of notebook paper and a writing utensil. Play the song "It's Closing Time." Explain to students the importance of reflecting on life events. Relate this principle to the day's activity. Ask students to write a reflection over the past year. Indicate to them that they need to address their growth, strengths, weaknesses, and the teacher's growths, strengths, and weaknesses. Give students a list of food items to bring in for the end of school class party.
180	**End of School Party** Given a non-threatening social environment, students will communicate with one another in English only with no speaking errors.	WIDA Standard 1 Grade 8 Level 3 VSOL: ENGL 8.2a, b, c, d, e, h TCA: 2(1a, b) 2(2d) 2(3h, g) 2(4j)	Music from the '60s, '70s, and '80s American food items	**MUS/COLL/DIV/ACT/T**—Play American rock'n'roll music from the '60s, '70s, and '80s for the entire class period. Indicate to students that they may only speak in English for the last class. Have students set their things in the corner of the room. Set up food and teach the students how to serve one another. Have the boys serve the girls and then have the girls serve the boys. Allow students to eat, ask questions, and converse with one another. Toward the end of class, ask students directed questions about their summer plans.

REFERENCES

AACTE. (2018). About edTPA: Overview. Retrieved from http://edtpa.aacte.org/about-edtpa#Overview-0

Ackerman, B. (2007). *P.R.A.I.S.E.: Effectively guiding student behavior.* Colorado Springs, CO: Purposeful Design Publications.

American Montessori Society. (2018). American Montessori Society: Education that transforms lives. Retrieved from https://amshq.org/Montessori-Education/Introduction-to-Montessori

Arreola, R. (1998). Writing learning objectives: A teaching resource document from the Office of the Vice Chancellor for planning and academic support. Retrieved from https://www.uwo.ca/tsc/graduate_student_programs/pdf/LearningObjectivesArreola.pdf

ASCD. (2018). Understanding by design. Retrieved from http://www.ascd.org/research-a-topic/understanding-by-design-resources.aspx

Beam, A. (2005). The analysis of inclusion versus pullout at the elementary level as determined by selected variables (Doctoral dissertation, George Washington University).

Beam, A., & Pinkie, E. (2015). *Secondary curriculum in practice: Developing with an integrated approach.* Boston, MA: Pearson.

Beam, A., Yocum, R., & Pinkie, E. (2016). Perspectives of pre-service teachers on students with emotional disabilities. *The Teachers Educators' Journal, 9,* 49–62.

Bloom, B., Engelhart, M., Furst, E., Hill, W., & Krathwohl, D. (1956). *Taxonomy of educational objectives, handbook I: The cognitive domain.* New York: David McKay Co Inc.

Carnegie Mellon University (CMU). (2016). What is the difference between formative and summative assessment? Retrieved from https://www.cmu.edu/teaching/assessment/basics/formative-summative.html

CAST, Inc. (2012). National center for universal design for learning. Retrieved from http://www.udlcenter.org/aboutudl/whatisudl

Character Education Partnership (CEP). (1999). Character education. Retrieved from http://www.doe.virginia.gov/instruction/character_ed/index.shtml

Clare Boothe Luce Policy Institute. (2015). *A brief history of education in America.* Retrieved from http://www.cblpi.org/ftp/School%20Choice/EdHistory.pdf

Clark, D. (2015). Bloom's Taxonomy of learning domains. Retrieved from http://www.nwlink.com/~donclark/hrd/bloom.html

Common Core Standards Initiative. (2018). Preparing America's students for success. Retrieved from http://www.corestandards.org/

Connell, J. (2005). Brain-based strategies to reach every learner. Adapted by Scholastic; retrieved from https://www.scholastic.com/teachers/articles/teaching-content/clip-save-checklist-learning-activities-connect-multiple-intelligences/

Crown. (2018). The New Zealand curriculum online. Retrieved from http://nzcurriculum.tki.org.nz/Archives/Curriculum-project-archives/Developing-the- draft/History-of-curriculum-development

Department of Mathematics. (2018). University of Northern Iowa: The math department mission statement. Retrieved from https://uni.edu/math/math-department-mission-statement

Education.com. (2018). The importance of recognizing tactile and kinesthetic learners. Retrieved from https://www.education.com/reference/article/tactual-kinesthetic-learners/

Essex, N. L. (2012). *School law and the public schools: A practical guide for educational leaders.* Boston, MA: Pearson.

Ferguson-Joseph, I. (2018). Problem based learning and assessment. Retrieved from http://assessment-in-education.wikispaces.com/%2A%2AProblem+Based+Learning+and+Assessment

Friend, M. (2007). Co-teaching connection. Retrieved from http://marilynfriend.com/approaches.htm

Friend, M. (2015). The power of two. DVD/video.

Gardner, H. (2006). *Multiple intelligences: New horizons.* New York, NY: Basic Books.

Gardner, H. (2014). *Multiple intelligence theory.* Retrieved from http://www.multipleintelligencetheory.co.uk

Hunter, M. (1982). *Mastery teaching.* Thousand Oaks, CA: Corwin Press.

Hunter, M. (1987). The Madeline Hunter model of mastery learning. Retrieved from https://www.doe.in.gov/sites/default/files/turnaround-principles/8-steps-effective-lesson-plan-design-madeline-hunter.pdf

IDEA. (2018). Individuals with Disabilities Act. Retrieved from https://sites.ed.gov/idea/

IFLTE. (2013). About the edTPA. Retrieved from http://www.flte.illinois.edu/edtpa/

Individuals with Disabilities Education Act, 20 U.S.C. § 1400 (2004).

International Society for Technology in Education (ISTE). (2018). Personalized vs. differentiated vs. individualized learning. Retrieved from https://www.iste.org/explore/articleDetail?articleid=124

Kelly, M. (2017). Pretests effective tools to target instruction. Retrieved from https://www.thoughtco.com/importance-and-uses-of-pretests-7674

Kidwell, L., Fisher, D., Braun, R., & Swanson, D. (2013). Developing learning objectives for accounting ethics using Bloom's Taxonomy. *Accounting Education, 22*(1), 48–50. doi:10.1080/09639284.2012.6984788

Liberty University. (2018). edTPA endorsement codes. Retrieved from http://www.liberty.edu.

National Association for Gifted Children (NAGC). (2018). Curriculum compacting. Retrieved from https://www.nagc.org/resources-publications/gifted-education-practices/curriculum-compacting

North Dakota State University (NDSU). (2013). English department mission statement. Retrieved from https://www.ndsu.edu/english/mission_statement/

North Shore Pediatric Therapy. (2011). What's the difference between positive and negative reinforcement? Retrieved from https://nspt4kids.com/parenting/the-difference-between-positive-and-negative-reinforcement/

Pacer Center, Inc. (2015). School accommodation and modification ideas for students who receive special education services. Retrieved from http://www.pacer.org/parent/php/PHP-c49a.pdf

Parentree. (2018). Teaching children through Naturalistic Intelligence (multiple intelligence)—Activities, toys, materials, examples. Retrieved from https://www.parentree.in/Blogs/876-teaching-children-through-naturalistic-intelligence-multiple-intelligence-activities-toys-materials-examples.

Positive Behavioral Interventions & Supports (PBIS). (2018). What is school-wide PBIS? Retrieved from https://www.pbis.org/school

Quotescape, Inc. (2018). School mission statements. Retrieved from https://www.missionstatements.com/school_mission_statements.html

Reis, S., & Renzulli, J. (2018). Curriculum compacting: A systematic procedure for modifying the curriculum for above average ability students. Retrieved from https://gifted.uconn.edu/schoolwide-enrichment-model/curriculum_compacting/

SCALE. (2018). Educative teacher performance assessment. Retrieved from https://scale.stanford.edu/

Spaulding, L.S., Mostert, M. P., & Beam, A. P. (2010). Is Brain Gym an effective educational intervention? *Exceptionality, 18,* 18–30.

Tomlinson, C. (2013). Differentiating instruction is . . . . Retrieved from http://caroltomlinson.com/

University of Washington. (2017). What is the difference between accommodation and modification for a student with a disability? Retrieved from https://www.washington.edu/doit/what-difference-between-accommodation-and-modification-student

U.S. Department of Education. (2015). Building the legacy: IDEA 2004. Retrieved from www.idea.ed.gov.

U.S. Department of Education. (2018). Protecting students with disabilities. Retrieved from https://www2.ed.gov/about/offices/list/ocr/504faq.html

Vanderbilt Peabody College. (2018). The Iris Center. Retrieved from https://iris.peabody.vanderbilt.edu/

Virginia Department of Education. (2018). Individualized education program (IEP). Retrieved from http://www.doe.virginia.gov/special_ed/iep_instruct_svcs/iep/

Weaver, B. (2018). Formal vs. informal assessments. Retrieved from https://www.scholastic.com/teachers/articles/teaching-content/formal-vs-informal-assessments/

Webster, J. (2018). ABC–Antecedent, behavior, and consequence. Retrieved from https://www.thoughtco.com/abc-antecedent-behavior-and-consequence-3111263

WIDA. (2012). 2012 amplification of the English language development standards. Retrieved from www.wida.us

Wiggins, G., & McTighe, J. (2011). *The understanding by design guide to creating high-quality units.* Alexandria, VA: ASCD.

Wilson, L. (2018). The second principle. Retrieved from https://thesecondprinciple.com/optimal-learning/ninth-intelligence-existential-cosmic-smarts-2/.

Wong, H. K., & Wong, R. T. (2009). *The first days of school: How to be an effective teacher.* Mountain View, CA: Harry K. Wong Publications, Inc.

Wright, P. (2018). Wrightslaw: Discrimination: Section 504 and ADA AA. Retrieved from http://www.wrightslaw.com/info/sec504.index.htm